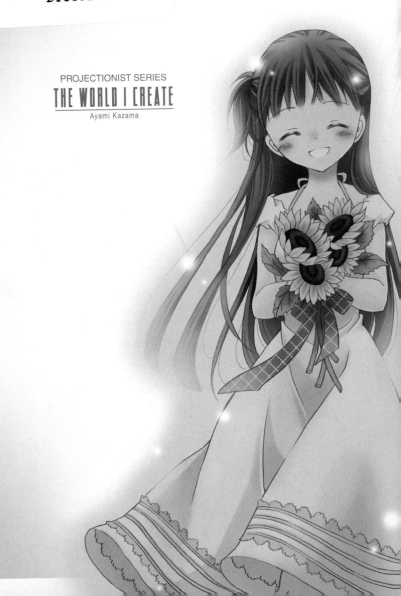

PROJECTIONIST SERIES

THE WORLD I CREATE

Ayami Kazama

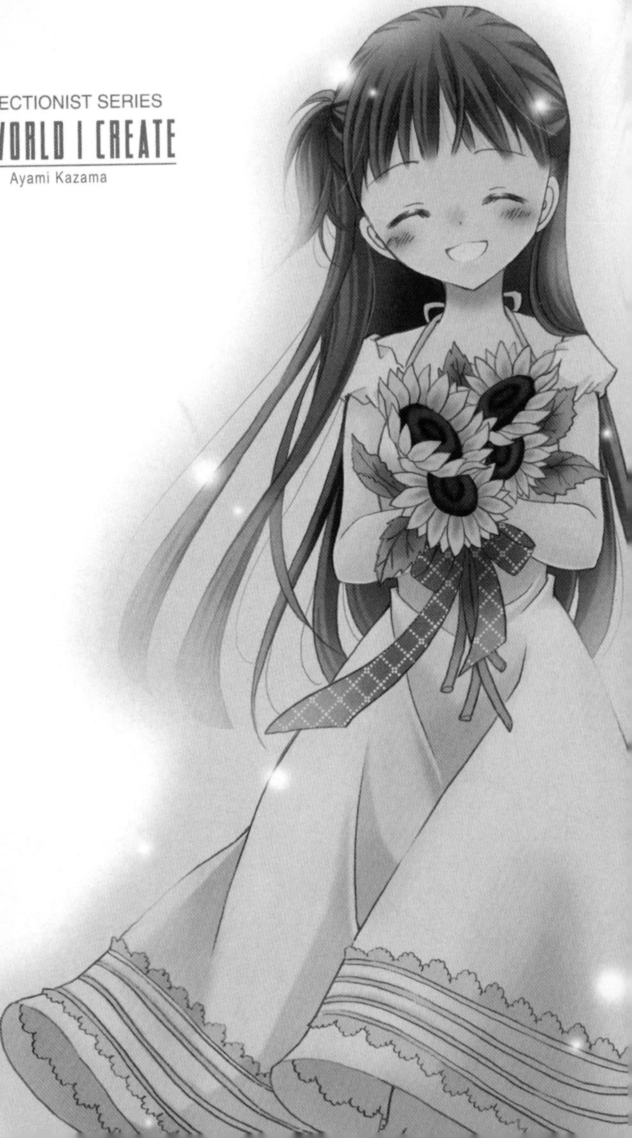

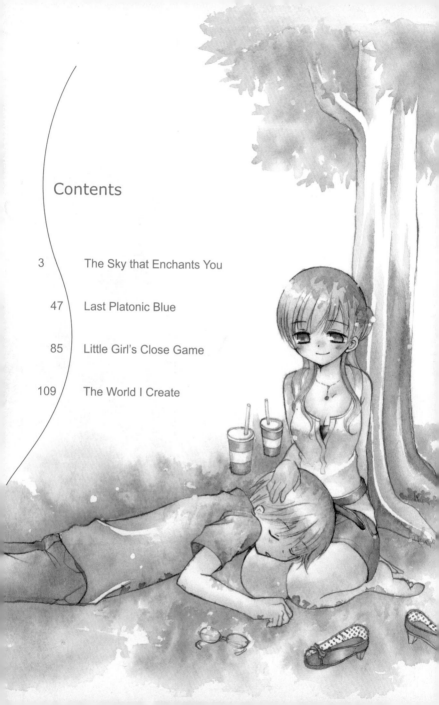

Contents

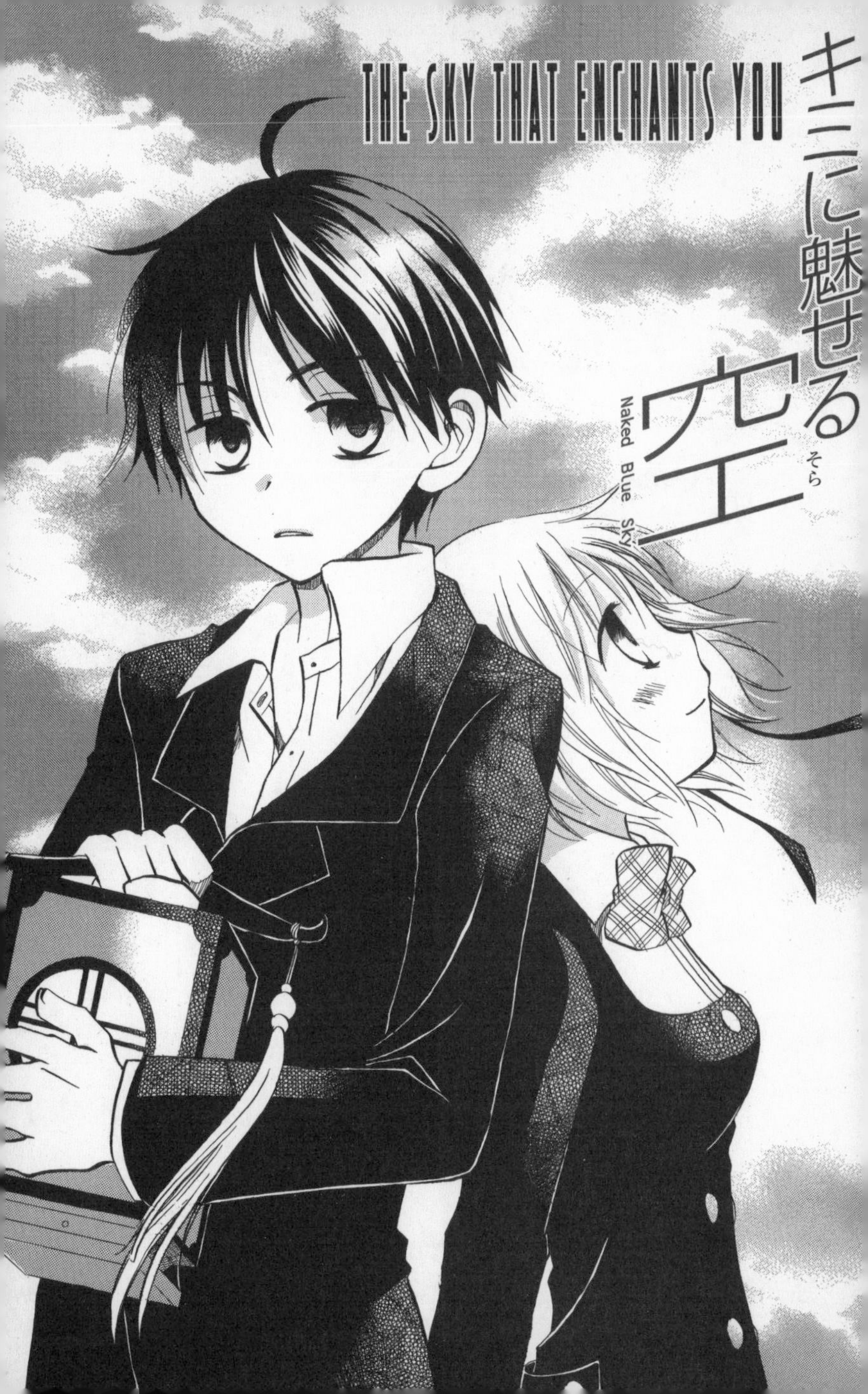
THE SKY THAT ENCHANTS YOU
きミに魅せる空
そら
Naked Blue Sky

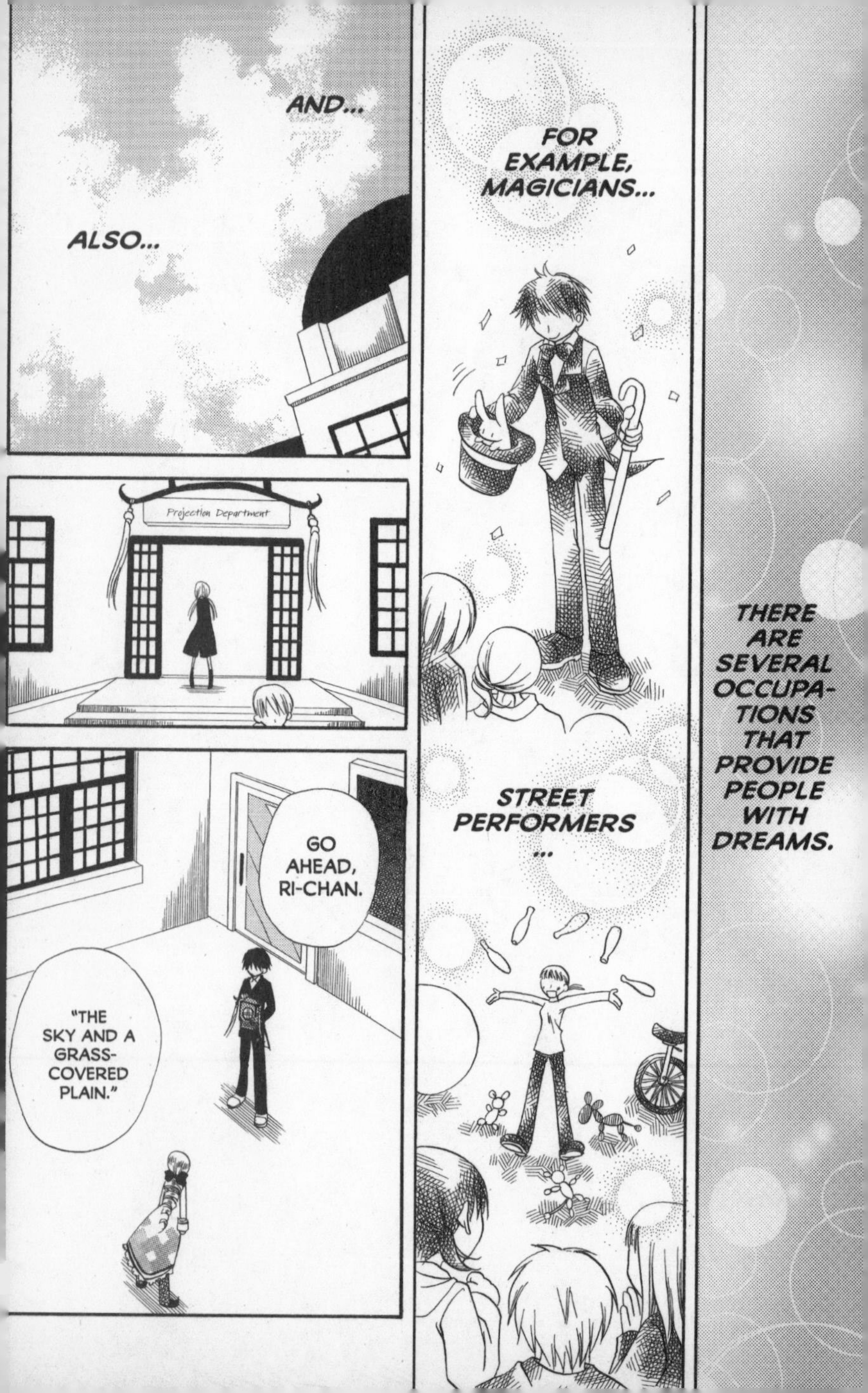
THERE ARE SEVERAL OCCUPATIONS THAT PROVIDE PEOPLE WITH DREAMS.
FOR EXAMPLE, MAGICIANS...
STREET PERFORMERS ...
AND...
ALSO...
Projection Department
GO AHEAD, RI-CHAN.
"THE SKY AND A GRASS-COVERED PLAIN."

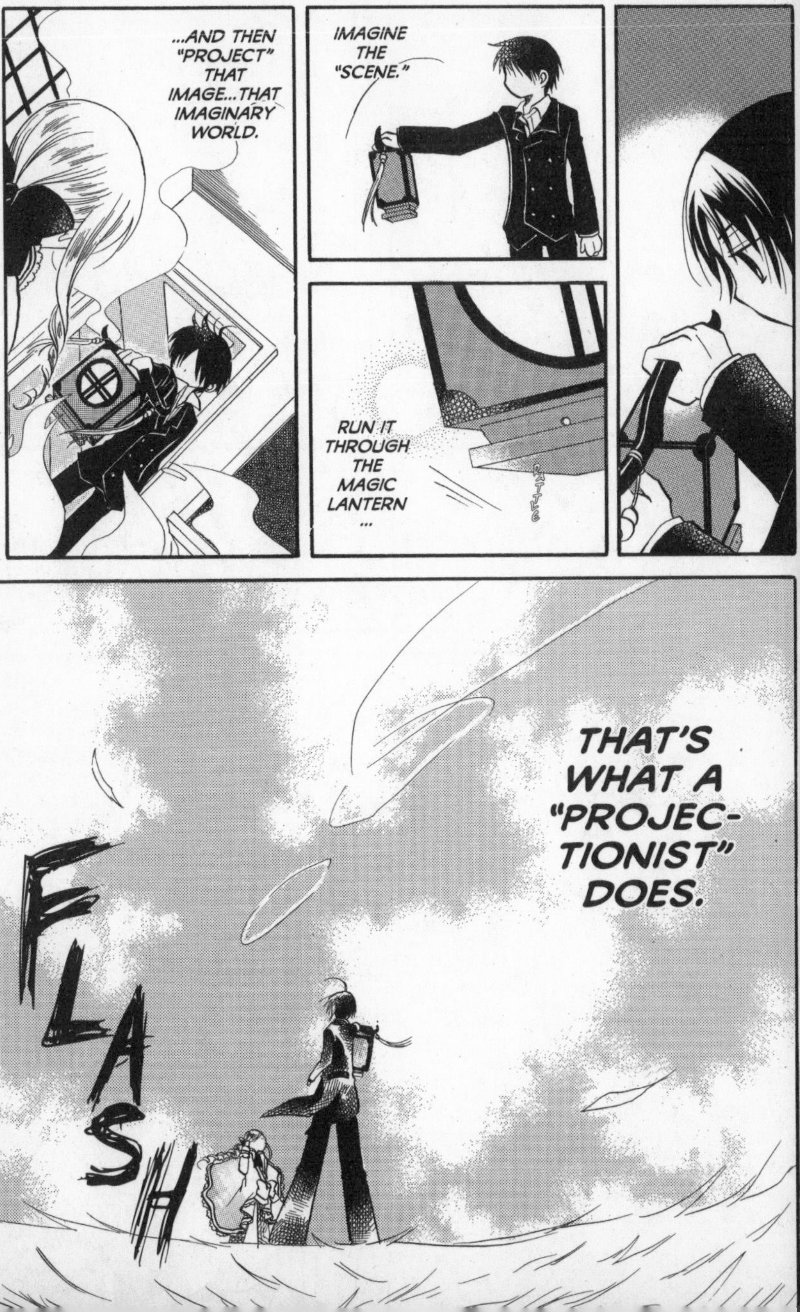
IMAGINE THE "SCENE."
RUN IT THROUGH THE MAGIC LANTERN ...
RATTLE
...AND THEN "PROJECT" THAT IMAGE...THAT IMAGINARY WORLD.
THAT'S WHAT A "PROJECTIONIST" DOES.
FLASH

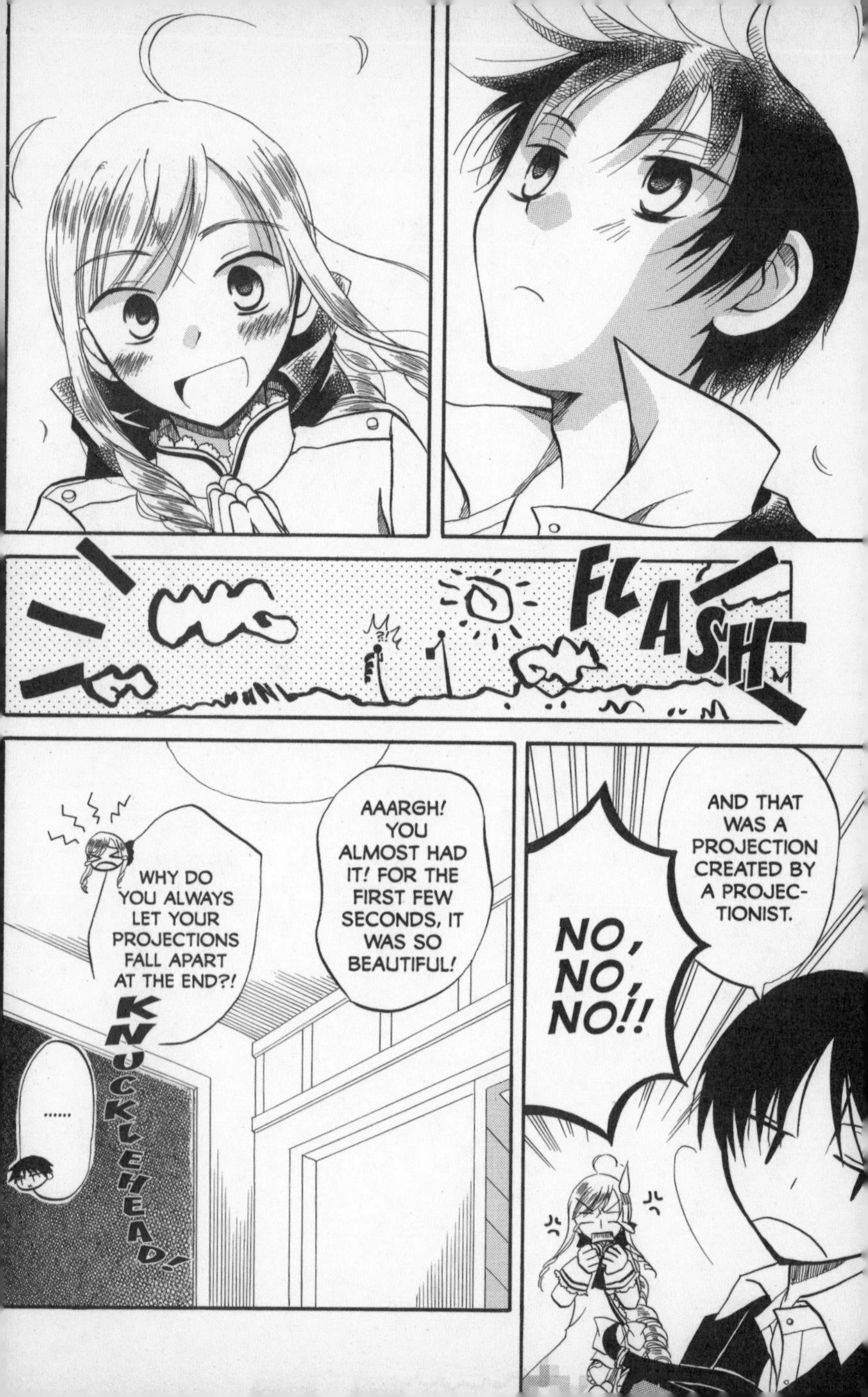
FLASH
AND THAT WAS A PROJECTION CREATED BY A PROJECTIONIST.
NO, NO, NO!!
AAARGH! YOU ALMOST HAD IT! FOR THE FIRST FEW SECONDS, IT WAS SO BEAUTIFUL!
WHY DO YOU ALWAYS LET YOUR PROJECTIONS FALL APART AT THE END?!
KNUCKLEHEAD!
......

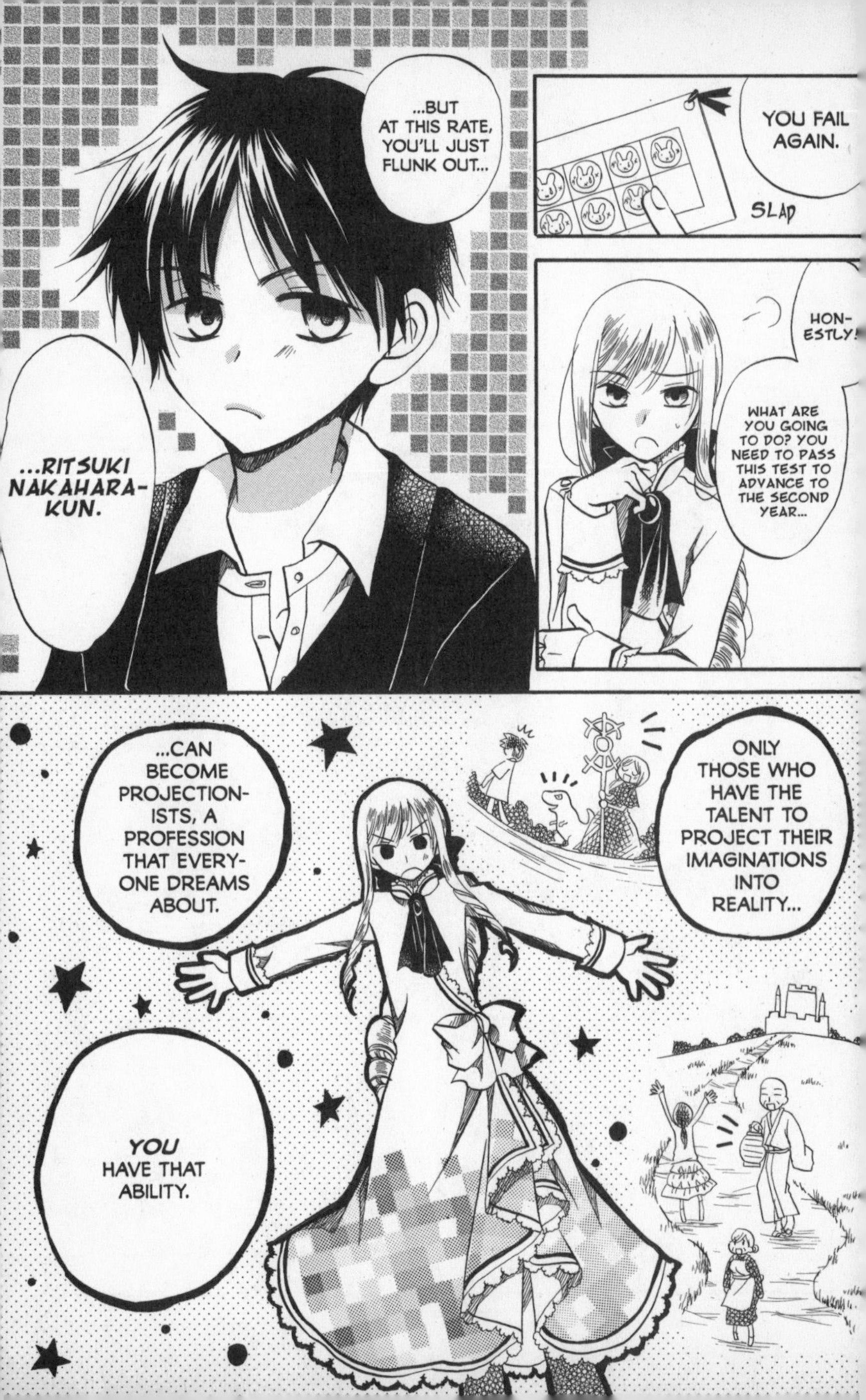
YOU FAIL AGAIN.
SLAP
HON-ESTLY!
WHAT ARE YOU GOING TO DO? YOU NEED TO PASS THIS TEST TO ADVANCE TO THE SECOND YEAR...
...BUT AT THIS RATE, YOU'LL JUST FLUNK OUT...
...RITSUKI NAKAHARA-KUN.
ONLY THOSE WHO HAVE THE TALENT TO PROJECT THEIR IMAGINATIONS INTO REALITY...
...CAN BECOME PROJECTION-ISTS, A PROFESSION THAT EVERY-ONE DREAMS ABOUT.
YOU HAVE THAT ABILITY.

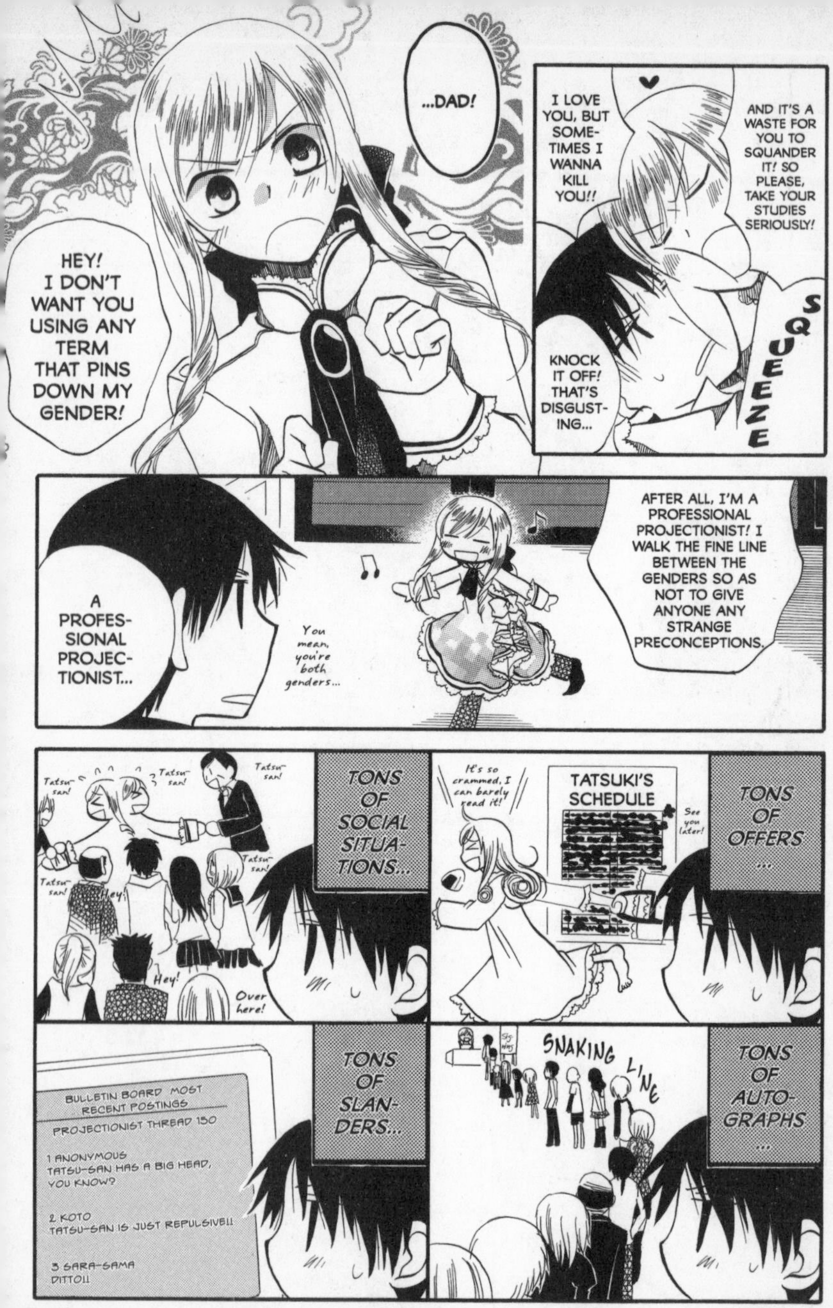
AND IT'S A WASTE FOR YOU TO SQUANDER IT! SO PLEASE, TAKE YOUR STUDIES SERIOUSLY!
I LOVE YOU, BUT SOMETIMES I WANNA KILL YOU!!
SQUEEZE
KNOCK IT OFF! THAT'S DISGUSTING...
...DAD!
HEY! I DON'T WANT YOU USING ANY TERM THAT PINS DOWN MY GENDER!
AFTER ALL, I'M A PROFESSIONAL PROJECTIONIST! I WALK THE FINE LINE BETWEEN THE GENDERS SO AS NOT TO GIVE ANYONE ANY STRANGE PRECONCEPTIONS.
You mean, you're both genders...
A PROFESSIONAL PROJECTIONIST...
TONS OF OFFERS...
See you later!
TATSUKI'S SCHEDULE
It's so crammed, I can barely read it!
TONS OF SOCIAL SITUATIONS...
Tatsu-san!
Tatsu-san!
Tatsu-san!
Tatsu-san!
Tatsu-san!
Hey!
Hey!
Over here!
TONS OF AUTOGRAPHS...
SNAKING LINE
TONS OF SLANDERS...
BULLETIN BOARD MOST RECENT POSTINGS
PROJECTIONIST THREAD 150
1 ANONYMOUS
TATSU-SAN HAS A BIG HEAD, YOU KNOW?
2 KOTO
TATSU-SAN IS JUST REPULSIVE!!
3 SARA-SAMA
DITTO!!

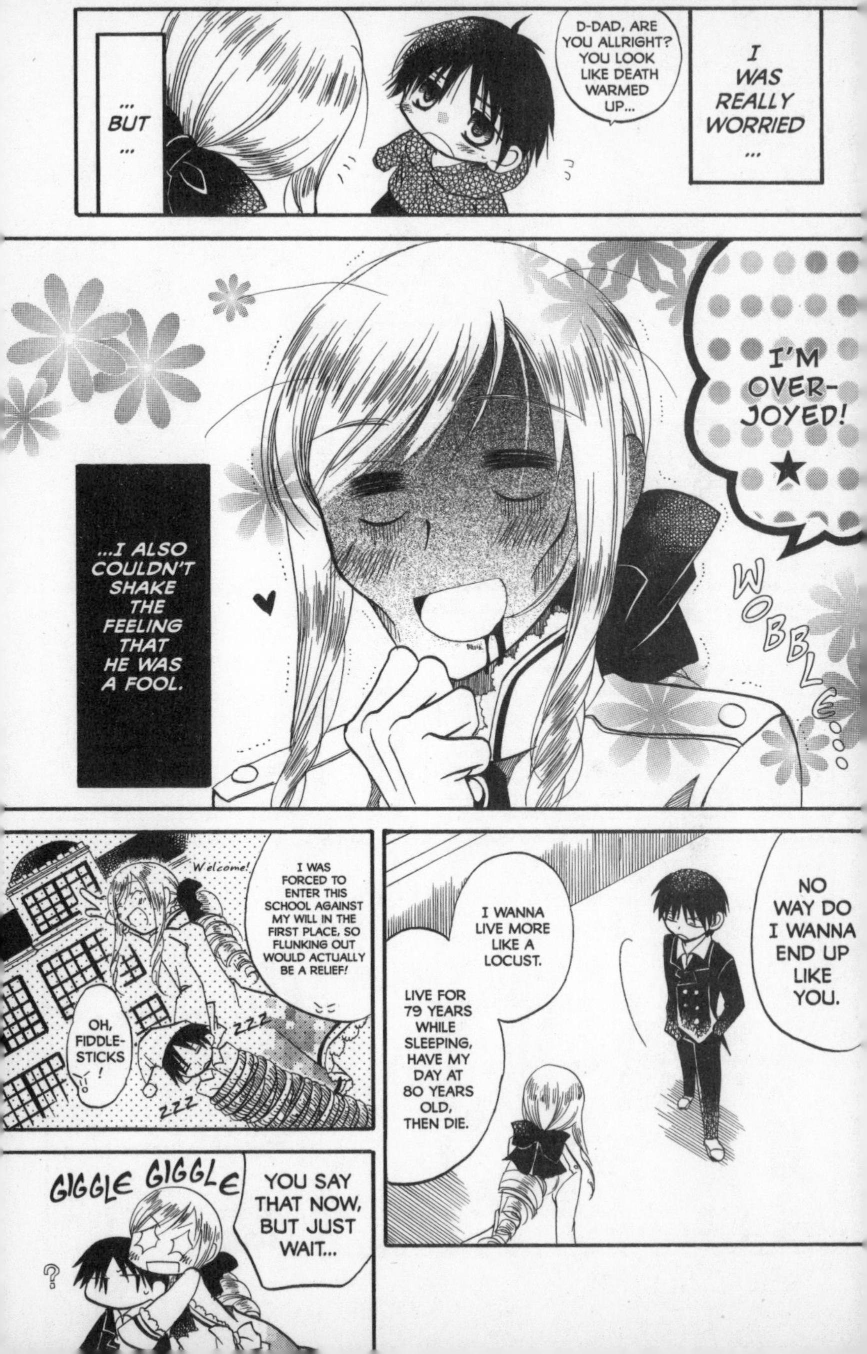
I WAS REALLY WORRIED...
D-DAD, ARE YOU ALLRIGHT? YOU LOOK LIKE DEATH WARMED UP...
...BUT...
I'M OVER-JOYED! ★
WOBBLE...
...I ALSO COULDN'T SHAKE THE FEELING THAT HE WAS A FOOL.
NO WAY DO I WANNA END UP LIKE YOU.
I WANNA LIVE MORE LIKE A LOCUST.
LIVE FOR 79 YEARS WHILE SLEEPING, HAVE MY DAY AT 80 YEARS OLD, THEN DIE.
Welcome!
I WAS FORCED TO ENTER THIS SCHOOL AGAINST MY WILL IN THE FIRST PLACE, SO FLUNKING OUT WOULD ACTUALLY BE A RELIEF!
OH, FIDDLE-STICKS!
ZZZ
ZZZ
YOU SAY THAT NOW, BUT JUST WAIT...
GIGGLE GIGGLE

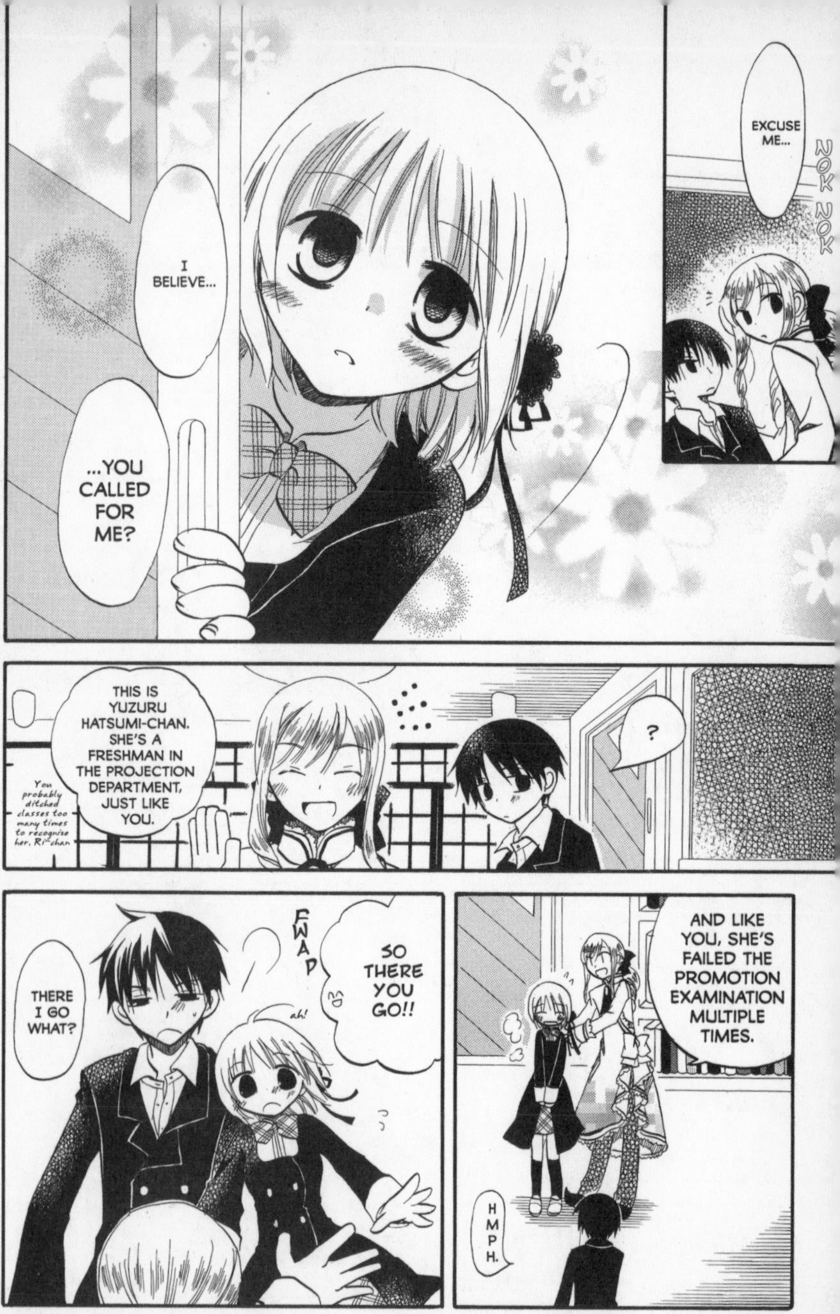
EXCUSE ME...
NOK NOK
I BELIEVE...
...YOU CALLED FOR ME?
?
THIS IS YUZURU HATSUMI-CHAN. SHE'S A FRESHMAN IN THE PROJECTION DEPARTMENT, JUST LIKE YOU.
You probably ditched classes too many times to recognize her, Ri-chan
AND LIKE YOU, SHE'S FAILED THE PROMOTION EXAMINATION MULTIPLE TIMES.
HMPH.
SO THERE YOU GO!!
FWAP
ah!
THERE I GO WHAT?

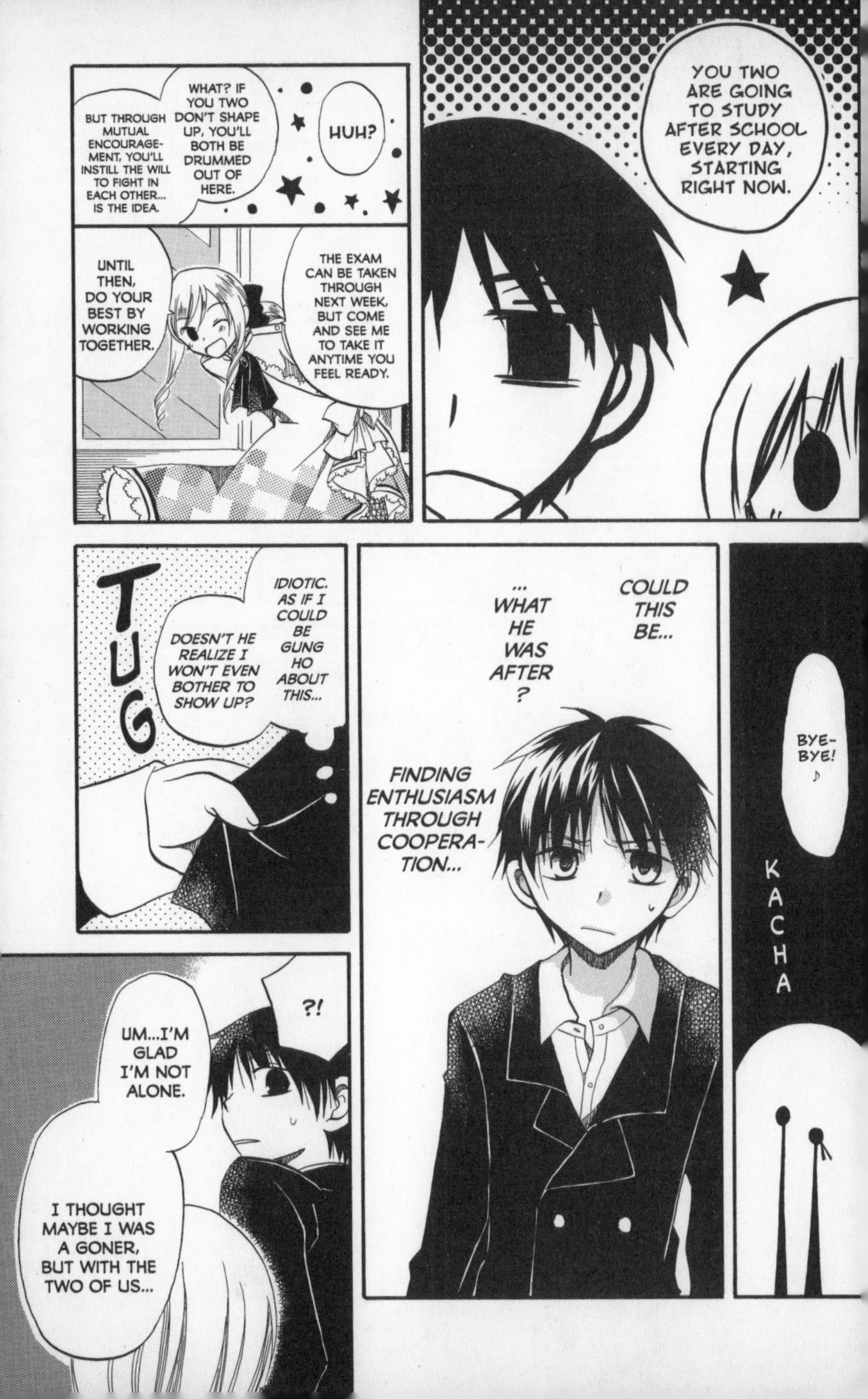
YOU TWO ARE GOING TO STUDY AFTER SCHOOL EVERY DAY, STARTING RIGHT NOW.
HUH?
WHAT? IF YOU TWO DON'T SHAPE UP, YOU'LL BOTH BE DRUMMED OUT OF HERE.
BUT THROUGH MUTUAL ENCOURAGEMENT, YOU'LL INSTILL THE WILL TO FIGHT IN EACH OTHER... IS THE IDEA.
THE EXAM CAN BE TAKEN THROUGH NEXT WEEK, BUT COME AND SEE ME TO TAKE IT ANYTIME YOU FEEL READY.
UNTIL THEN, DO YOUR BEST BY WORKING TOGETHER.
BYE-BYE! ♪
KACHA
COULD THIS BE...
...WHAT HE WAS AFTER?
FINDING ENTHUSIASM THROUGH COOPERATION...
IDIOTIC. AS IF I COULD BE GUNG HO ABOUT THIS...
DOESN'T HE REALIZE I WON'T EVEN BOTHER TO SHOW UP?
TUG
?!
UM...I'M GLAD I'M NOT ALONE.
I THOUGHT MAYBE I WAS A GONER, BUT WITH THE TWO OF US...

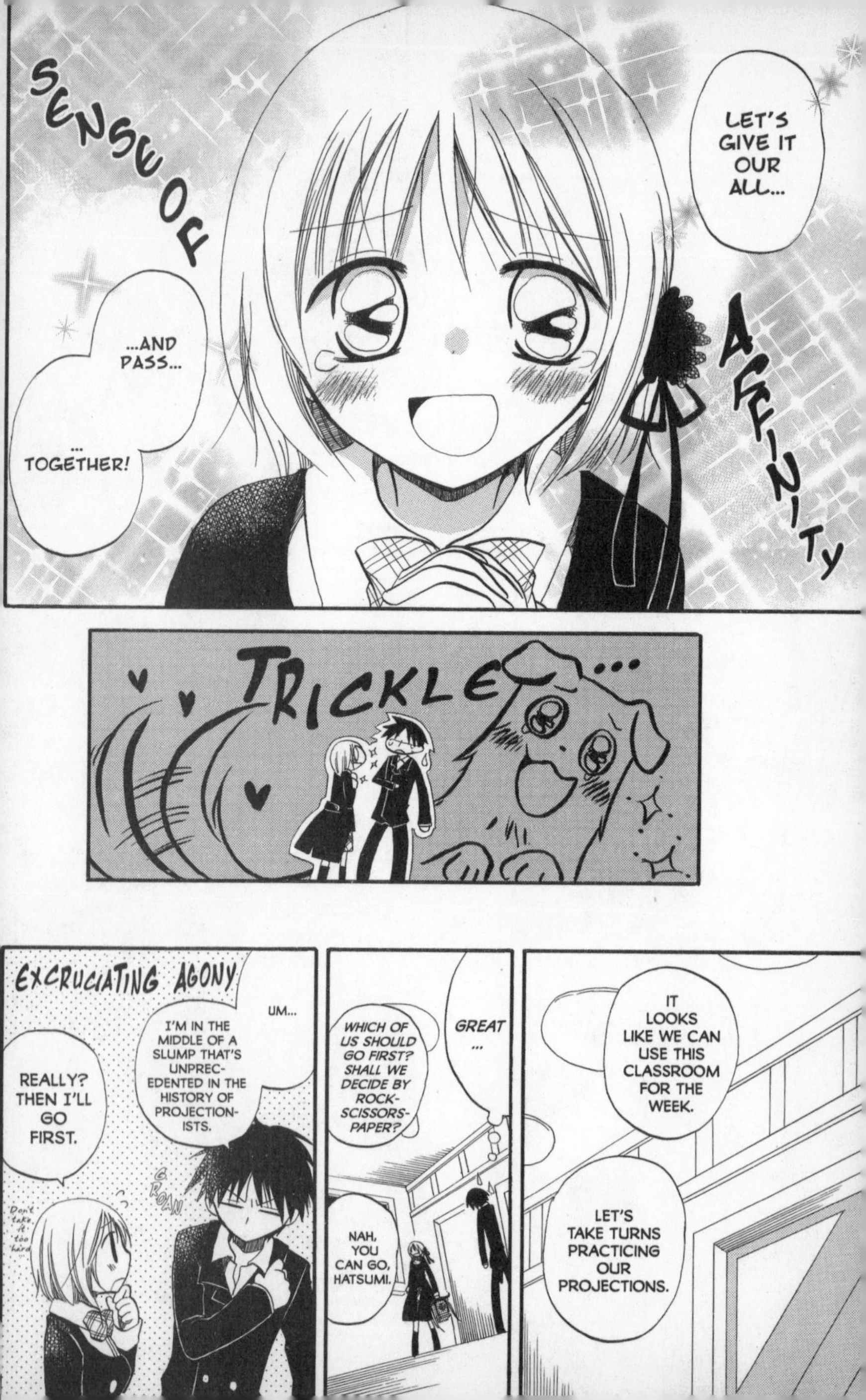
LET'S GIVE IT OUR ALL...
SENSE OF
...AND PASS...
... TOGETHER!
AFFINITY
TRICKLE...
IT LOOKS LIKE WE CAN USE THIS CLASSROOM FOR THE WEEK.
LET'S TAKE TURNS PRACTICING OUR PROJECTIONS.
GREAT ...
WHICH OF US SHOULD GO FIRST? SHALL WE DECIDE BY ROCK-SCISSORS-PAPER?
NAH, YOU CAN GO, HATSUMI.
UM...
I'M IN THE MIDDLE OF A SLUMP THAT'S UNPRECEDENTED IN THE HISTORY OF PROJECTIONISTS.
EXCRUCIATING AGONY
REALLY? THEN I'LL GO FIRST.
GROAN
Don't take it too hard...

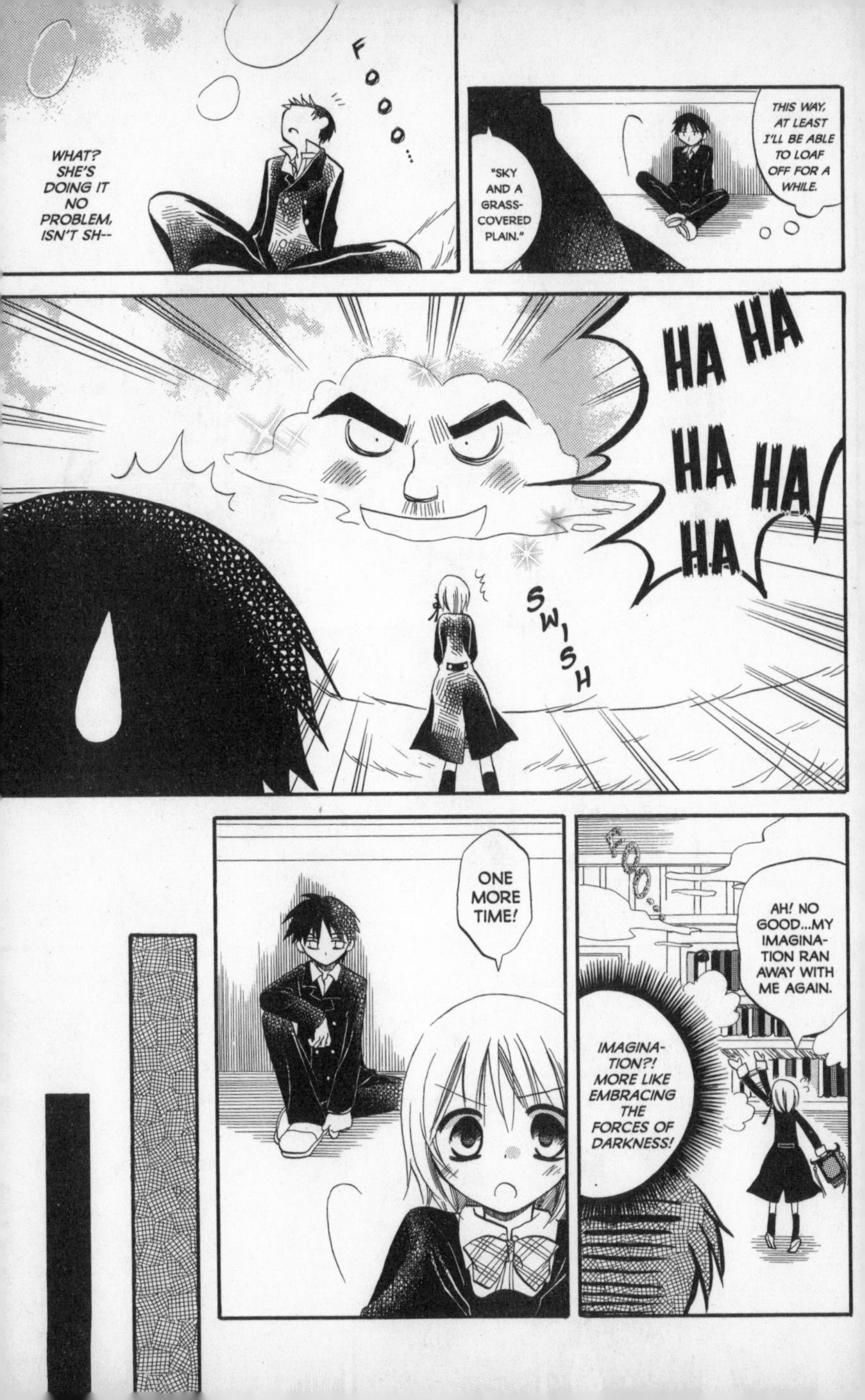
THIS WAY, AT LEAST I'LL BE ABLE TO LOAF OFF FOR A WHILE.
"SKY AND A GRASS-COVERED PLAIN."
FOOO...
WHAT? SHE'S DOING IT NO PROBLEM, ISN'T SH--
HA HA HA HA HA HA
SWISH
AH! NO GOOD...MY IMAGINATION RAN AWAY WITH ME AGAIN.
FOOO...
IMAGINATION?! MORE LIKE EMBRACING THE FORCES OF DARKNESS!
ONE MORE TIME!

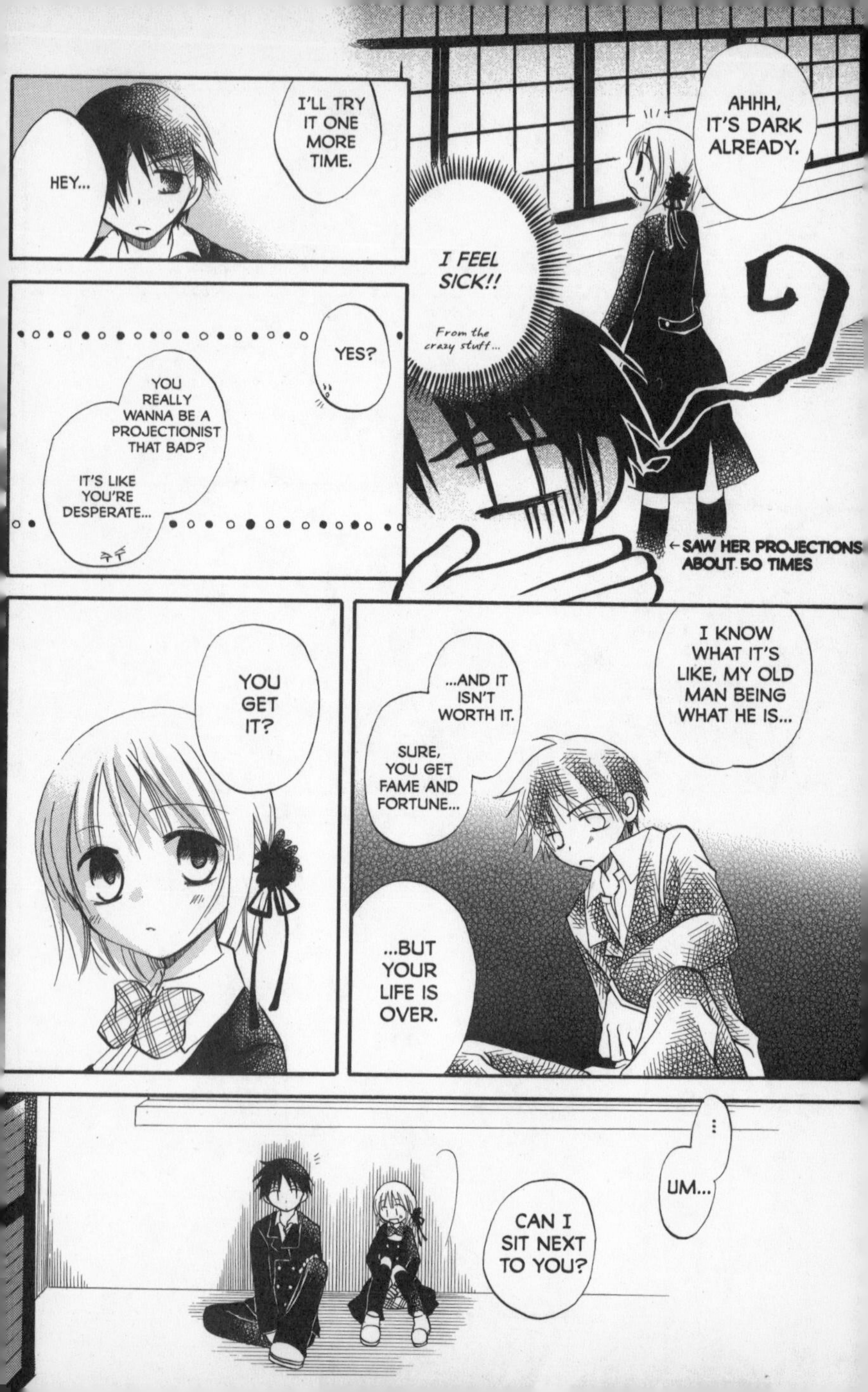
AHHH, IT'S DARK ALREADY.
I FEEL SICK!!
From the crazy stuff...
← SAW HER PROJECTIONS ABOUT 50 TIMES
I'LL TRY IT ONE MORE TIME.
HEY...
YES?
YOU REALLY WANNA BE A PROJECTIONIST THAT BAD?
IT'S LIKE YOU'RE DESPERATE...
I KNOW WHAT IT'S LIKE, MY OLD MAN BEING WHAT HE IS...
...AND IT ISN'T WORTH IT.
SURE, YOU GET FAME AND FORTUNE...
...BUT YOUR LIFE IS OVER.
YOU GET IT?
...
UM...
CAN I SIT NEXT TO YOU?

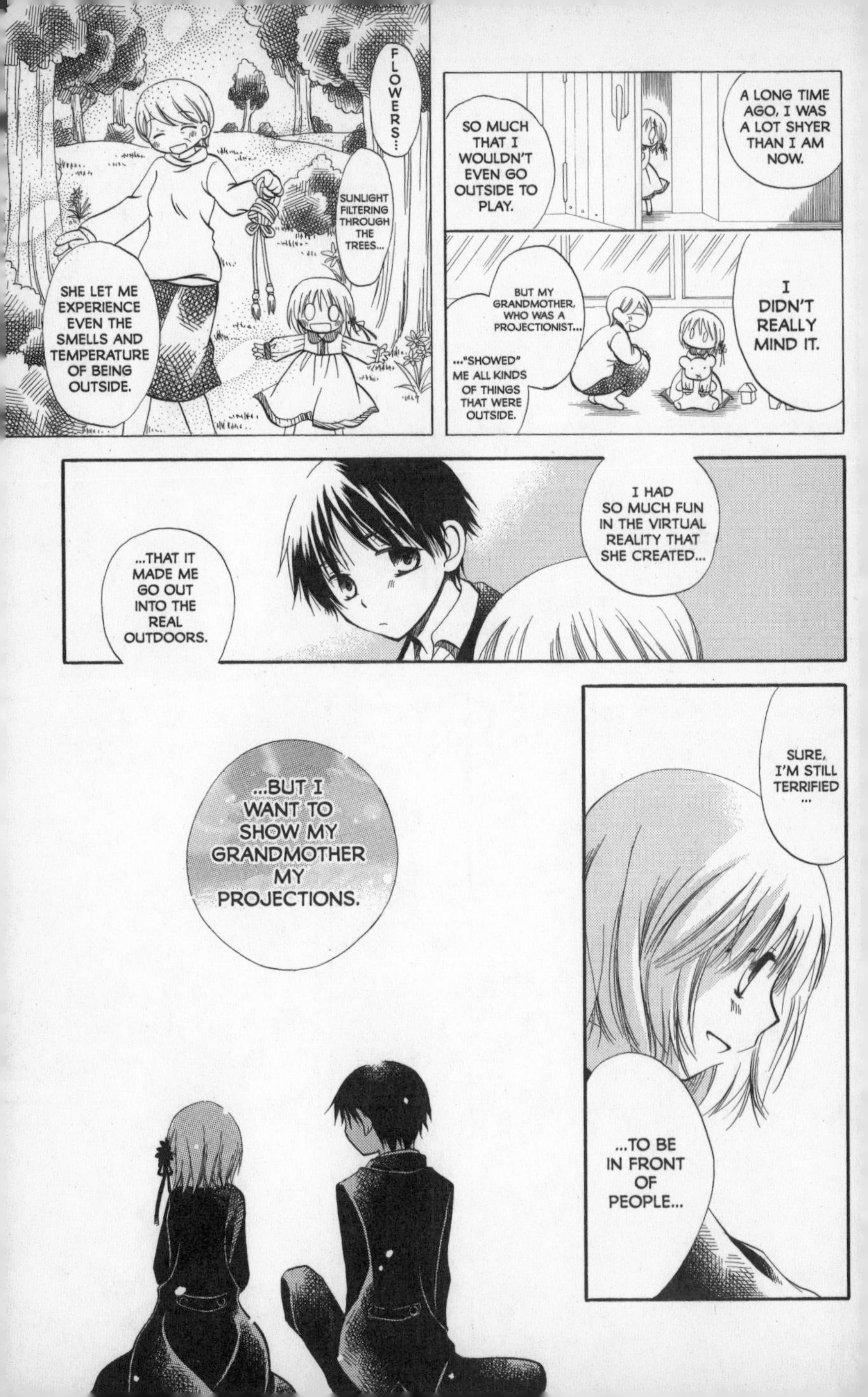
A LONG TIME AGO, I WAS A LOT SHYER THAN I AM NOW.
SO MUCH THAT I WOULDN'T EVEN GO OUTSIDE TO PLAY.
I DIDN'T REALLY MIND IT.
BUT MY GRANDMOTHER, WHO WAS A PROJECTIONIST...
..."SHOWED" ME ALL KINDS OF THINGS THAT WERE OUTSIDE.
FLOWERS...
SUNLIGHT FILTERING THROUGH THE TREES...
SHE LET ME EXPERIENCE EVEN THE SMELLS AND TEMPERATURE OF BEING OUTSIDE.
I HAD SO MUCH FUN IN THE VIRTUAL REALITY THAT SHE CREATED...
...THAT IT MADE ME GO OUT INTO THE REAL OUTDOORS.
SURE, I'M STILL TERRIFIED ...
...TO BE IN FRONT OF PEOPLE...
...BUT I WANT TO SHOW MY GRANDMOTHER MY PROJECTIONS.

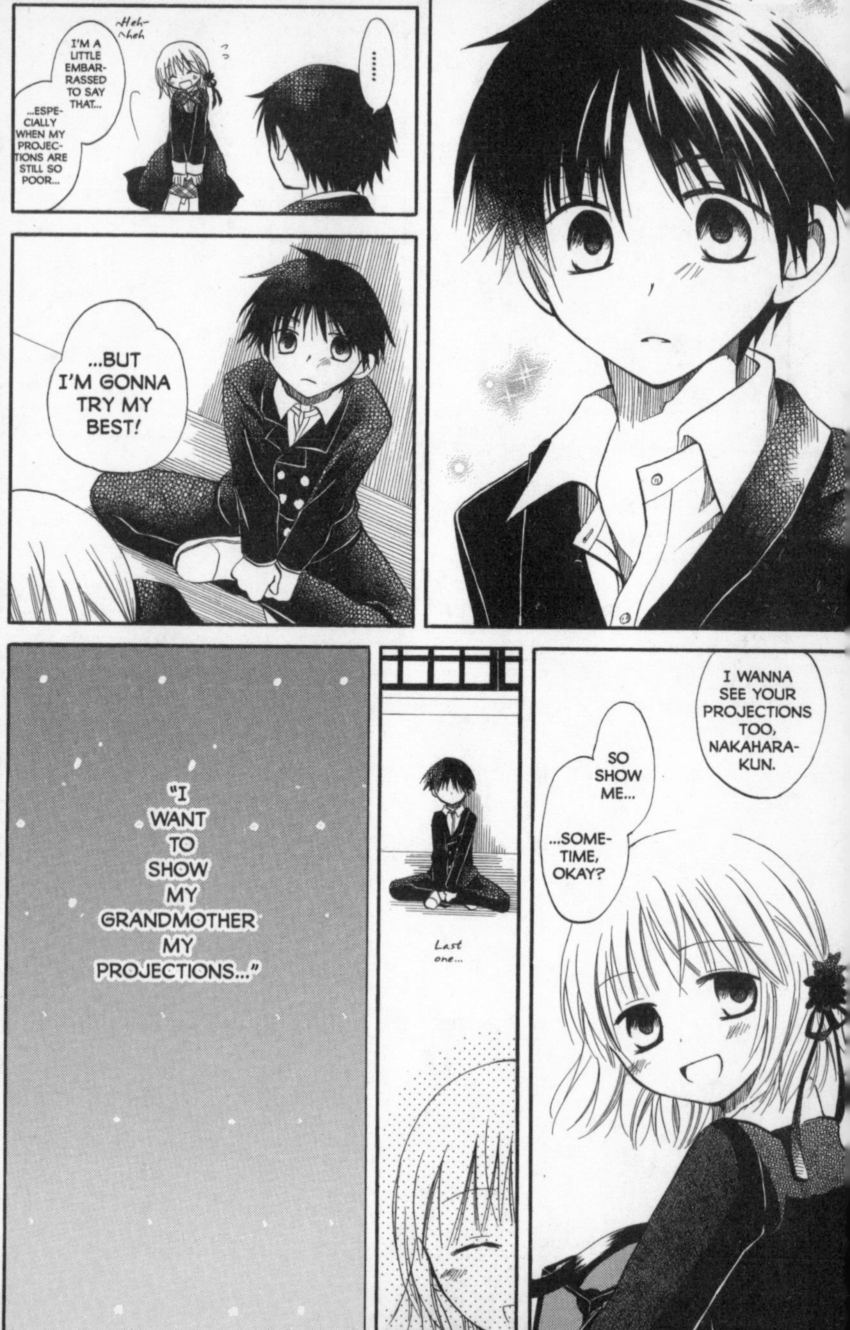
......
Heh-heh
I'M A LITTLE EMBARRASSED TO SAY THAT...
...ESPECIALLY WHEN MY PROJECTIONS ARE STILL SO POOR...
...BUT I'M GONNA TRY MY BEST!
I WANNA SEE YOUR PROJECTIONS TOO, NAKAHARA-KUN.
SO SHOW ME...
...SOMETIME, OKAY?
Last one...
"I WANT TO SHOW MY GRANDMOTHER MY PROJECTIONS..."

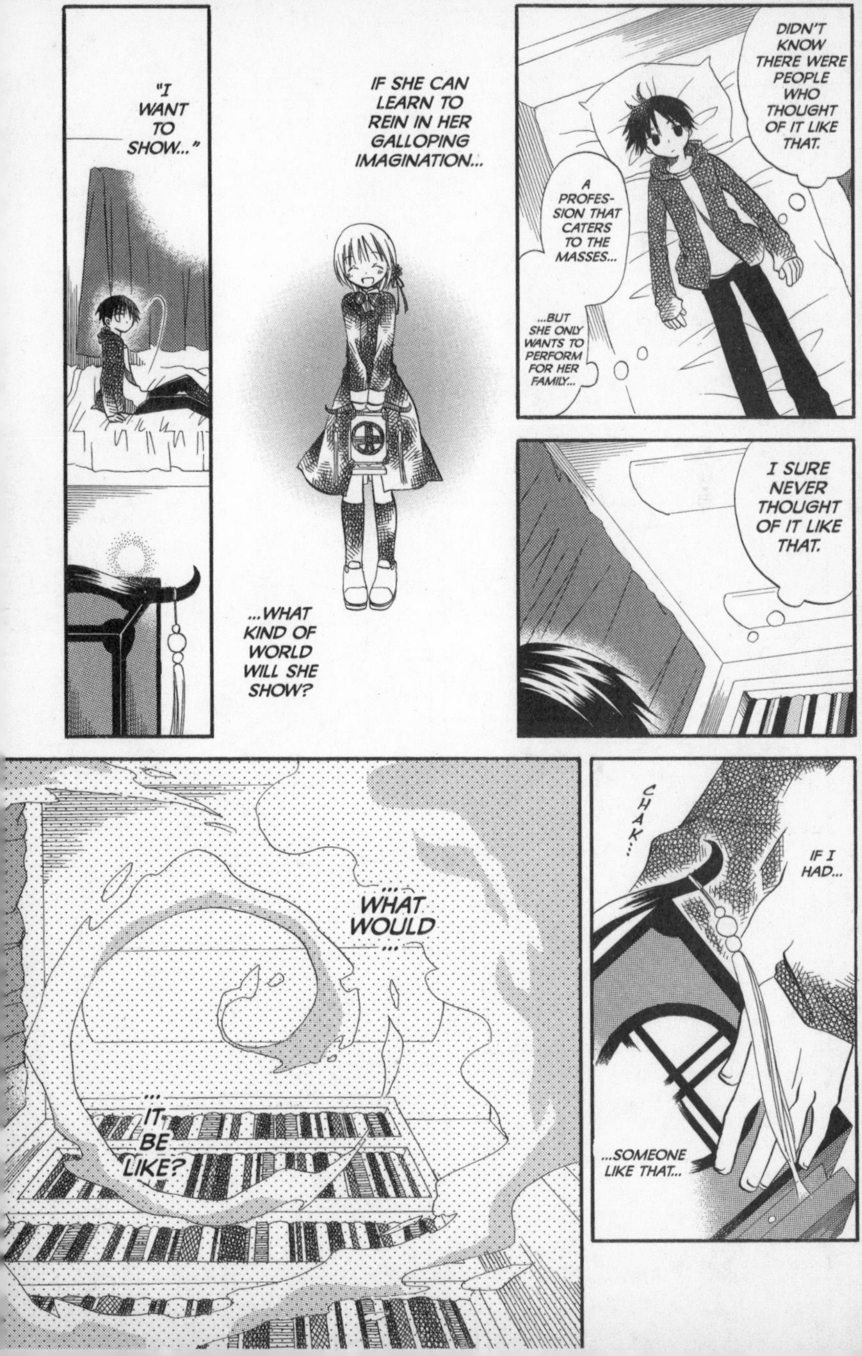
DIDN'T KNOW THERE WERE PEOPLE WHO THOUGHT OF IT LIKE THAT.
A PROFES-SION THAT CATERS TO THE MASSES...
...BUT SHE ONLY WANTS TO PERFORM FOR HER FAMILY...
I SURE NEVER THOUGHT OF IT LIKE THAT.
IF SHE CAN LEARN TO REIN IN HER GALLOPING IMAGINATION...
...WHAT KIND OF WORLD WILL SHE SHOW?
"I WANT TO SHOW..."
CHAK...
IF I HAD...
...SOMEONE LIKE THAT...
...WHAT WOULD...
...IT BE LIKE?

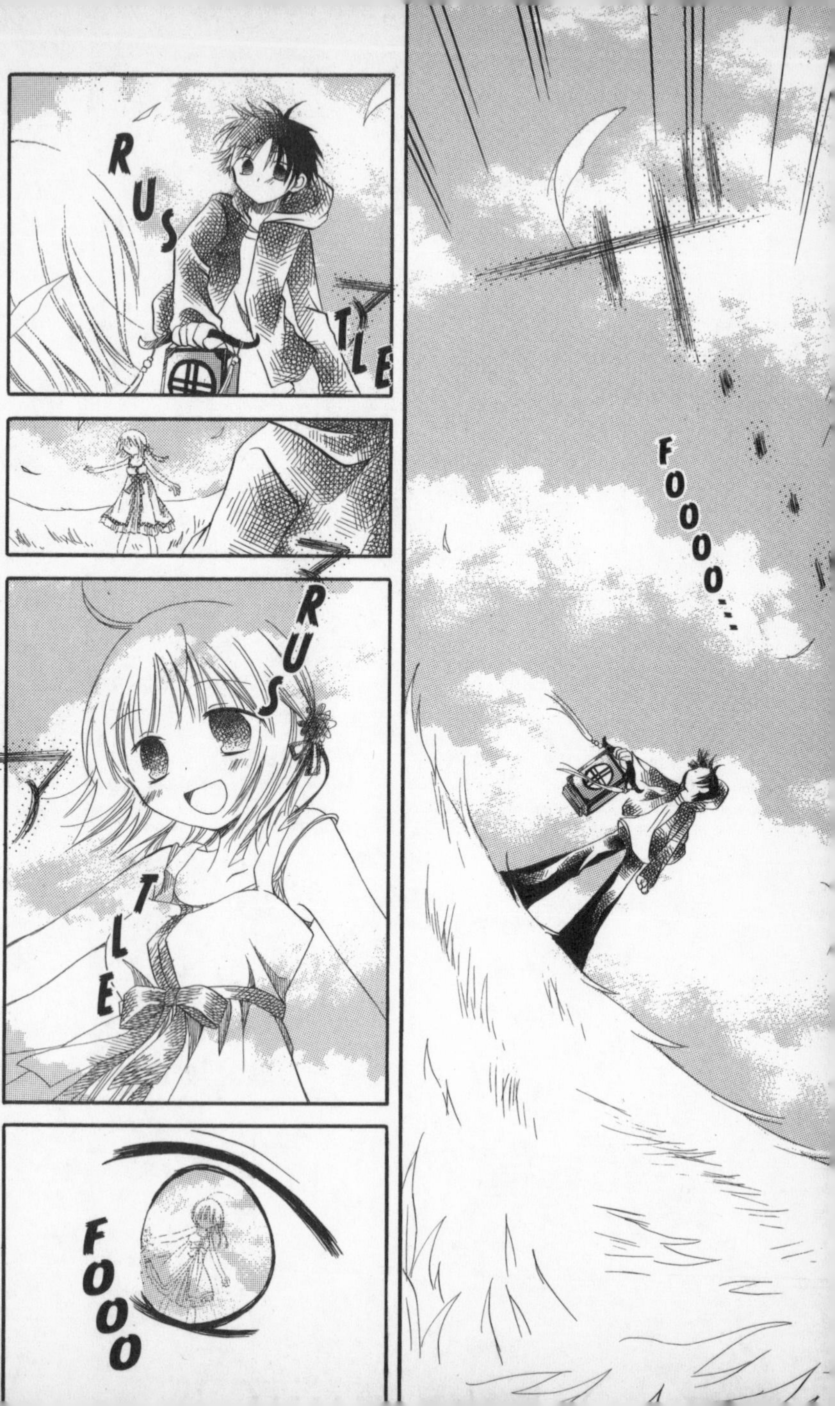
FOOOO...
RUSTLE
RUSTLE
FOOO

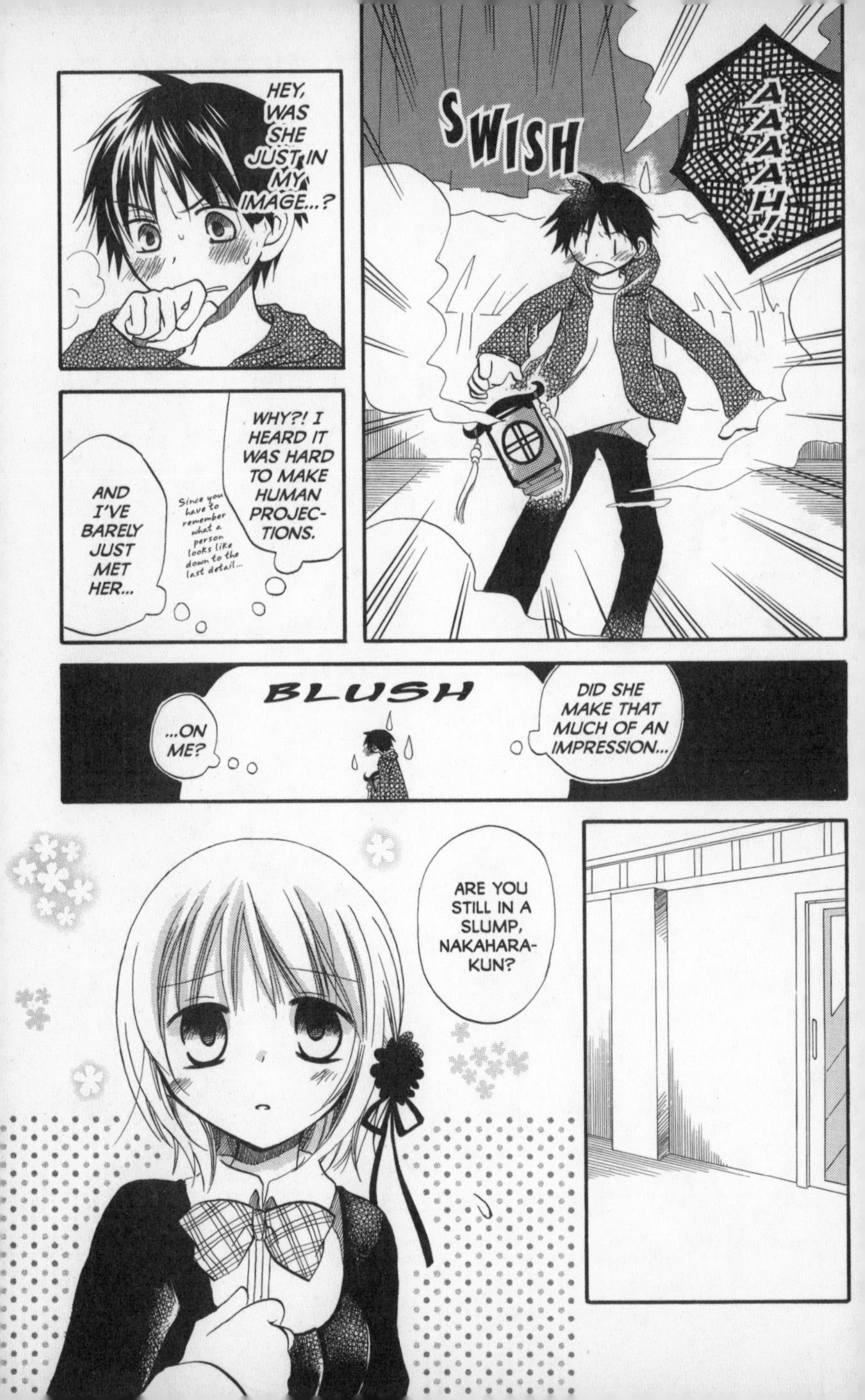
AAAAH!
SWISH
HEY, WAS SHE JUST IN MY IMAGE...?
WHY?! I HEARD IT WAS HARD TO MAKE HUMAN PROJECTIONS.
Since you have to remember what a person looks like down to the last detail...
AND I'VE BARELY JUST MET HER...
DID SHE MAKE THAT MUCH OF AN IMPRESSION...
BLUSH
...ON ME?
ARE YOU STILL IN A SLUMP, NAKAHARA-KUN?

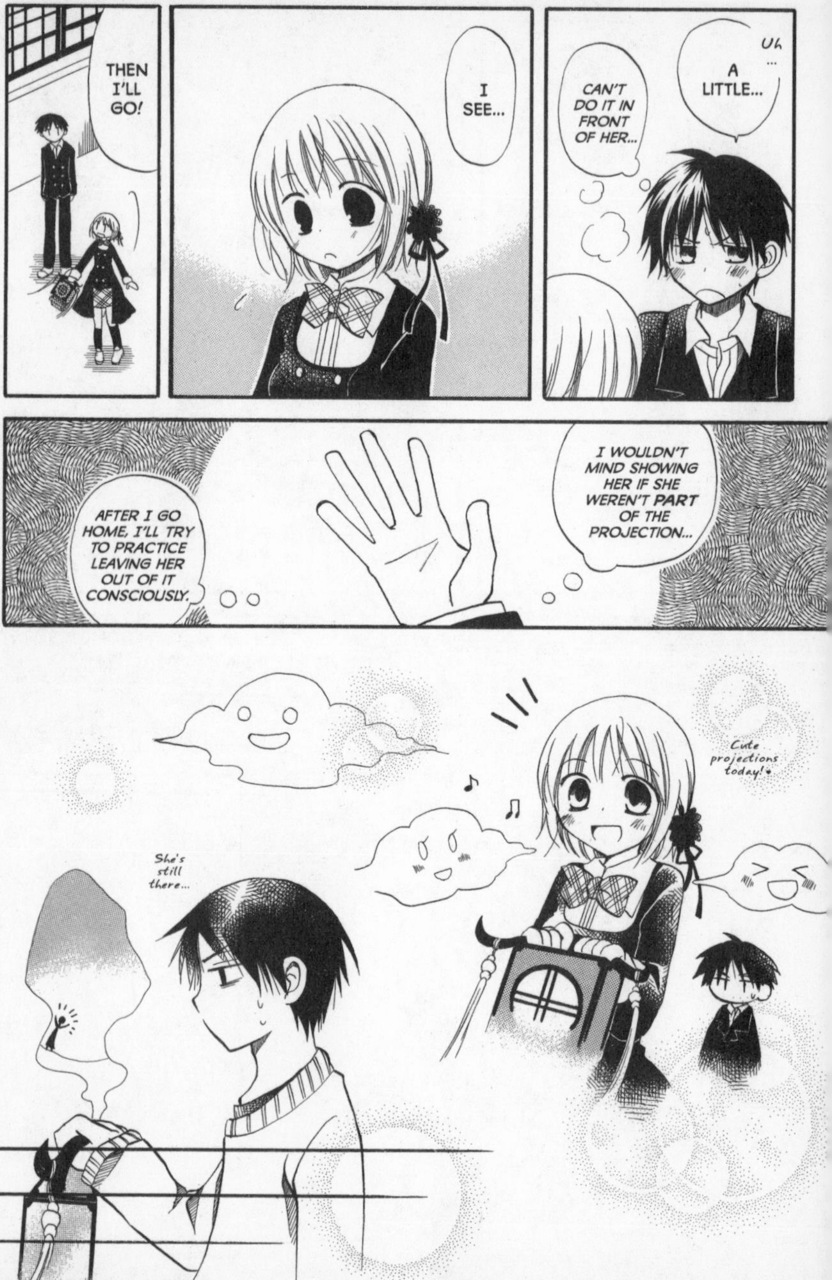
Uh ...
A LITTLE...
CAN'T DO IT IN FRONT OF HER...
I SEE...
THEN I'LL GO!
I WOULDN'T MIND SHOWING HER IF SHE WEREN'T **PART** OF THE PROJECTION...
AFTER I GO HOME, I'LL TRY TO PRACTICE LEAVING HER OUT OF IT CONSCIOUSLY.
Cute projections today!
She's still there...

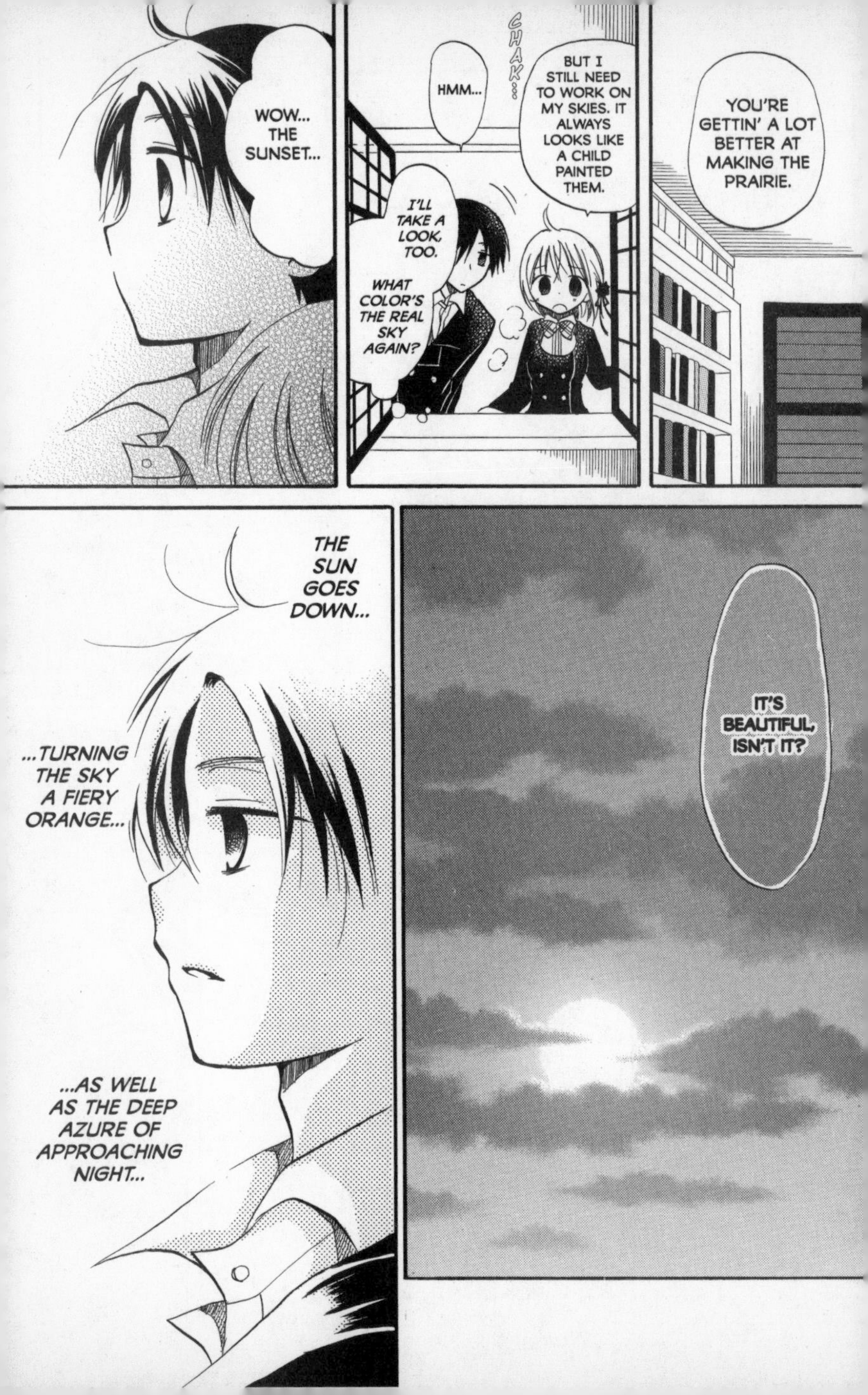
YOU'RE GETTIN' A LOT BETTER AT MAKING THE PRAIRIE.
CHAK...
BUT I STILL NEED TO WORK ON MY SKIES. IT ALWAYS LOOKS LIKE A CHILD PAINTED THEM.
HMM...
I'LL TAKE A LOOK, TOO.
WHAT COLOR'S THE REAL SKY AGAIN?
WOW... THE SUNSET...
IT'S BEAUTIFUL, ISN'T IT?
THE SUN GOES DOWN...
...TURNING THE SKY A FIERY ORANGE...
...AS WELL AS THE DEEP AZURE OF APPROACHING NIGHT...

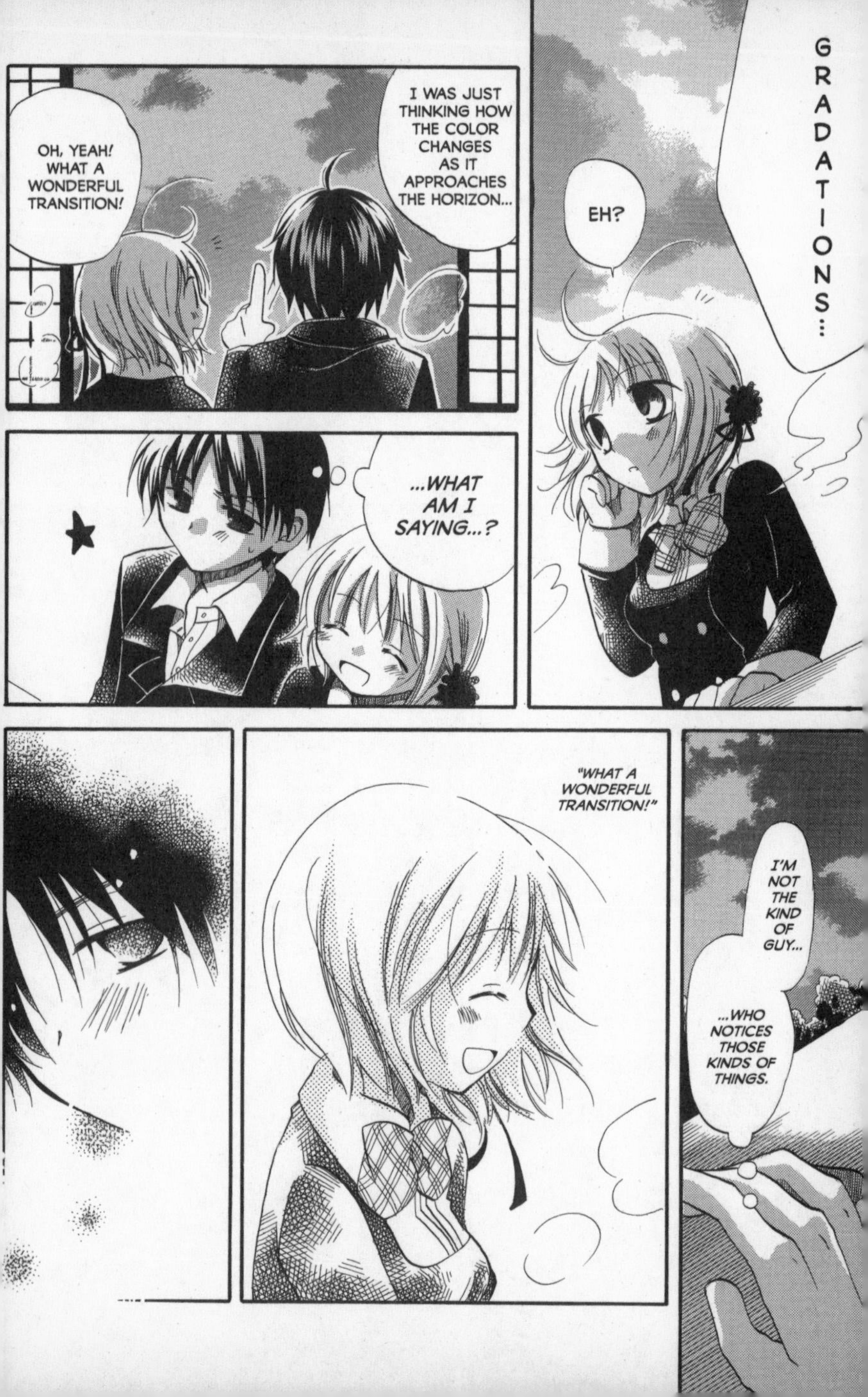
GRADATIONS...
EH?
I WAS JUST THINKING HOW THE COLOR CHANGES AS IT APPROACHES THE HORIZON...
OH, YEAH! WHAT A WONDERFUL TRANSITION!
...WHAT AM I SAYING...?
I'M NOT THE KIND OF GUY...
...WHO NOTICES THOSE KINDS OF THINGS.
"WHAT A WONDERFUL TRANSITION!"

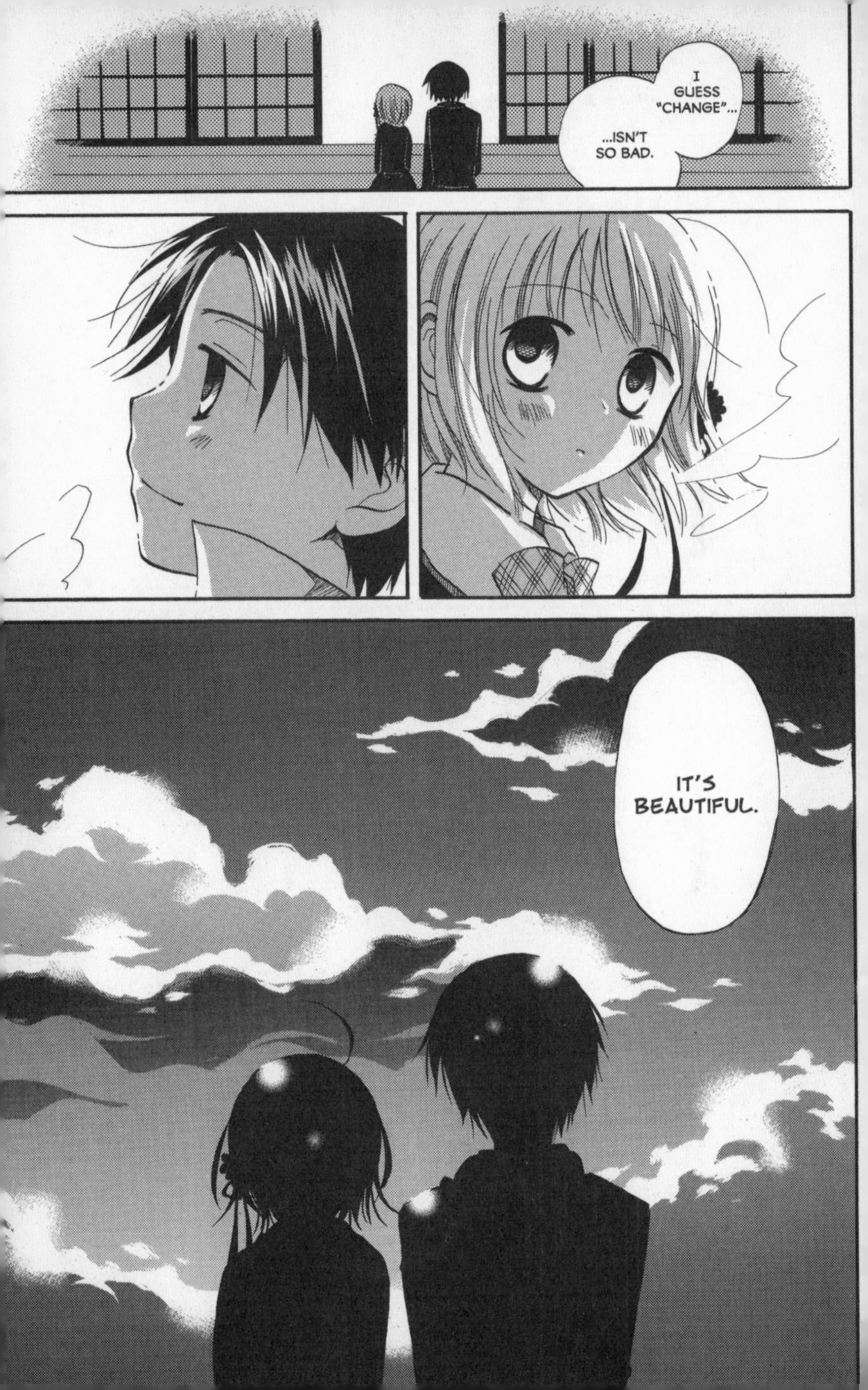
I GUESS "CHANGE"...
...ISN'T SO BAD.
IT'S BEAUTIFUL.

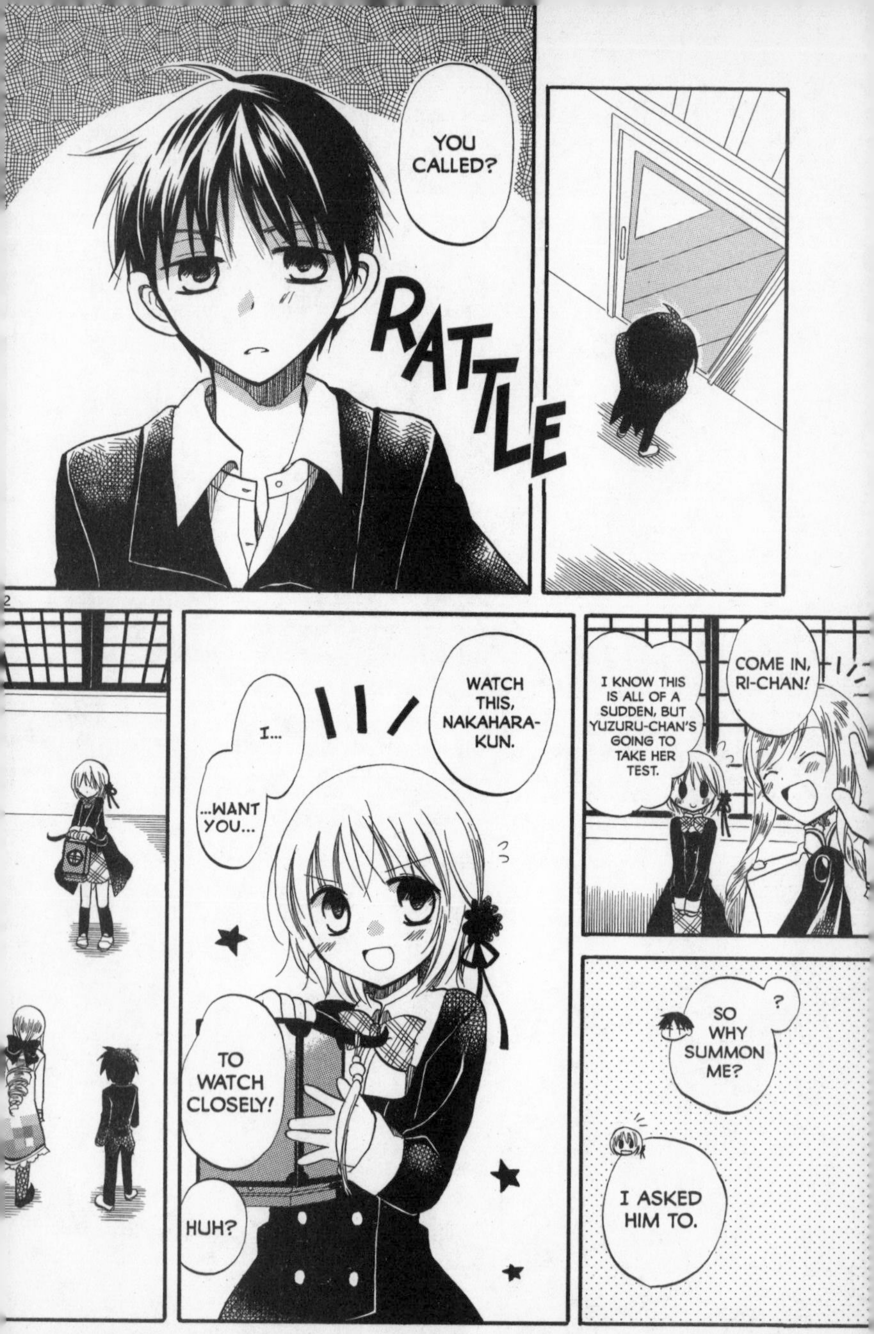
RATTLE
YOU CALLED?
COME IN, RI-CHAN!
I KNOW THIS IS ALL OF A SUDDEN, BUT YUZURU-CHAN'S GOING TO TAKE HER TEST.
SO WHY SUMMON ME?
I ASKED HIM TO.
WATCH THIS, NAKAHARA-KUN.
I...
...WANT YOU...
TO WATCH CLOSELY!
HUH?

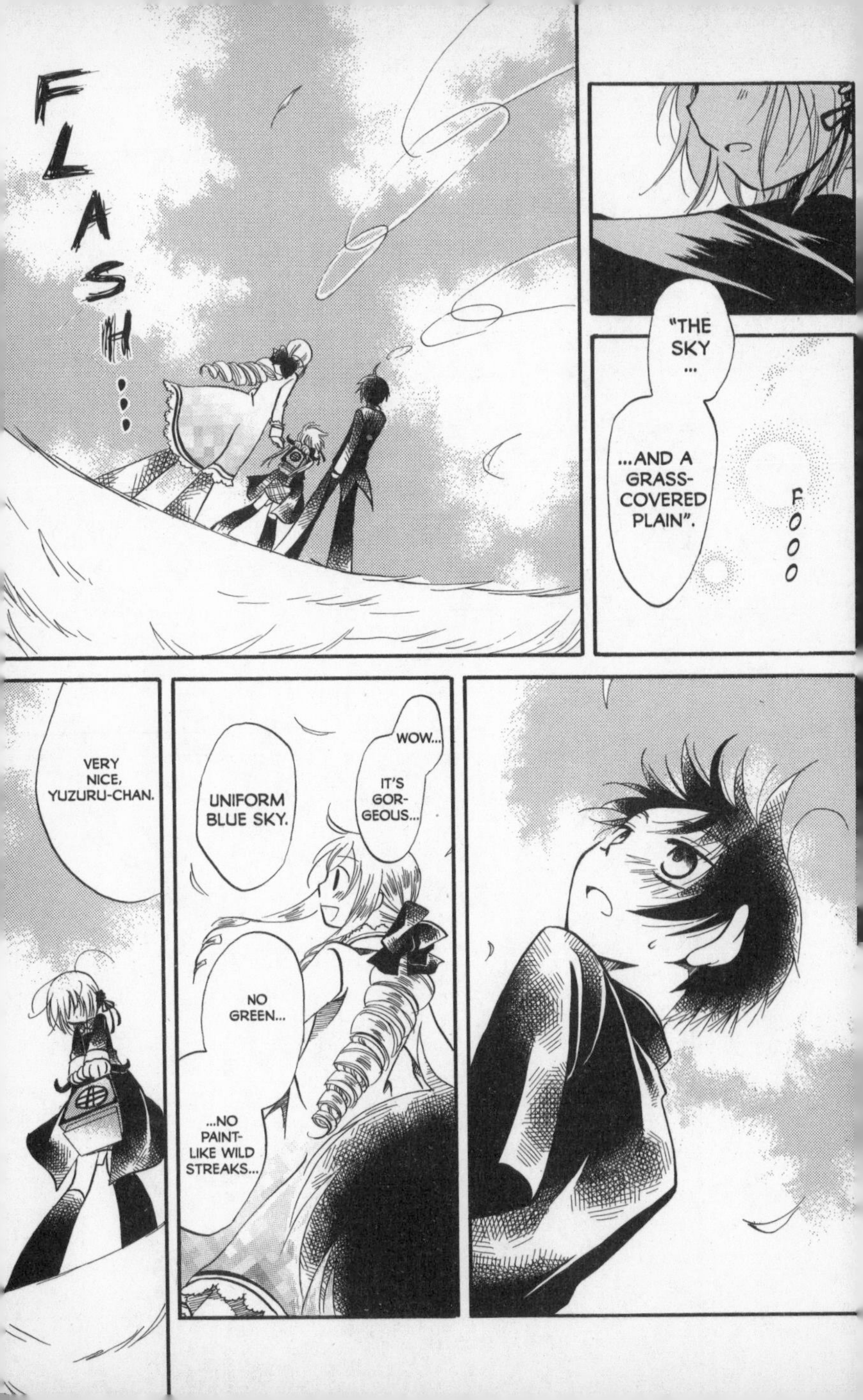
"THE SKY ...
...AND A GRASS-COVERED PLAIN".
FOOO
FLASH...
WOW...
IT'S GORGEOUS...
UNIFORM BLUE SKY.
NO GREEN...
...NO PAINT-LIKE WILD STREAKS...
VERY NICE, YUZURU-CHAN.

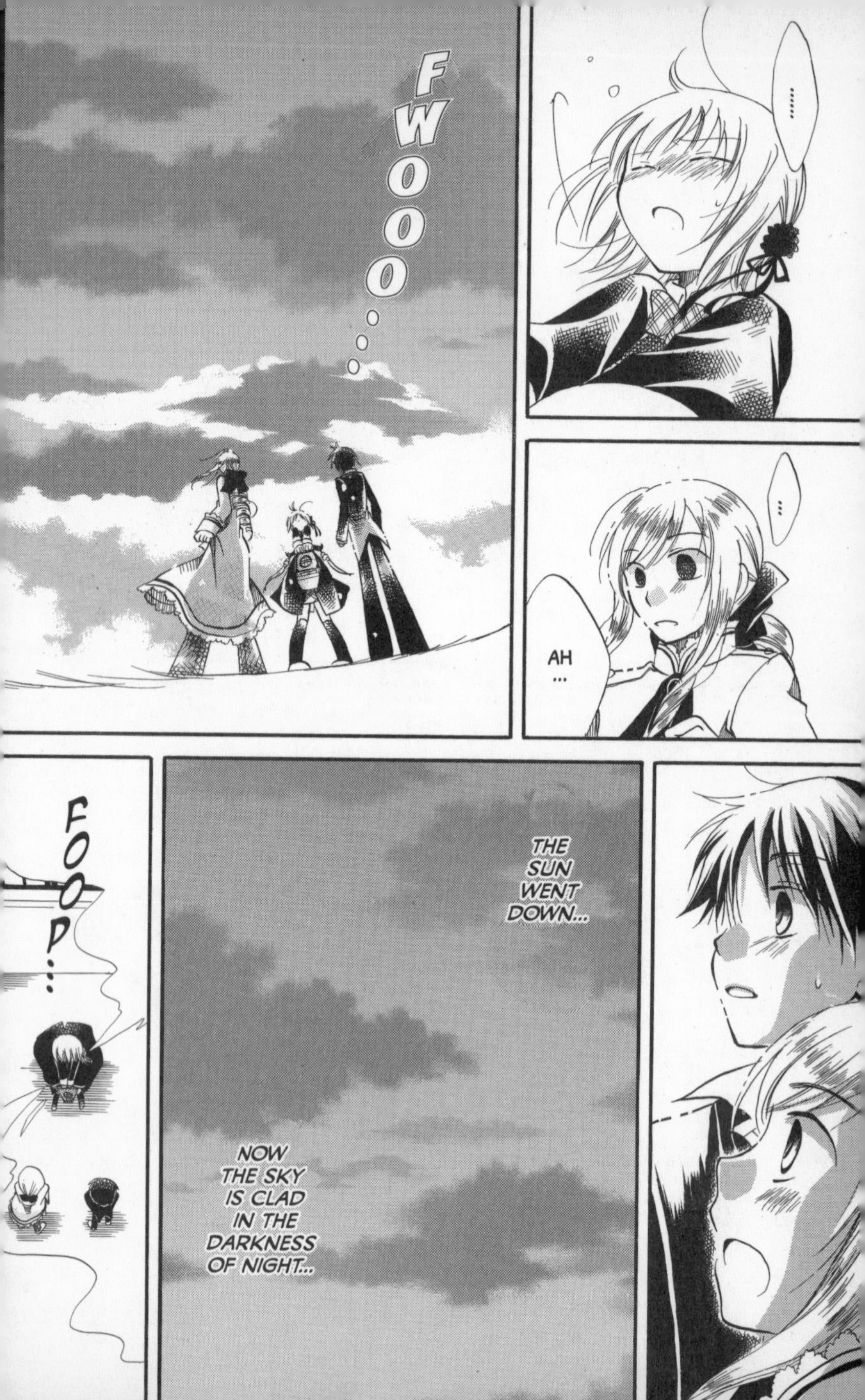
......
...
AH ...
FWOOO...
THE SUN WENT DOWN...
NOW THE SKY IS CLAD IN THE DARKNESS OF NIGHT...
FOOP...

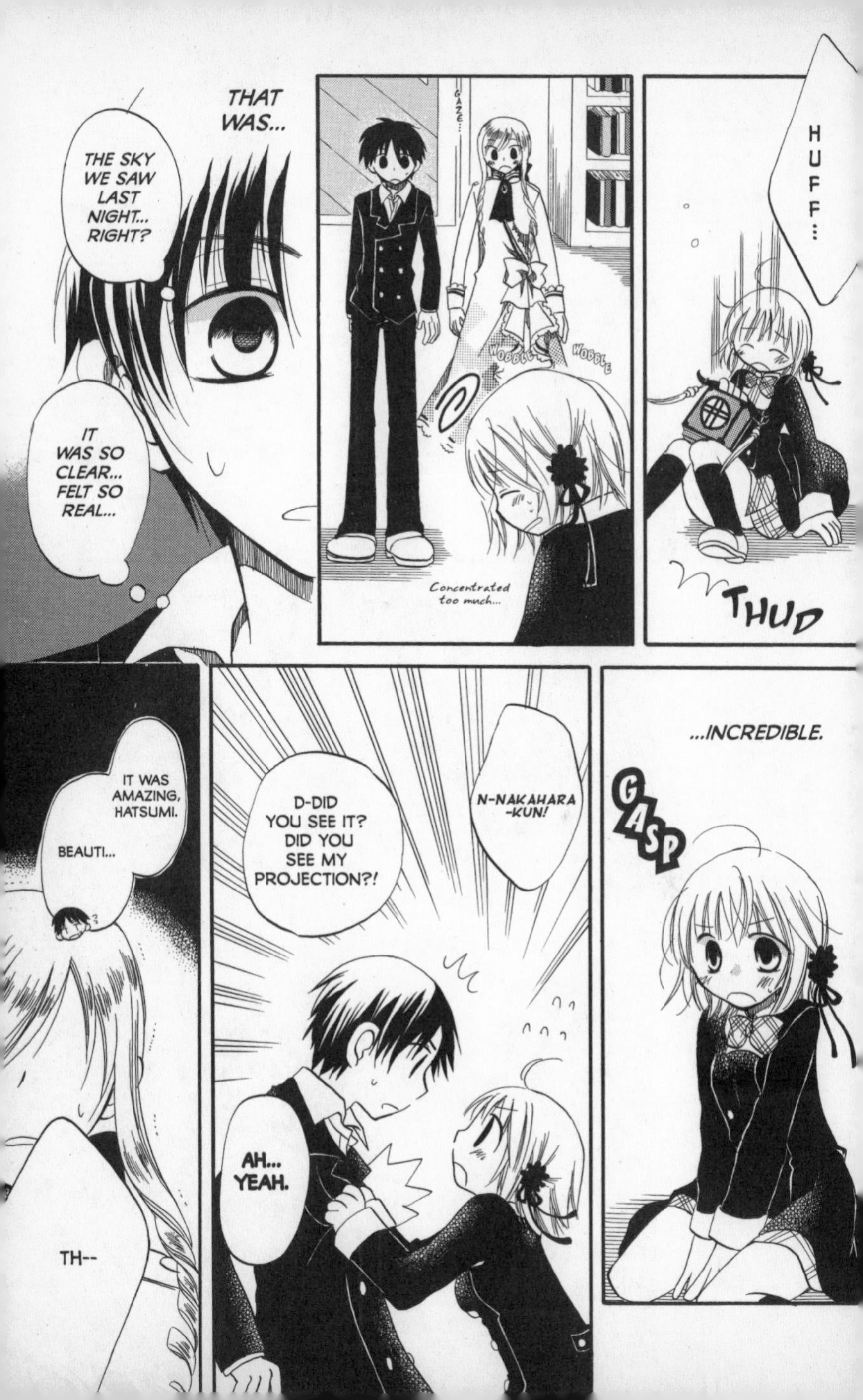
HUFF...
THUD
GAZE...
WOBBLE
WOBBLE
Concentrated too much...
THAT WAS...
THE SKY WE SAW LAST NIGHT... RIGHT?
IT WAS SO CLEAR... FELT SO REAL...
...INCREDIBLE.
GASP
N-NAKAHARA-KUN!
D-DID YOU SEE IT? DID YOU SEE MY PROJECTION?!
AH... YEAH.
IT WAS AMAZING, HATSUMI.
BEAUTI...
TH--

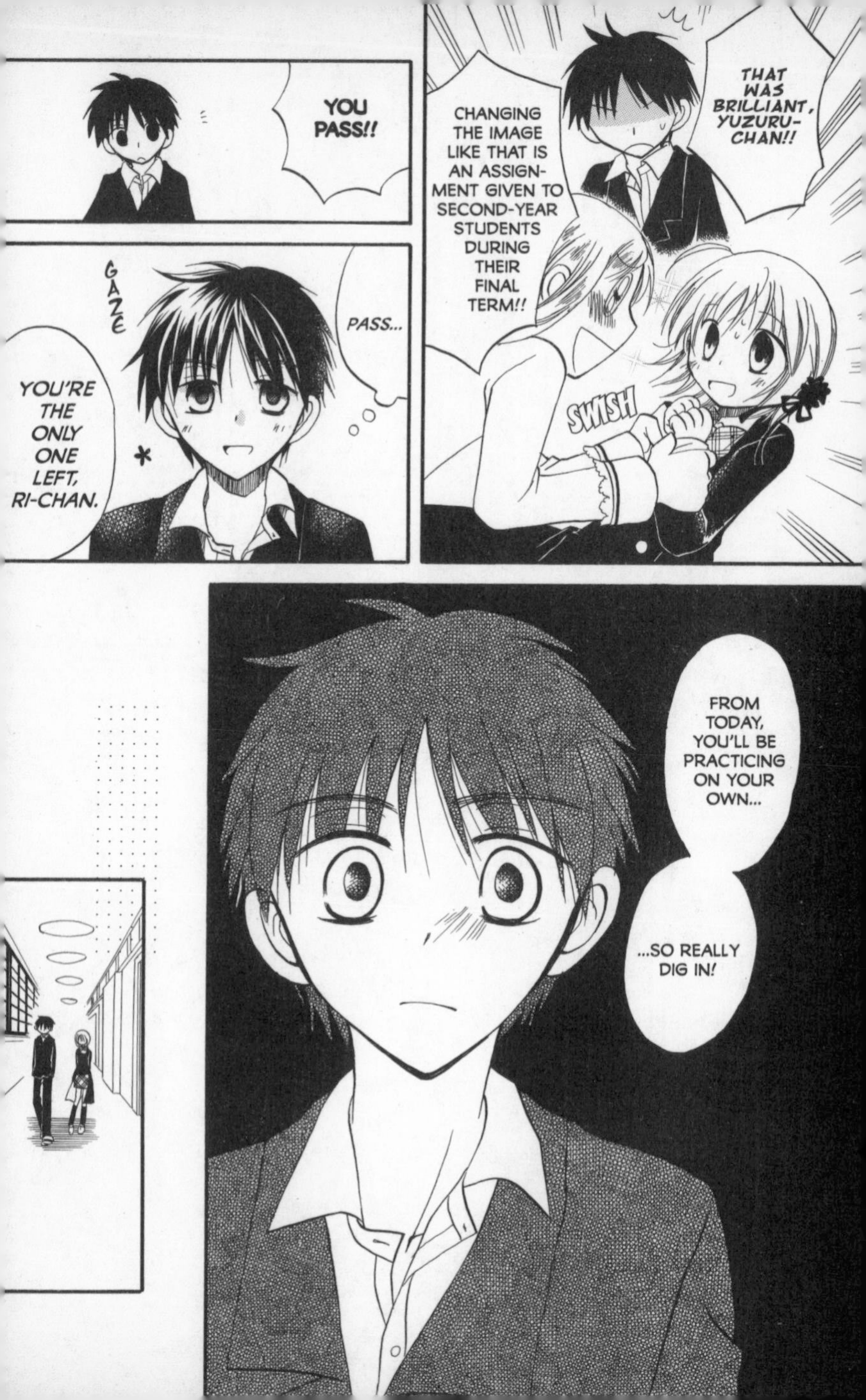
THAT WAS BRILLIANT, YUZURU-CHAN!!
CHANGING THE IMAGE LIKE THAT IS AN ASSIGNMENT GIVEN TO SECOND-YEAR STUDENTS DURING THEIR FINAL TERM!!
SWISH
YOU PASS!!
PASS...
GAZE
YOU'RE THE ONLY ONE LEFT, RI-CHAN.
FROM TODAY, YOU'LL BE PRACTICING ON YOUR OWN...
...SO REALLY DIG IN!

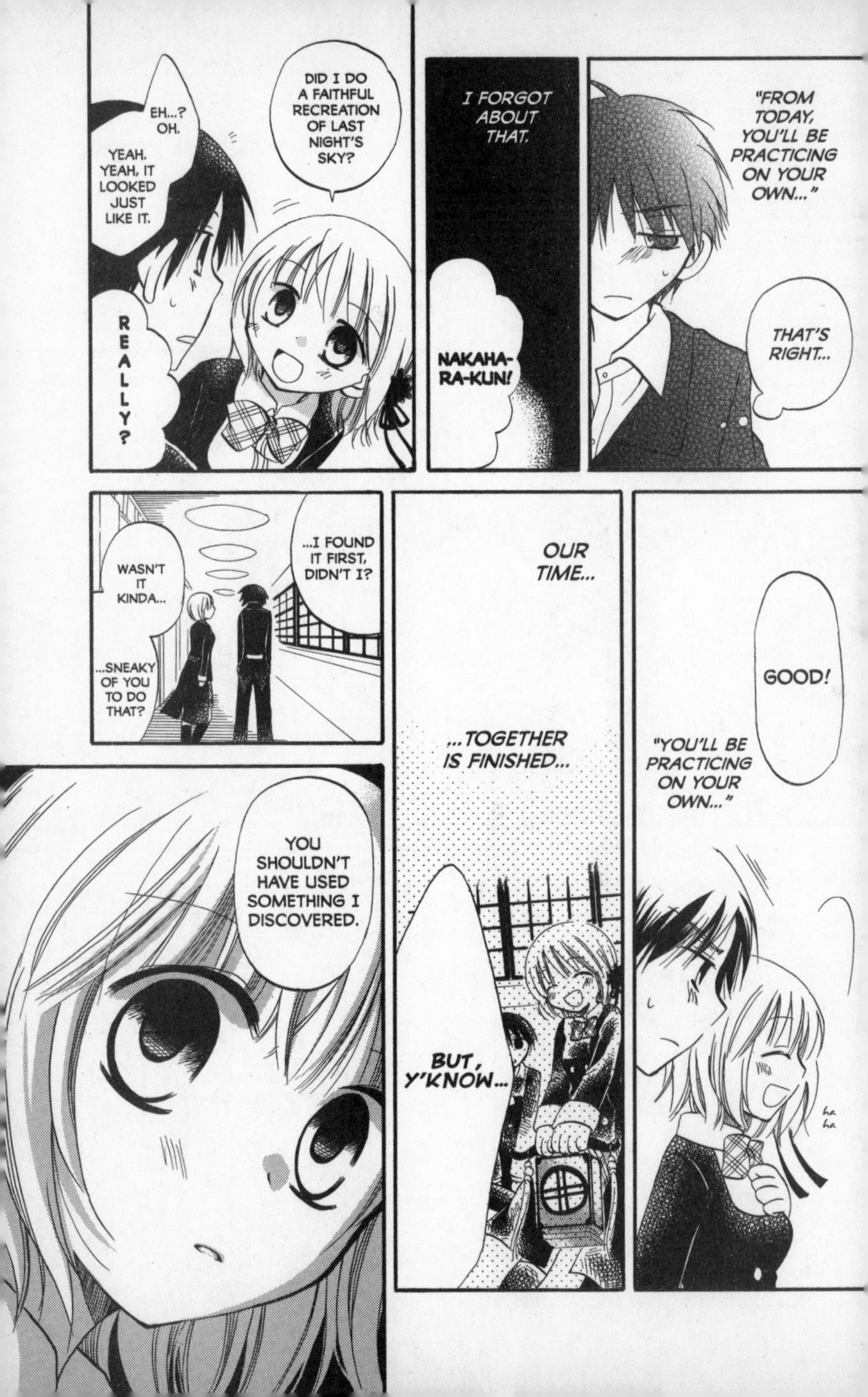
"FROM TODAY, YOU'LL BE PRACTICING ON YOUR OWN..."
THAT'S RIGHT...
I FORGOT ABOUT THAT.
NAKAHARA-KUN!
DID I DO A FAITHFUL RECREATION OF LAST NIGHT'S SKY?
EH...? OH.
YEAH. YEAH, IT LOOKED JUST LIKE IT.
REALLY?
GOOD!
"YOU'LL BE PRACTICING ON YOUR OWN..."
ha ha
OUR TIME...
...TOGETHER IS FINISHED...
BUT, Y'KNOW...
...I FOUND IT FIRST, DIDN'T I?
WASN'T IT KINDA...
...SNEAKY OF YOU TO DO THAT?
YOU SHOULDN'T HAVE USED SOMETHING I DISCOVERED.

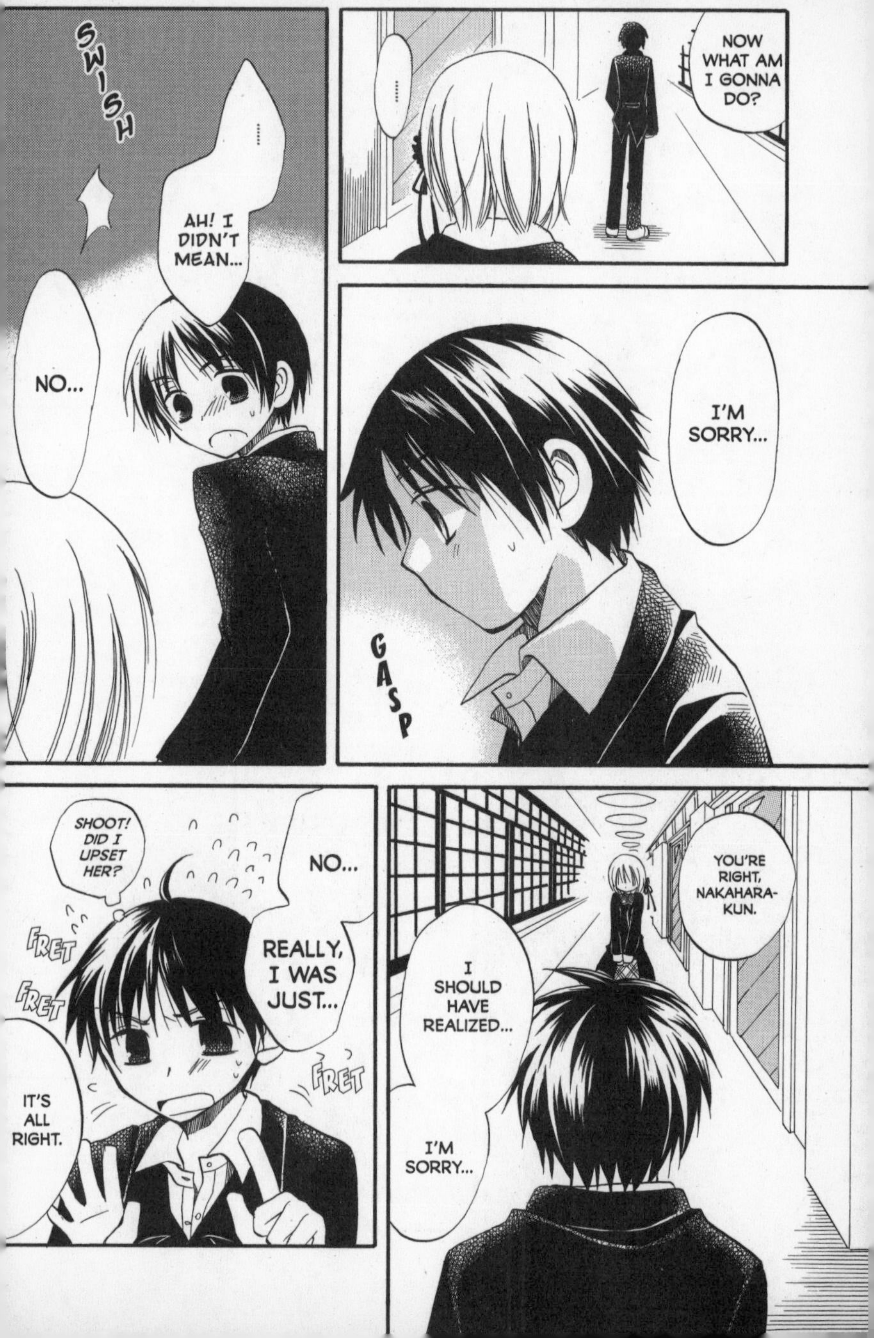
NOW WHAT AM I GONNA DO?
...
I'M SORRY...
GASP
SWISH
...
AH! I DIDN'T MEAN...
NO...
YOU'RE RIGHT, NAKAHARA-KUN.
I SHOULD HAVE REALIZED...
I'M SORRY...
NO...
REALLY, I WAS JUST...
SHOOT! DID I UPSET HER?
FRET
FRET
FRET
IT'S ALL RIGHT.

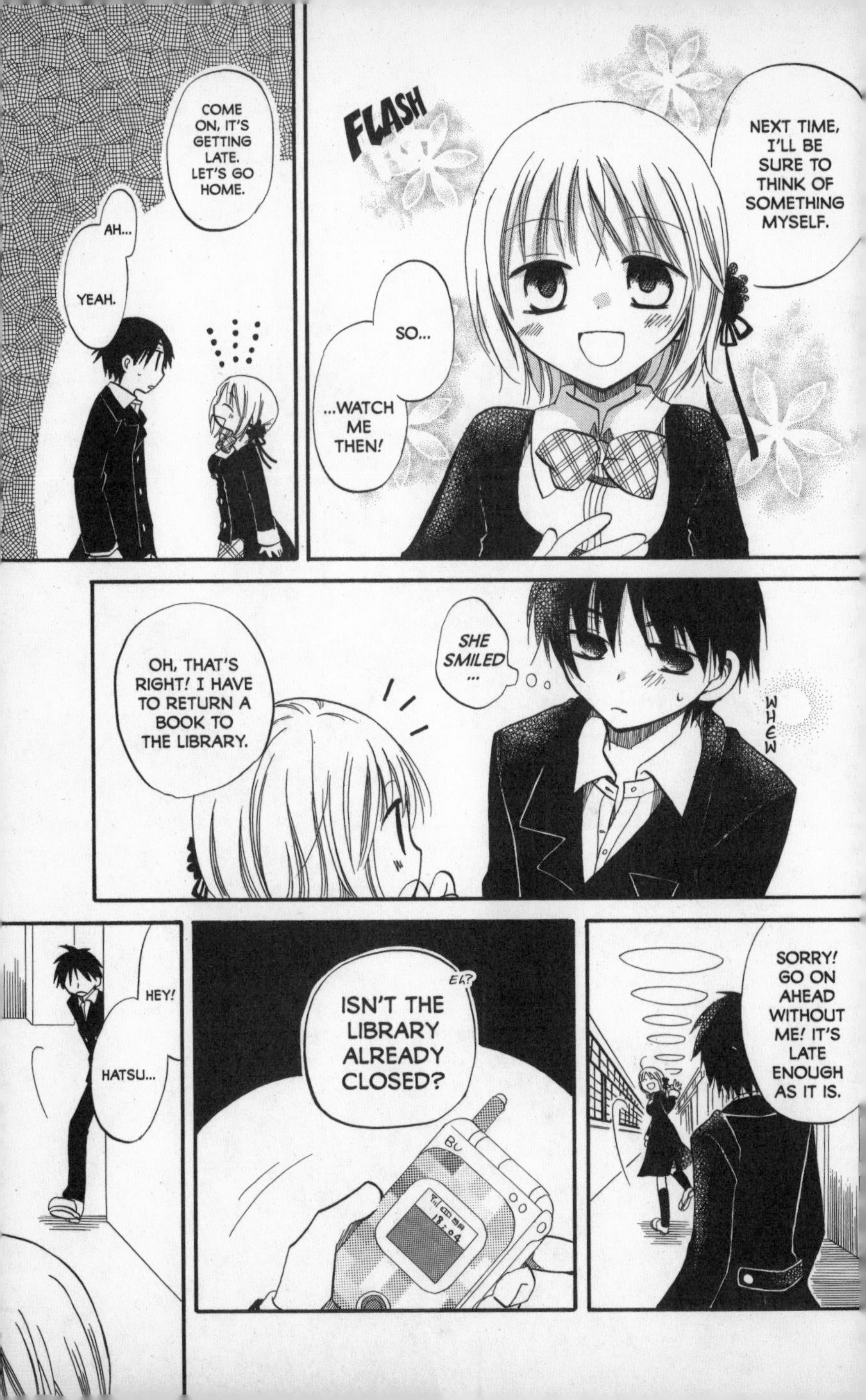
FLASH
NEXT TIME, I'LL BE SURE TO THINK OF SOMETHING MYSELF.
SO...
...WATCH ME THEN!
COME ON, IT'S GETTING LATE. LET'S GO HOME.
AH...
YEAH.
WHEW
SHE SMILED...
OH, THAT'S RIGHT! I HAVE TO RETURN A BOOK TO THE LIBRARY.
SORRY! GO ON AHEAD WITHOUT ME! IT'S LATE ENOUGH AS IT IS.
Eh?
ISN'T THE LIBRARY ALREADY CLOSED?
HEY!
HATSU...

"YOU
SHOULDN'T
HAVE USED
SOMETHING I
DISCOVERED."

"WASN'T
IT KINDA
SNEAKY
OF YOU
TO DO
THAT?"

"...I'M
SORRY."

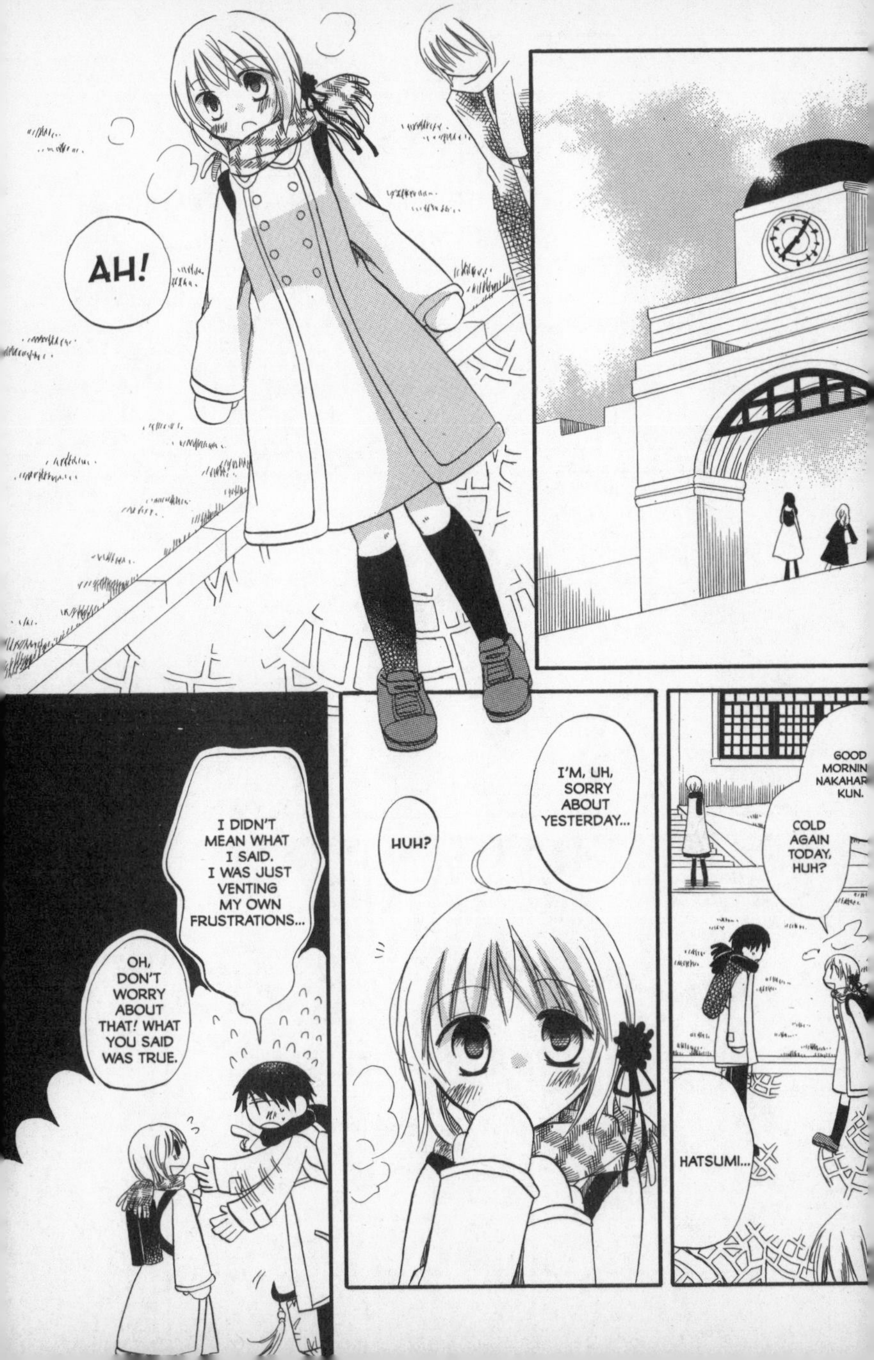
AH!
GOOD MORNIN NAKAHAR KUN.
COLD AGAIN TODAY, HUH?
HATSUMI...
I'M, UH, SORRY ABOUT YESTERDAY...
HUH?
I DIDN'T MEAN WHAT I SAID. I WAS JUST VENTING MY OWN FRUSTRATIONS...
OH, DON'T WORRY ABOUT THAT! WHAT YOU SAID WAS TRUE.

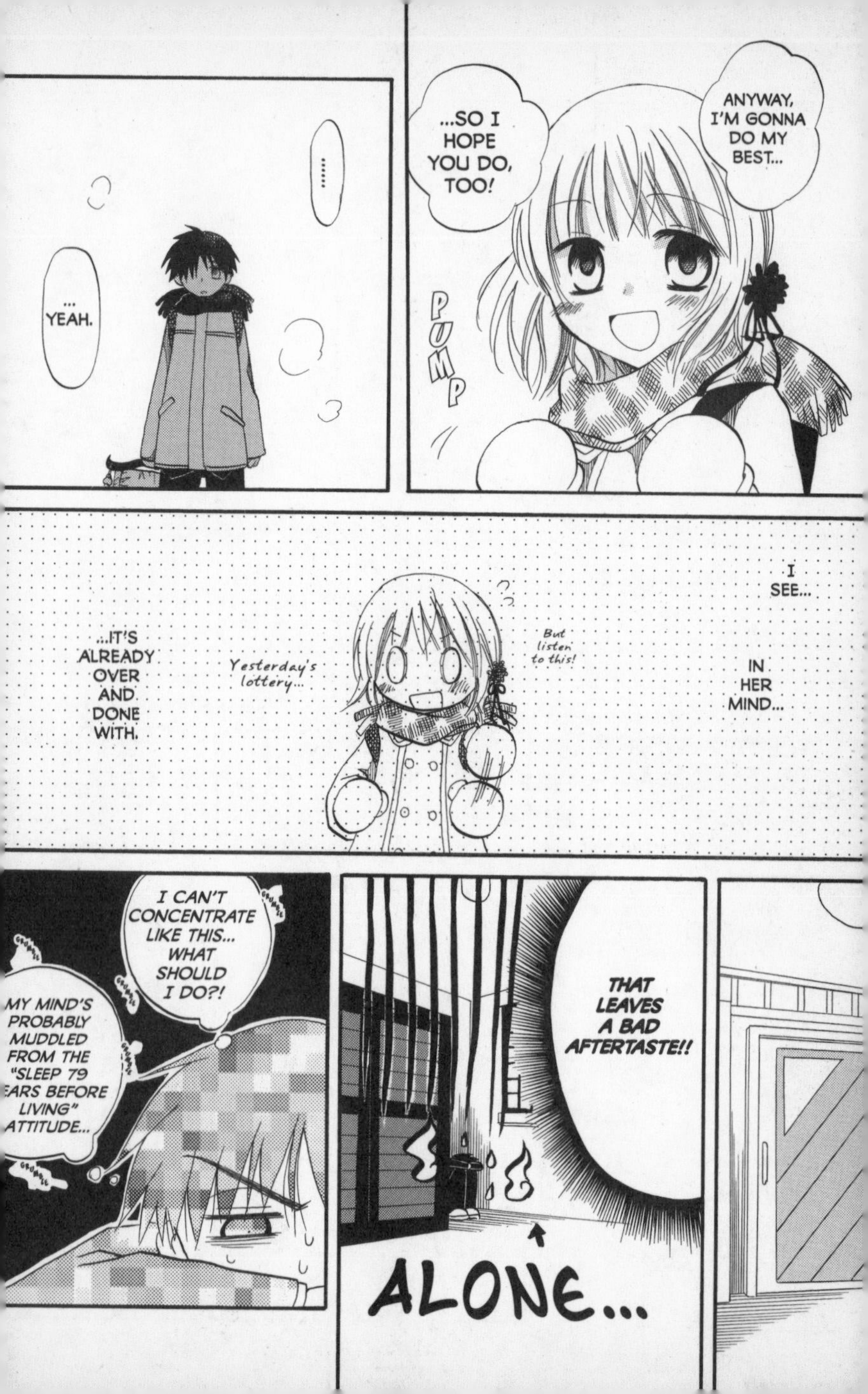
ANYWAY, I'M GONNA DO MY BEST...
...SO I HOPE YOU DO, TOO!
PUMP
......
... YEAH.
I SEE...
IN HER MIND...
But listen to this!
Yesterday's lottery...
...IT'S ALREADY OVER AND DONE WITH.
THAT LEAVES A BAD AFTERTASTE!!
ALONE...
I CAN'T CONCENTRATE LIKE THIS... WHAT SHOULD I DO?!
MY MIND'S PROBABLY MUDDLED FROM THE "SLEEP 79 EARS BEFORE LIVING" ATTITUDE...

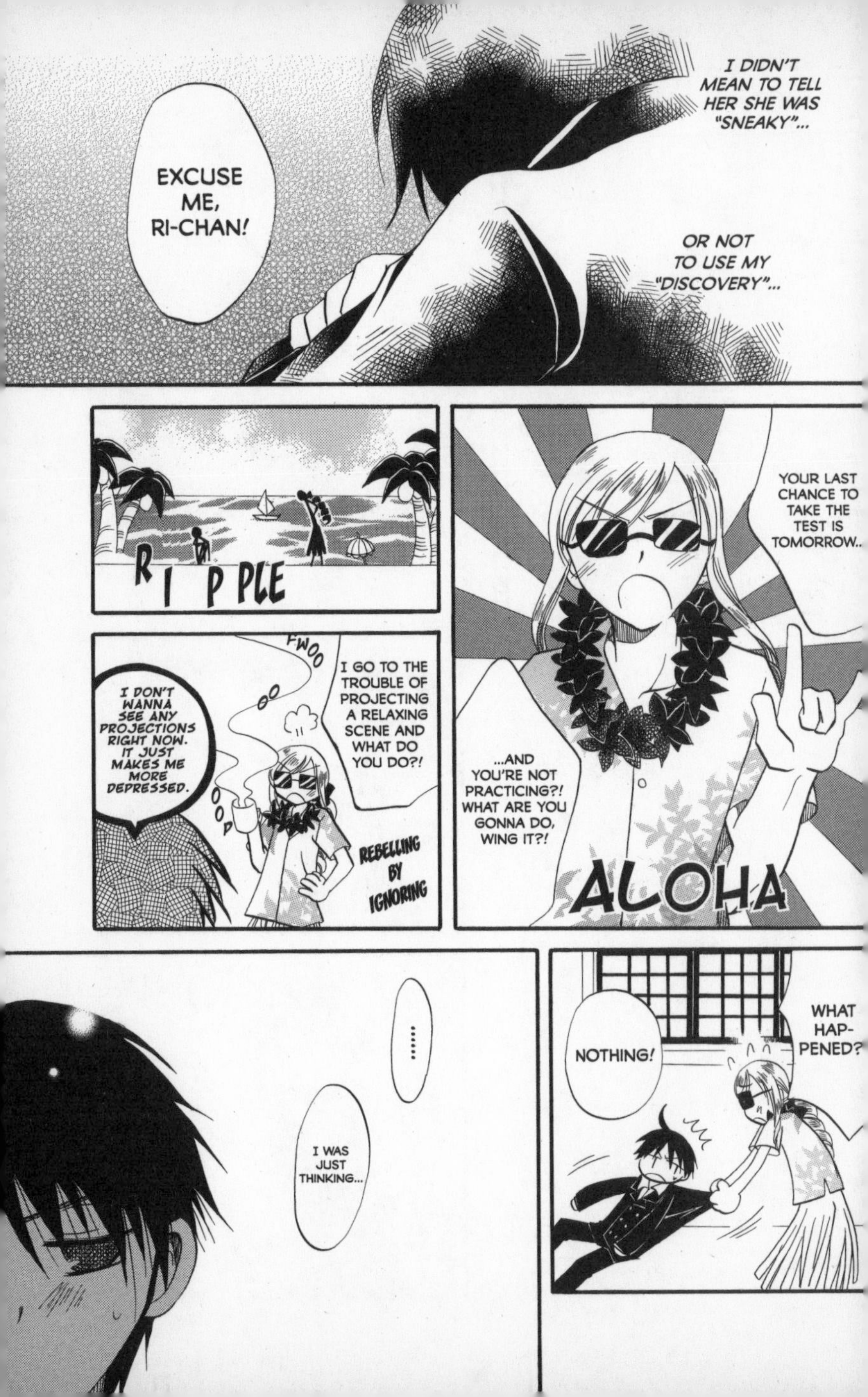
I DIDN'T MEAN TO TELL HER SHE WAS "SNEAKY"...
OR NOT TO USE MY "DISCOVERY"...
EXCUSE ME, RI-CHAN!
YOUR LAST CHANCE TO TAKE THE TEST IS TOMORROW..
...AND YOU'RE NOT PRACTICING?! WHAT ARE YOU GONNA DO, WING IT?!
ALOHA
RIPPLE
FWOO
I GO TO THE TROUBLE OF PROJECTING A RELAXING SCENE AND WHAT DO YOU DO?!
I DON'T WANNA SEE ANY PROJECTIONS RIGHT NOW. IT JUST MAKES ME MORE DEPRESSED.
REBELLING BY IGNORING
WHAT HAP-PENED?
NOTHING!
......
I WAS JUST THINKING...

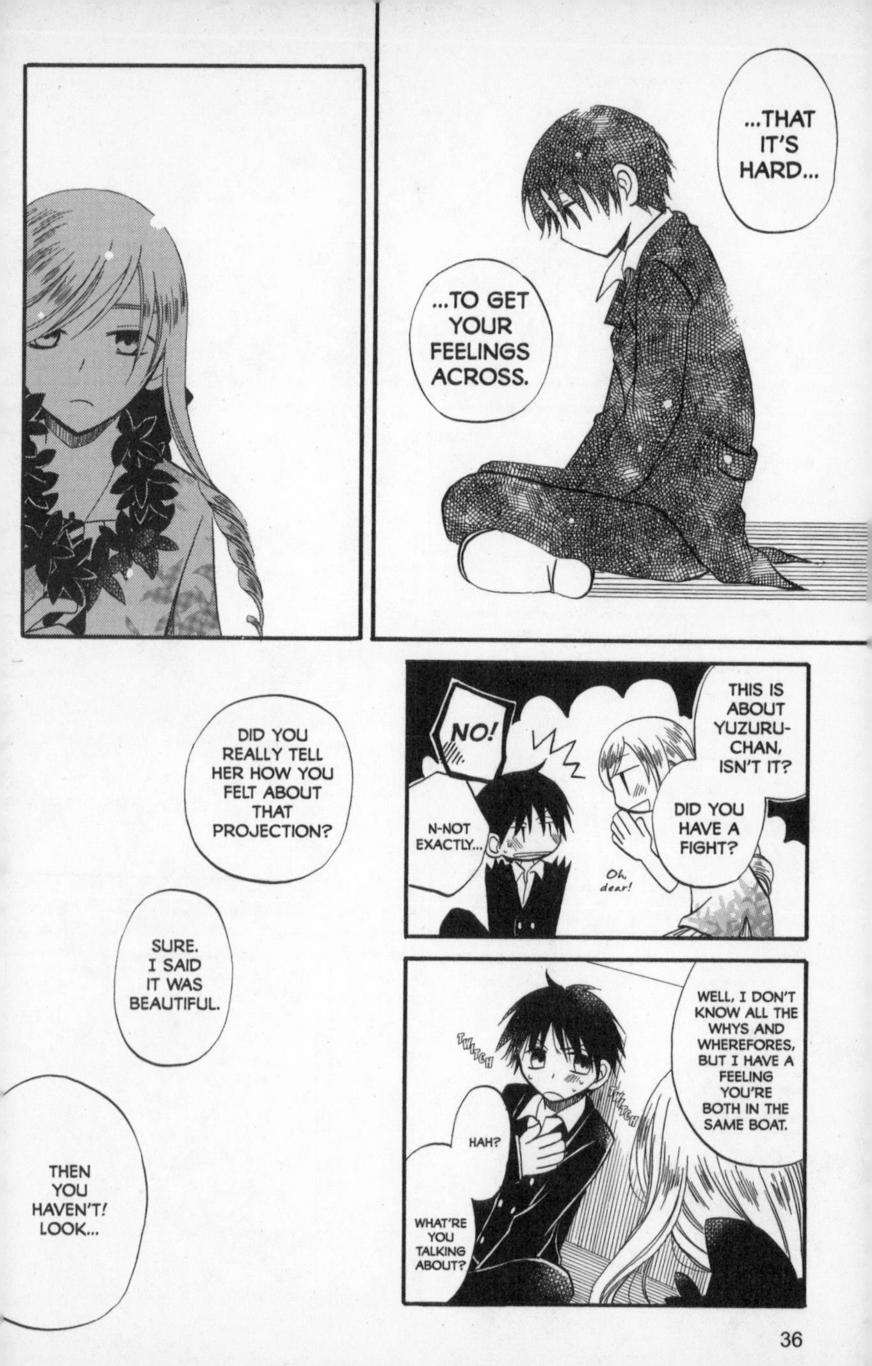
...THAT IT'S HARD...
...TO GET YOUR FEELINGS ACROSS.
THIS IS ABOUT YUZURU-CHAN, ISN'T IT?
NO!
DID YOU HAVE A FIGHT?
Oh, dear!
N-NOT EXACTLY...
WELL, I DON'T KNOW ALL THE WHYS AND WHEREFORES, BUT I HAVE A FEELING YOU'RE BOTH IN THE SAME BOAT.
TWITCH
TWITCH
HAH?
WHAT'RE YOU TALKING ABOUT?
DID YOU REALLY TELL HER HOW YOU FELT ABOUT THAT PROJECTION?
SURE. I SAID IT WAS BEAUTIFUL.
THEN YOU HAVEN'T! LOOK...

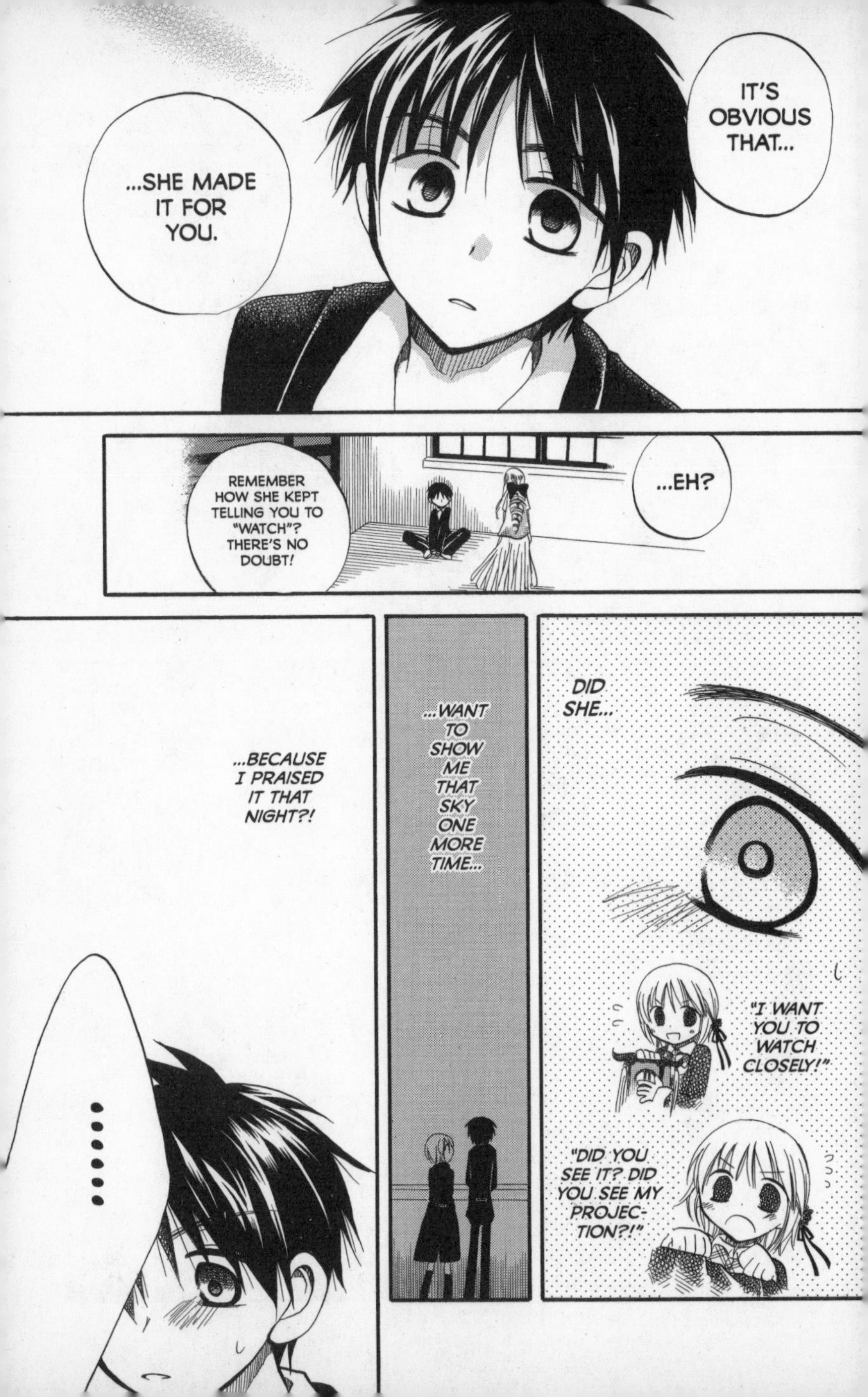
IT'S OBVIOUS THAT...
...SHE MADE IT FOR YOU.
...EH?
REMEMBER HOW SHE KEPT TELLING YOU TO "WATCH"? THERE'S NO DOUBT!
DID SHE...
"I WANT YOU TO WATCH CLOSELY!"
"DID YOU SEE IT? DID YOU SEE MY PROJEC-TION?!"
...WANT TO SHOW ME THAT SKY ONE MORE TIME...
...BECAUSE I PRAISED IT THAT NIGHT?!
.....

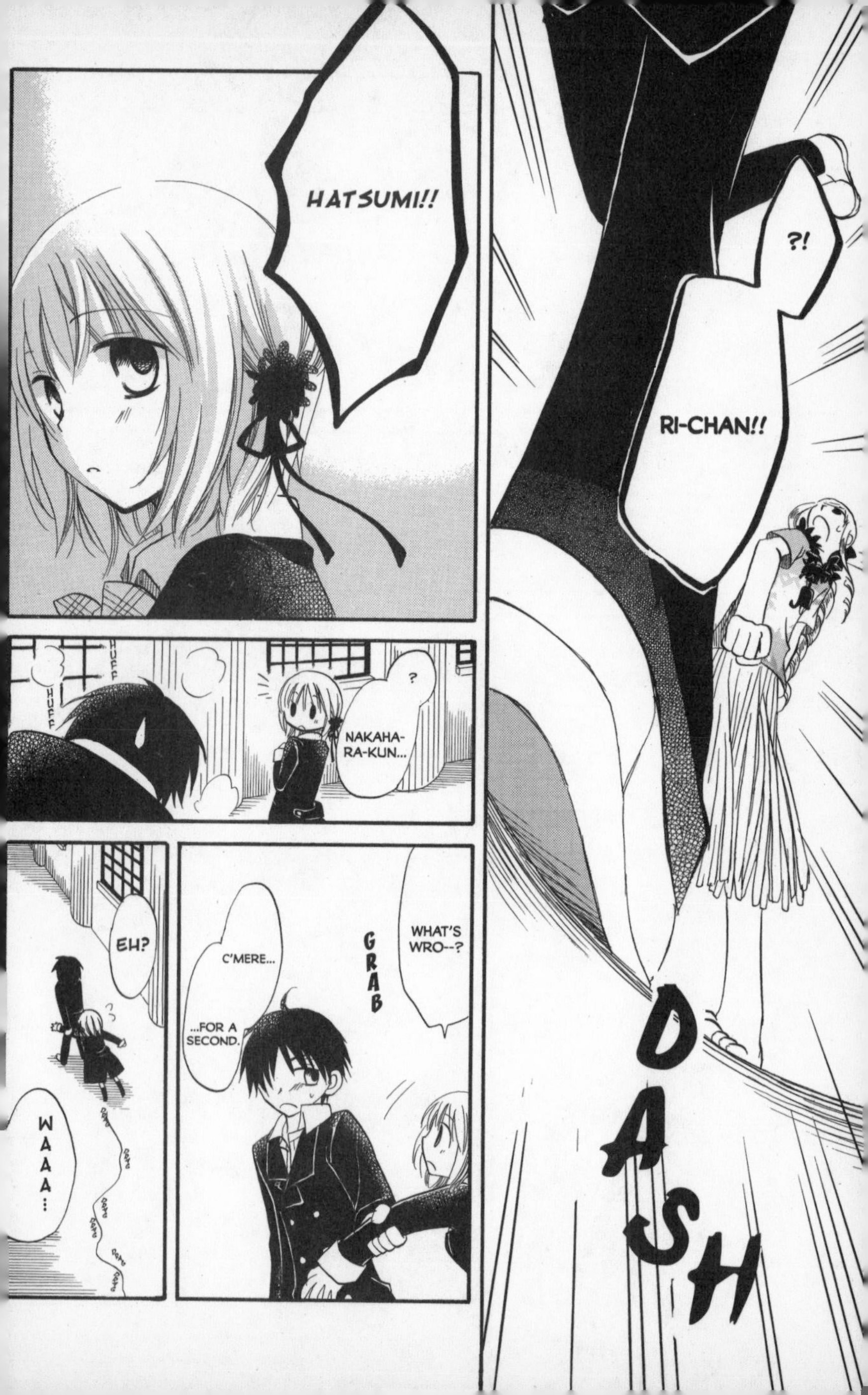
?!
RI-CHAN!!
DASH
HATSUMI!!
HUFF
HUFF
?
NAKAHARA-RA-KUN...
WHAT'S WRO--?
GRAB
C'MERE...
...FOR A SECOND.
EH?
WAAA...

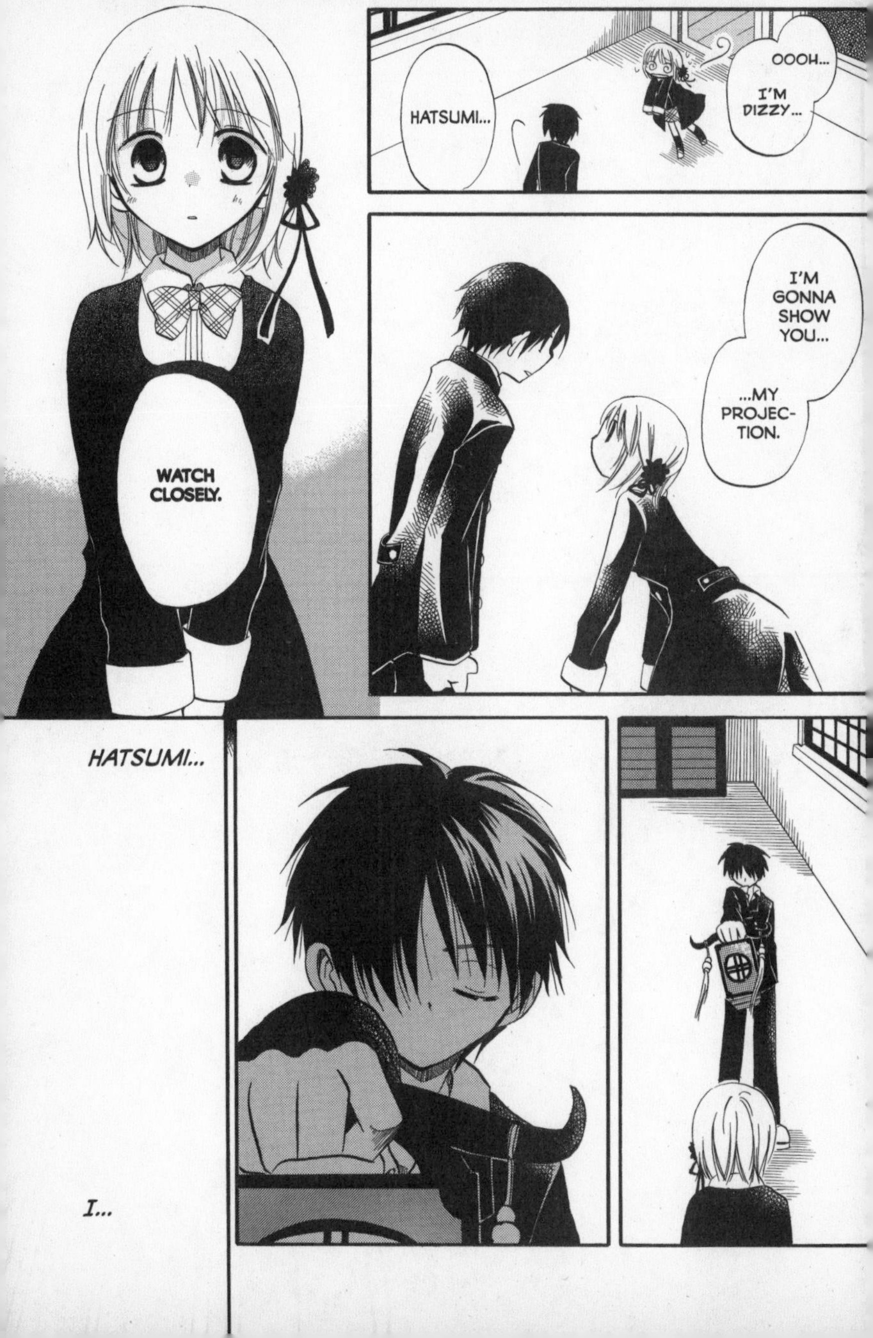
OOOH... I'M DIZZY...
HATSUMI...
I'M GONNA SHOW YOU...
...MY PROJECTION.
WATCH CLOSELY.
HATSUMI...
I...

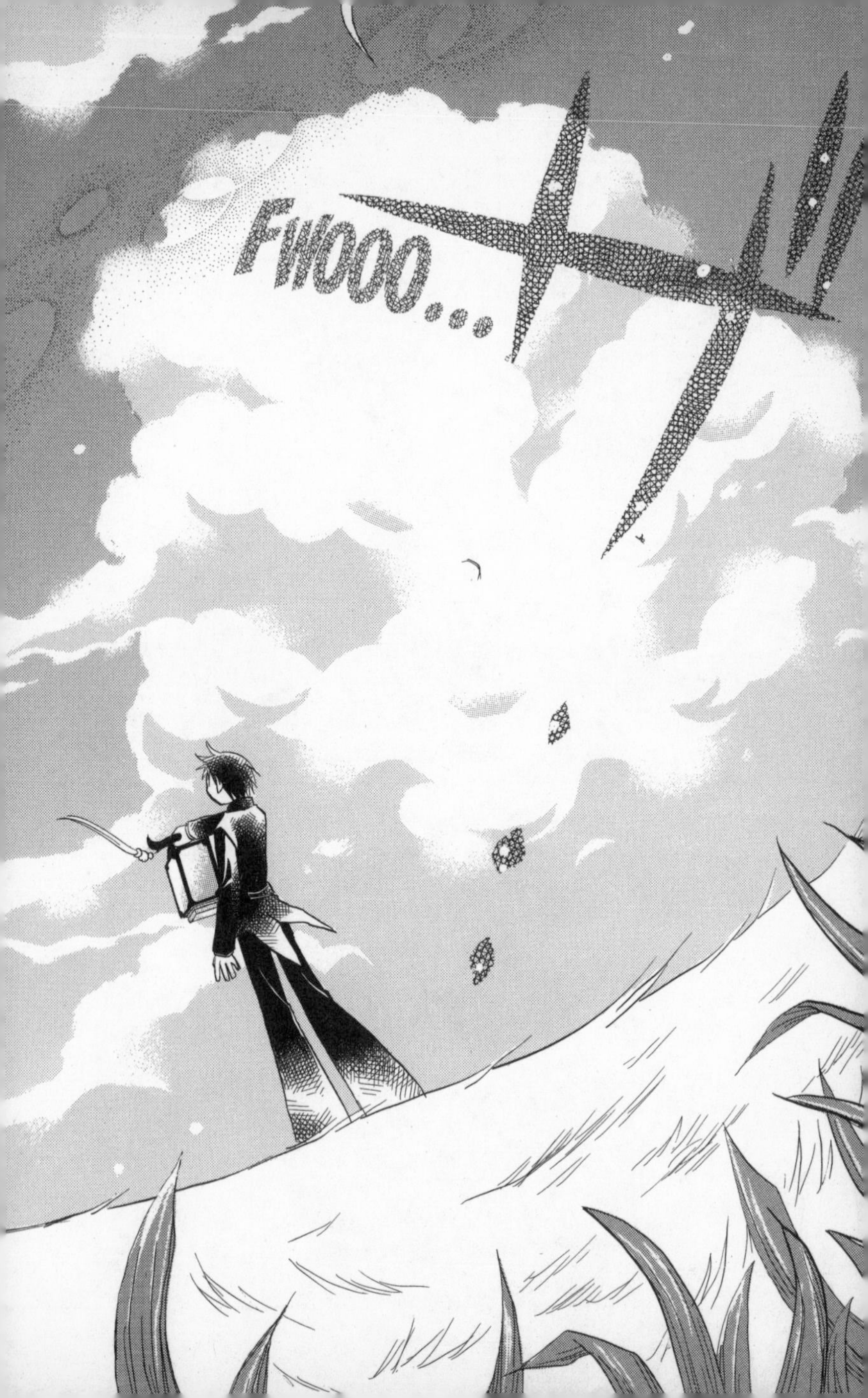
FWOOO...

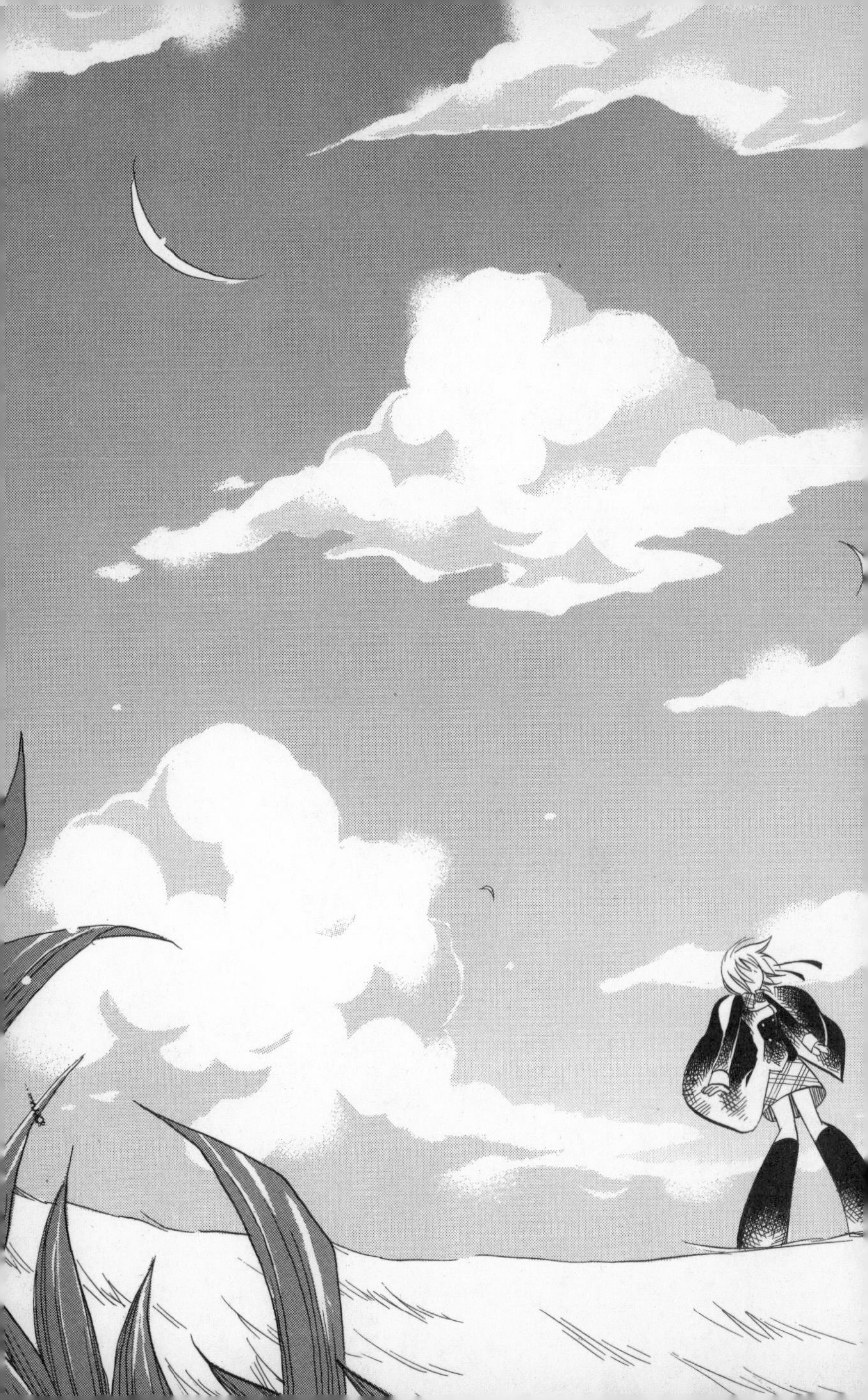

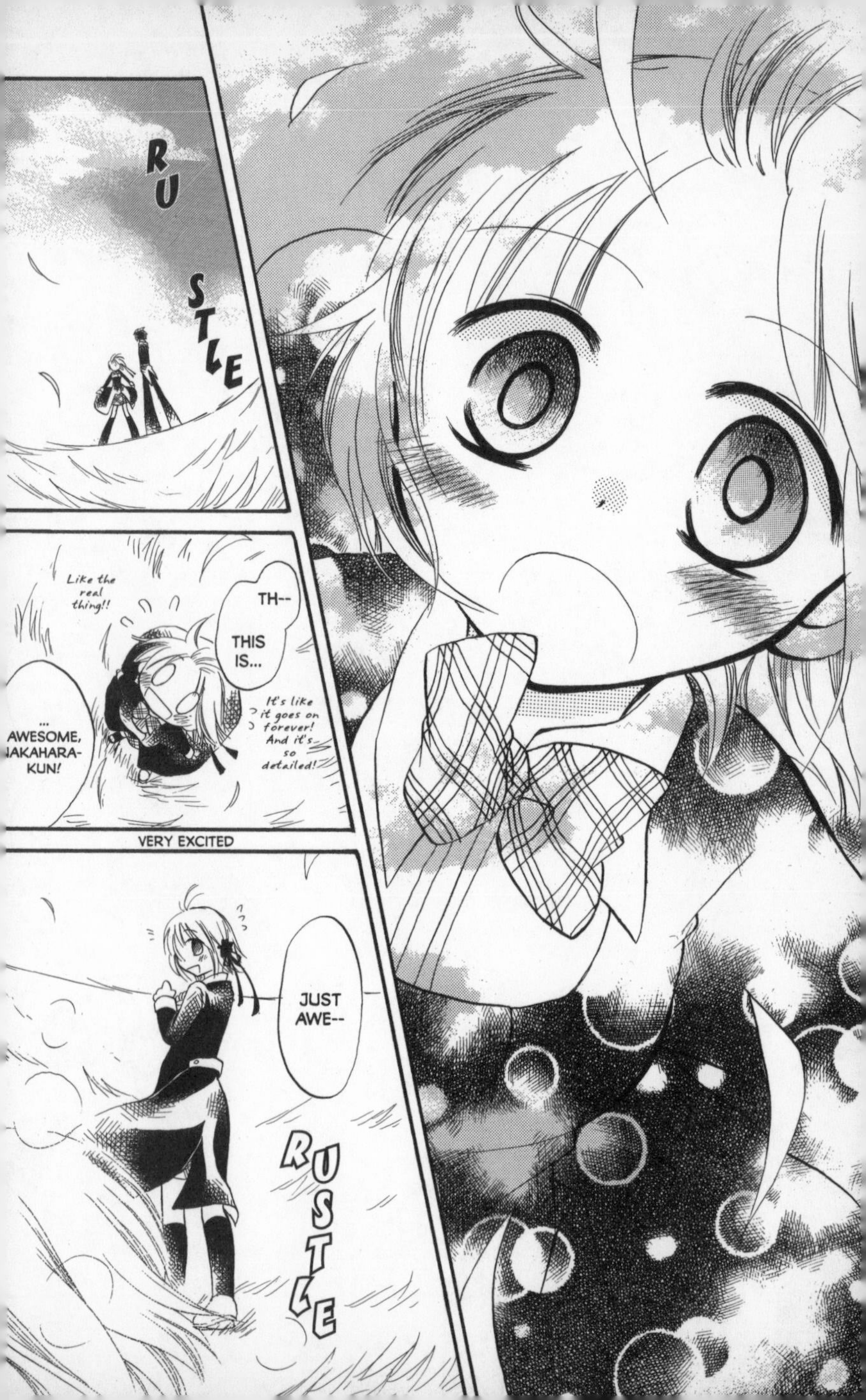
RUSTLE
TH-- THIS IS...
Like the real thing!!
It's like it goes on forever! And it's so detailed!
... AWESOME, NAKAHARA-KUN!
VERY EXCITED
JUST AWE--
RUSTLE

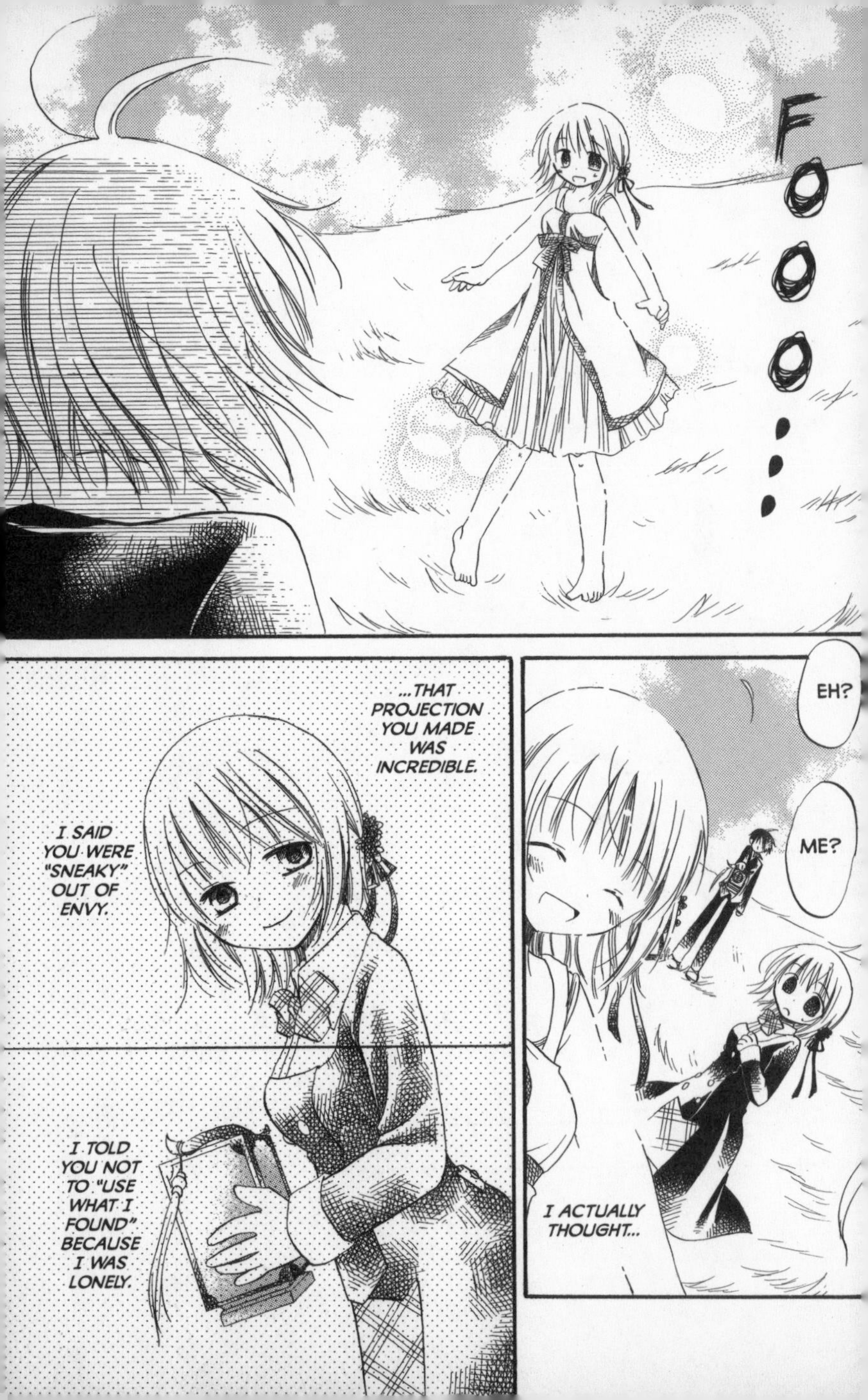
FOOO...
EH?
ME?
I ACTUALLY THOUGHT...
...THAT PROJECTION YOU MADE WAS INCREDIBLE.
I SAID YOU WERE "SNEAKY" OUT OF ENVY.
I TOLD YOU NOT TO "USE WHAT I FOUND" BECAUSE I WAS LONELY.

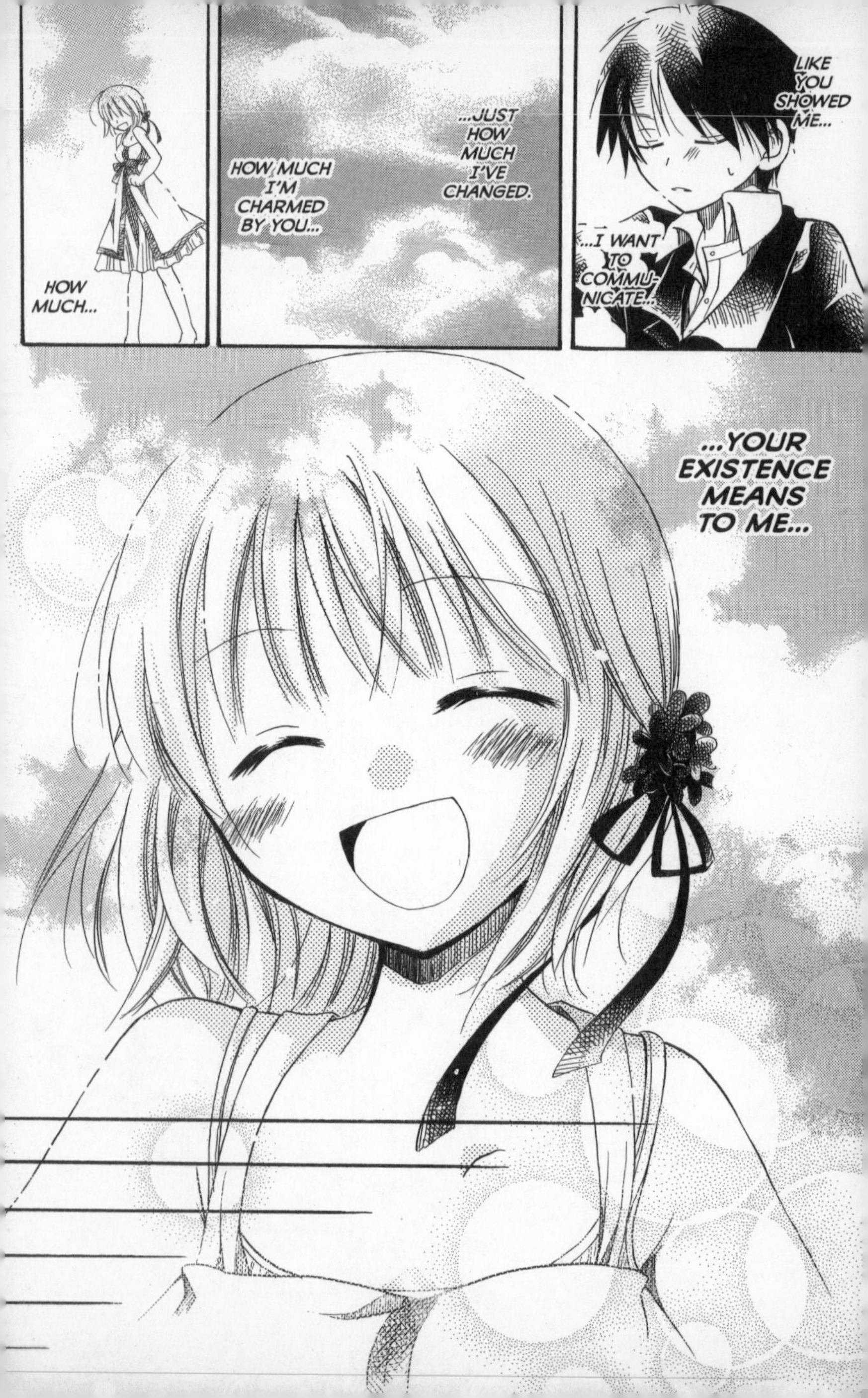
LIKE YOU SHOWED ME...
...I WANT TO COMMUNICATE...
...JUST HOW MUCH I'VE CHANGED.
HOW MUCH I'M CHARMED BY YOU...
HOW MUCH...
...YOUR EXISTENCE MEANS TO ME...

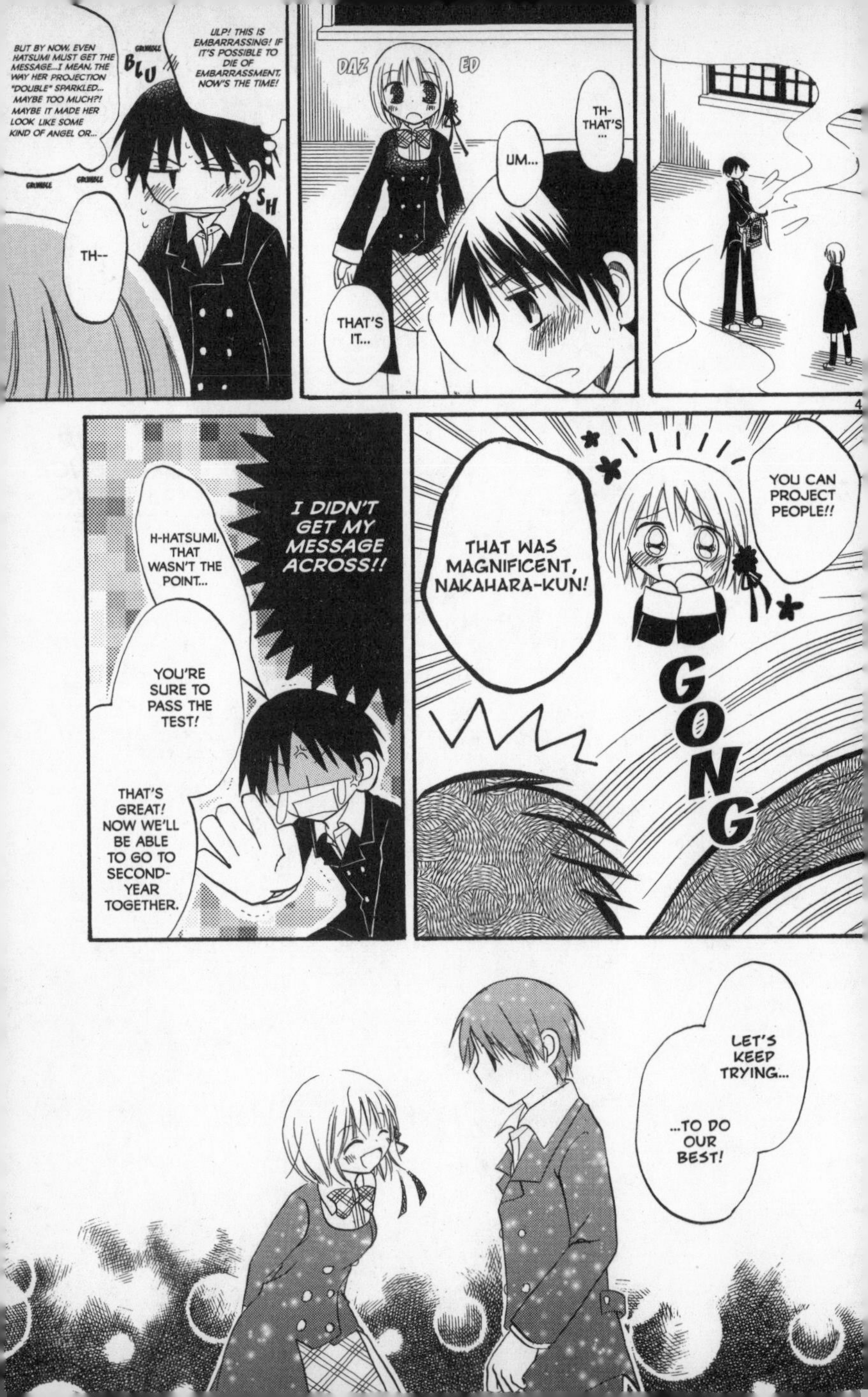
DAZED
TH-THAT'S...
UM...
THAT'S IT...
ULP! THIS IS EMBARRASSING! IF IT'S POSSIBLE TO DIE OF EMBARRASSMENT, NOW'S THE TIME!
BUT BY NOW, EVEN HATSUMI MUST GET THE MESSAGE...I MEAN, THE WAY HER PROJECTION "DOUBLE" SPARKLED... MAYBE TOO MUCH?! MAYBE IT MADE HER LOOK LIKE SOME KIND OF ANGEL OR...
GRUMBLE
BLUSH
GRUMBLE GRUMBLE
TH--
YOU CAN PROJECT PEOPLE!!
THAT WAS MAGNIFICENT, NAKAHARA-KUN!
GONG
I DIDN'T GET MY MESSAGE ACROSS!!
H-HATSUMI, THAT WASN'T THE POINT...
YOU'RE SURE TO PASS THE TEST!
THAT'S GREAT! NOW WE'LL BE ABLE TO GO TO SECOND-YEAR TOGETHER.
LET'S KEEP TRYING...
...TO DO OUR BEST!

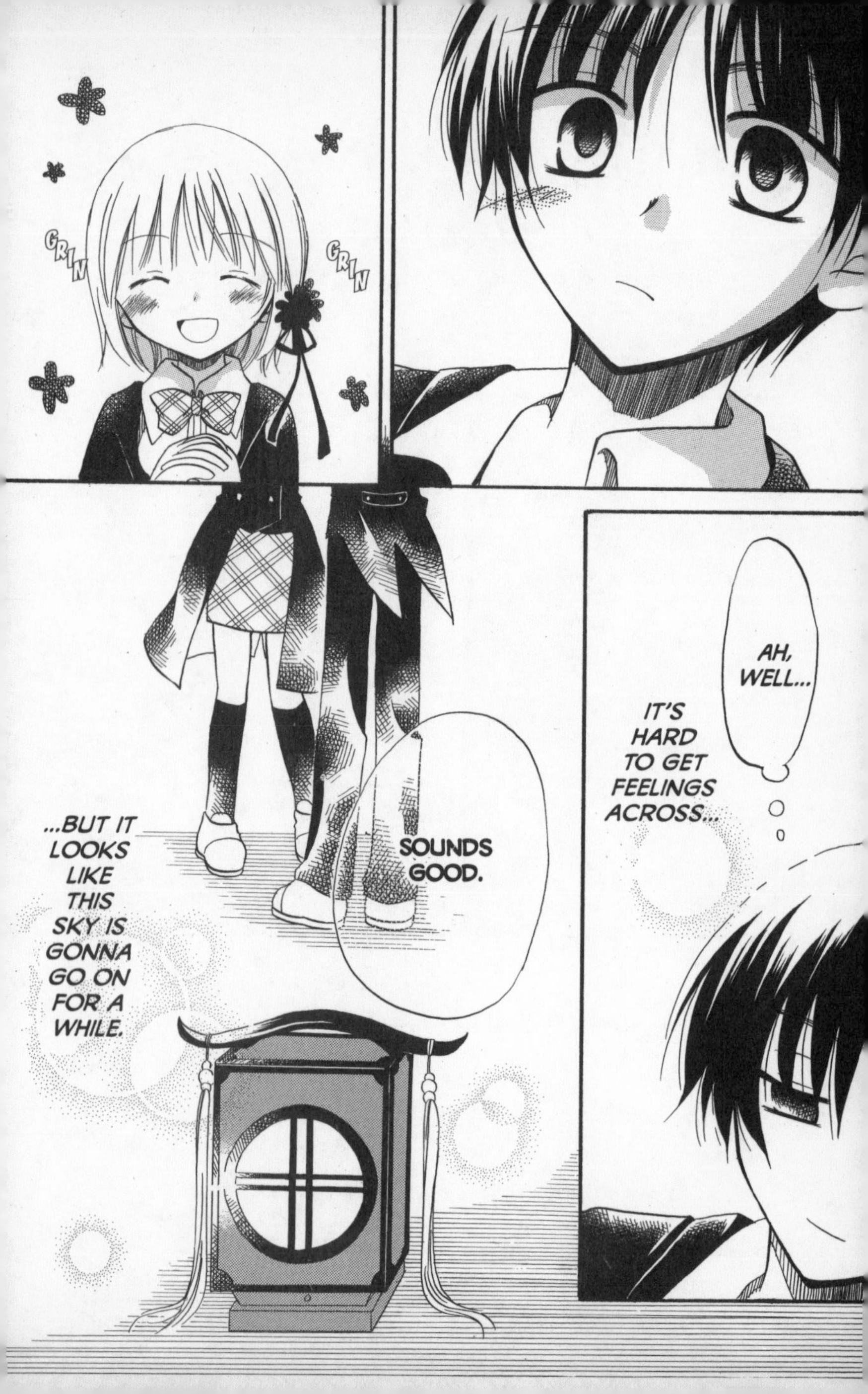
GRIN
GRIN
AH, WELL...
IT'S HARD TO GET FEELINGS ACROSS...
SOUNDS GOOD.
...BUT IT LOOKS LIKE THIS SKY IS GONNA GO ON FOR A WHILE.

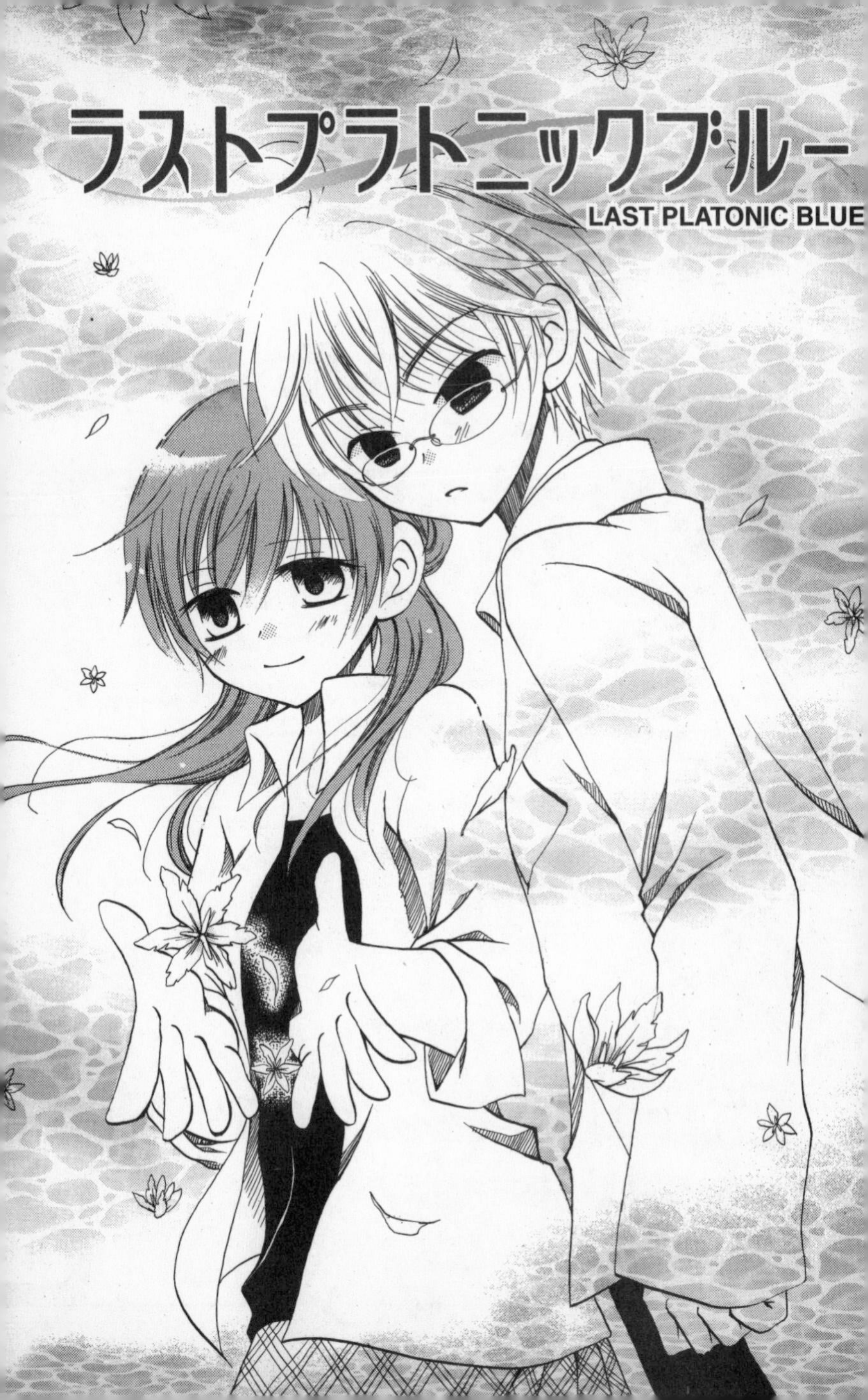
ラストプラトニックブルー
LAST PLATONIC BLUE

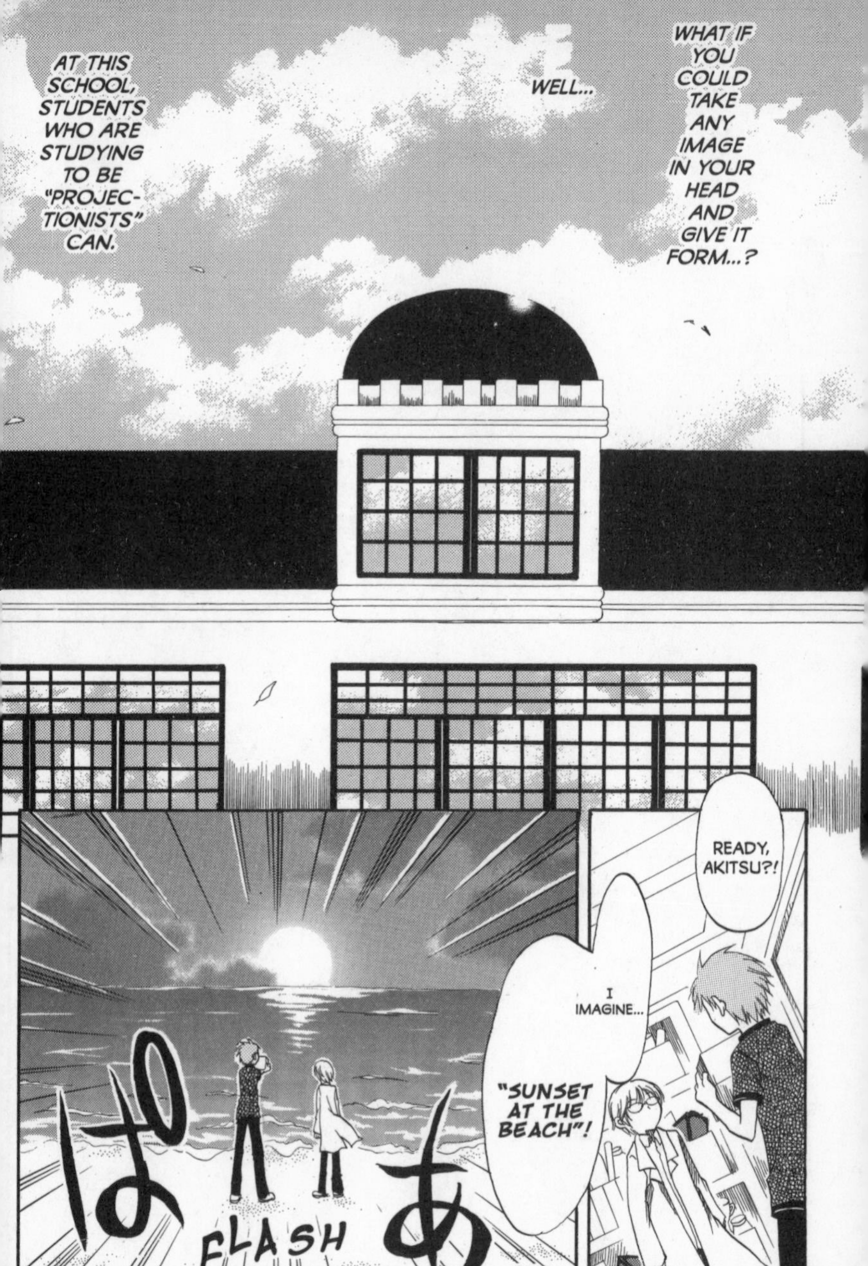
WHAT IF YOU COULD TAKE ANY IMAGE IN YOUR HEAD AND GIVE IT FORM...?
WELL...
AT THIS SCHOOL, STUDENTS WHO ARE STUDYING TO BE "PROJECTIONISTS" CAN.
READY, AKITSU?!
I IMAGINE...
"SUNSET AT THE BEACH"!
ぱあッ
FLASH

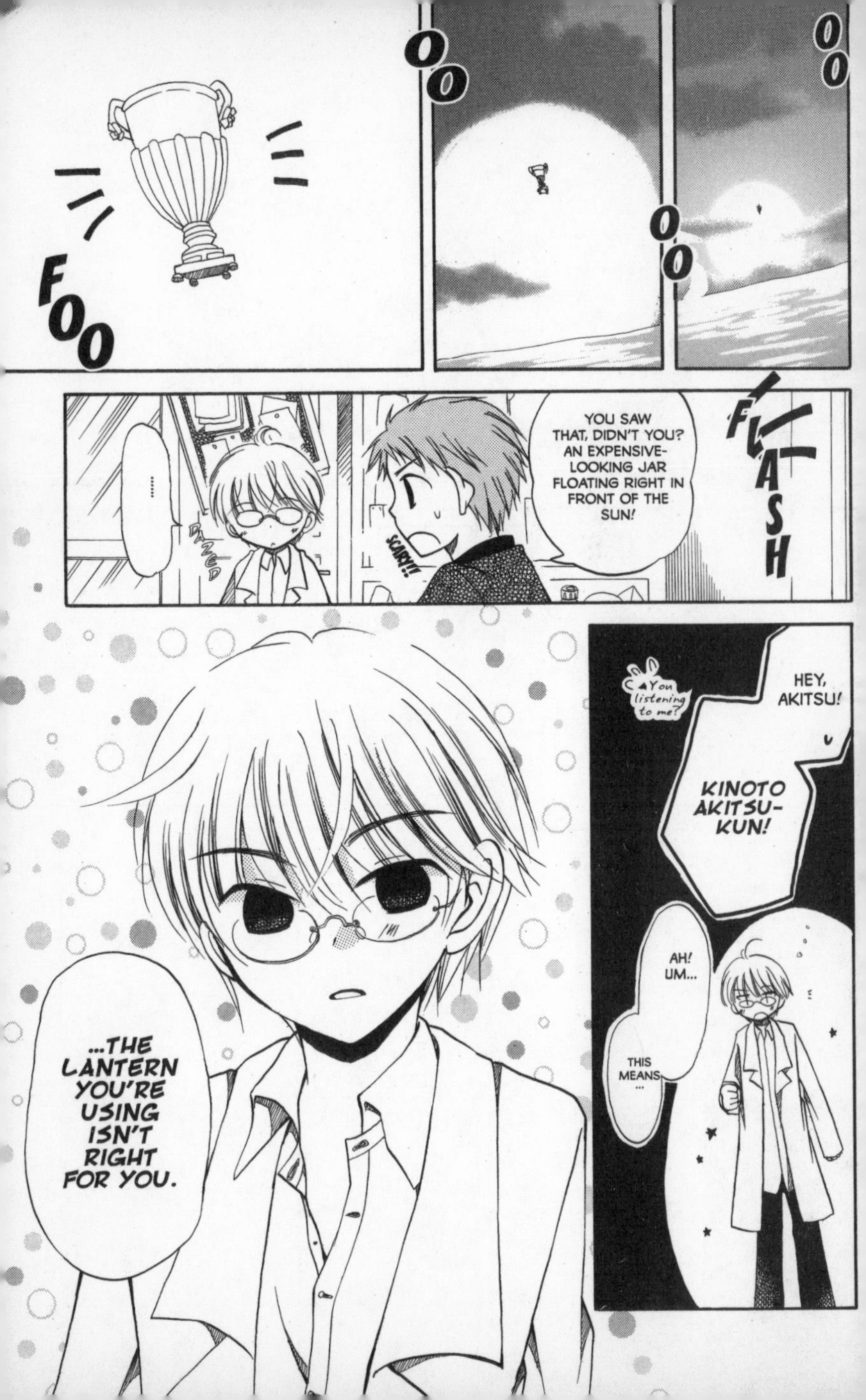
OO
OO
OO
FOO
FLASH
YOU SAW THAT, DIDN'T YOU? AN EXPENSIVE-LOOKING JAR FLOATING RIGHT IN FRONT OF THE SUN!
SCARY!!
DAZED
......
HEY, AKITSU!
You listening to me?
KINOTO AKITSU-KUN!
AH! UM...
THIS MEANS...
...THE LANTERN YOU'RE USING ISN'T RIGHT FOR YOU.

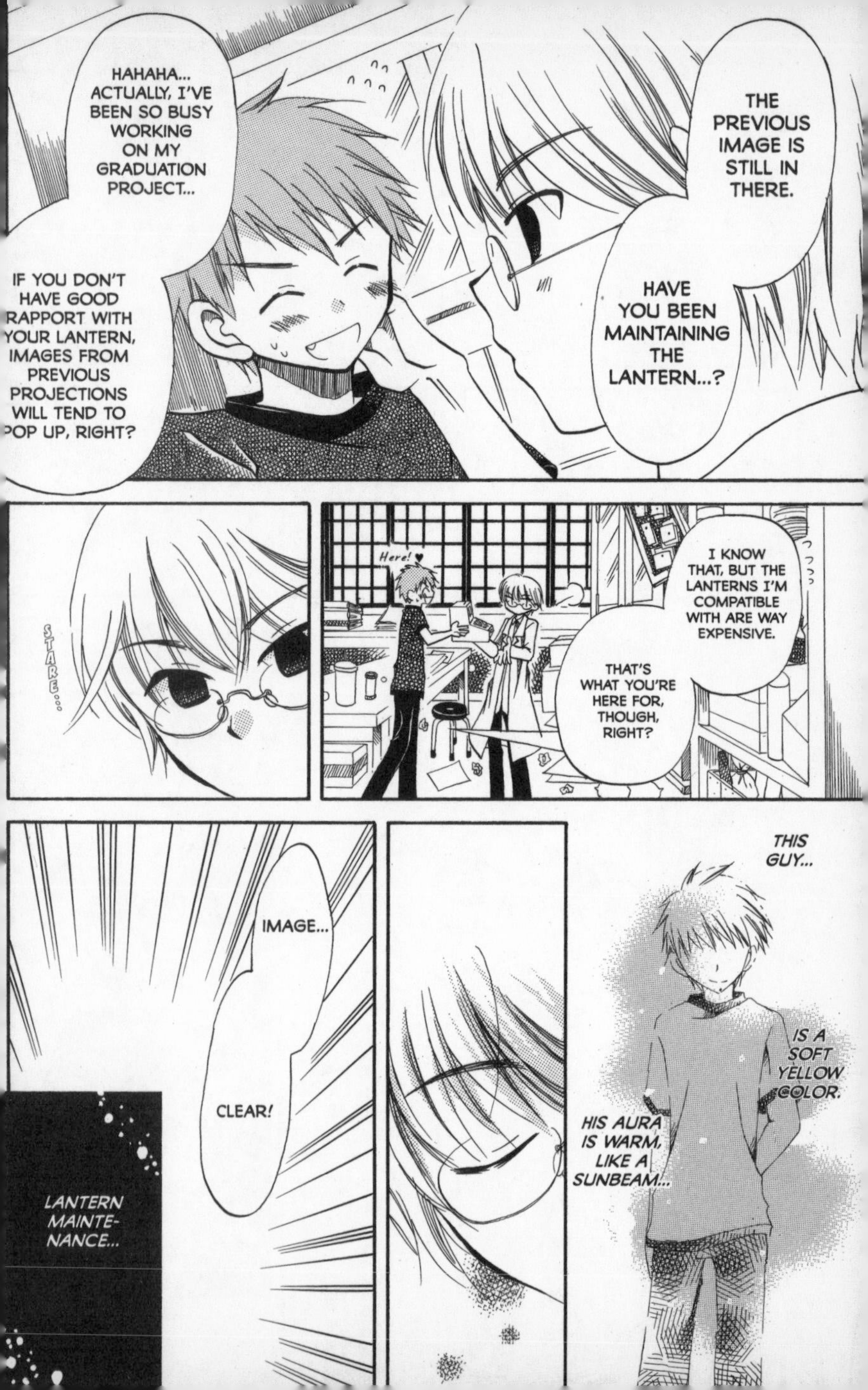
THE PREVIOUS IMAGE IS STILL IN THERE.
HAVE YOU BEEN MAINTAINING THE LANTERN...?
HAHAHA... ACTUALLY, I'VE BEEN SO BUSY WORKING ON MY GRADUATION PROJECT...
IF YOU DON'T HAVE GOOD RAPPORT WITH YOUR LANTERN, IMAGES FROM PREVIOUS PROJECTIONS WILL TEND TO POP UP, RIGHT?
I KNOW THAT, BUT THE LANTERNS I'M COMPATIBLE WITH ARE WAY EXPENSIVE.
Here! ♥
THAT'S WHAT YOU'RE HERE FOR, THOUGH, RIGHT?
STARE...
THIS GUY...
IS A SOFT YELLOW COLOR.
HIS AURA IS WARM, LIKE A SUNBEAM...
IMAGE...
CLEAR!
LANTERN MAINTE-NANCE...

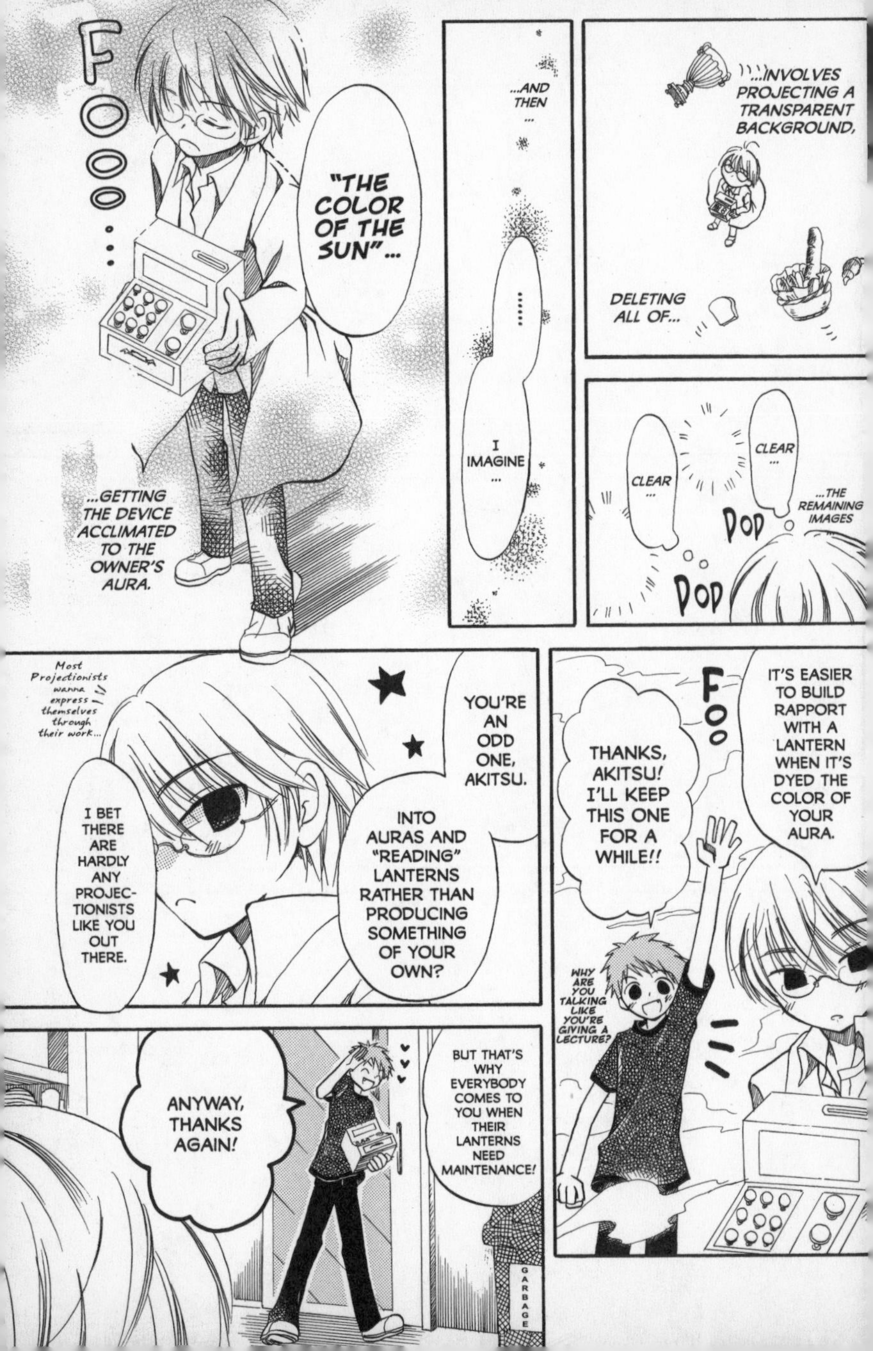
...INVOLVES PROJECTING A TRANSPARENT BACKGROUND,
DELETING ALL OF...
...THE REMAINING IMAGES
CLEAR...
CLEAR...
DOP
DOP
...AND THEN ...
......
I IMAGINE ...
FOOO...
"THE COLOR OF THE SUN"...
...GETTING THE DEVICE ACCLIMATED TO THE OWNER'S AURA.
IT'S EASIER TO BUILD RAPPORT WITH A LANTERN WHEN IT'S DYED THE COLOR OF YOUR AURA.
FOO
THANKS, AKITSU! I'LL KEEP THIS ONE FOR A WHILE!!
WHY ARE YOU TALKING LIKE YOU'RE GIVING A LECTURE?
YOU'RE AN ODD ONE, AKITSU.
INTO AURAS AND "READING" LANTERNS RATHER THAN PRODUCING SOMETHING OF YOUR OWN?
Most Projectionists wanna express themselves through their work...
I BET THERE ARE HARDLY ANY PROJECTIONISTS LIKE YOU OUT THERE.
BUT THAT'S WHY EVERYBODY COMES TO YOU WHEN THEIR LANTERNS NEED MAINTENANCE!
ANYWAY, THANKS AGAIN!
GARBAGE

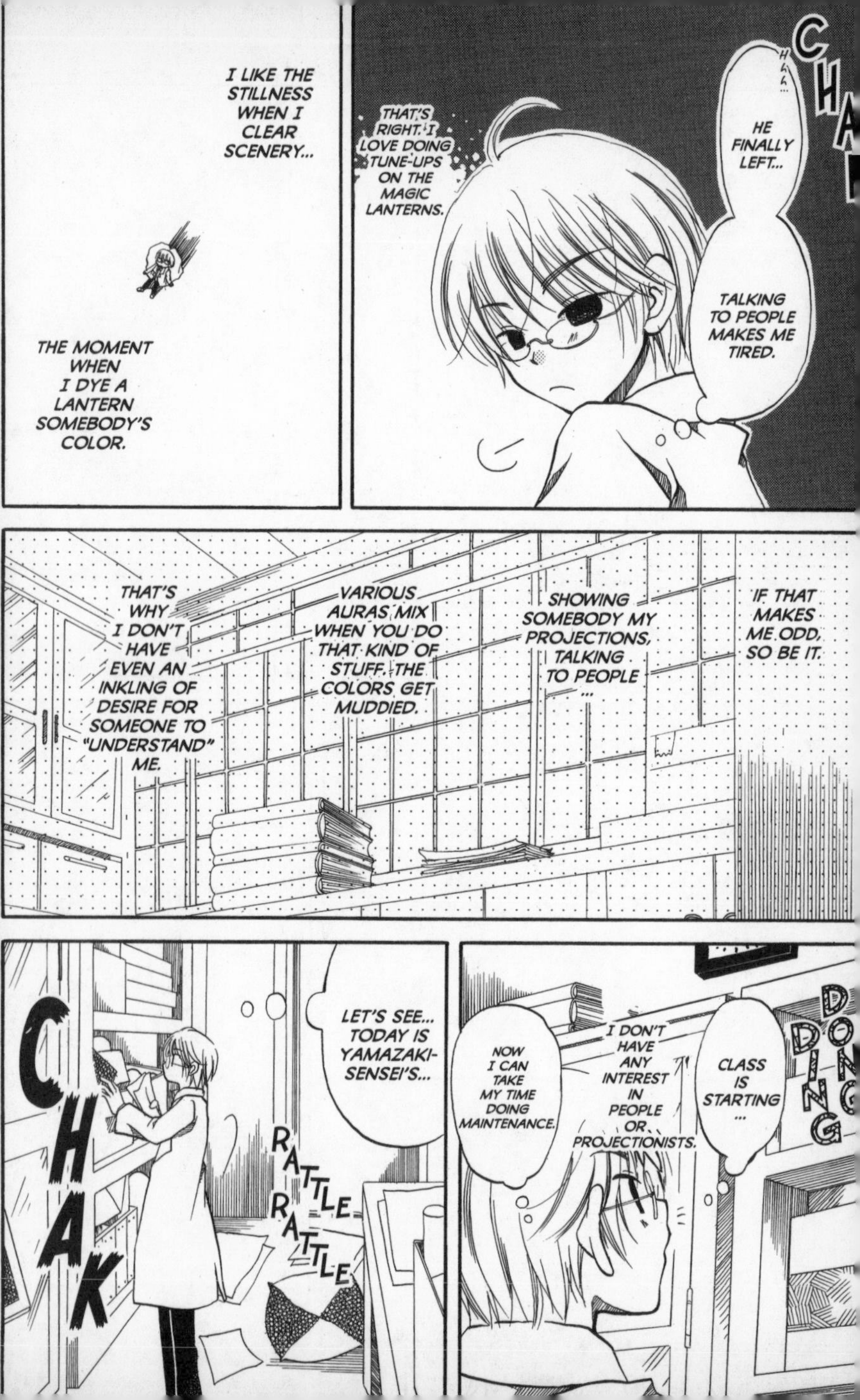

CHA
HE FINALLY LEFT...
TALKING TO PEOPLE MAKES ME TIRED.
THAT'S RIGHT. I LOVE DOING TUNE-UPS ON THE MAGIC LANTERNS.
I LIKE THE STILLNESS WHEN I CLEAR SCENERY...
THE MOMENT WHEN I DYE A LANTERN SOMEBODY'S COLOR.
IF THAT MAKES ME ODD, SO BE IT.
SHOWING SOMEBODY MY PROJECTIONS, TALKING TO PEOPLE...
VARIOUS AURAS MIX WHEN YOU DO THAT KIND OF STUFF. THE COLORS GET MUDDIED.
THAT'S WHY I DON'T HAVE EVEN AN INKLING OF DESIRE FOR SOMEONE TO "UNDERSTAND" ME.
DING DONG DING DONG
CLASS IS STARTING...
I DON'T HAVE ANY INTEREST IN PEOPLE OR PROJECTIONISTS.
NOW I CAN TAKE MY TIME DOING MAINTENANCE.
LET'S SEE... TODAY IS YAMAZAKI-SENSEI'S...
RATTLE RATTLE
CHAK

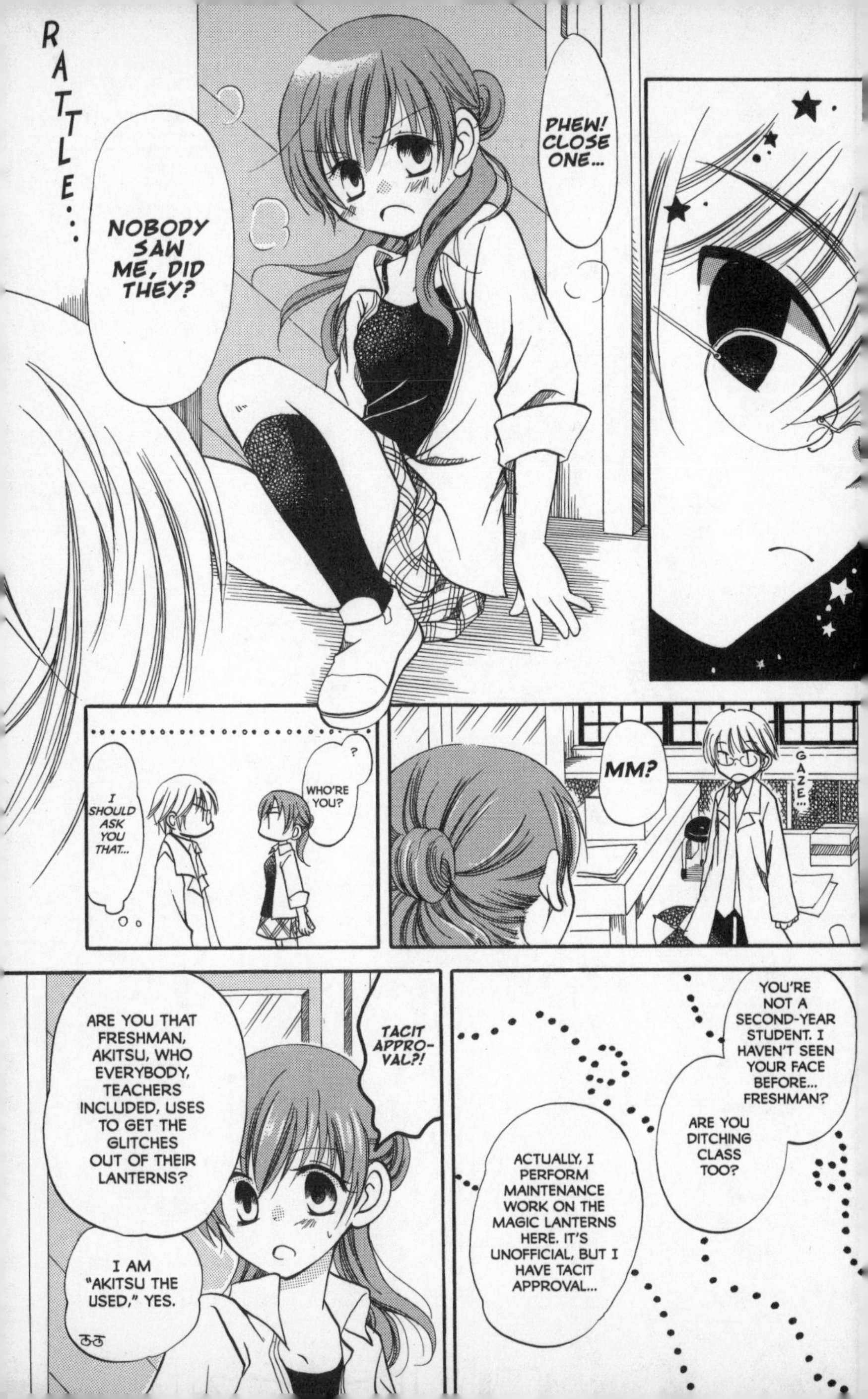
RATTLE...
PHEW! CLOSE ONE...
NOBODY SAW ME, DID THEY?
MM?
GAZE...
....
?
WHO'RE YOU?
I SHOULD ASK YOU THAT...
YOU'RE NOT A SECOND-YEAR STUDENT. I HAVEN'T SEEN YOUR FACE BEFORE... FRESHMAN?
ARE YOU DITCHING CLASS TOO?
ACTUALLY, I PERFORM MAINTENANCE WORK ON THE MAGIC LANTERNS HERE. IT'S UNOFFICIAL, BUT I HAVE TACIT APPROVAL...
TACIT APPROVAL?!
ARE YOU THAT FRESHMAN, AKITSU, WHO EVERYBODY, TEACHERS INCLUDED, USES TO GET THE GLITCHES OUT OF THEIR LANTERNS?
I AM "AKITSU THE USED," YES.

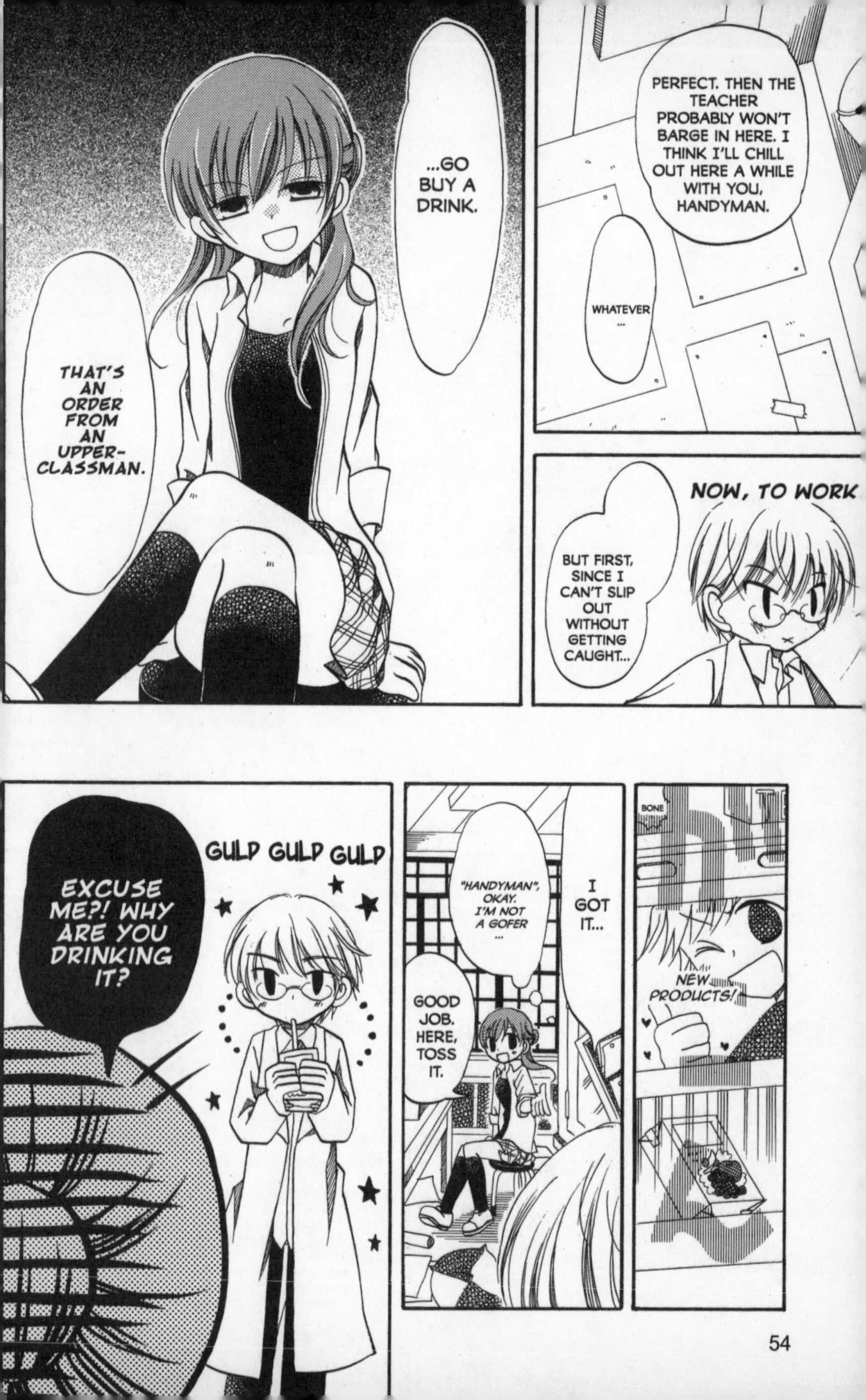
PERFECT. THEN THE TEACHER PROBABLY WON'T BARGE IN HERE. I THINK I'LL CHILL OUT HERE A WHILE WITH YOU, HANDYMAN.
WHATEVER...
NOW, TO WORK
BUT FIRST, SINCE I CAN'T SLIP OUT WITHOUT GETTING CAUGHT...
...GO BUY A DRINK.
THAT'S AN ORDER FROM AN UPPER-CLASSMAN.
BONE
NEW PRODUCTS!
I GOT IT...
"HANDYMAN", OKAY. I'M NOT A GOFER...
GOOD JOB. HERE, TOSS IT.
GULP GULP GULP
EXCUSE ME?! WHY ARE YOU DRINKING IT?

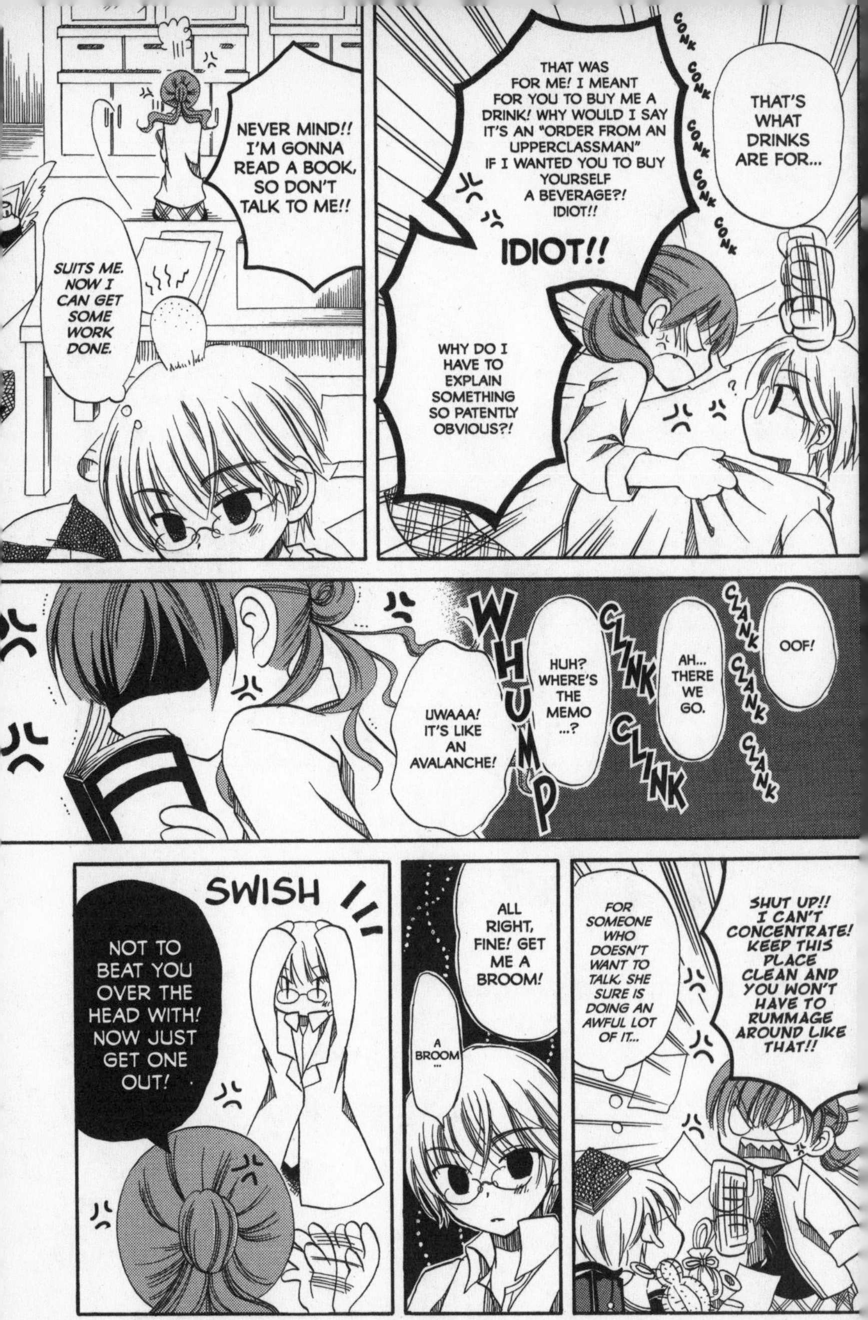
THAT'S WHAT DRINKS ARE FOR...
CONK CONK CONK CONK CONK CONK
THAT WAS FOR ME! I MEANT FOR YOU TO BUY ME A DRINK! WHY WOULD I SAY IT'S AN "ORDER FROM AN UPPERCLASSMAN" IF I WANTED YOU TO BUY YOURSELF A BEVERAGE?! IDIOT!!
IDIOT!!
WHY DO I HAVE TO EXPLAIN SOMETHING SO PATENTLY OBVIOUS?!
NEVER MIND!! I'M GONNA READ A BOOK, SO DON'T TALK TO ME!!
SUITS ME. NOW I CAN GET SOME WORK DONE.
OOF!
CLANK CLANK CLANK
AH... THERE WE GO.
CLINK CLINK
HUH? WHERE'S THE MEMO ...?
WHUMP
UWAAA! IT'S LIKE AN AVALANCHE!
SHUT UP!! I CAN'T CONCENTRATE! KEEP THIS PLACE CLEAN AND YOU WON'T HAVE TO RUMMAGE AROUND LIKE THAT!!
FOR SOMEONE WHO DOESN'T WANT TO TALK, SHE SURE IS DOING AN AWFUL LOT OF IT...
ALL RIGHT, FINE! GET ME A BROOM!
A BROOM ...
SWISH
NOT TO BEAT YOU OVER THE HEAD WITH! NOW JUST GET ONE OUT!

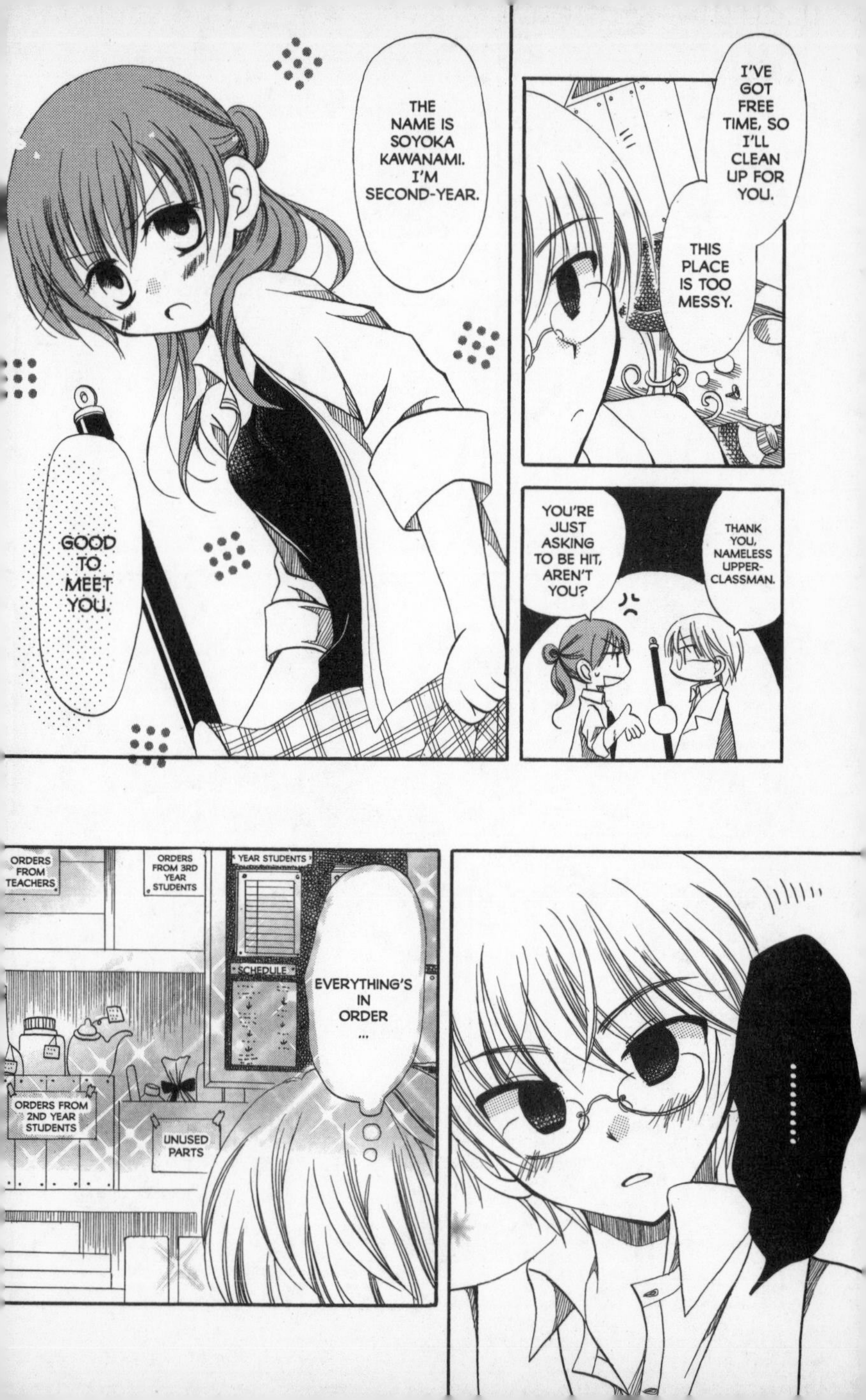
I'VE GOT FREE TIME, SO I'LL CLEAN UP FOR YOU.
THIS PLACE IS TOO MESSY.
THANK YOU, NAMELESS UPPER-CLASSMAN.
YOU'RE JUST ASKING TO BE HIT, AREN'T YOU?
THE NAME IS SOYOKA KAWANAMI. I'M SECOND-YEAR.
GOOD TO MEET YOU.
....
ORDERS FROM TEACHERS
ORDERS FROM 3RD YEAR STUDENTS
YEAR STUDENTS
SCHEDULE
EVERYTHING'S IN ORDER ...
ORDERS FROM 2ND YEAR STUDENTS
UNUSED PARTS

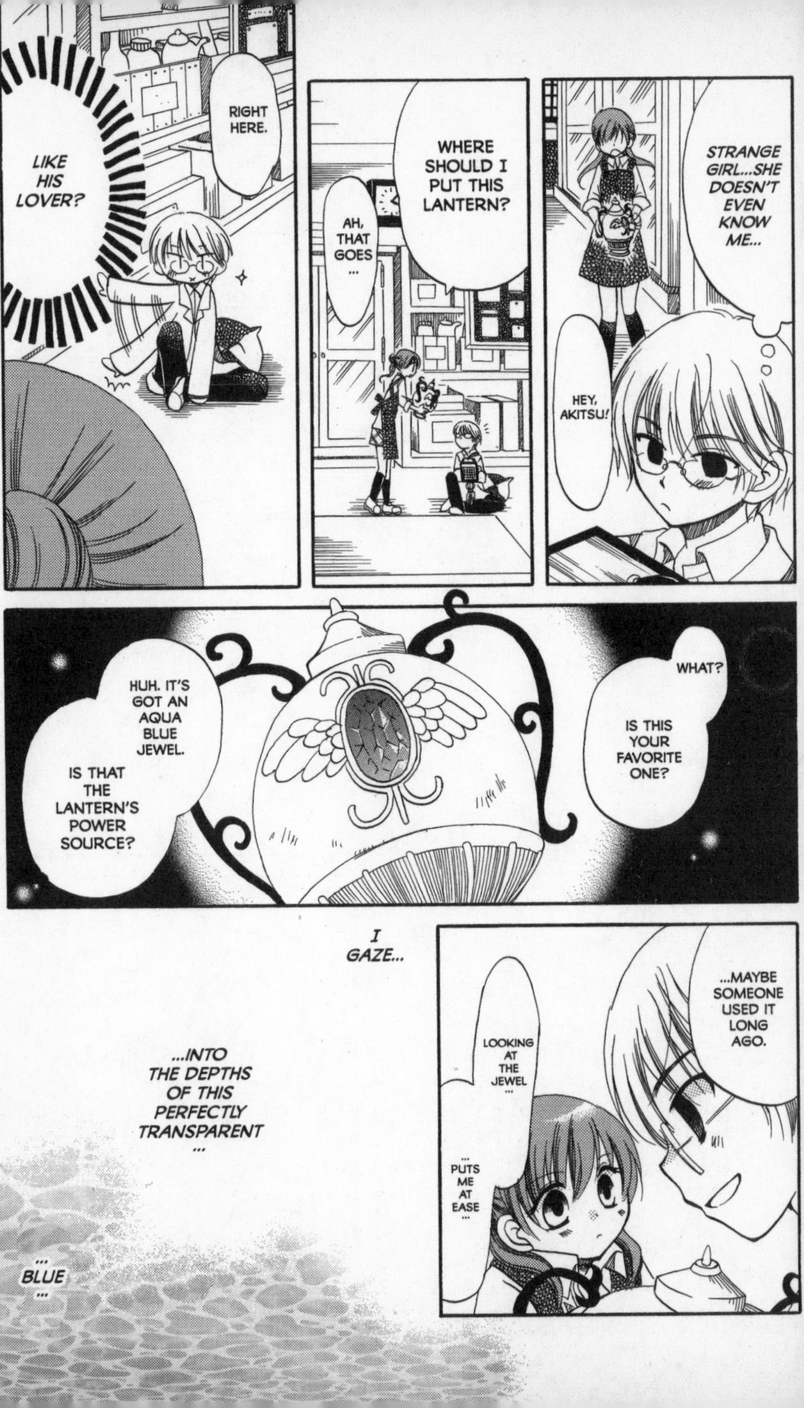
STRANGE GIRL...SHE DOESN'T EVEN KNOW ME...
HEY, AKITSU!
WHERE SHOULD I PUT THIS LANTERN?
AH, THAT GOES ...
RIGHT HERE.
LIKE HIS LOVER?
WHAT?
IS THIS YOUR FAVORITE ONE?
HUH. IT'S GOT AN AQUA BLUE JEWEL.
IS THAT THE LANTERN'S POWER SOURCE?
...MAYBE SOMEONE USED IT LONG AGO.
LOOKING AT THE JEWEL ...
... PUTS ME AT EASE ...
I GAZE...
...INTO THE DEPTHS OF THIS PERFECTLY TRANSPARENT ...
... BLUE ...

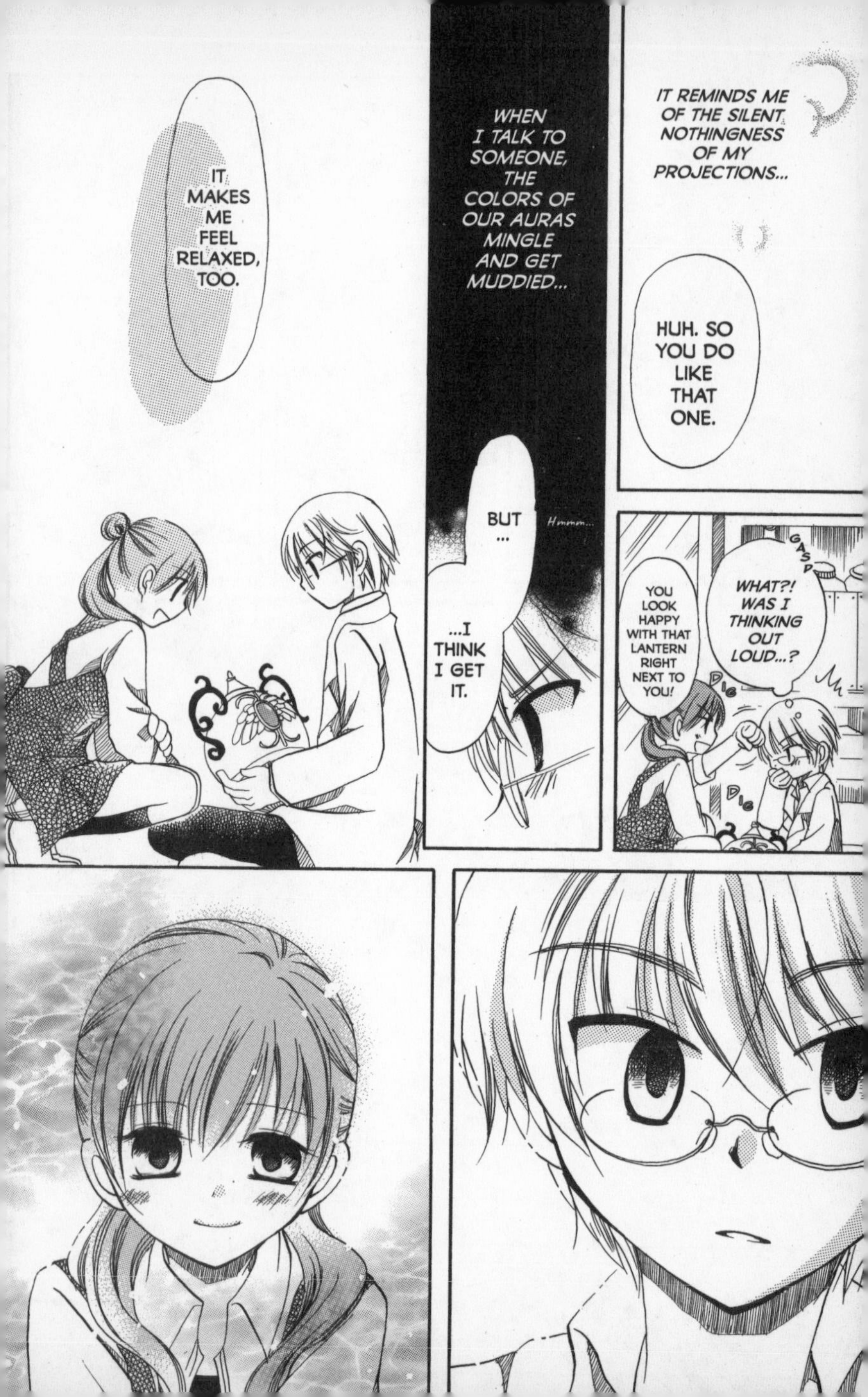
IT REMINDS ME OF THE SILENT NOTHINGNESS OF MY PROJECTIONS...
HUH. SO YOU DO LIKE THAT ONE.
GASP
WHAT?! WAS I THINKING OUT LOUD...?
YOU LOOK HAPPY WITH THAT LANTERN RIGHT NEXT TO YOU!
DIG
DIG
WHEN I TALK TO SOMEONE, THE COLORS OF OUR AURAS MINGLE AND GET MUDDIED...
Hmmm...
BUT ...
...I THINK I GET IT.
IT MAKES ME FEEL RELAXED, TOO.

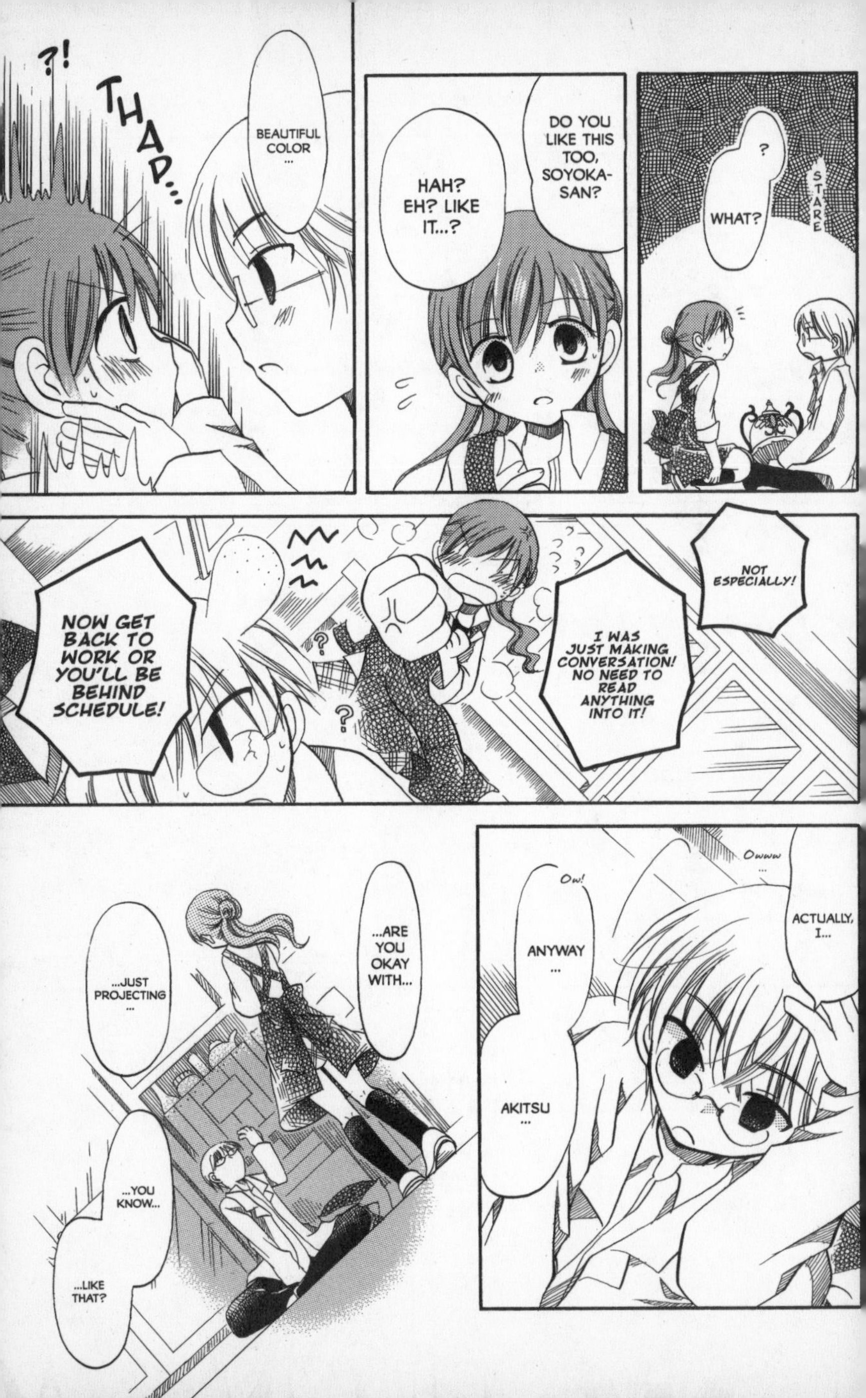
?
WHAT?
STARE
DO YOU LIKE THIS TOO, SOYOKA-SAN?
HAH? EH? LIKE IT...?
BEAUTIFUL COLOR ...
THAP...
?!
NOT ESPECIALLY!
I WAS JUST MAKING CONVERSATION! NO NEED TO READ ANYTHING INTO IT!
NOW GET BACK TO WORK OR YOU'LL BE BEHIND SCHEDULE!
Owww ...
ACTUALLY, I...
Ow!
ANYWAY ...
AKITSU ...
...ARE YOU OKAY WITH...
...JUST PROJECTING ...
...YOU KNOW...
...LIKE THAT?

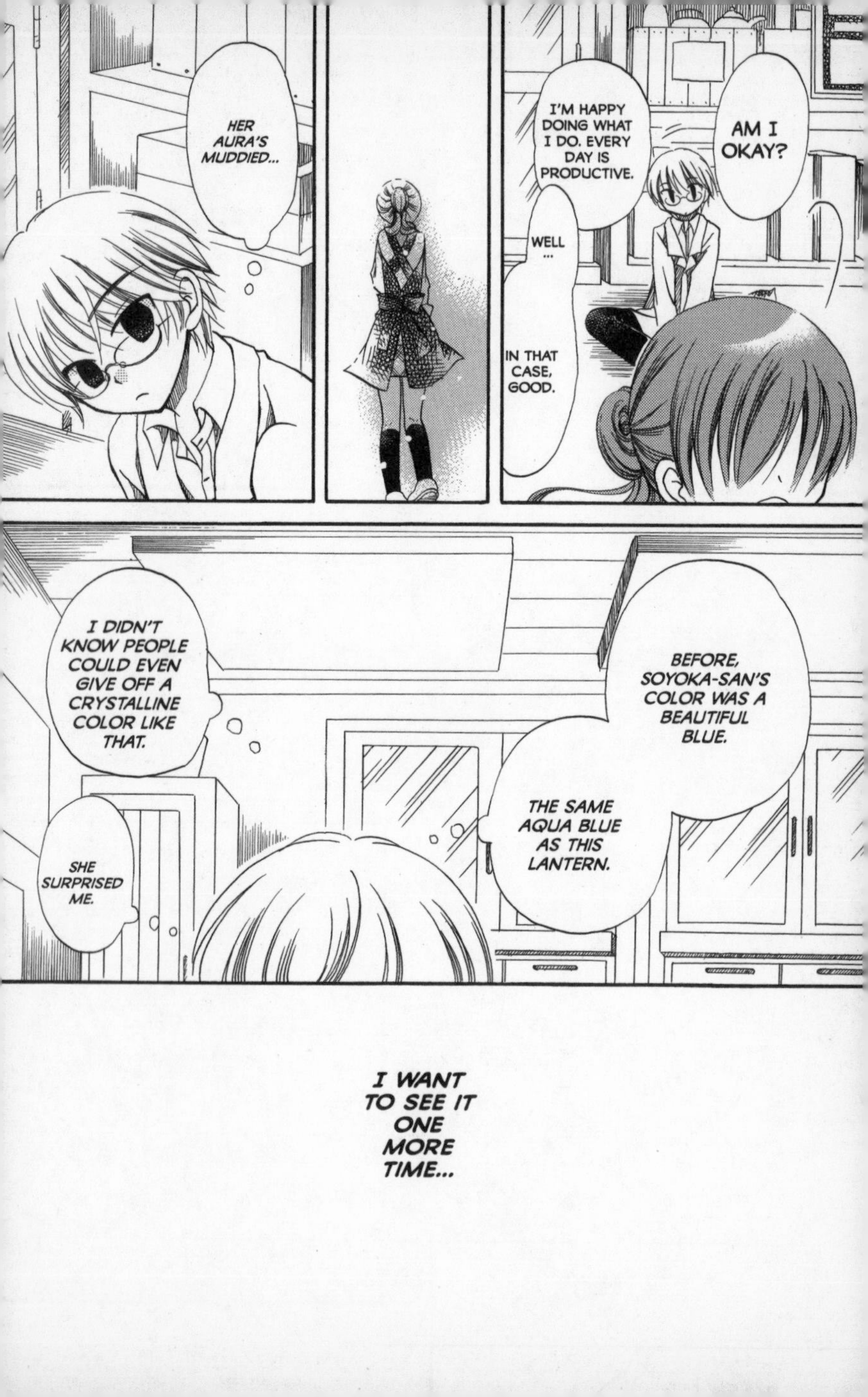
AM I OKAY?
I'M HAPPY DOING WHAT I DO. EVERY DAY IS PRODUCTIVE.
WELL...
IN THAT CASE, GOOD.
HER AURA'S MUDDIED...
BEFORE, SOYOKA-SAN'S COLOR WAS A BEAUTIFUL BLUE.
THE SAME AQUA BLUE AS THIS LANTERN.
I DIDN'T KNOW PEOPLE COULD EVEN GIVE OFF A CRYSTALLINE COLOR LIKE THAT.
SHE SURPRISED ME.
I WANT TO SEE IT ONE MORE TIME...

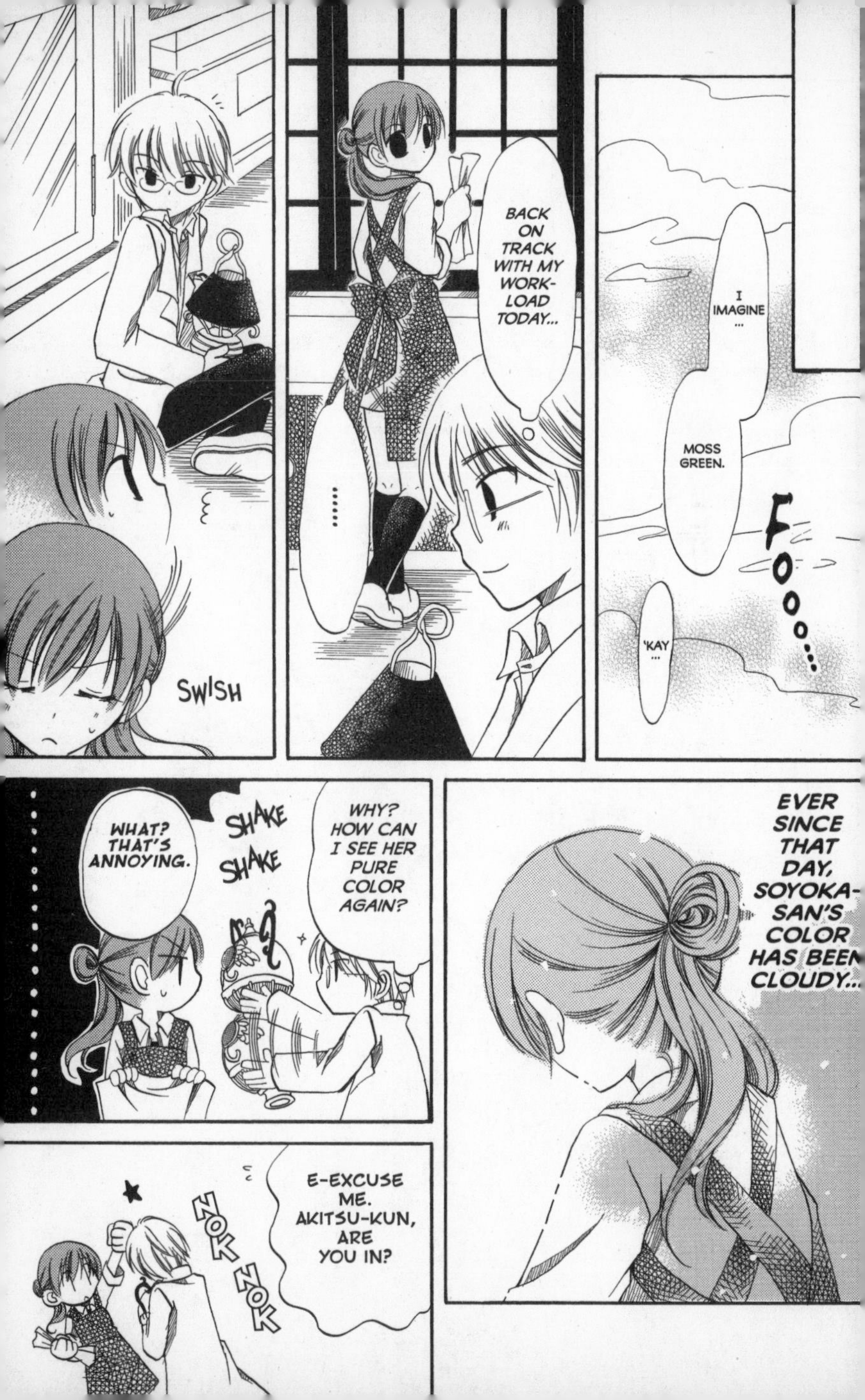
I IMAGINE...
MOSS GREEN.
FOOO...
'KAY...
BACK ON TRACK WITH MY WORKLOAD TODAY...
......
SWISH
EVER SINCE THAT DAY, SOYOKA-SAN'S COLOR HAS BEEN CLOUDY...
WHY? HOW CAN I SEE HER PURE COLOR AGAIN?
SHAKE SHAKE
WHAT? THAT'S ANNOYING.
E-EXCUSE ME. AKITSU-KUN, ARE YOU IN?
NOK NOK

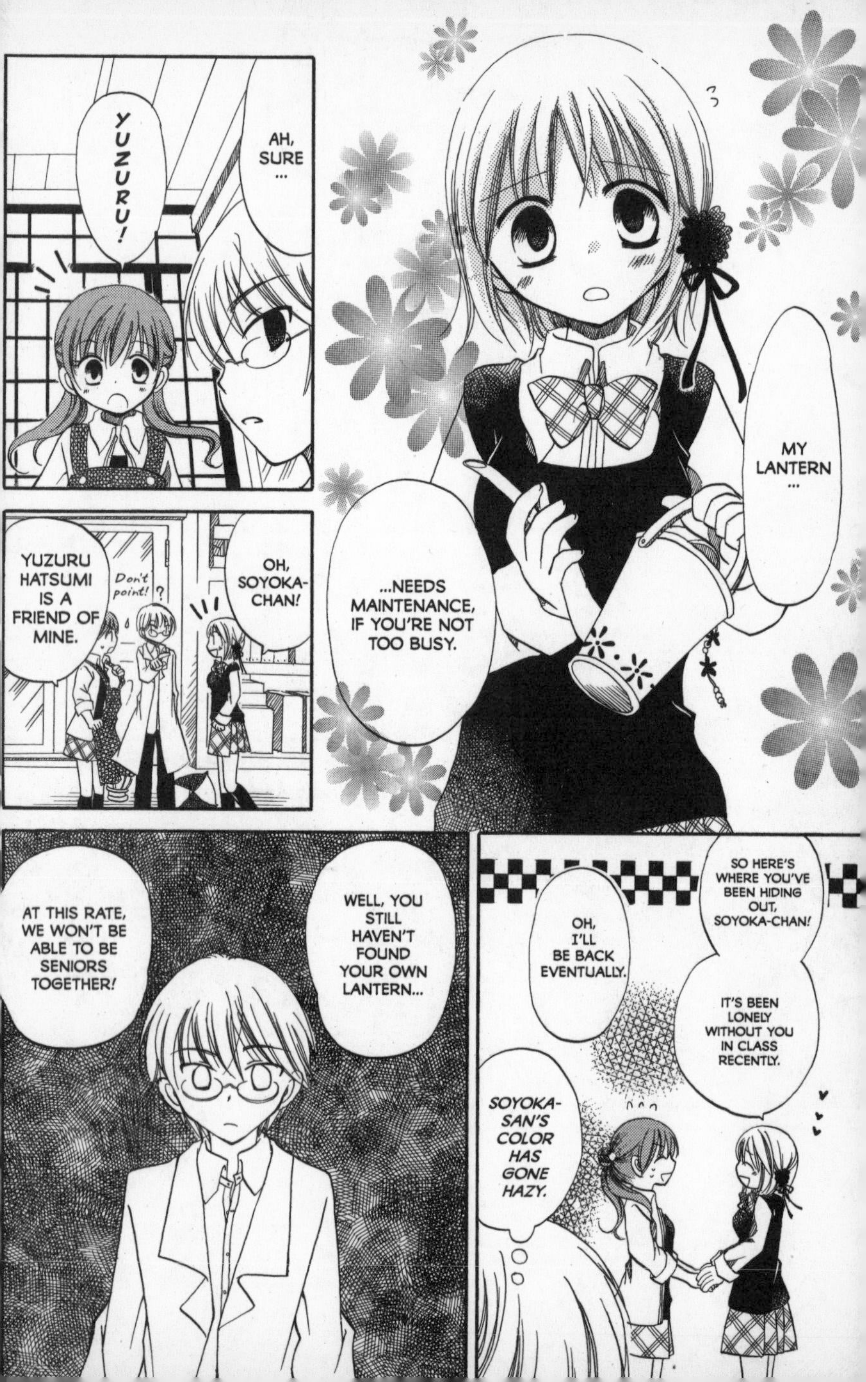
MY LANTERN ...
...NEEDS MAINTENANCE, IF YOU'RE NOT TOO BUSY.
AH, SURE ...
YUZURU!
OH, SOYOKA-CHAN!
YUZURU HATSUMI IS A FRIEND OF MINE.
Don't point!
SO HERE'S WHERE YOU'VE BEEN HIDING OUT, SOYOKA-CHAN!
OH, I'LL BE BACK EVENTUALLY.
IT'S BEEN LONELY WITHOUT YOU IN CLASS RECENTLY.
SOYOKA-SAN'S COLOR HAS GONE HAZY.
WELL, YOU STILL HAVEN'T FOUND YOUR OWN LANTERN...
AT THIS RATE, WE WON'T BE ABLE TO BE SENIORS TOGETHER!

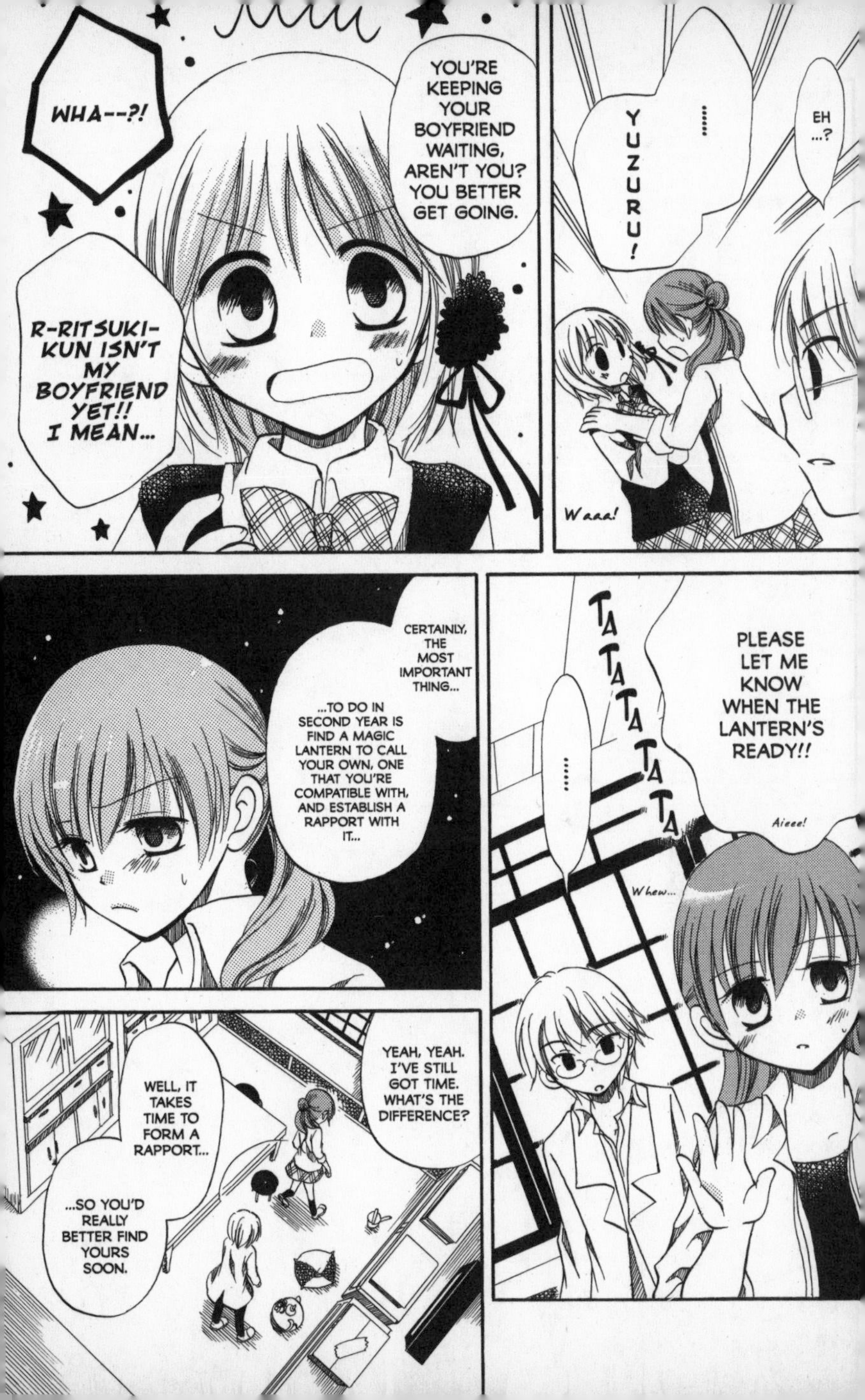
EH ...?
......
YUZURU!
Waaa!
YOU'RE KEEPING YOUR BOYFRIEND WAITING, AREN'T YOU? YOU BETTER GET GOING.
WHA--?!
R-RITSUKI-KUN ISN'T MY BOYFRIEND YET!! I MEAN...
PLEASE LET ME KNOW WHEN THE LANTERN'S READY!!
Aieee!
TATATATATATA
......
Whew...
CERTAINLY, THE MOST IMPORTANT THING...
...TO DO IN SECOND YEAR IS FIND A MAGIC LANTERN TO CALL YOUR OWN, ONE THAT YOU'RE COMPATIBLE WITH, AND ESTABLISH A RAPPORT WITH IT...
YEAH, YEAH. I'VE STILL GOT TIME. WHAT'S THE DIFFERENCE?
WELL, IT TAKES TIME TO FORM A RAPPORT...
...SO YOU'D REALLY BETTER FIND YOURS SOON.

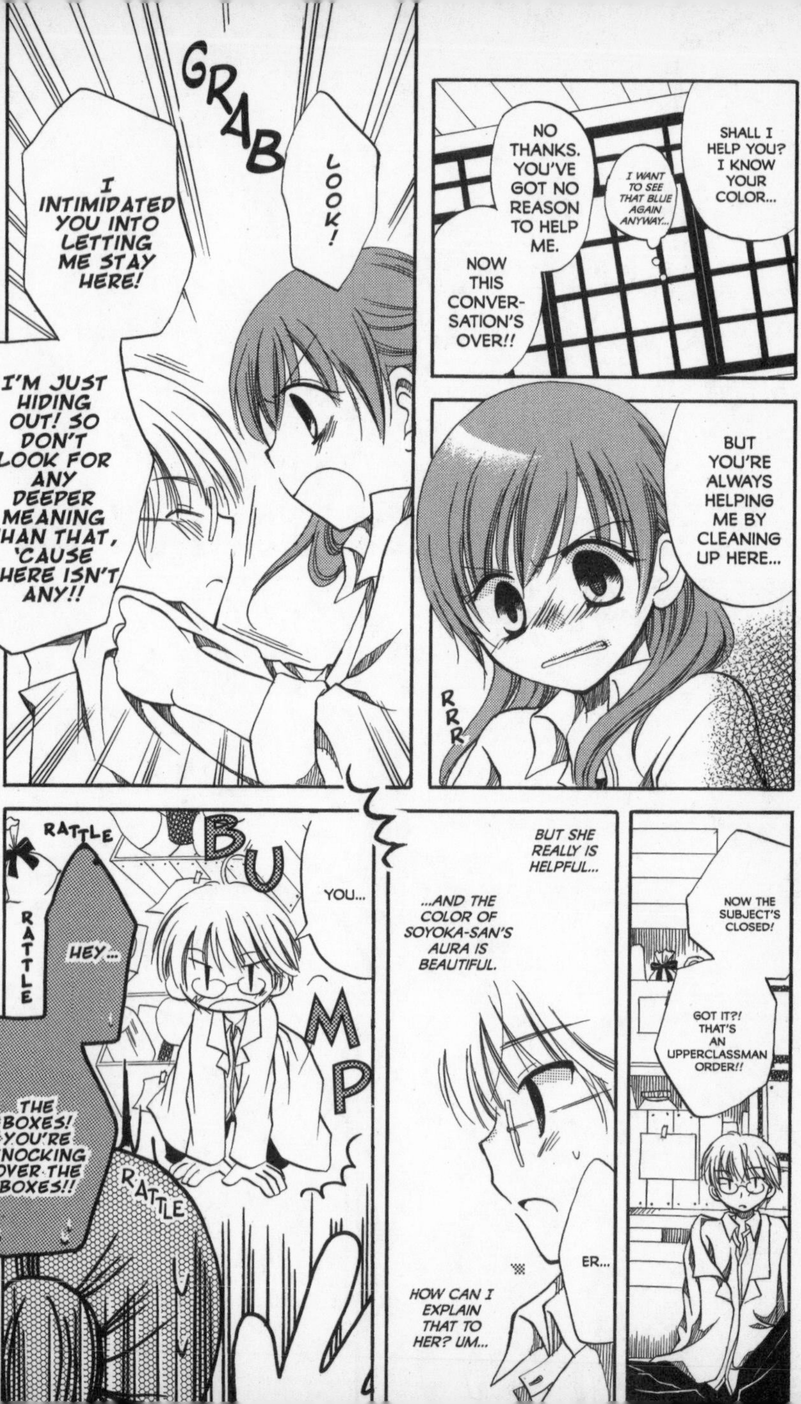
SHALL I HELP YOU? I KNOW YOUR COLOR...
I WANT TO SEE THAT BLUE AGAIN ANYWAY...
NO THANKS. YOU'VE GOT NO REASON TO HELP ME.
NOW THIS CONVERSATION'S OVER!!
BUT YOU'RE ALWAYS HELPING ME BY CLEANING UP HERE...
RRR
GRAB
LOOK!
I INTIMIDATED YOU INTO LETTING ME STAY HERE!
I'M JUST HIDING OUT! SO DON'T LOOK FOR ANY DEEPER MEANING THAN THAT, 'CAUSE THERE ISN'T ANY!!
NOW THE SUBJECT'S CLOSED!
GOT IT?! THAT'S AN UPPERCLASSMAN ORDER!!
BUT SHE REALLY IS HELPFUL...
...AND THE COLOR OF SOYOKA-SAN'S AURA IS BEAUTIFUL.
ER...
HOW CAN I EXPLAIN THAT TO HER? UM...
BUMP
YOU...
RATTLE
RATTLE
HEY...
THE BOXES! YOU'RE KNOCKING OVER THE BOXES!!
RATTLE

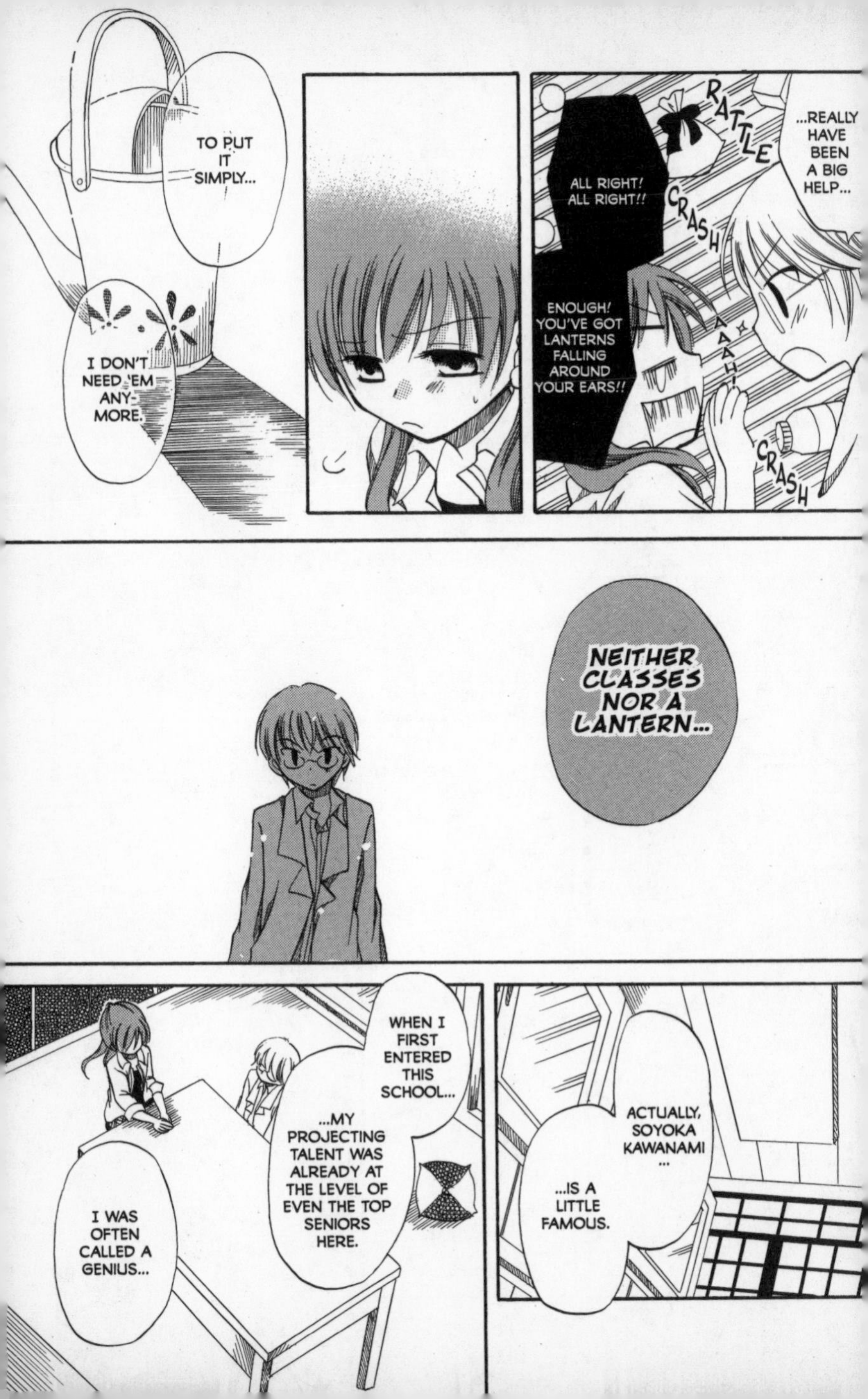
...REALLY HAVE BEEN A BIG HELP...
RATTLE
CRASH
ALL RIGHT! ALL RIGHT!!
ENOUGH! YOU'VE GOT LANTERNS FALLING AROUND YOUR EARS!!
AAAH!
CRASH
TO PUT IT SIMPLY...
I DON'T NEED 'EM ANYMORE.
NEITHER CLASSES NOR A LANTERN...
ACTUALLY, SOYOKA KAWANAMI ...
...IS A LITTLE FAMOUS.
WHEN I FIRST ENTERED THIS SCHOOL...
...MY PROJECTING TALENT WAS ALREADY AT THE LEVEL OF EVEN THE TOP SENIORS HERE.
I WAS OFTEN CALLED A GENIUS...

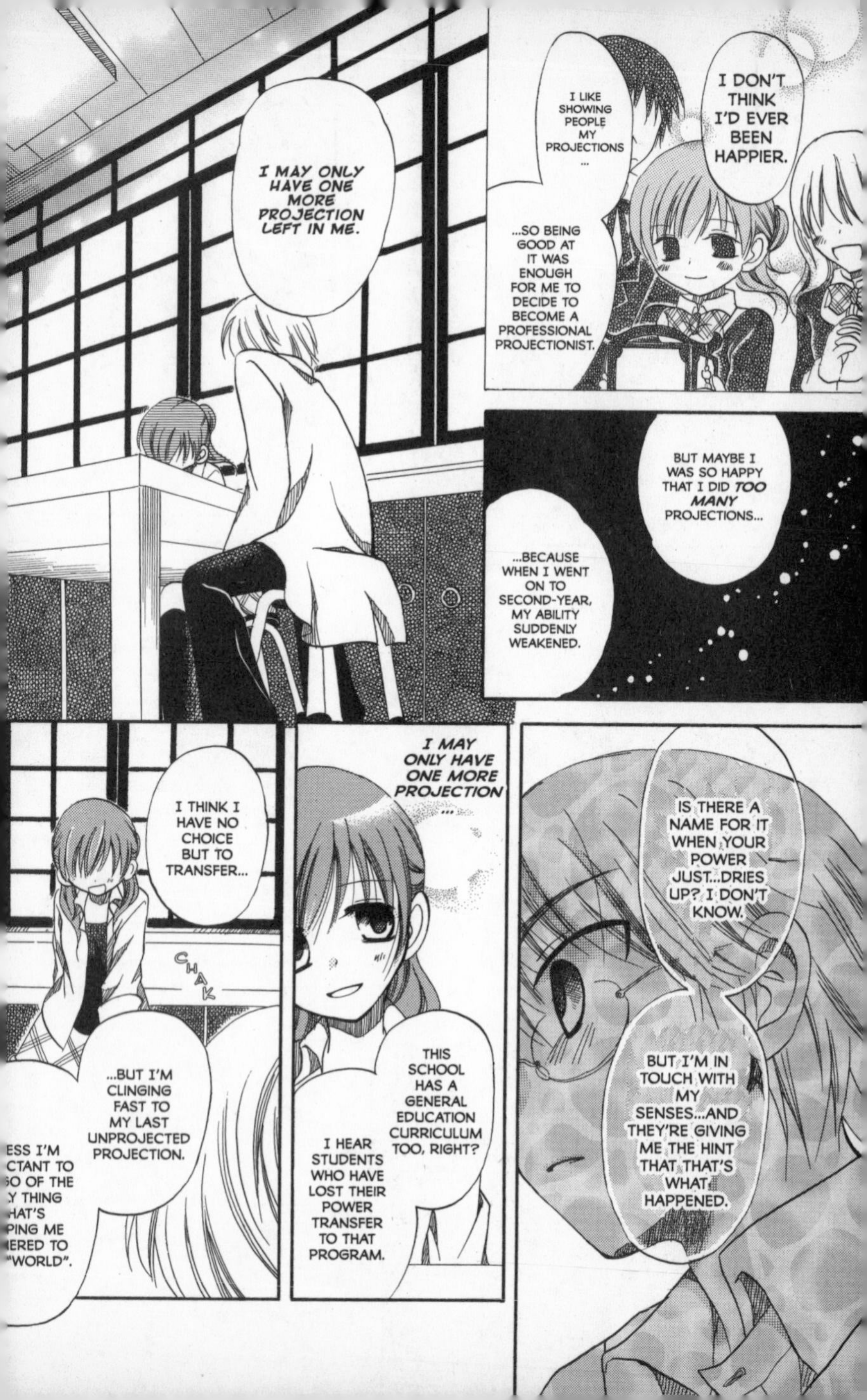
I DON'T THINK I'D EVER BEEN HAPPIER.
I LIKE SHOWING PEOPLE MY PROJECTIONS...
...SO BEING GOOD AT IT WAS ENOUGH FOR ME TO DECIDE TO BECOME A PROFESSIONAL PROJECTIONIST.
BUT MAYBE I WAS SO HAPPY THAT I DID *TOO MANY* PROJECTIONS...
...BECAUSE WHEN I WENT ON TO SECOND-YEAR, MY ABILITY SUDDENLY WEAKENED.
I MAY ONLY HAVE ONE MORE PROJECTION LEFT IN ME.
IS THERE A NAME FOR IT WHEN YOUR POWER JUST...DRIES UP? I DON'T KNOW.
BUT I'M IN TOUCH WITH MY SENSES...AND THEY'RE GIVING ME THE HINT THAT THAT'S WHAT HAPPENED.
I MAY ONLY HAVE ONE MORE PROJECTION...
THIS SCHOOL HAS A GENERAL EDUCATION CURRICULUM TOO, RIGHT?
I HEAR STUDENTS WHO HAVE LOST THEIR POWER TRANSFER TO THAT PROGRAM.
I THINK I HAVE NO CHOICE BUT TO TRANSFER...
CHAK
...BUT I'M CLINGING FAST TO MY LAST UNPROJECTED PROJECTION.
ESS I'M
CTANT TO
GO OF THE
Y THING
HAT'S
PING ME
ERED TO
"WORLD".

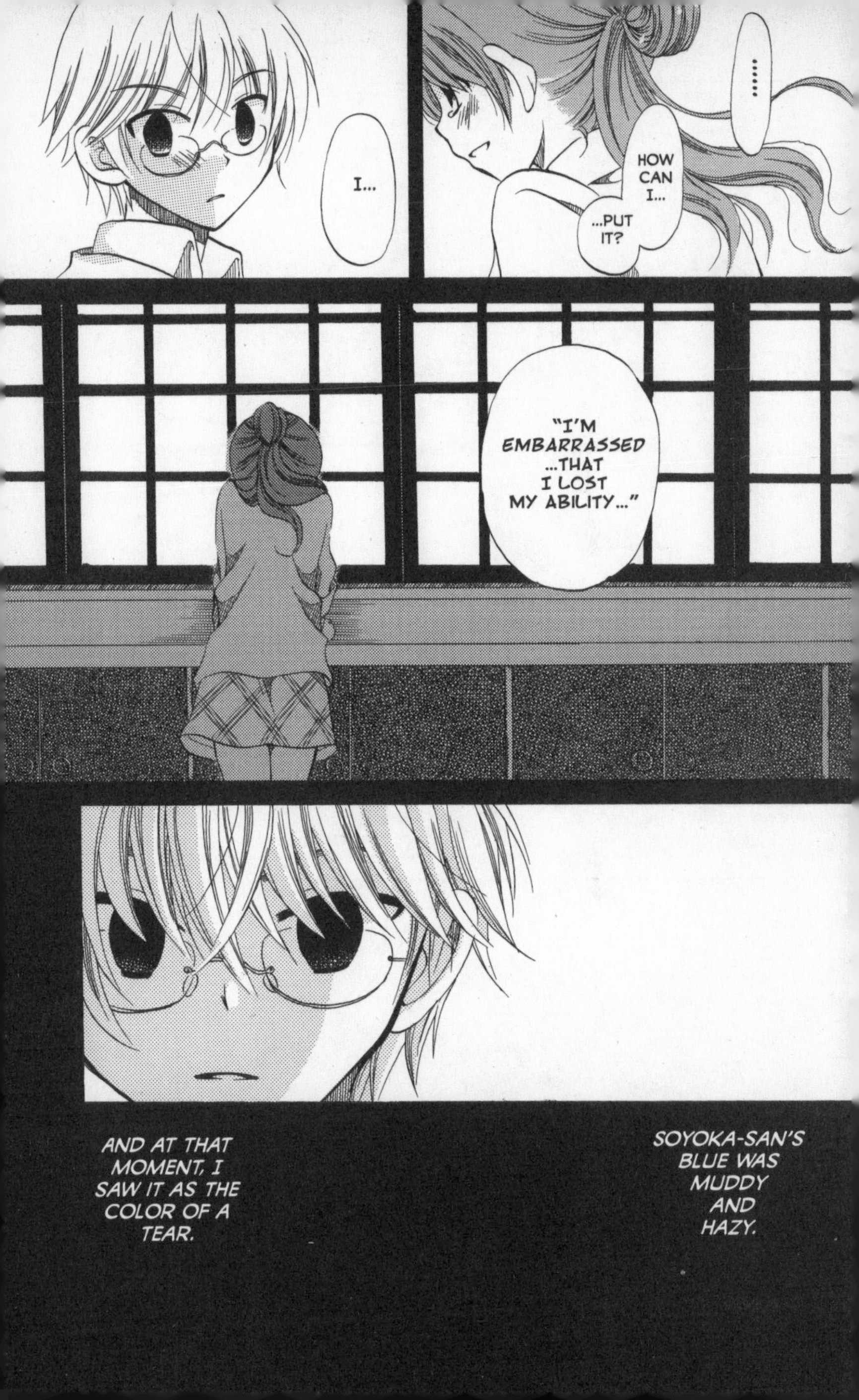
......
HOW CAN I...
...PUT IT?
I...
"I'M EMBARRASSED ...THAT I LOST MY ABILITY..."
SOYOKA-SAN'S BLUE WAS MUDDY AND HAZY.
AND AT THAT MOMENT, I SAW IT AS THE COLOR OF A TEAR.

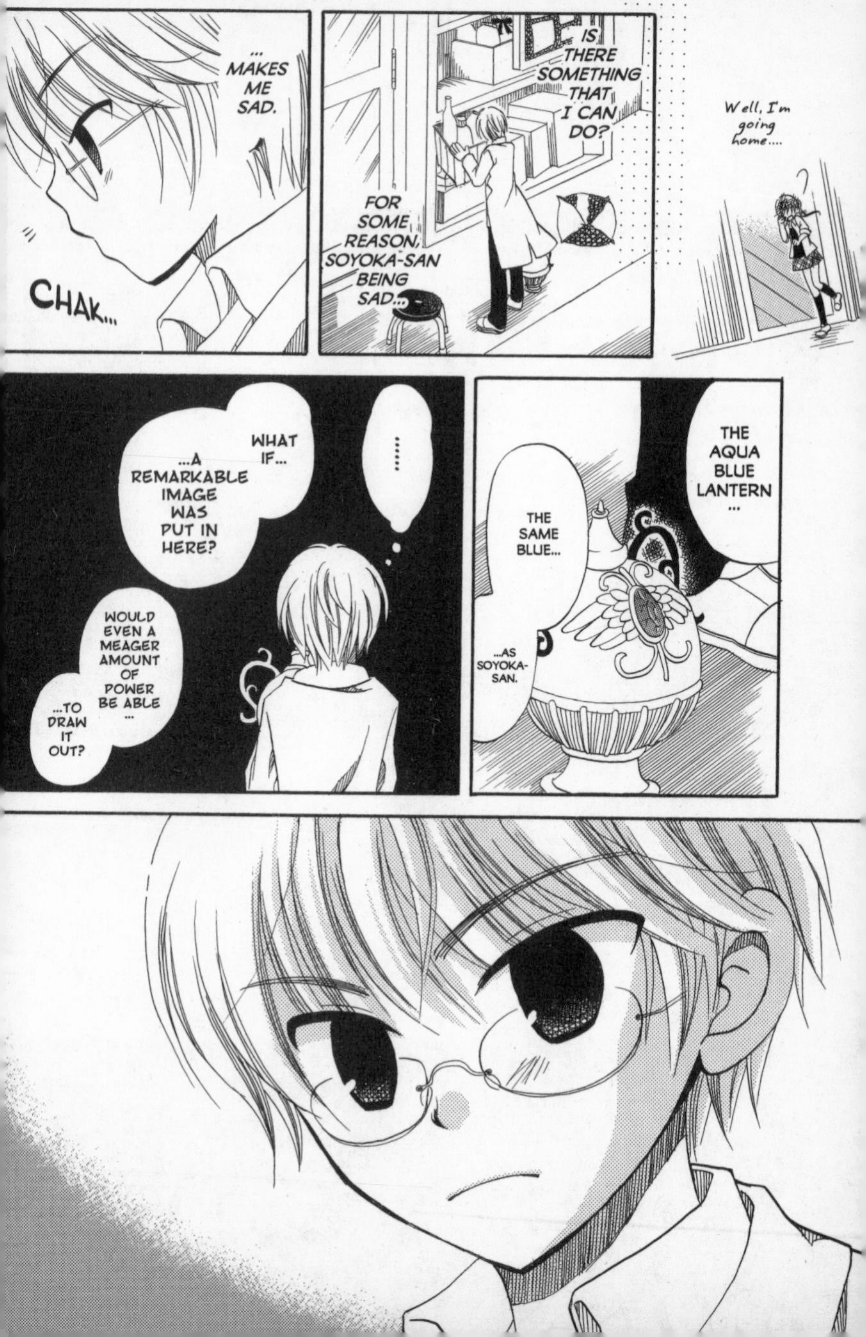
Well, I'm going home....
IS THERE SOMETHING THAT I CAN DO?
FOR SOME REASON, SOYOKA-SAN BEING SAD...
... MAKES ME SAD.
CHAK...
THE AQUA BLUE LANTERN ...
THE SAME BLUE...
...AS SOYOKA-SAN.
......
WHAT IF...
...A REMARKABLE IMAGE WAS PUT IN HERE?
WOULD EVEN A MEAGER AMOUNT OF POWER BE ABLE ...
...TO DRAW IT OUT?

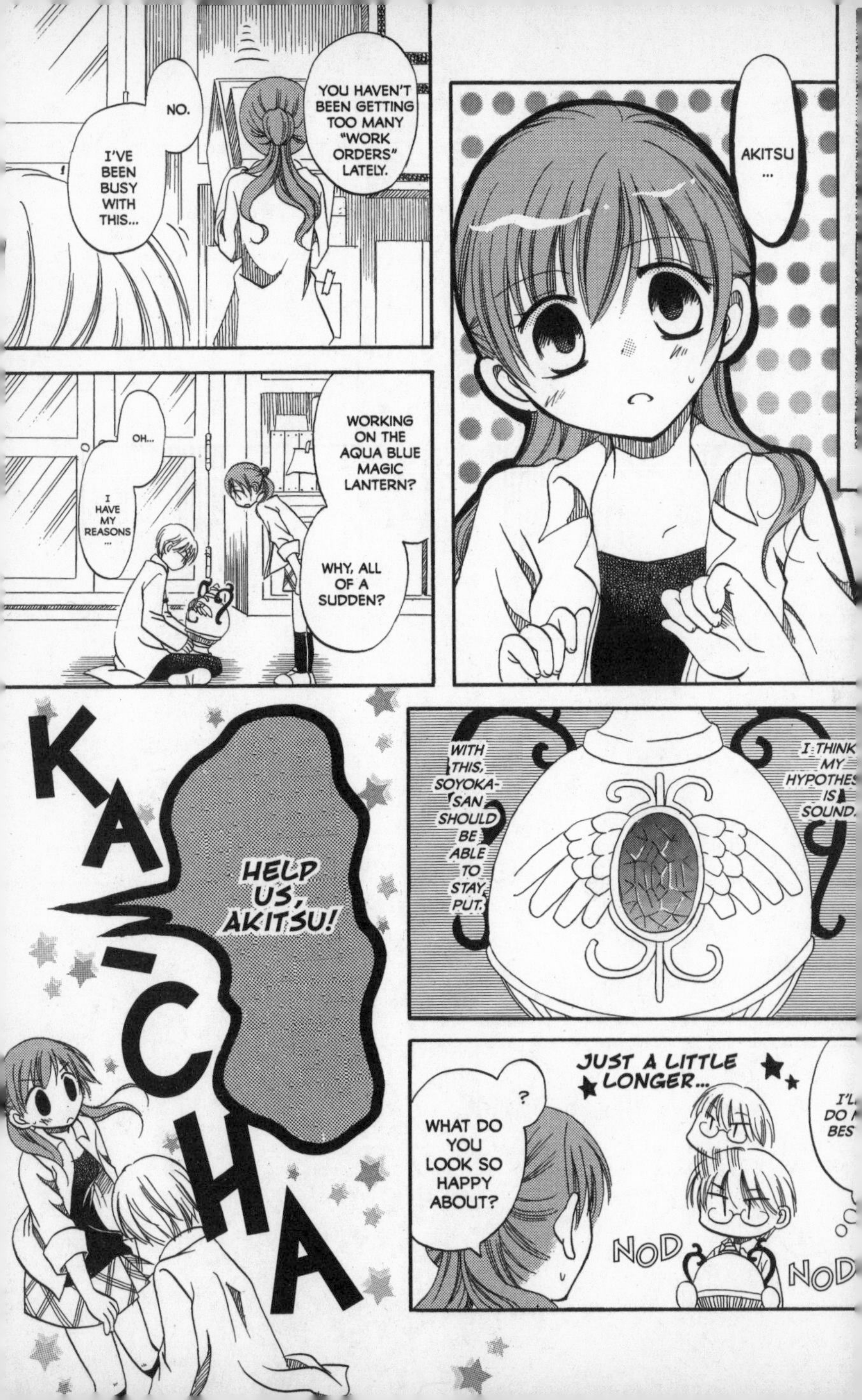
AKITSU ...
YOU HAVEN'T BEEN GETTING TOO MANY "WORK ORDERS" LATELY.
NO.
I'VE BEEN BUSY WITH THIS...
WORKING ON THE AQUA BLUE MAGIC LANTERN?
WHY, ALL OF A SUDDEN?
OH...
I HAVE MY REASONS ...
I THINK MY HYPOTHES IS SOUND.
WITH THIS, SOYOKA-SAN SHOULD BE ABLE TO STAY PUT.
I'L DO I BES
JUST A LITTLE LONGER...
?
WHAT DO YOU LOOK SO HAPPY ABOUT?
NOD
NOD
KA-CHA
HELP US, AKITSU!

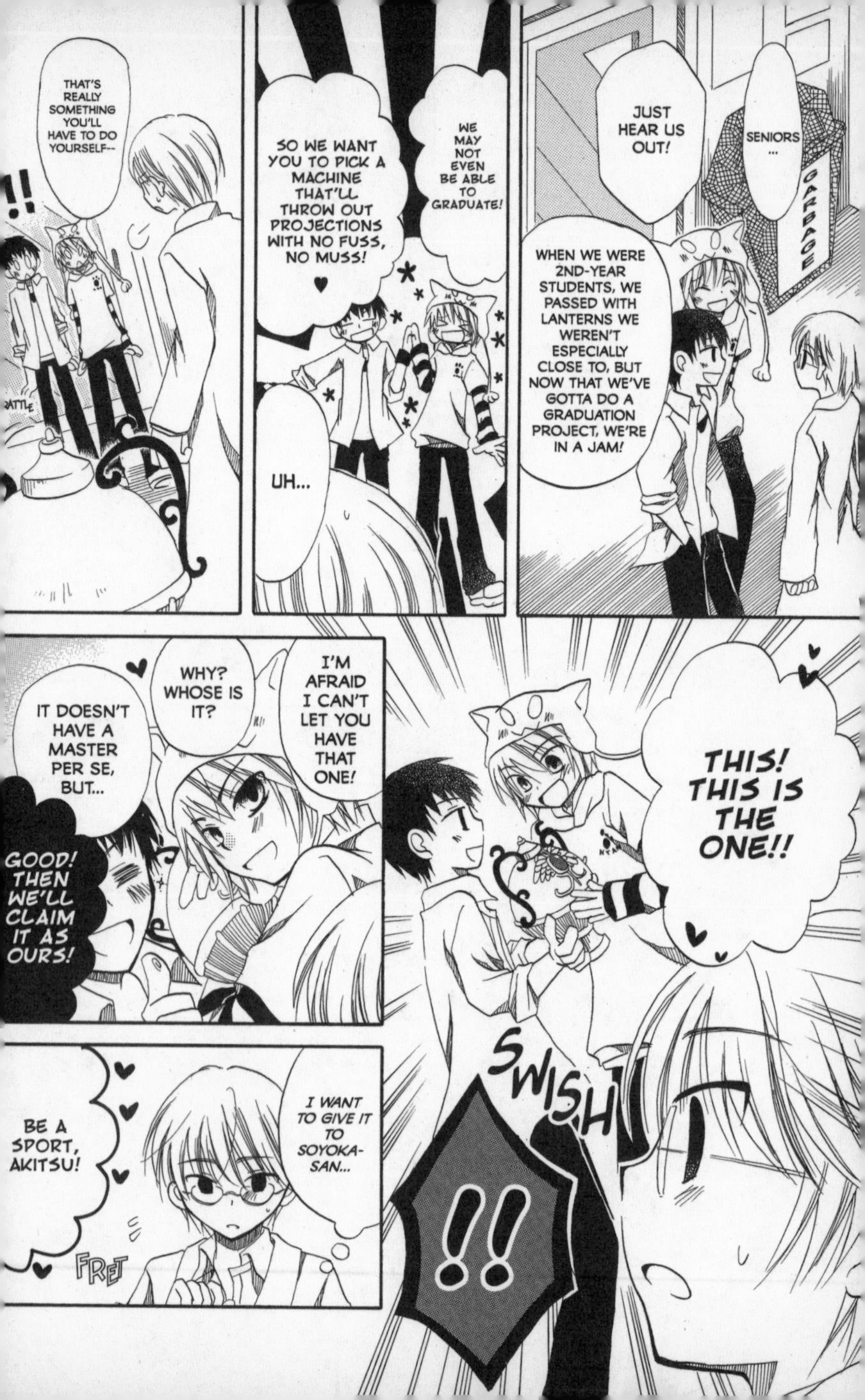
SENIORS...
JUST HEAR US OUT!
GARBAGE
WHEN WE WERE 2ND-YEAR STUDENTS, WE PASSED WITH LANTERNS WE WEREN'T ESPECIALLY CLOSE TO, BUT NOW THAT WE'VE GOTTA DO A GRADUATION PROJECT, WE'RE IN A JAM!
WE MAY NOT EVEN BE ABLE TO GRADUATE!
SO WE WANT YOU TO PICK A MACHINE THAT'LL THROW OUT PROJECTIONS WITH NO FUSS, NO MUSS!
UH...
THAT'S REALLY SOMETHING YOU'LL HAVE TO DO YOURSELF--
!!
THIS! THIS IS THE ONE!!
I'M AFRAID I CAN'T LET YOU HAVE THAT ONE!
WHY? WHOSE IS IT?
IT DOESN'T HAVE A MASTER PER SE, BUT...
GOOD! THEN WE'LL CLAIM IT AS OURS!
SWISH
!!
I WANT TO GIVE IT TO SOYOKA-SAN...
BE A SPORT, AKITSU!
FRET

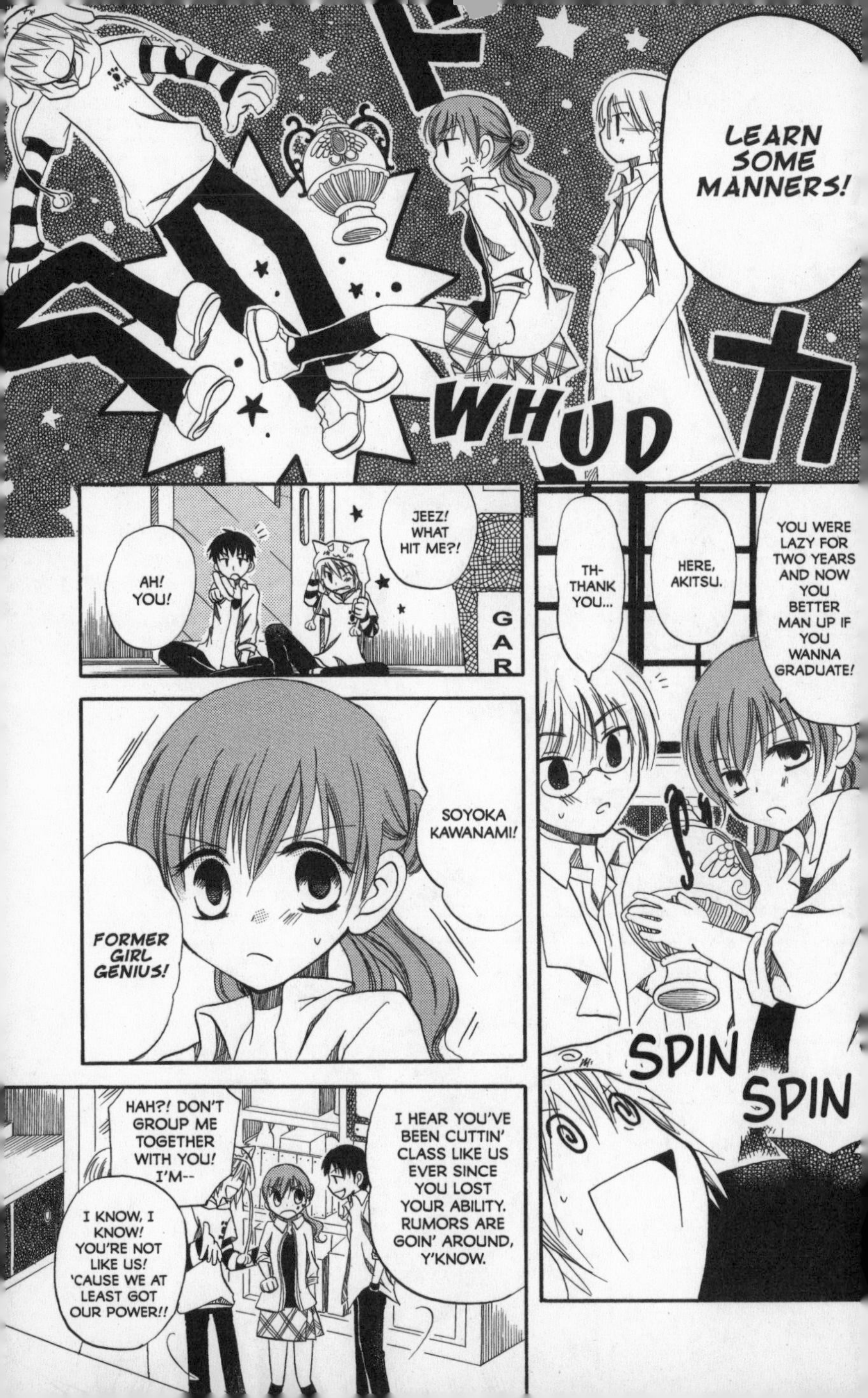
LEARN SOME MANNERS!
ド
カ
WHUD
YOU WERE LAZY FOR TWO YEARS AND NOW YOU BETTER MAN UP IF YOU WANNA GRADUATE!
HERE, AKITSU.
TH- THANK YOU...
SPIN
SPIN
JEEZ! WHAT HIT ME?!
AH! YOU!
GAR
SOYOKA KAWANAMI!
FORMER GIRL GENIUS!
I HEAR YOU'VE BEEN CUTTIN' CLASS LIKE US EVER SINCE YOU LOST YOUR ABILITY. RUMORS ARE GOIN' AROUND, Y'KNOW.
HAH?! DON'T GROUP ME TOGETHER WITH YOU! I'M--
I KNOW, I KNOW! YOU'RE NOT LIKE US! 'CAUSE WE AT LEAST GOT OUR POWER!!

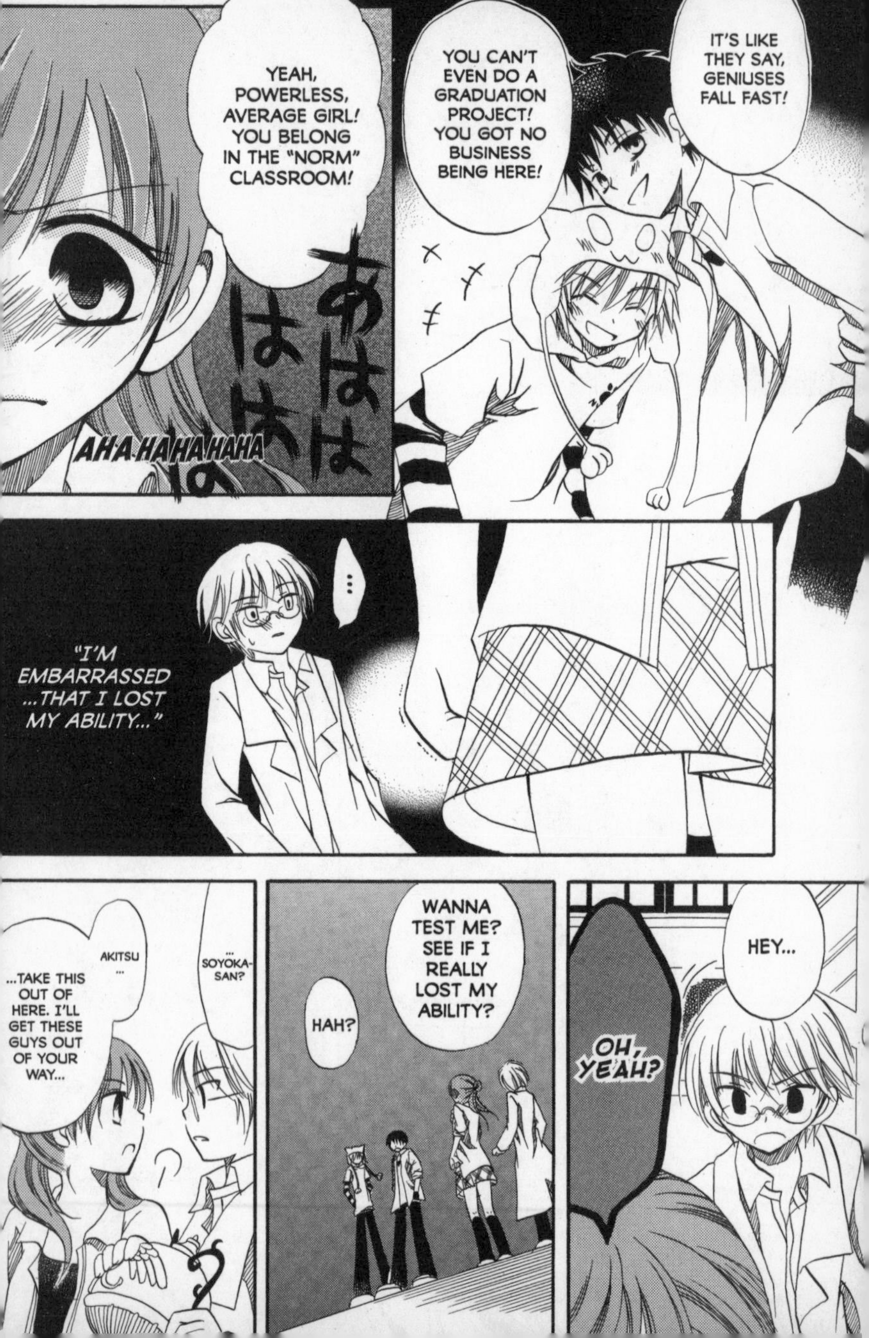
IT'S LIKE THEY SAY, GENIUSES FALL FAST!
YOU CAN'T EVEN DO A GRADUATION PROJECT! YOU GOT NO BUSINESS BEING HERE!
YEAH, POWERLESS, AVERAGE GIRL! YOU BELONG IN THE "NORM" CLASSROOM!
あははは
AHA HAHA HAHA
...
"I'M EMBARRASSED ...THAT I LOST MY ABILITY..."
HEY...
OH, YEAH?
WANNA TEST ME? SEE IF I REALLY LOST MY ABILITY?
HAH?
... SOYOKA-SAN?
AKITSU ...
...TAKE THIS OUT OF HERE. I'LL GET THESE GUYS OUT OF YOUR WAY...

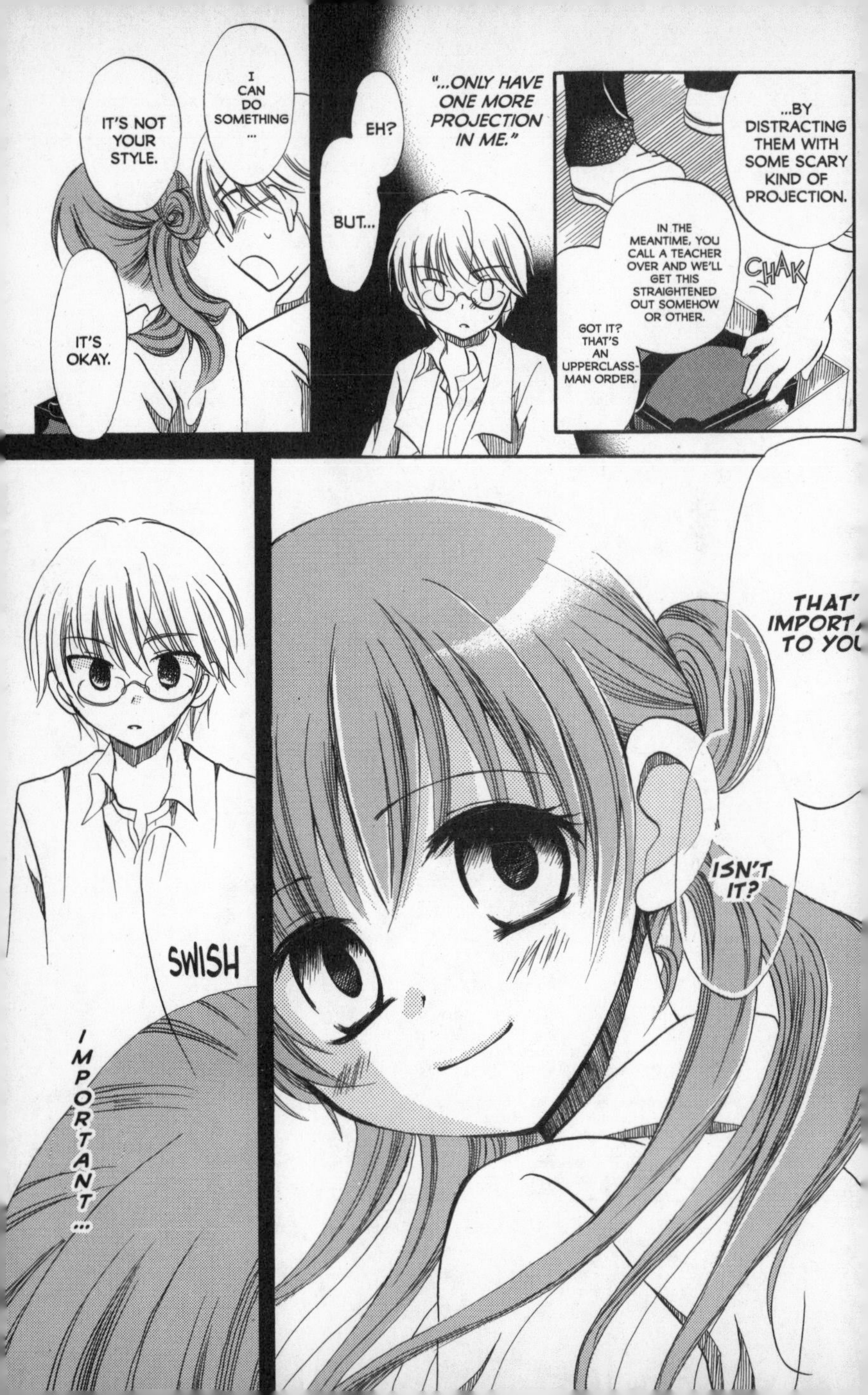
...BY DISTRACTING THEM WITH SOME SCARY KIND OF PROJECTION.
IN THE MEANTIME, YOU CALL A TEACHER OVER AND WE'LL GET THIS STRAIGHTENED OUT SOMEHOW OR OTHER.
CHAK
GOT IT? THAT'S AN UPPERCLASSMAN ORDER.
"...ONLY HAVE ONE MORE PROJECTION IN ME."
EH?
BUT...
I CAN DO SOMETHING ...
IT'S NOT YOUR STYLE.
IT'S OKAY.
THAT' IMPORT TO YO
ISN'T IT?
SWISH
IMPORTANT...

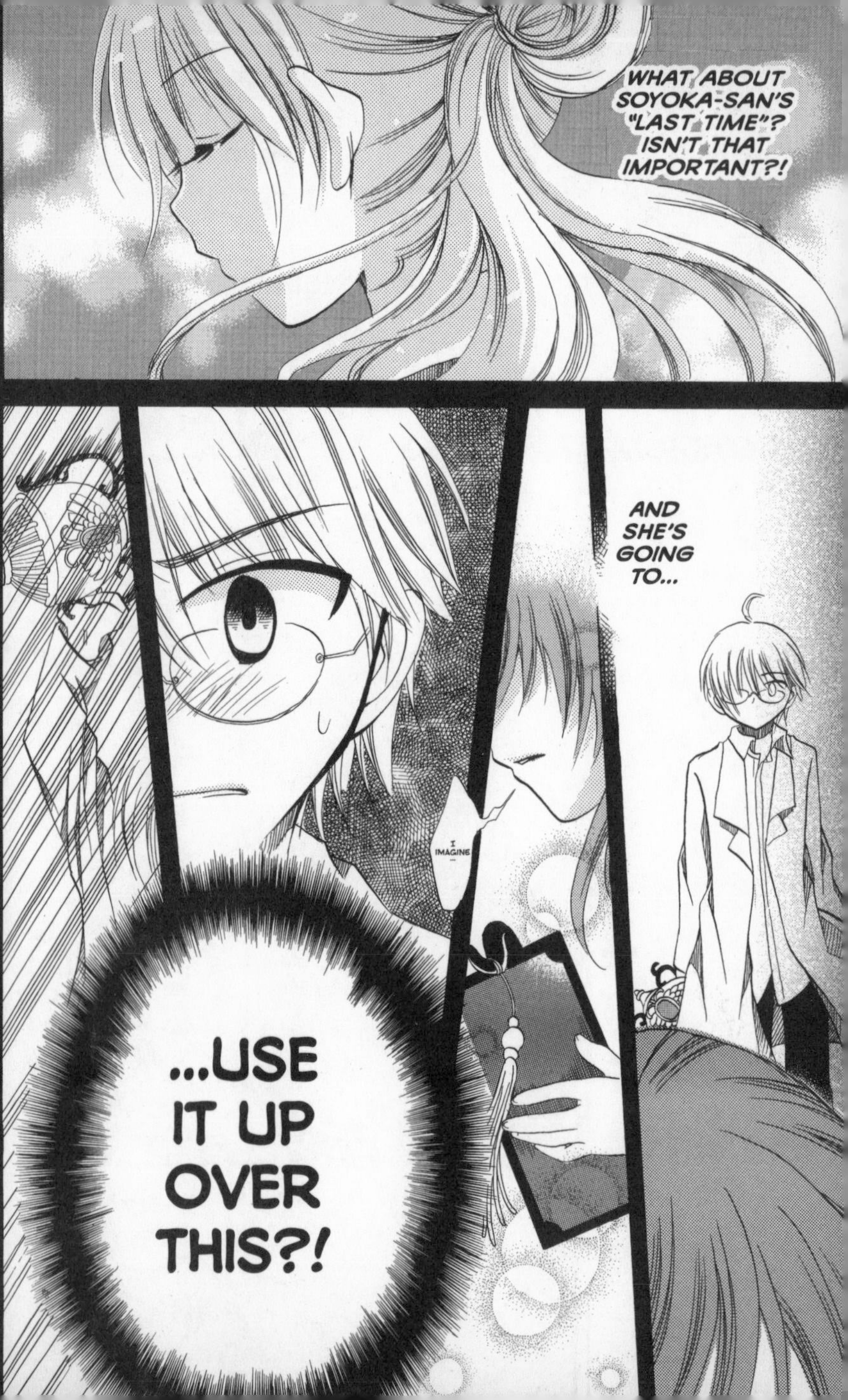
WHAT ABOUT SOYOKA-SAN'S "LAST TIME"? ISN'T THAT IMPORTANT?!
AND SHE'S GOING TO...
I IMAGINE...
...USE IT UP OVER THIS?!

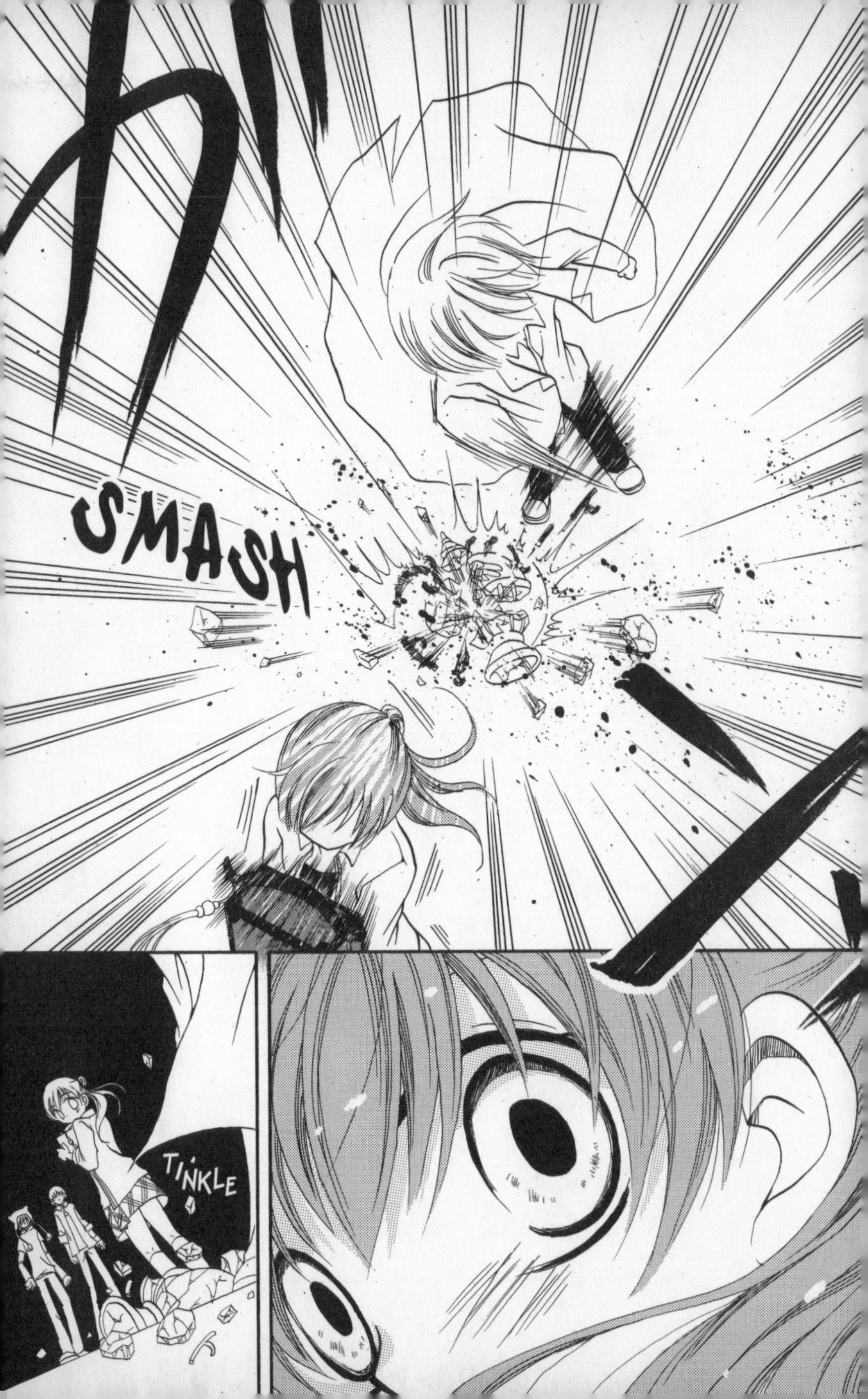
SMASH
TINKLE

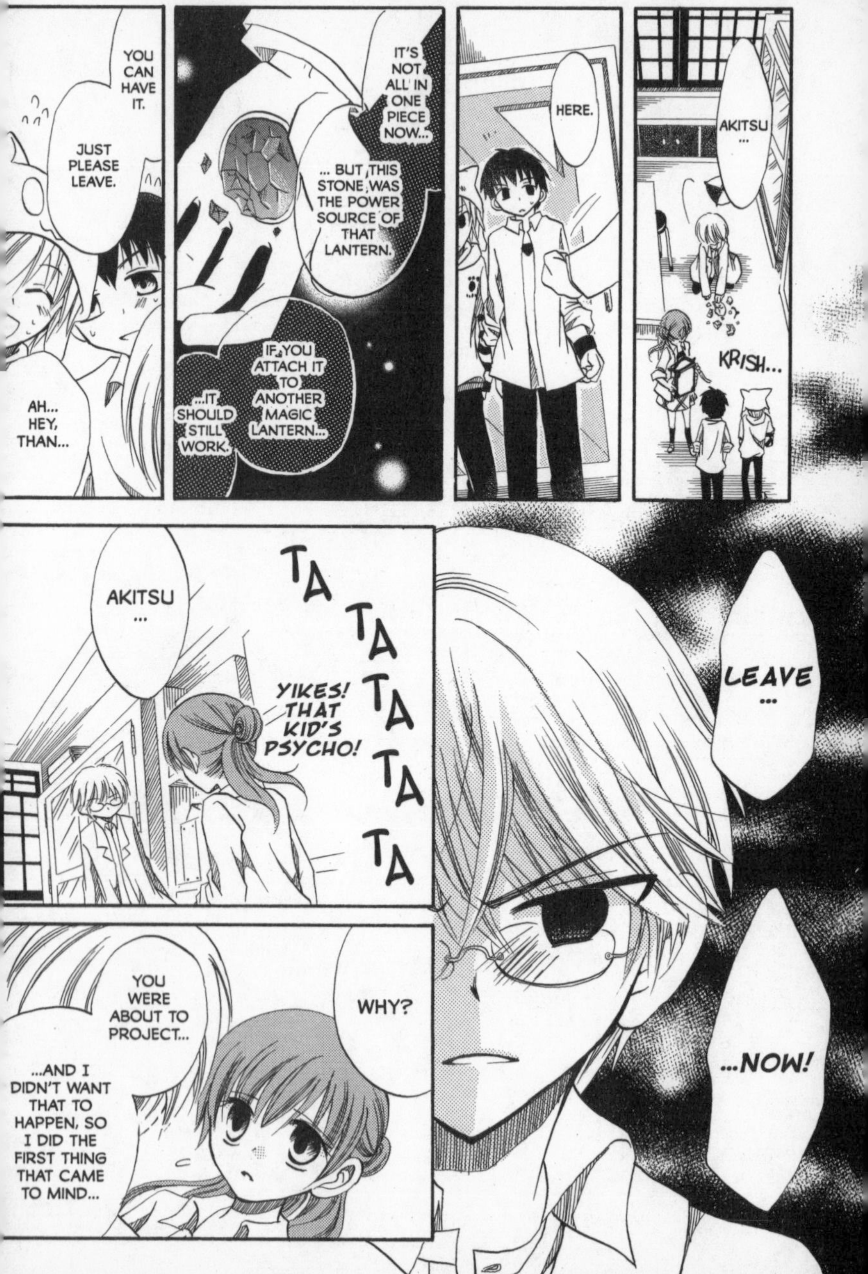
AKITSU ...
KRISH...
HERE.
IT'S NOT ALL IN ONE PIECE NOW...
... BUT THIS STONE WAS THE POWER SOURCE OF THAT LANTERN.
IF YOU ATTACH IT TO ANOTHER MAGIC LANTERN...
...IT SHOULD STILL WORK.
YOU CAN HAVE IT.
JUST PLEASE LEAVE.
AH... HEY, THAN...
LEAVE ...
...NOW!
AKITSU ...
TA TA TA TA TA TA
YIKES! THAT KID'S PSYCHO!
WHY?
YOU WERE ABOUT TO PROJECT...
...AND I DIDN'T WANT THAT TO HAPPEN, SO I DID THE FIRST THING THAT CAME TO MIND...

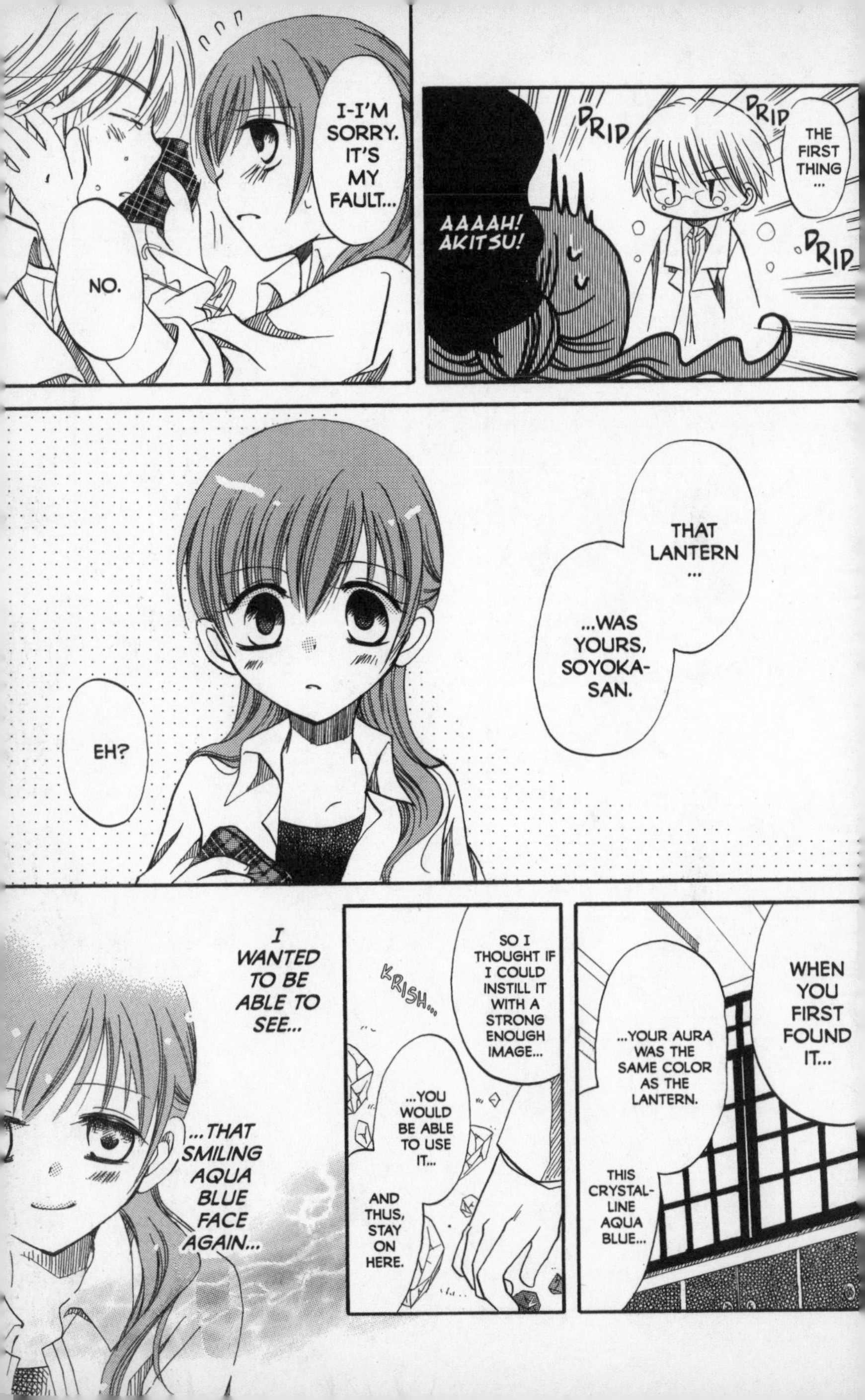
THE FIRST THING...
DRIP
DRIP
DRIP
AAAAH! AKITSU!
I-I'M SORRY. IT'S MY FAULT...
NO.
THAT LANTERN...
...WAS YOURS, SOYOKA-SAN.
EH?
WHEN YOU FIRST FOUND IT...
...YOUR AURA WAS THE SAME COLOR AS THE LANTERN.
THIS CRYSTAL-LINE AQUA BLUE...
SO I THOUGHT IF I COULD INSTILL IT WITH A STRONG ENOUGH IMAGE...
KRISH...
...YOU WOULD BE ABLE TO USE IT...
AND THUS, STAY ON HERE.
I WANTED TO BE ABLE TO SEE...
...THAT SMILING AQUA BLUE FACE AGAIN...

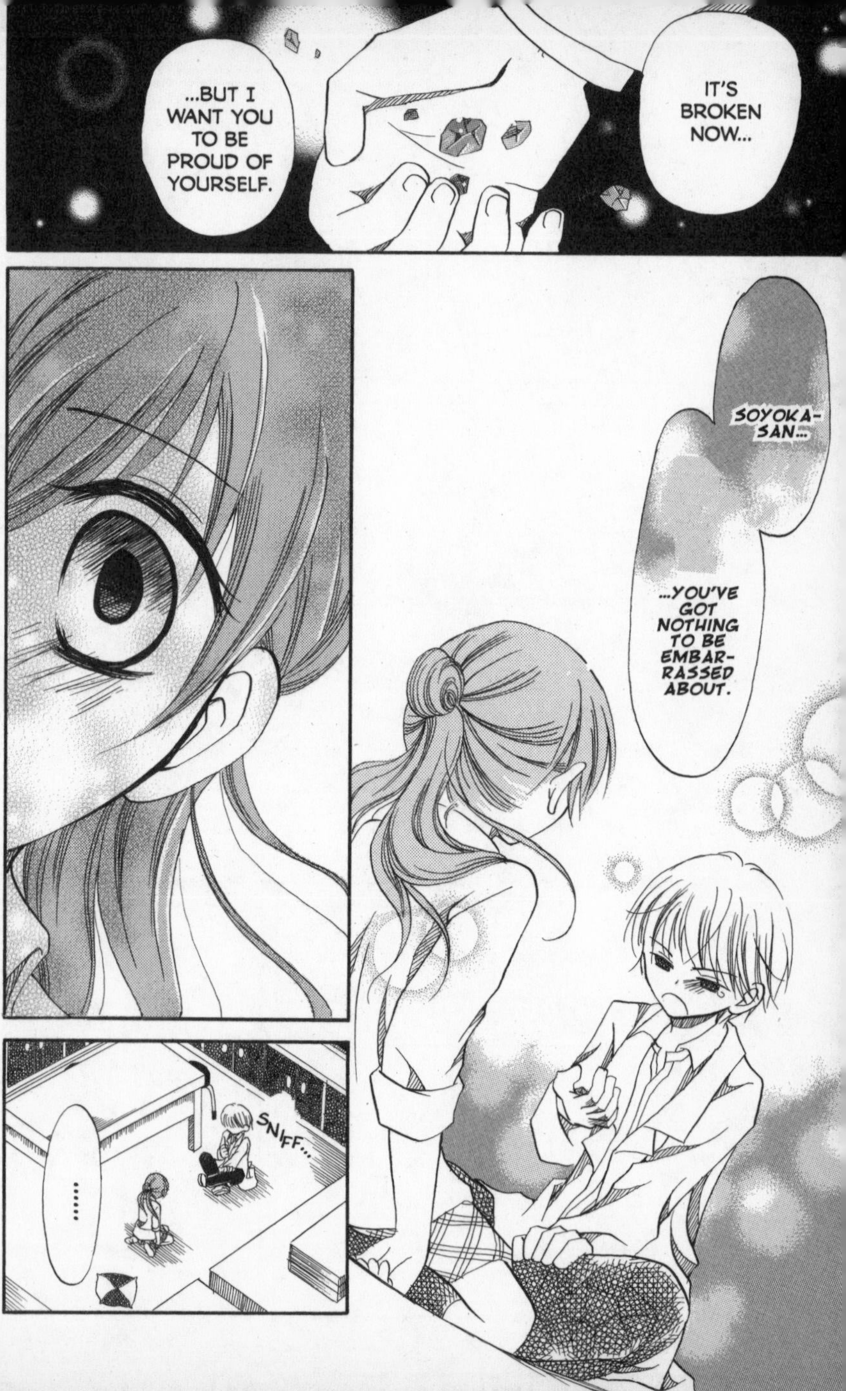
IT'S BROKEN NOW...
...BUT I WANT YOU TO BE PROUD OF YOURSELF.
SOYOKA-SAN...
...YOU'VE GOT NOTHING TO BE EMBARRASSED ABOUT.
SNIFF...
......

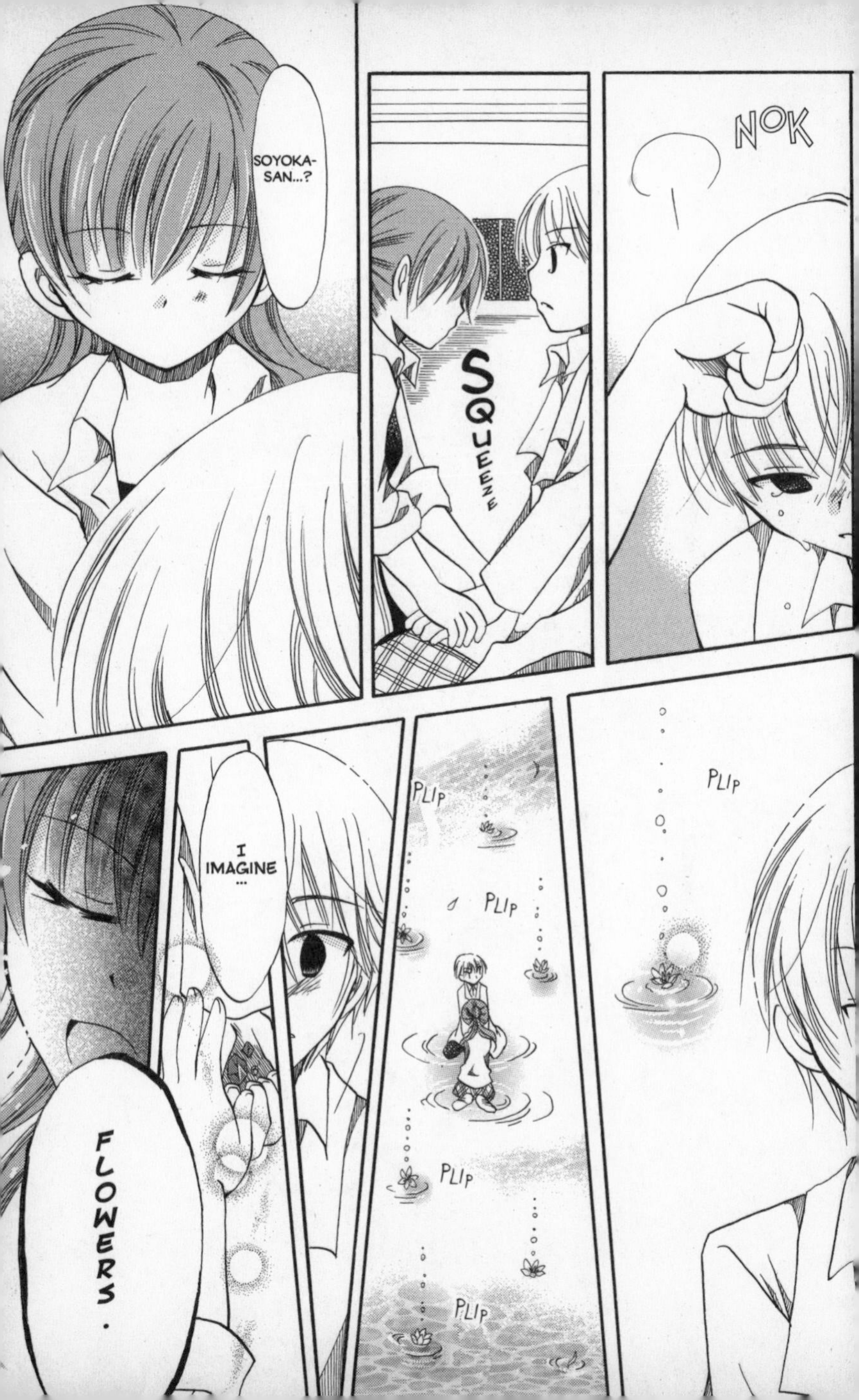
NOK
SQUEEZE
SOYOKA-SAN...?
PLIP
PLIP
PLIP
PLIP
PLIP
I IMAGINE ...
FLOWERS.

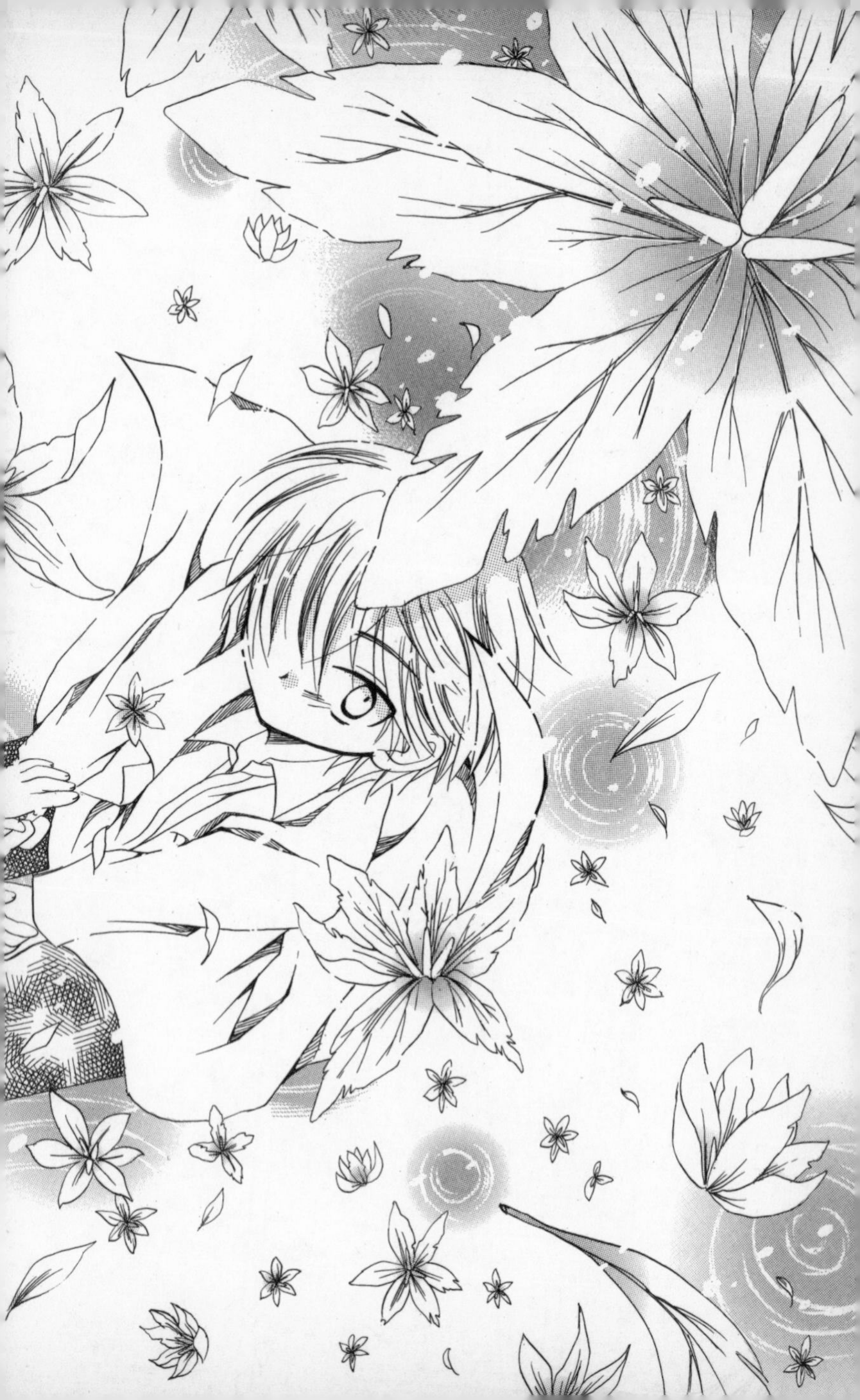

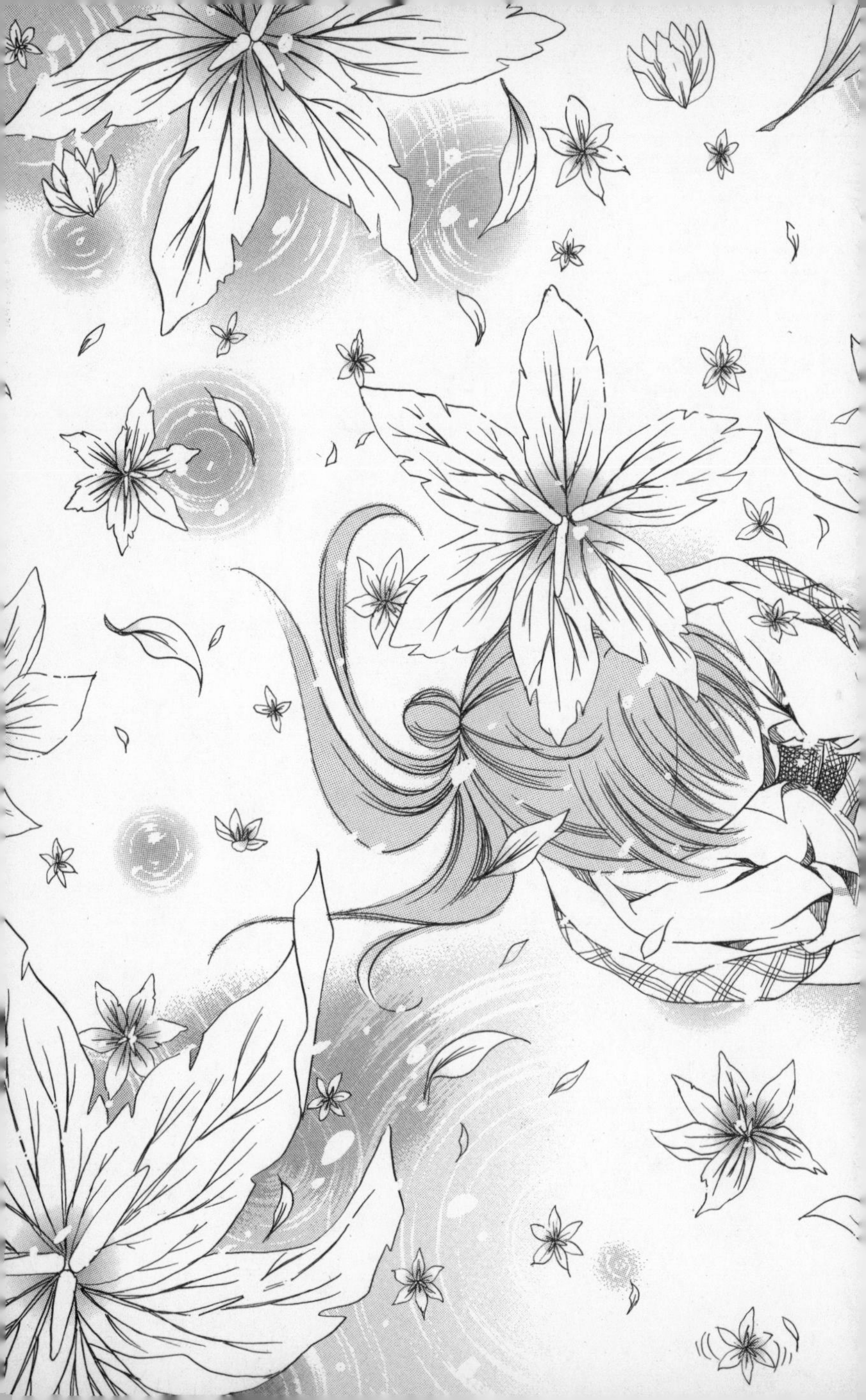

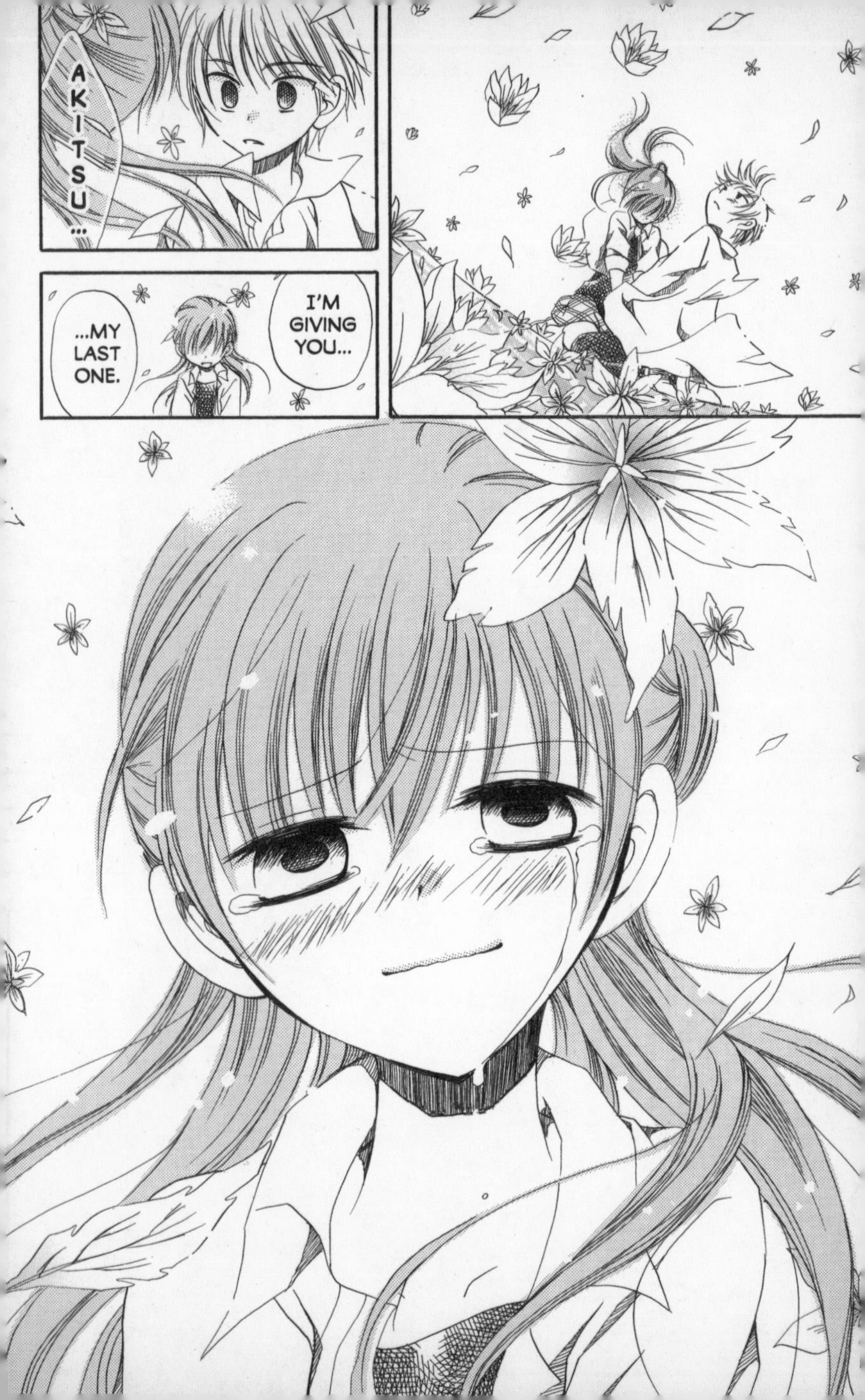
AKITSU...
I'M GIVING YOU...
...MY LAST ONE.

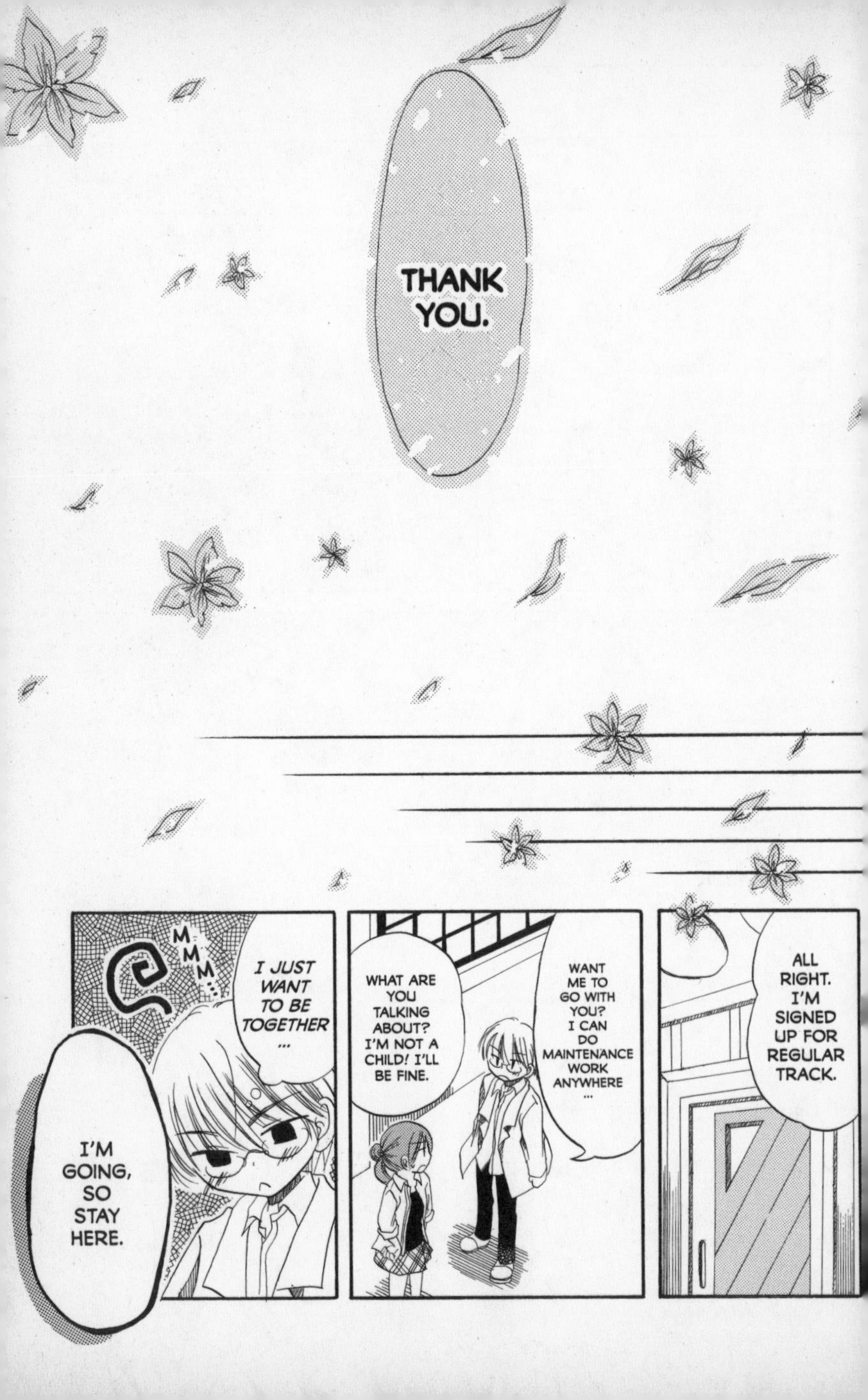
THANK YOU.
ALL RIGHT. I'M SIGNED UP FOR REGULAR TRACK.
WANT ME TO GO WITH YOU? I CAN DO MAINTENANCE WORK ANYWHERE ...
WHAT ARE YOU TALKING ABOUT? I'M NOT A CHILD! I'LL BE FINE.
I JUST WANT TO BE TOGETHER ...
MMM...
I'M GOING, SO STAY HERE.

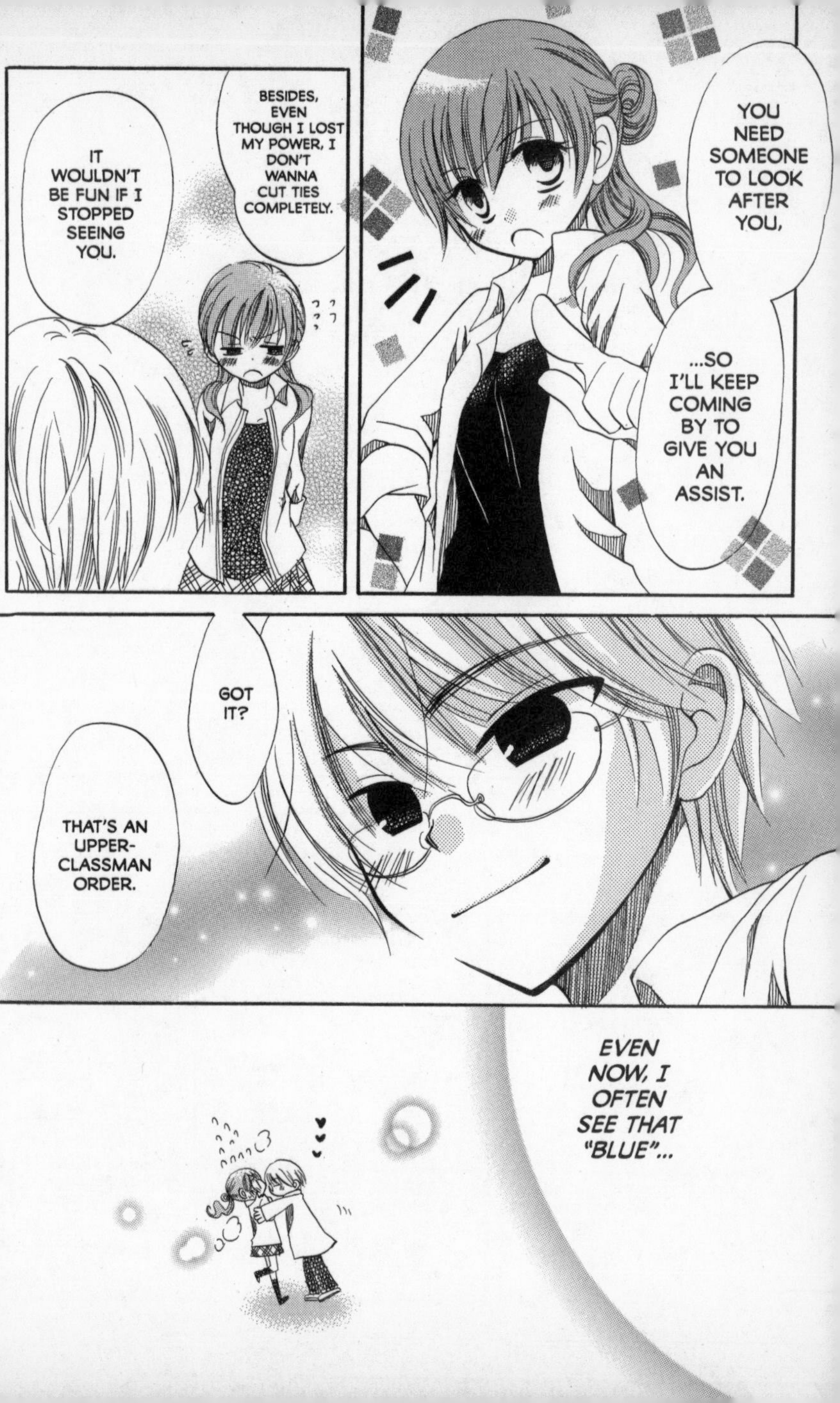
YOU NEED SOMEONE TO LOOK AFTER YOU,
...SO I'LL KEEP COMING BY TO GIVE YOU AN ASSIST.
BESIDES, EVEN THOUGH I LOST MY POWER, I DON'T WANNA CUT TIES COMPLETELY.
IT WOULDN'T BE FUN IF I STOPPED SEEING YOU.
GOT IT?
THAT'S AN UPPER-CLASSMAN ORDER.
EVEN NOW, I OFTEN SEE THAT "BLUE"...

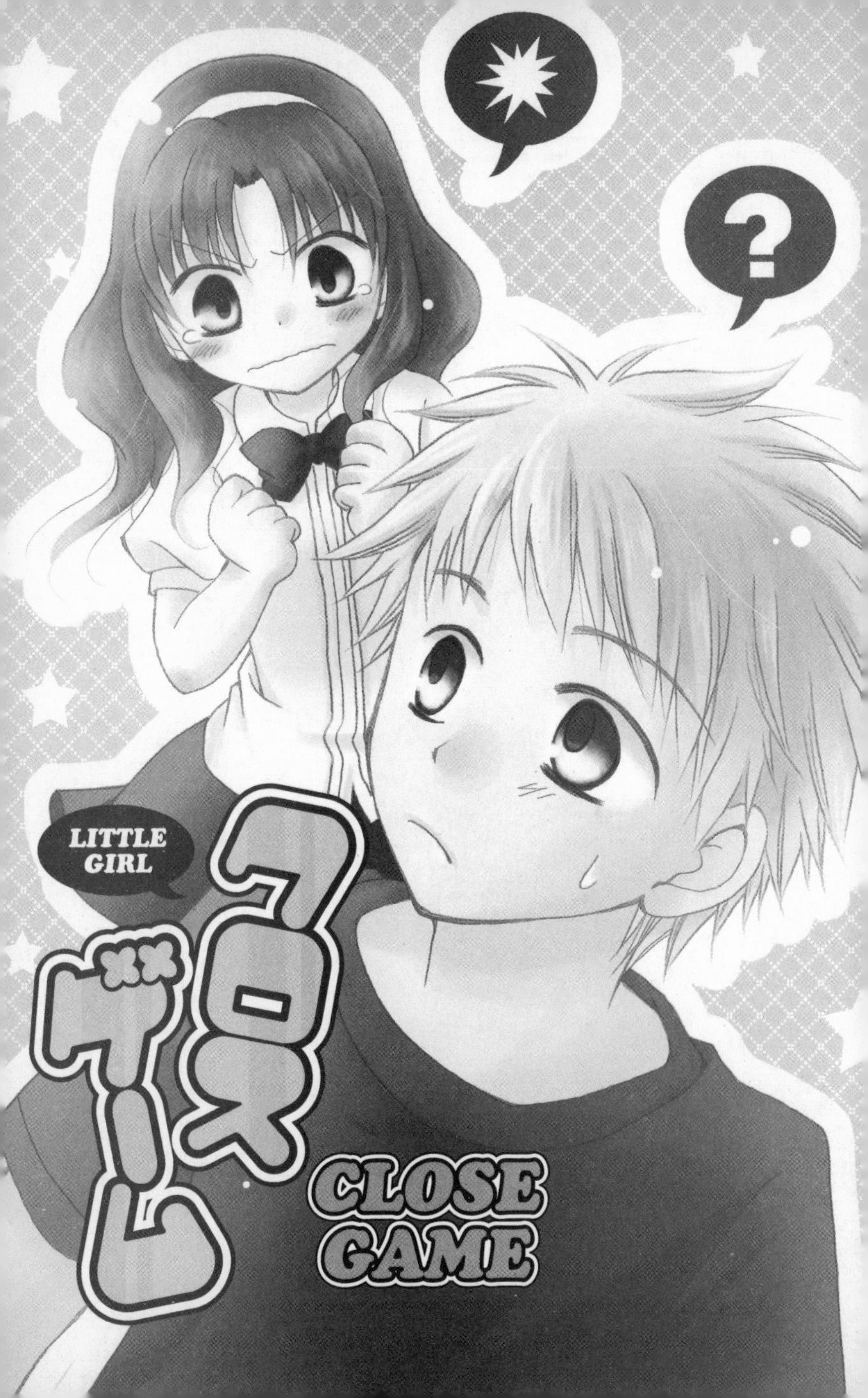
?
LITTLE GIRL
クロス××ゲーム
CLOSE GAME

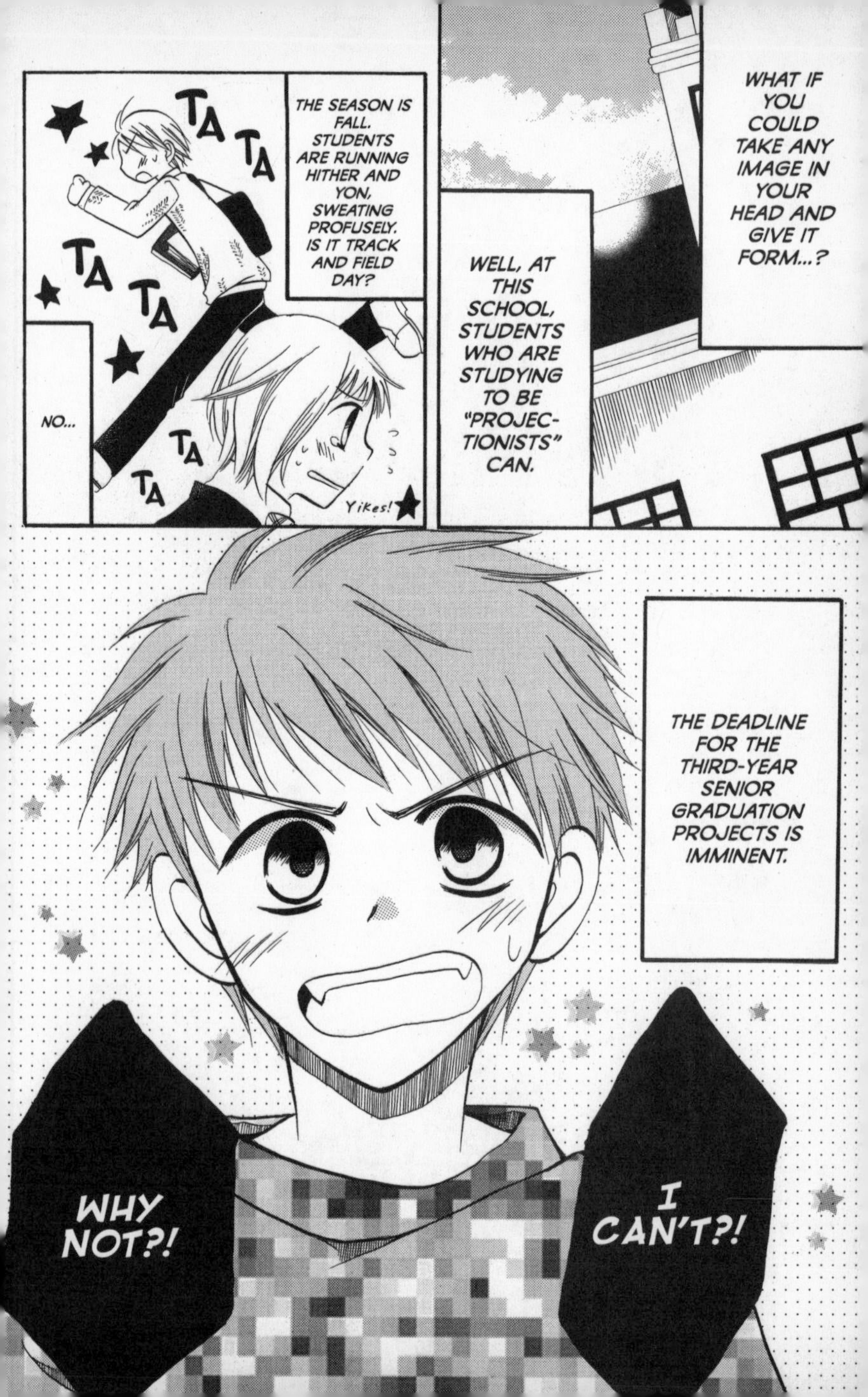

WHAT IF YOU COULD TAKE ANY IMAGE IN YOUR HEAD AND GIVE IT FORM...?
WELL, AT THIS SCHOOL, STUDENTS WHO ARE STUDYING TO BE "PROJECTIONISTS" CAN.
THE SEASON IS FALL. STUDENTS ARE RUNNING HITHER AND YON, SWEATING PROFUSELY. IS IT TRACK AND FIELD DAY?
TA TA
TA TA
NO...
TA TA
Yikes!
THE DEADLINE FOR THE THIRD-YEAR SENIOR GRADUATION PROJECTS IS IMMINENT.
I CAN'T?!
WHY NOT?!

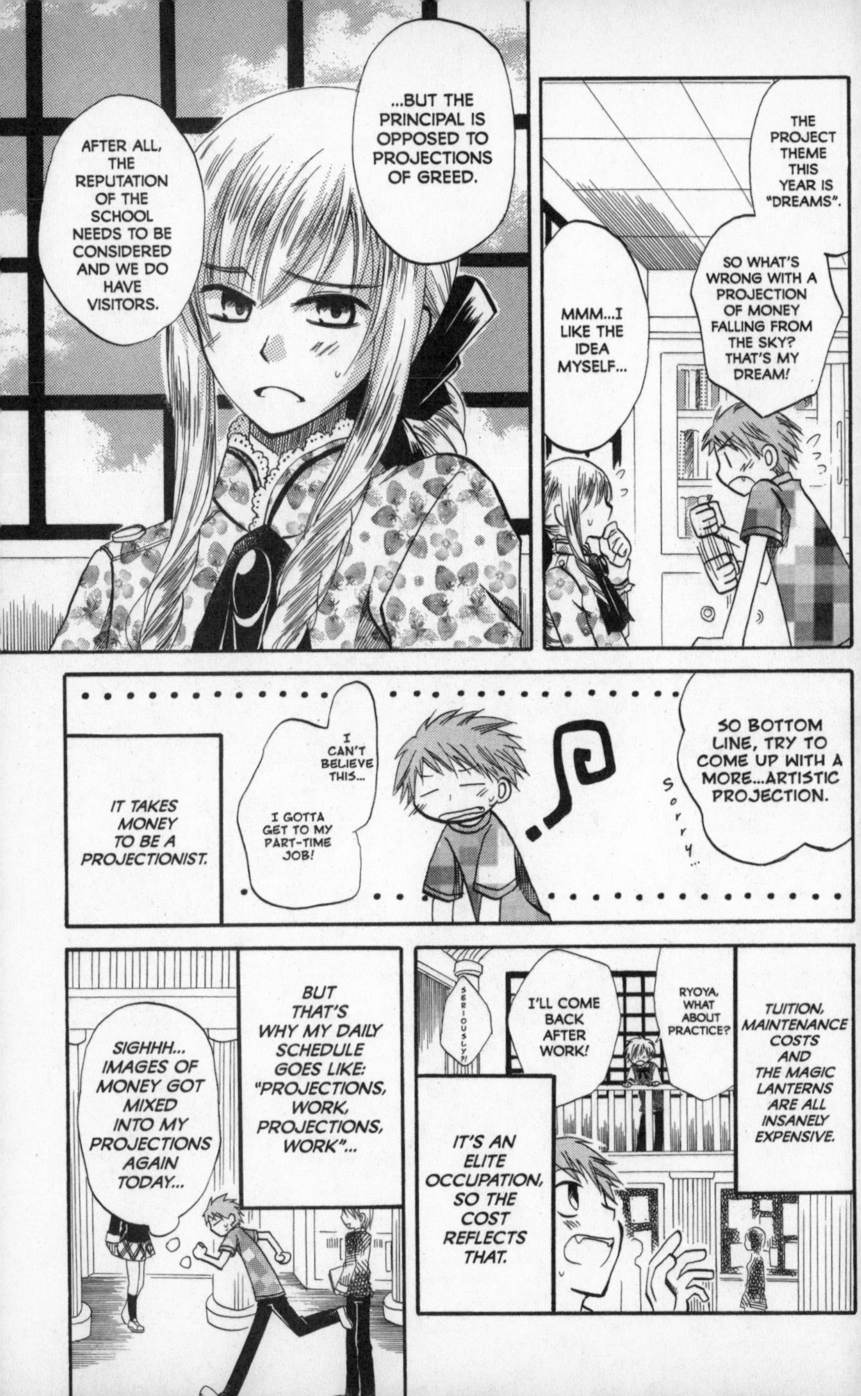
THE PROJECT THEME THIS YEAR IS "DREAMS".
SO WHAT'S WRONG WITH A PROJECTION OF MONEY FALLING FROM THE SKY? THAT'S MY DREAM!
MMM...I LIKE THE IDEA MYSELF...
...BUT THE PRINCIPAL IS OPPOSED TO PROJECTIONS OF GREED.
AFTER ALL, THE REPUTATION OF THE SCHOOL NEEDS TO BE CONSIDERED AND WE DO HAVE VISITORS.
SO BOTTOM LINE, TRY TO COME UP WITH A MORE...ARTISTIC PROJECTION.
Sorry...
I CAN'T BELIEVE THIS...
I GOTTA GET TO MY PART-TIME JOB!
IT TAKES MONEY TO BE A PROJECTIONIST.
TUITION, MAINTENANCE COSTS AND THE MAGIC LANTERNS ARE ALL INSANELY EXPENSIVE.
RYOYA, WHAT ABOUT PRACTICE?
I'LL COME BACK AFTER WORK!
SERIOUSLY?!
IT'S AN ELITE OCCUPATION, SO THE COST REFLECTS THAT.
BUT THAT'S WHY MY DAILY SCHEDULE GOES LIKE: "PROJECTIONS, WORK, PROJECTIONS, WORK"...
SIGHHH... IMAGES OF MONEY GOT MIXED INTO MY PROJECTIONS AGAIN TODAY...

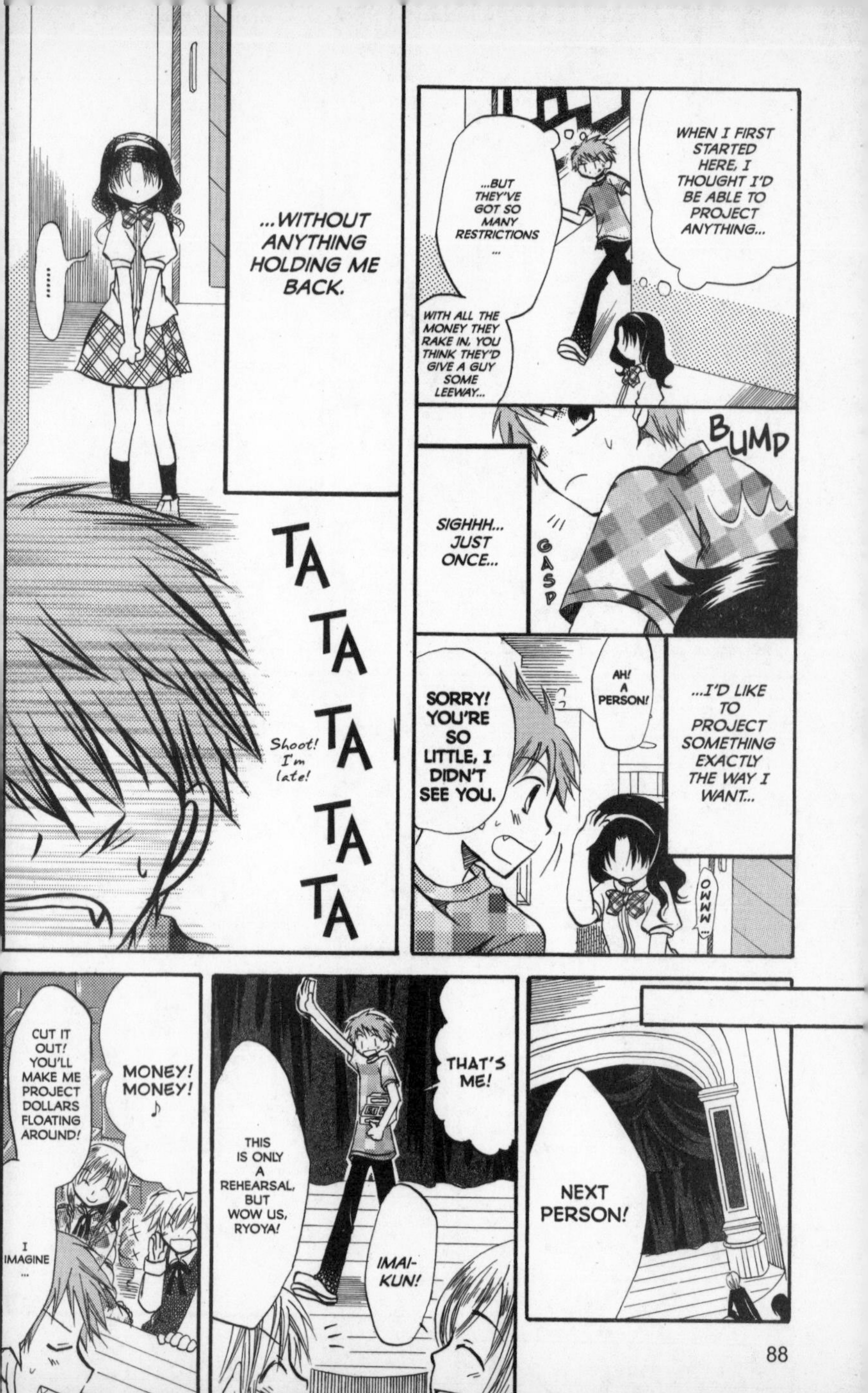
WHEN I FIRST STARTED HERE, I THOUGHT I'D BE ABLE TO PROJECT ANYTHING...
...BUT THEY'VE GOT SO MANY RESTRICTIONS ...
WITH ALL THE MONEY THEY RAKE IN, YOU THINK THEY'D GIVE A GUY SOME LEEWAY...
BUMP
SIGHHH... JUST ONCE...
GASP
...I'D LIKE TO PROJECT SOMETHING EXACTLY THE WAY I WANT...
AH! A PERSON!
SORRY! YOU'RE SO LITTLE, I DIDN'T SEE YOU.
OWWW...
...WITHOUT ANYTHING HOLDING ME BACK.
......
TA TA TA TA TA
Shoot! I'm late!
NEXT PERSON!
THAT'S ME!
THIS IS ONLY A REHEARSAL, BUT WOW US, RYOYA!
IMAI-KUN!
MONEY! MONEY! ♪
CUT IT OUT! YOU'LL MAKE ME PROJECT DOLLARS FLOATING AROUND!
I IMAGINE ...

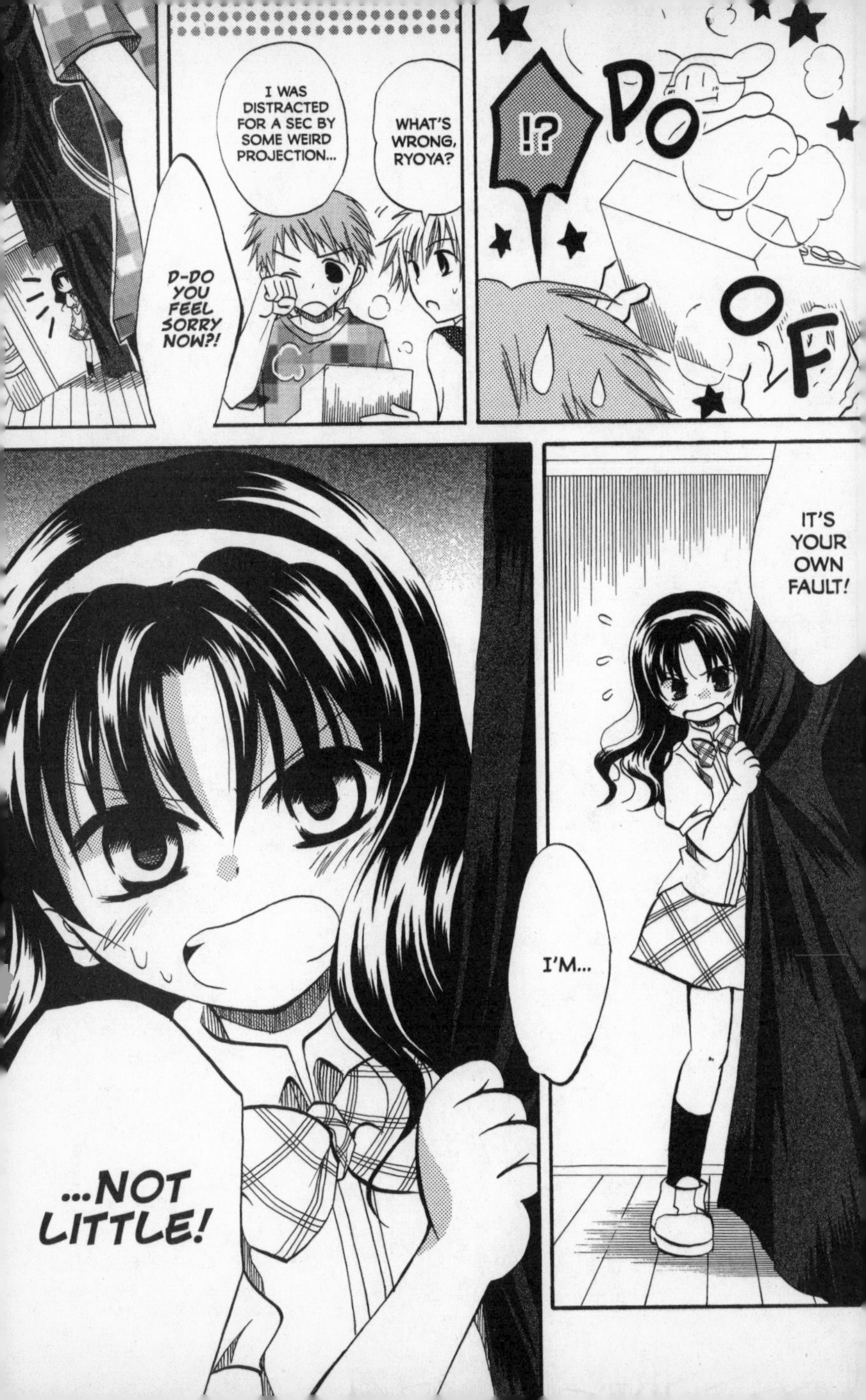
!?
DOOF
WHAT'S WRONG, RYOYA?
I WAS DISTRACTED FOR A SEC BY SOME WEIRD PROJECTION...
D-DO YOU FEEL SORRY NOW?!
IT'S YOUR OWN FAULT!
I'M...
...NOT LITTLE!

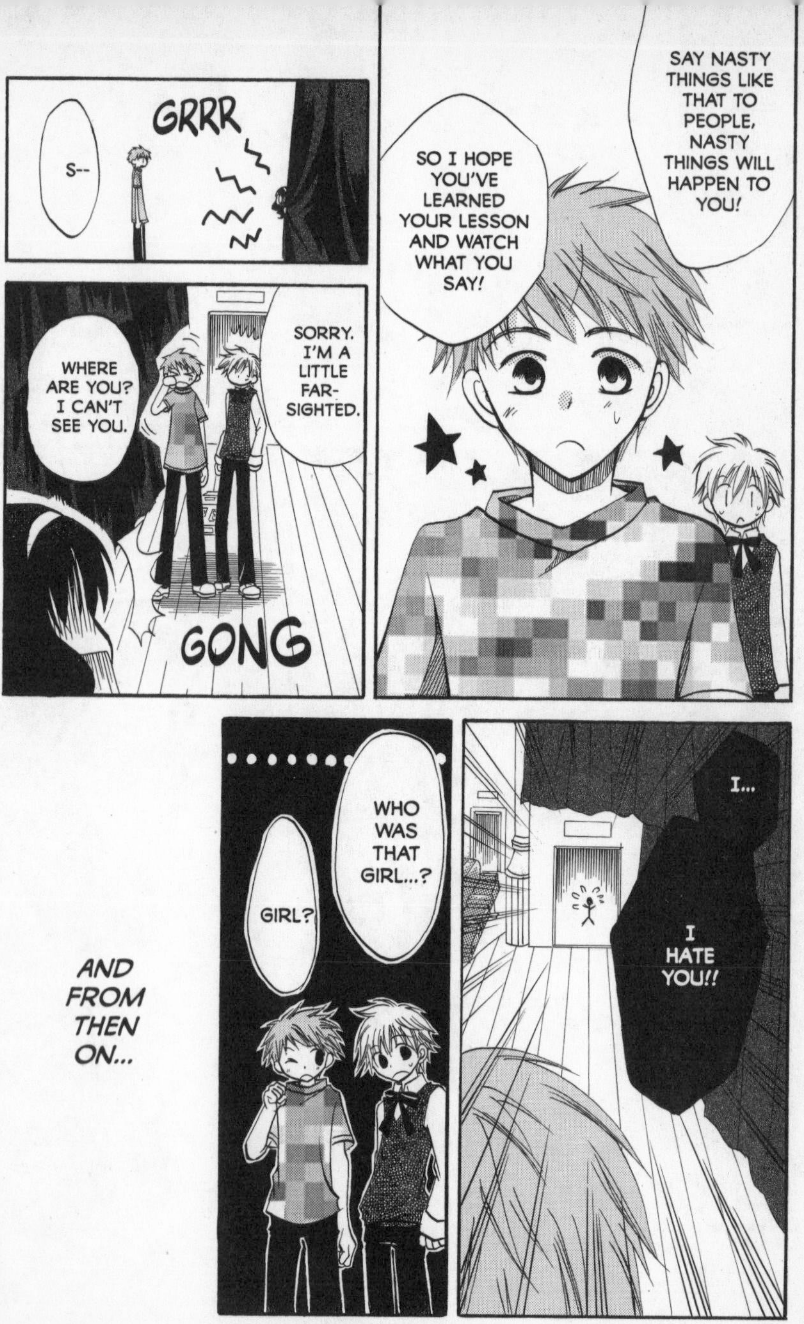

SAY NASTY THINGS LIKE THAT TO PEOPLE, NASTY THINGS WILL HAPPEN TO YOU!
SO I HOPE YOU'VE LEARNED YOUR LESSON AND WATCH WHAT YOU SAY!
GRRR
S--
SORRY. I'M A LITTLE FAR-SIGHTED.
WHERE ARE YOU? I CAN'T SEE YOU.
GONG
I...
I HATE YOU!!
....
WHO WAS THAT GIRL...?
GIRL?
AND FROM THEN ON...

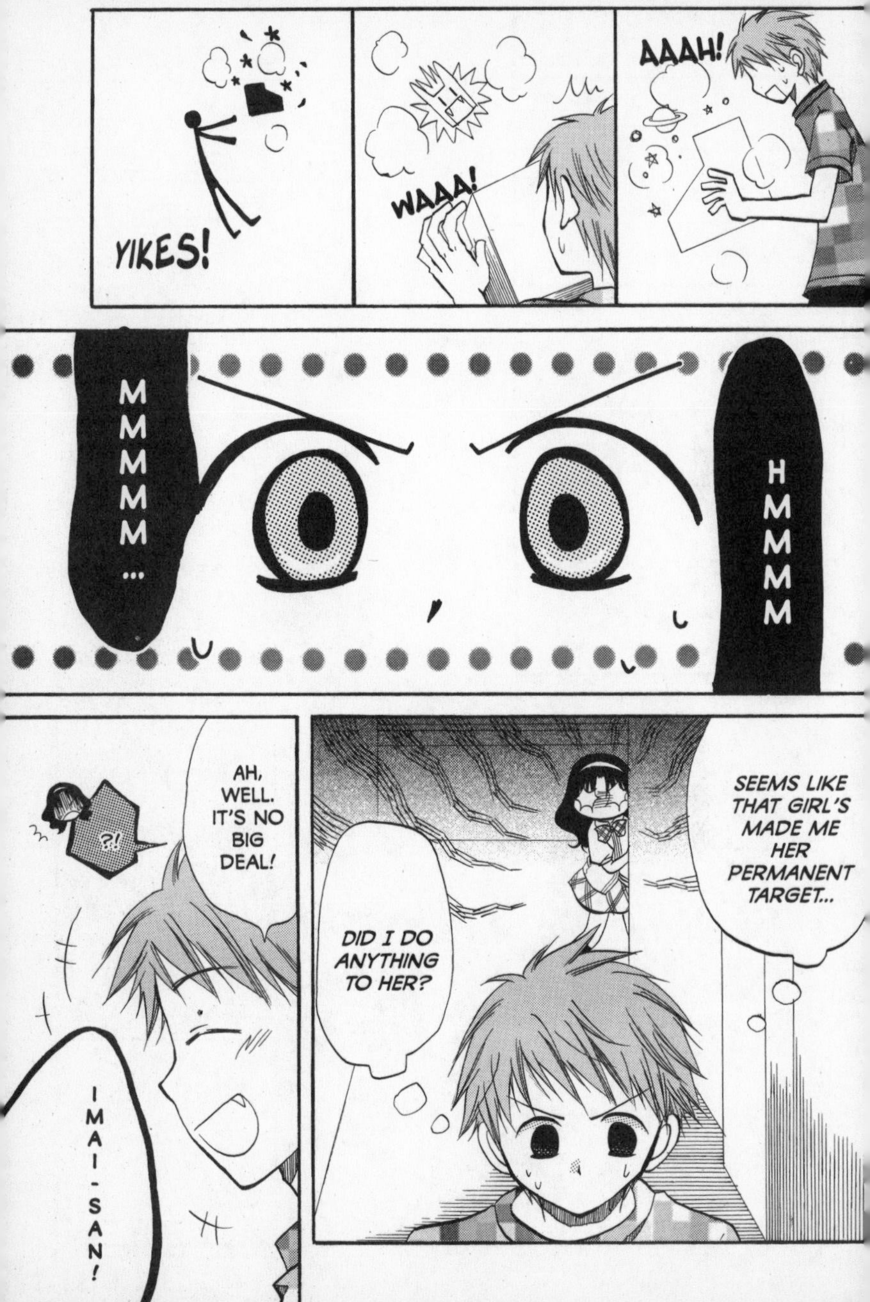
AAAH!
WAAA!
YIKES!
HMMMM
MMMMM...
SEEMS LIKE THAT GIRL'S MADE ME HER PERMANENT TARGET...
DID I DO ANYTHING TO HER?
AH, WELL. IT'S NO BIG DEAL!
?!
IMAI-SAN!

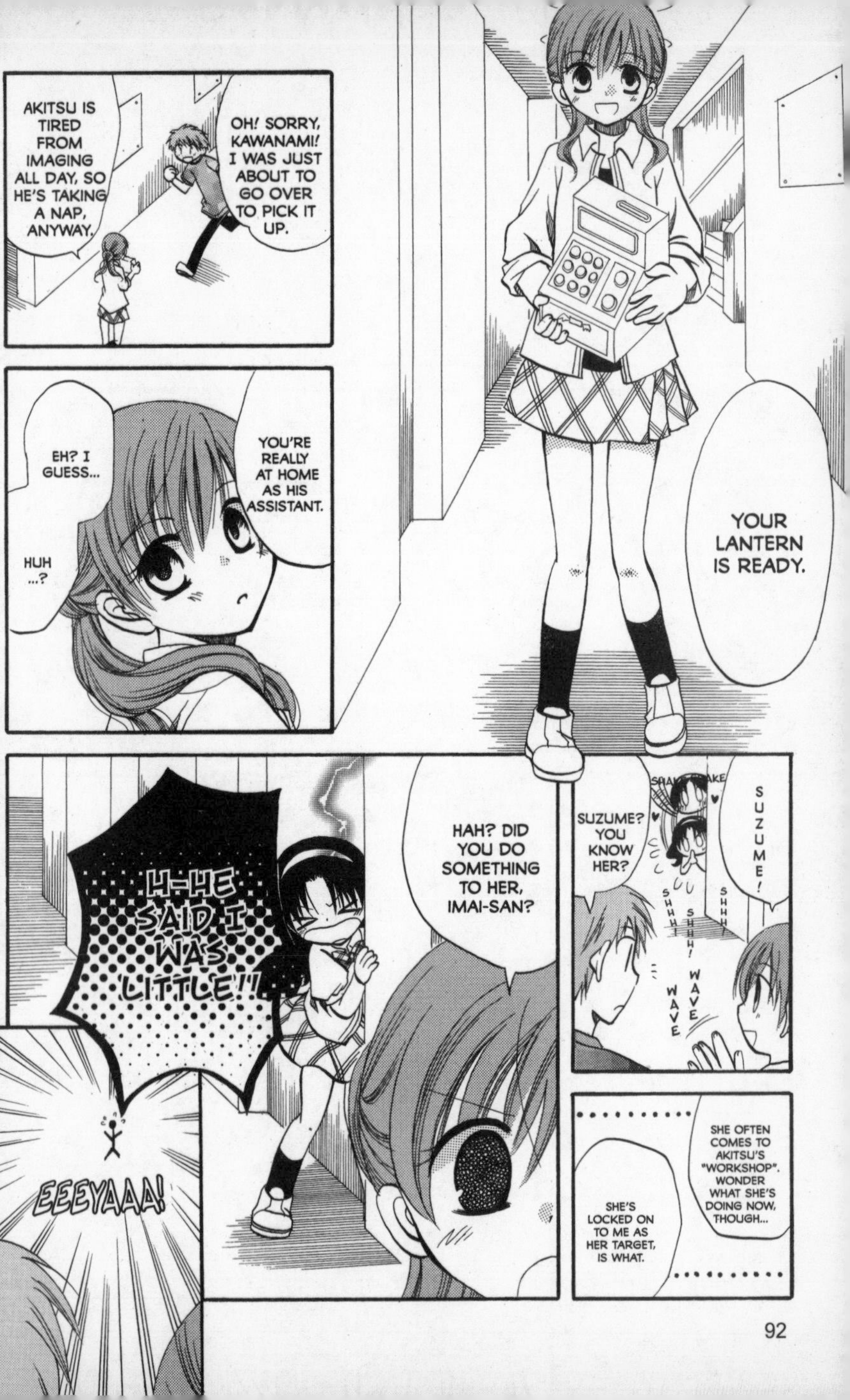

YOUR LANTERN IS READY.
OH! SORRY, KAWANAMI! I WAS JUST ABOUT TO GO OVER TO PICK IT UP.
AKITSU IS TIRED FROM IMAGING ALL DAY, SO HE'S TAKING A NAP, ANYWAY.
YOU'RE REALLY AT HOME AS HIS ASSISTANT.
EH? I GUESS...
HUH ...?
SHAKE SHAKE
SUZUME!
SUZUME? YOU KNOW HER?
SHHH! SHHH! SHHH!
WAVE WAVE
......
SHE OFTEN COMES TO AKITSU'S "WORKSHOP". WONDER WHAT SHE'S DOING NOW, THOUGH...
SHE'S LOCKED ON TO ME AS HER TARGET, IS WHAT.
......
HAH? DID YOU DO SOMETHING TO HER, IMAI-SAN?
H-HE SAID I WAS LITTLE!!
EEEYAAA!

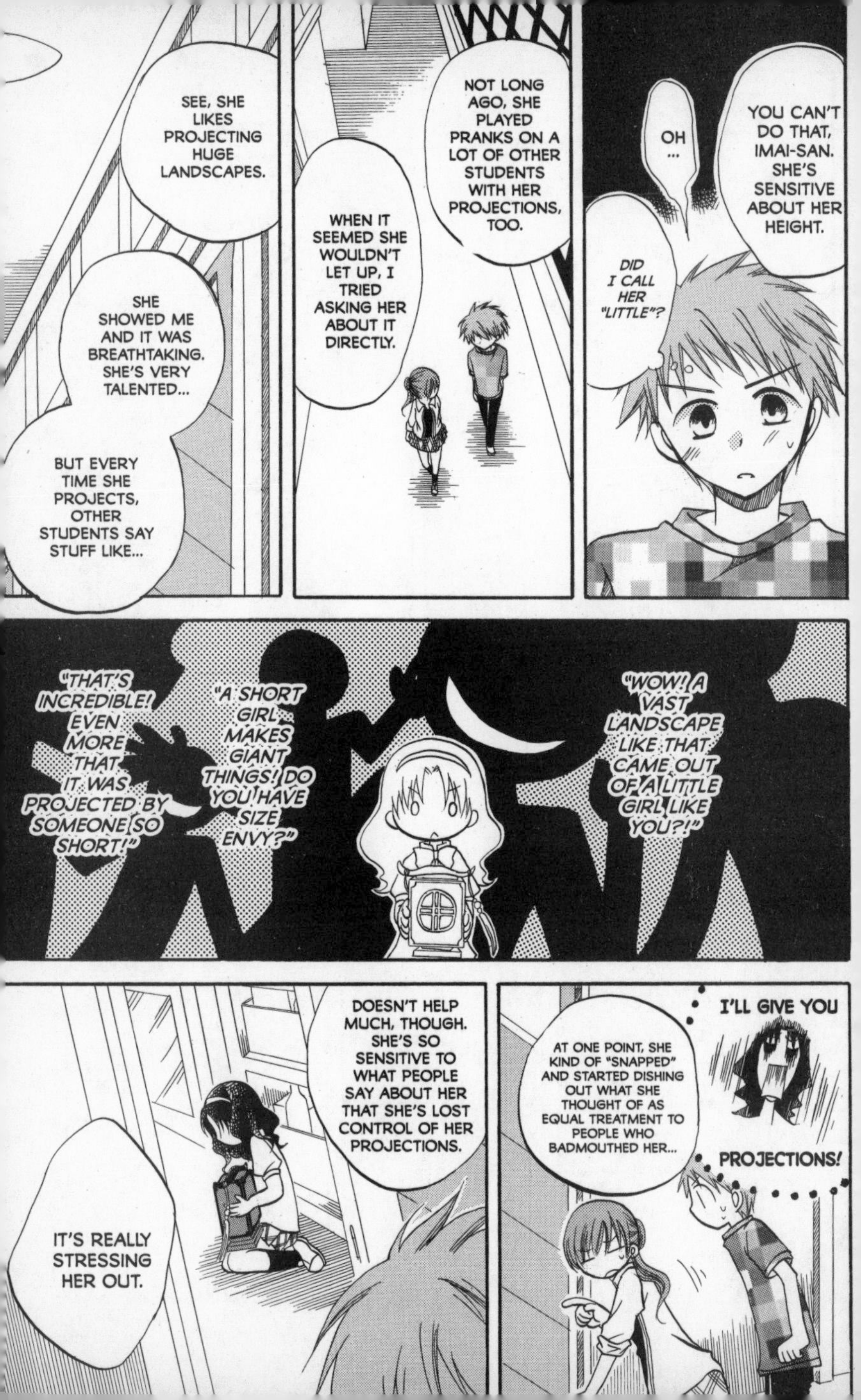
YOU CAN'T DO THAT, IMAI-SAN. SHE'S SENSITIVE ABOUT HER HEIGHT.
OH ...
DID I CALL HER "LITTLE"?
NOT LONG AGO, SHE PLAYED PRANKS ON A LOT OF OTHER STUDENTS WITH HER PROJECTIONS, TOO.
WHEN IT SEEMED SHE WOULDN'T LET UP, I TRIED ASKING HER ABOUT IT DIRECTLY.
SEE, SHE LIKES PROJECTING HUGE LANDSCAPES.
SHE SHOWED ME AND IT WAS BREATHTAKING. SHE'S VERY TALENTED...
BUT EVERY TIME SHE PROJECTS, OTHER STUDENTS SAY STUFF LIKE...
"WOW! A VAST LANDSCAPE LIKE THAT CAME OUT OF A LITTLE GIRL LIKE YOU?!"
"A SHORT GIRL MAKES GIANT THINGS! DO YOU HAVE SIZE ENVY?"
"THAT'S INCREDIBLE! EVEN MORE THAT IT WAS PROJECTED BY SOMEONE SO SHORT!"
AT ONE POINT, SHE KIND OF "SNAPPED" AND STARTED DISHING OUT WHAT SHE THOUGHT OF AS EQUAL TREATMENT TO PEOPLE WHO BADMOUTHED HER...
I'LL GIVE YOU PROJECTIONS!
DOESN'T HELP MUCH, THOUGH. SHE'S SO SENSITIVE TO WHAT PEOPLE SAY ABOUT HER THAT SHE'S LOST CONTROL OF HER PROJECTIONS.
IT'S REALLY STRESSING HER OUT.

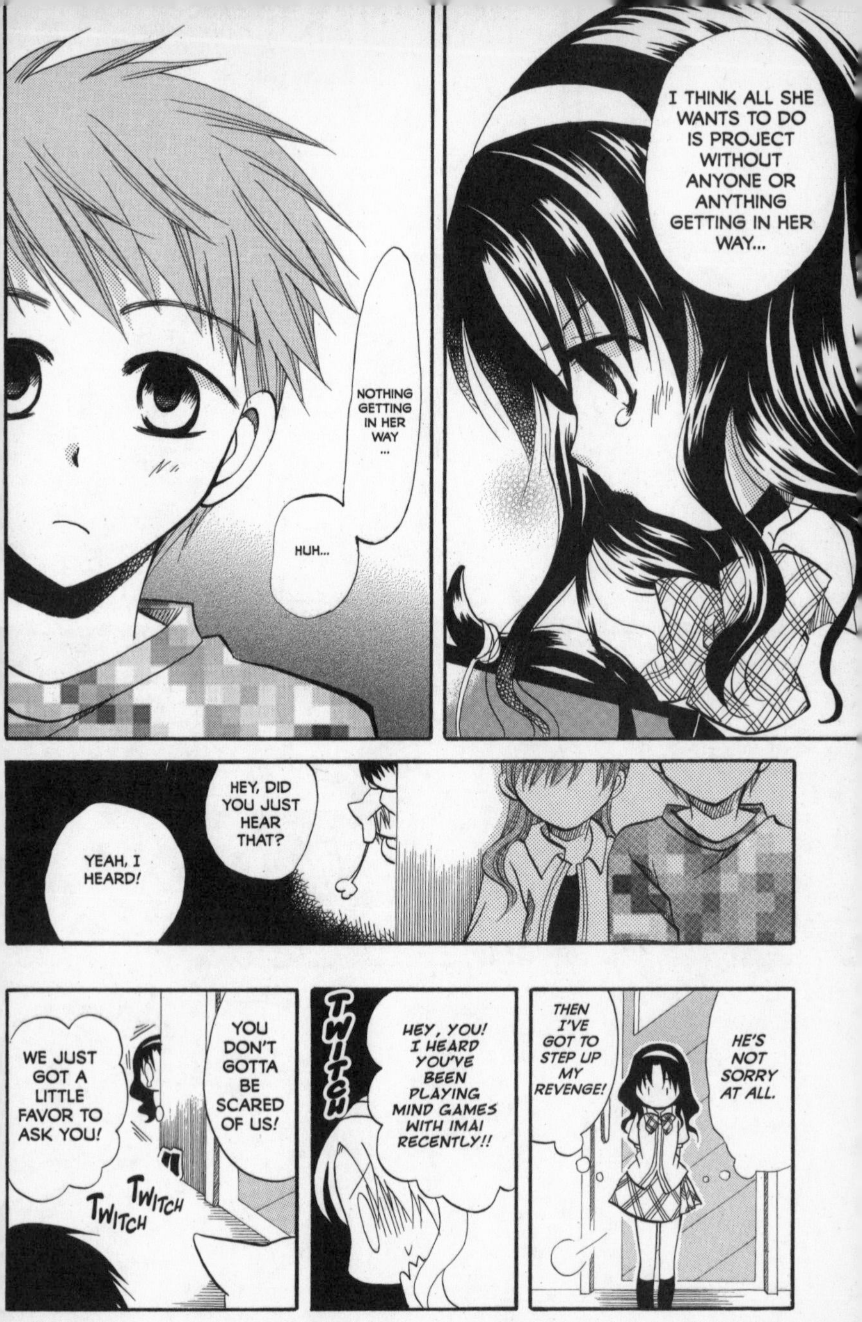
I THINK ALL SHE WANTS TO DO IS PROJECT WITHOUT ANYONE OR ANYTHING GETTING IN HER WAY...
NOTHING GETTING IN HER WAY ...
HUH...
HEY, DID YOU JUST HEAR THAT?
YEAH, I HEARD!
HE'S NOT SORRY AT ALL.
THEN I'VE GOT TO STEP UP MY REVENGE!
TWITCH
HEY, YOU! I HEARD YOU'VE BEEN PLAYING MIND GAMES WITH IMAI RECENTLY!!
YOU DON'T GOTTA BE SCARED OF US!
WE JUST GOT A LITTLE FAVOR TO ASK YOU!
TWITCH
TWITCH

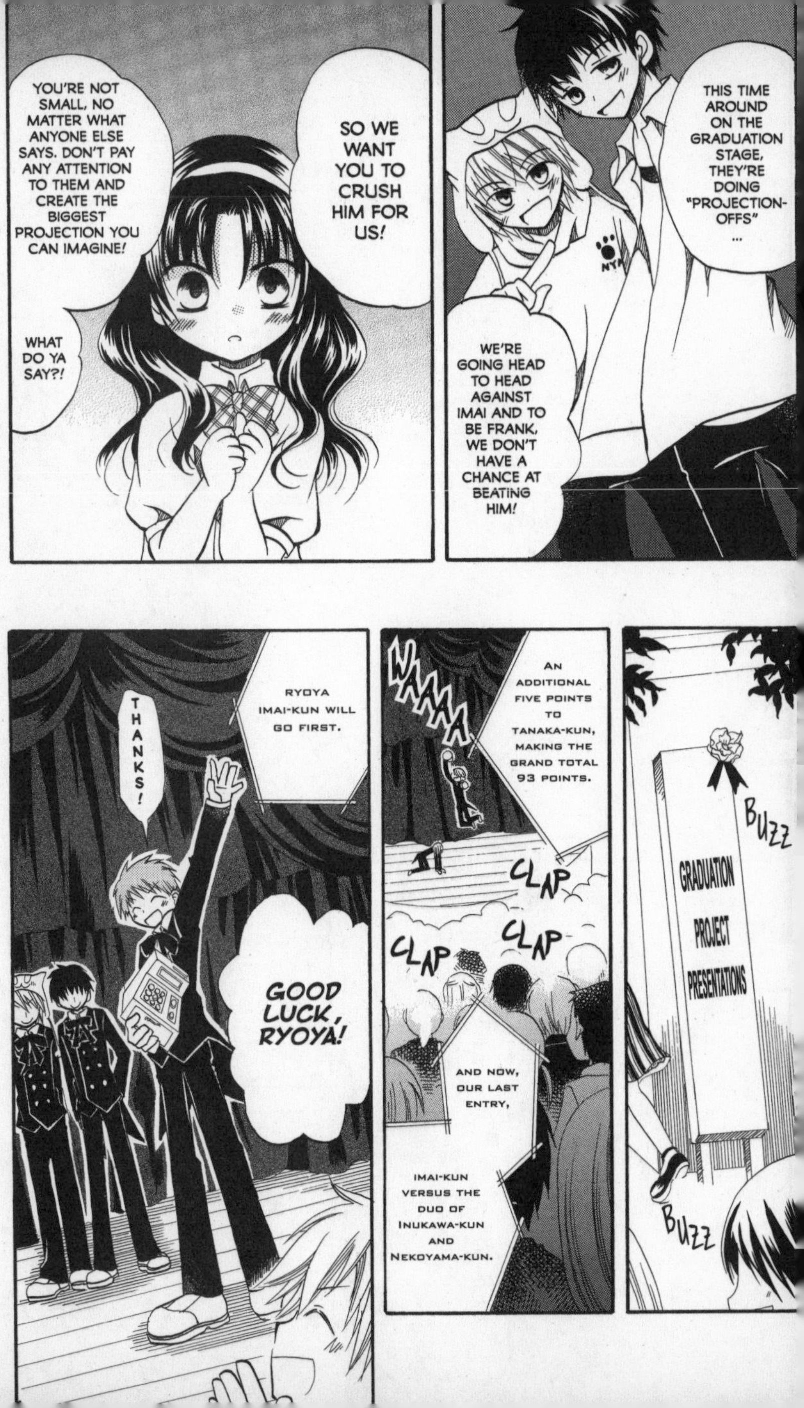
THIS TIME AROUND ON THE GRADUATION STAGE, THEY'RE DOING "PROJECTION-OFFS" ...
WE'RE GOING HEAD TO HEAD AGAINST IMAI AND TO BE FRANK, WE DON'T HAVE A CHANCE AT BEATING HIM!
SO WE WANT YOU TO CRUSH HIM FOR US!
YOU'RE NOT SMALL, NO MATTER WHAT ANYONE ELSE SAYS. DON'T PAY ANY ATTENTION TO THEM AND CREATE THE BIGGEST PROJECTION YOU CAN IMAGINE!
WHAT DO YA SAY?!
BUZZ
GRADUATION PROJECT PRESENTATIONS
BUZZ
WAAAAA
AN ADDITIONAL FIVE POINTS TO TANAKA-KUN, MAKING THE GRAND TOTAL 93 POINTS.
CLAP
CLAP
CLAP
AND NOW, OUR LAST ENTRY,
IMAI-KUN VERSUS THE DUO OF INUKAWA-KUN AND NEKOYAMA-KUN.
RYOYA IMAI-KUN WILL GO FIRST.
THANKS!
GOOD LUCK, RYOYA!

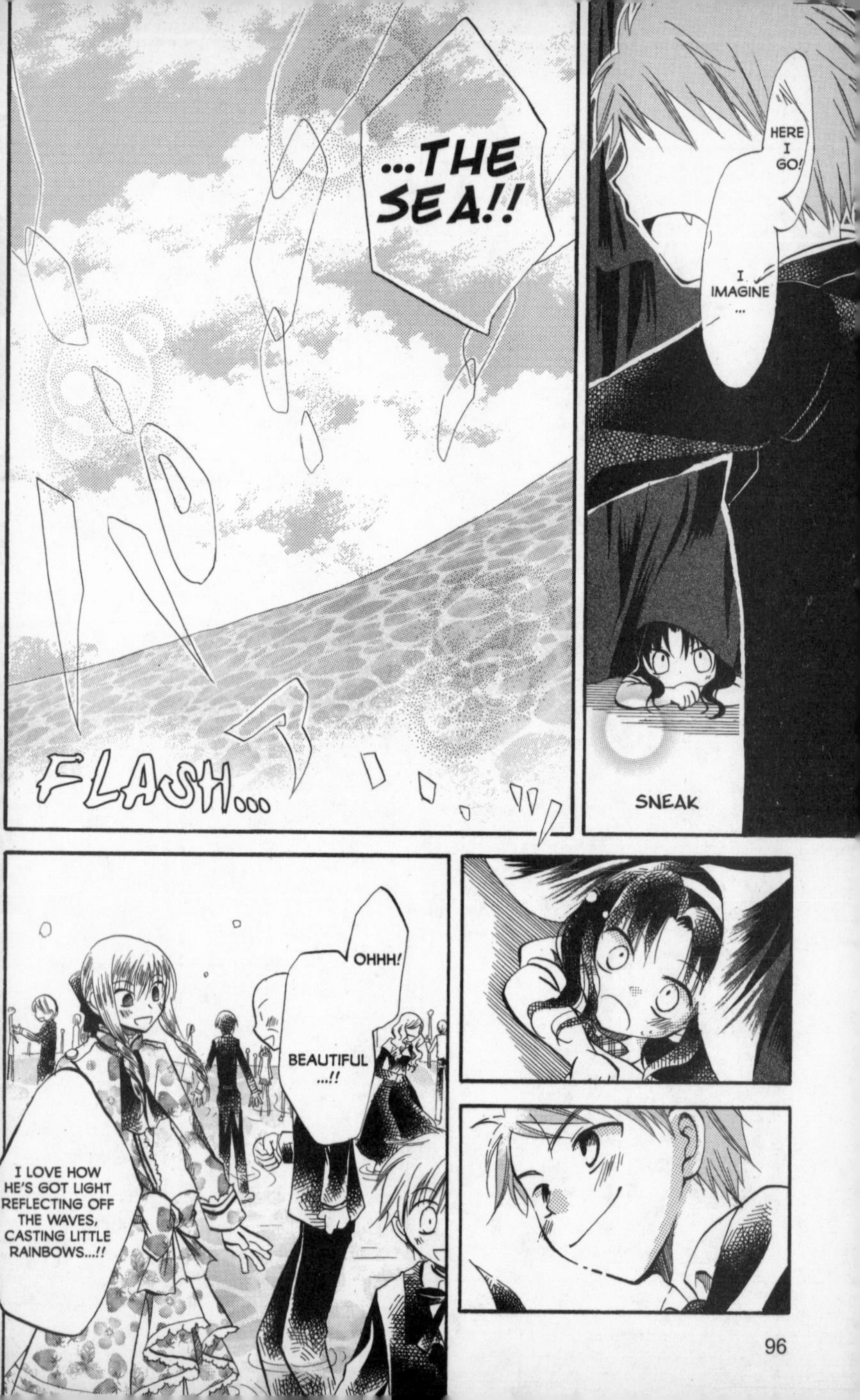
HERE I GO!
I IMAGINE ...
SNEAK
...THE SEA!!
FLASH...
OHHH!
BEAUTIFUL ...!!
I LOVE HOW HE'S GOT LIGHT REFLECTING OFF THE WAVES, CASTING LITTLE RAINBOWS...!!

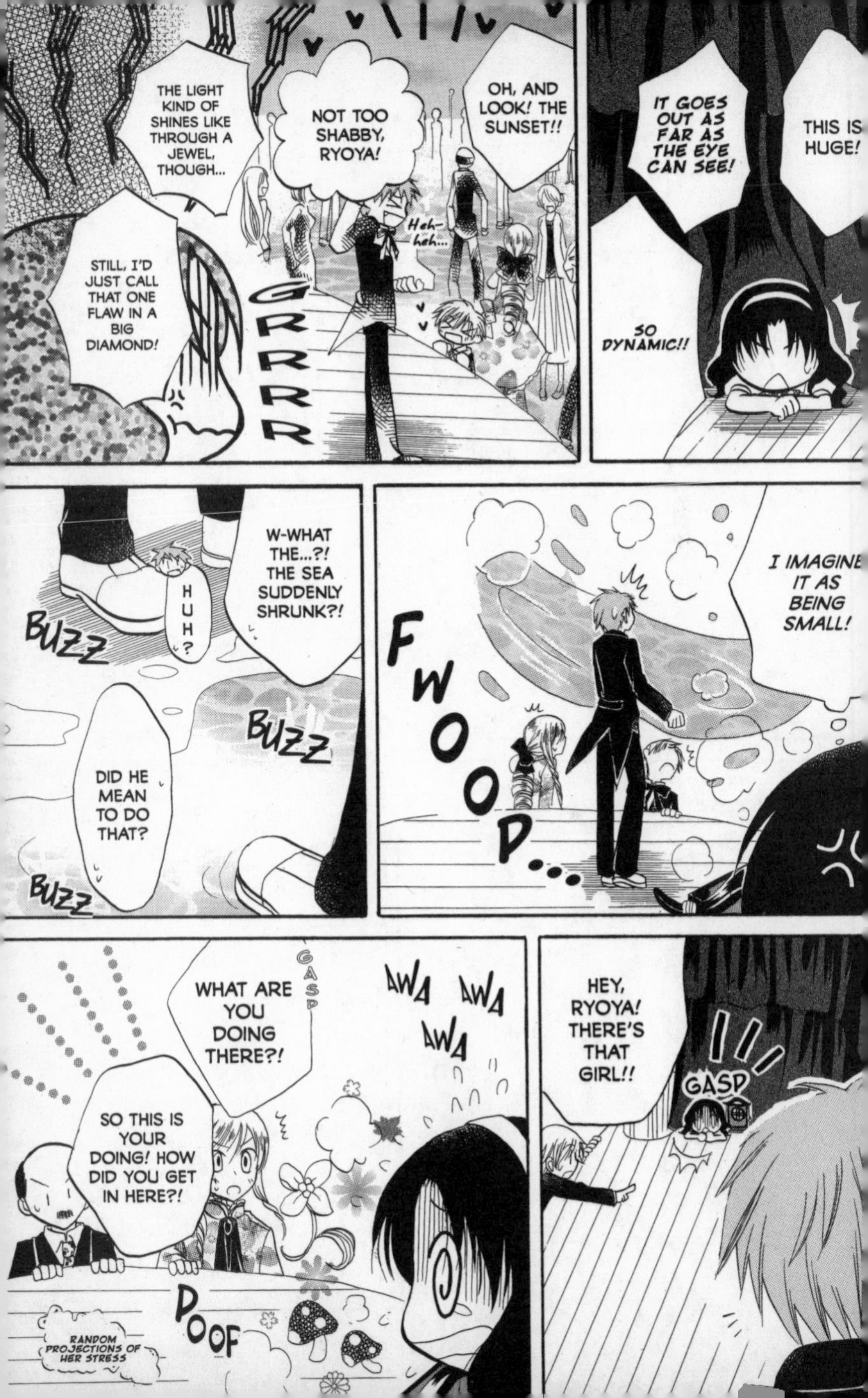
THIS IS HUGE!
IT GOES OUT AS FAR AS THE EYE CAN SEE!
SO DYNAMIC!!
OH, AND LOOK! THE SUNSET!!
NOT TOO SHABBY, RYOYA!
Heh-heh...
THE LIGHT KIND OF SHINES LIKE THROUGH A JEWEL, THOUGH...
STILL, I'D JUST CALL THAT ONE FLAW IN A BIG DIAMOND!
GRRRR
I IMAGINE IT AS BEING SMALL!
FWOOP...
W-WHAT THE...?! THE SEA SUDDENLY SHRUNK?!
HUH?
BUZZ
BUZZ
DID HE MEAN TO DO THAT?
BUZZ
HEY, RYOYA! THERE'S THAT GIRL!!
GASP
AWA AWA AWA
GASP
WHAT ARE YOU DOING THERE?!
SO THIS IS YOUR DOING! HOW DID YOU GET IN HERE?!
POOF
RANDOM PROJECTIONS OF HER STRESS

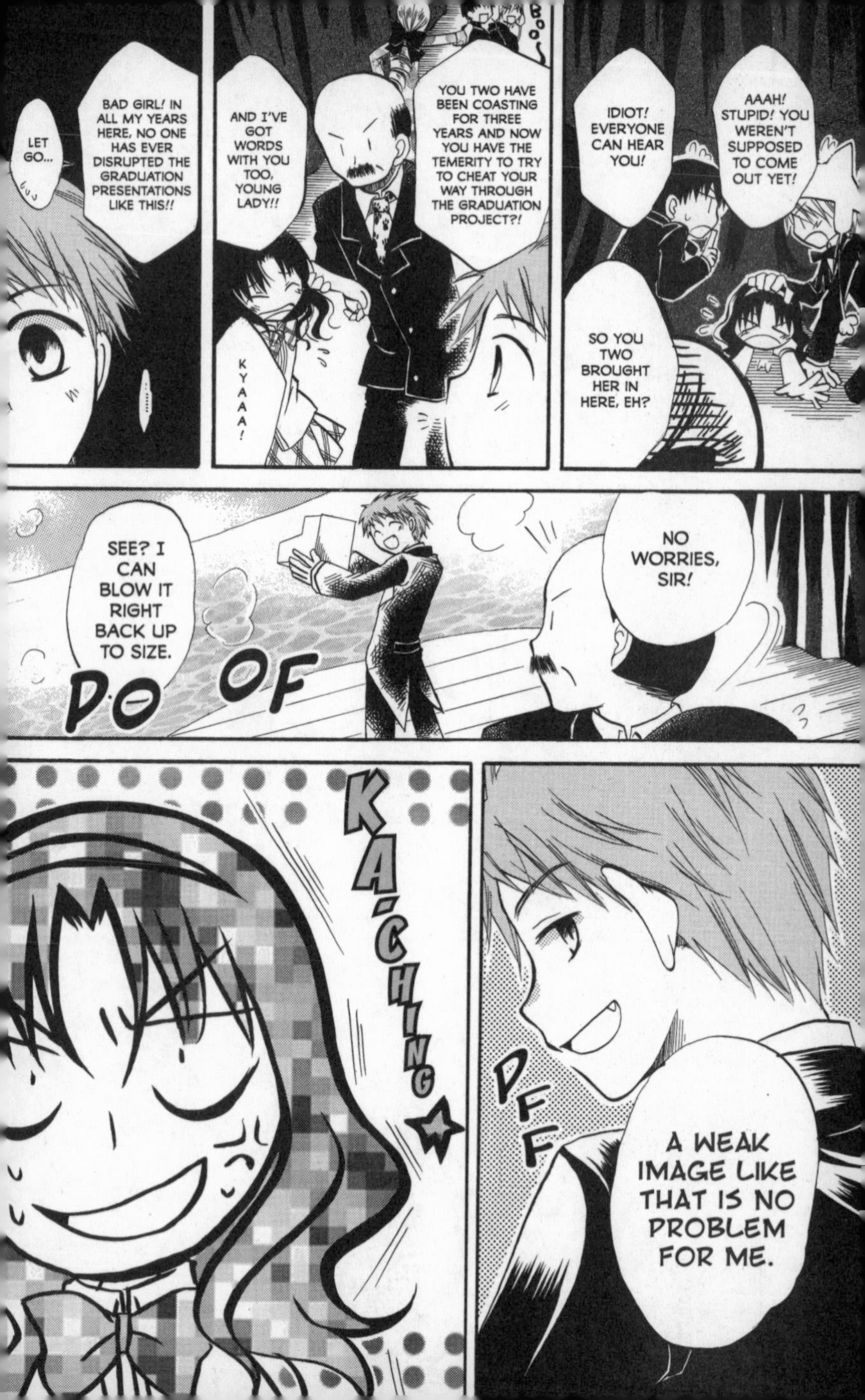

AAAH! STUPID! YOU WEREN'T SUPPOSED TO COME OUT YET!
IDIOT! EVERYONE CAN HEAR YOU!
SO YOU TWO BROUGHT HER IN HERE, EH?
YOU TWO HAVE BEEN COASTING FOR THREE YEARS AND NOW YOU HAVE THE TEMERITY TO TRY TO CHEAT YOUR WAY THROUGH THE GRADUATION PROJECT?!
AND I'VE GOT WORDS WITH YOU TOO, YOUNG LADY!!
KYAAAA!
BAD GIRL! IN ALL MY YEARS HERE, NO ONE HAS EVER DISRUPTED THE GRADUATION PRESENTATIONS LIKE THIS!!
LET GO...
......
NO WORRIES, SIR!
SEE? I CAN BLOW IT RIGHT BACK UP TO SIZE.
DOOF
A WEAK IMAGE LIKE THAT IS NO PROBLEM FOR ME.
DFF
KA-CHING

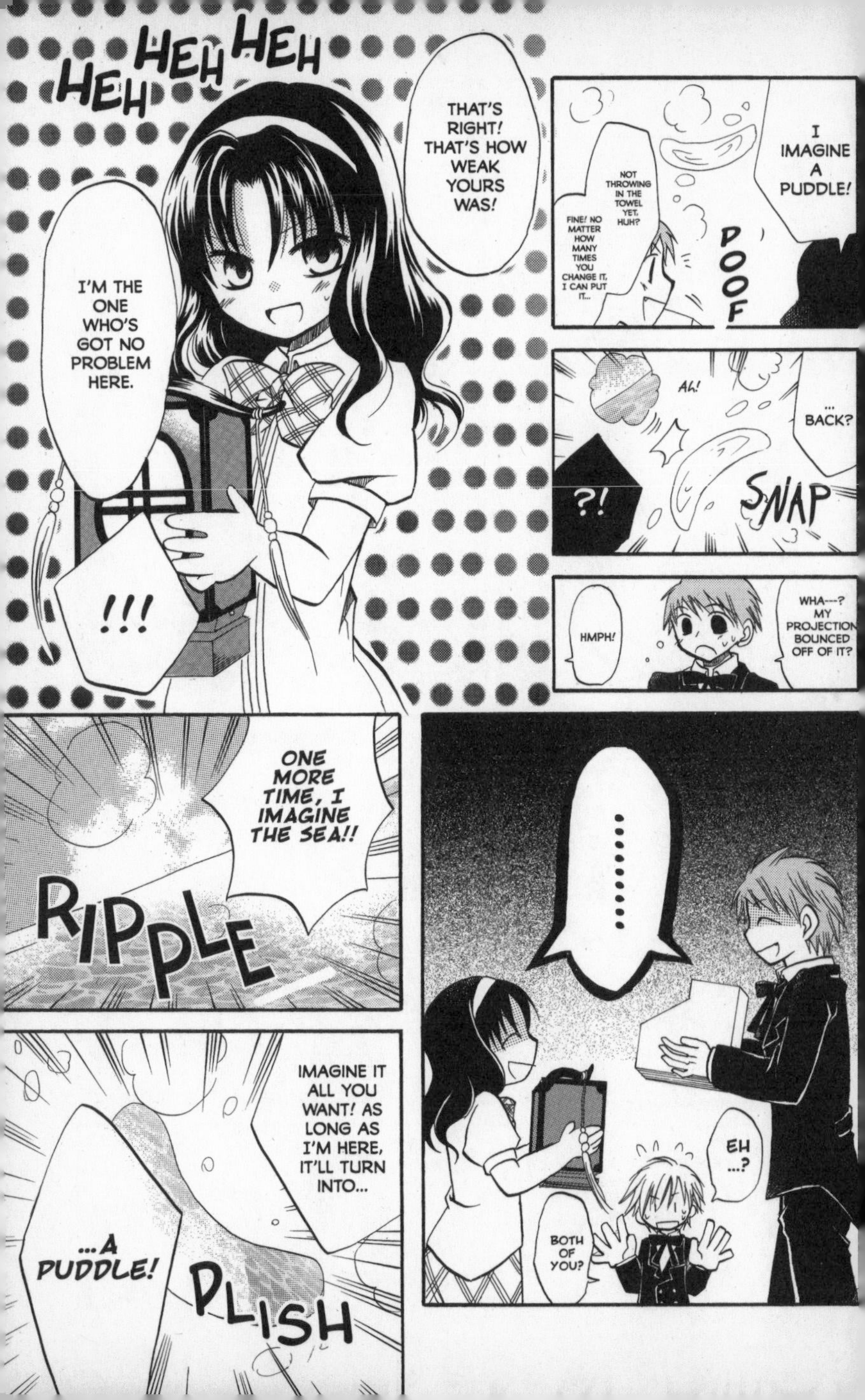

I IMAGINE A PUDDLE!
NOT THROWING IN THE TOWEL YET, HUH?
FINE! NO MATTER HOW MANY TIMES YOU CHANGE IT, I CAN PUT IT...
POOF
... BACK?
AH!
SNAP
?!
WHA---? MY PROJECTION BOUNCED OFF OF IT?
HMPH!
THAT'S RIGHT! THAT'S HOW WEAK YOURS WAS!
HEH HEH HEH HEH
I'M THE ONE WHO'S GOT NO PROBLEM HERE.
!!!
....
EH ...?
BOTH OF YOU?
ONE MORE TIME, I IMAGINE THE SEA!!
RIPPLE
IMAGINE IT ALL YOU WANT! AS LONG AS I'M HERE, IT'LL TURN INTO...
...A PUDDLE!
PLISH

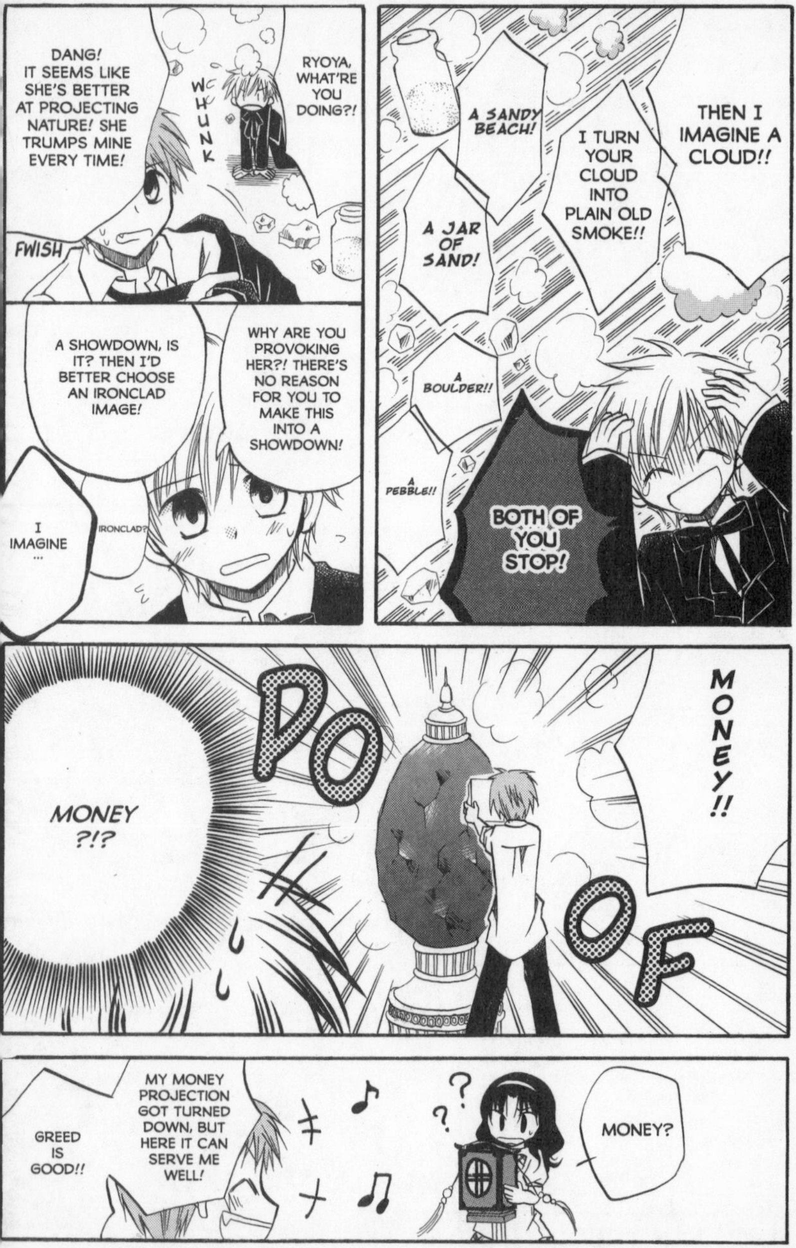
THEN I IMAGINE A CLOUD!!
I TURN YOUR CLOUD INTO PLAIN OLD SMOKE!!
A SANDY BEACH!
A JAR OF SAND!
A BOULDER!!
A PEBBLE!!
BOTH OF YOU STOP!
RYOYA, WHAT'RE YOU DOING?!
WHUNK
DANG! IT SEEMS LIKE SHE'S BETTER AT PROJECTING NATURE! SHE TRUMPS MINE EVERY TIME!
FWISH
WHY ARE YOU PROVOKING HER?! THERE'S NO REASON FOR YOU TO MAKE THIS INTO A SHOWDOWN!
A SHOWDOWN, IS IT? THEN I'D BETTER CHOOSE AN IRONCLAD IMAGE!
IRONCLAD?
I IMAGINE ...
MONEY!!
POOF
MONEY ?!?
MONEY?
MY MONEY PROJECTION GOT TURNED DOWN, BUT HERE IT CAN SERVE ME WELL!
GREED IS GOOD!!

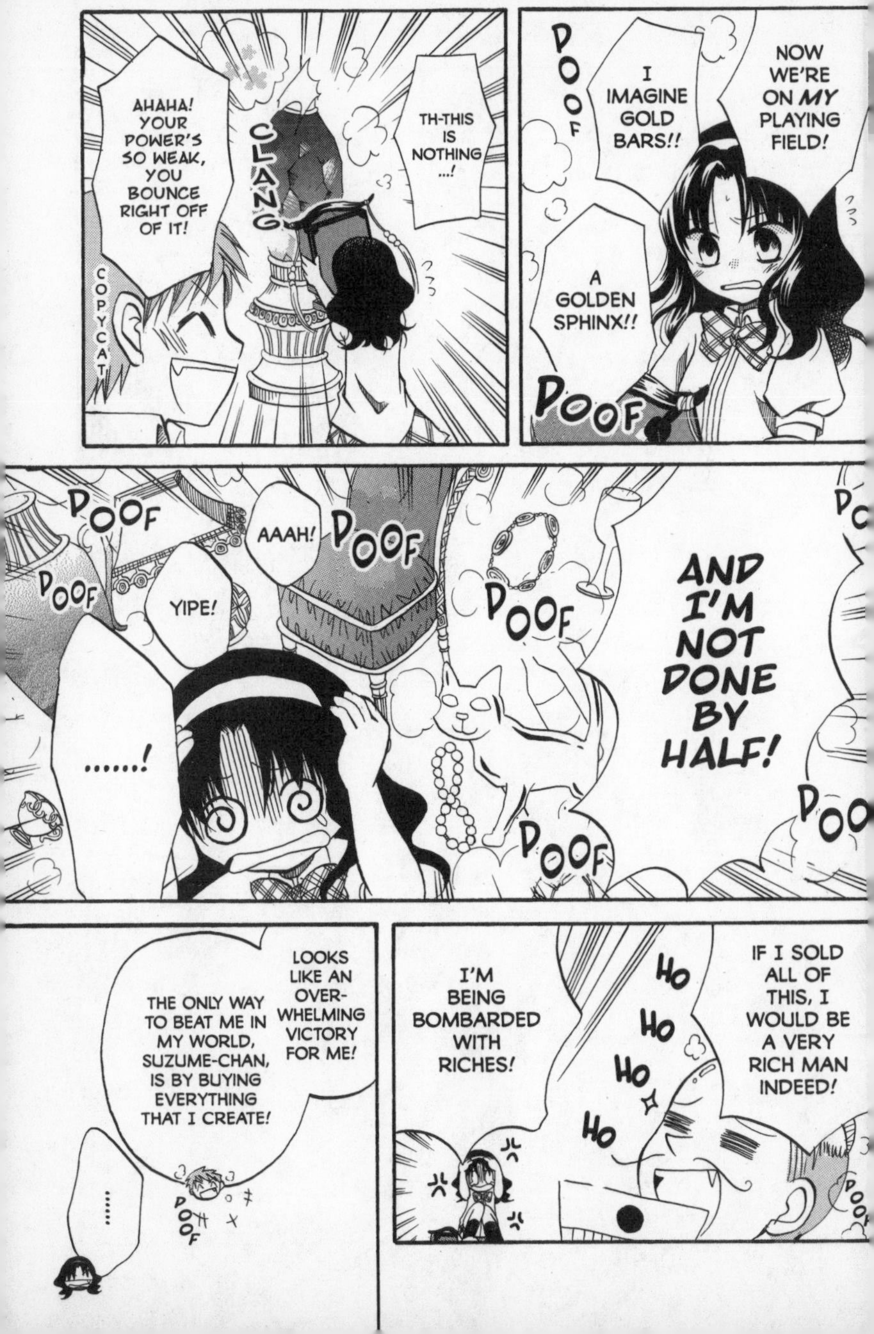
NOW WE'RE ON MY PLAYING FIELD!
I IMAGINE GOLD BARS!!
POOF
A GOLDEN SPHINX!!
POOF
TH-THIS IS NOTHING...!
CLANG
AHAHA! YOUR POWER'S SO WEAK, YOU BOUNCE RIGHT OFF OF IT!
COPYCAT
AND I'M NOT DONE BY HALF!
POOF
POOF
AAAH!
POOF
YIPE!
POOF
POOF
......!
POOF
IF I SOLD ALL OF THIS, I WOULD BE A VERY RICH MAN INDEED!
HO HO HO HO
I'M BEING BOMBARDED WITH RICHES!
LOOKS LIKE AN OVERWHELMING VICTORY FOR ME!
THE ONLY WAY TO BEAT ME IN MY WORLD, SUZUME-CHAN, IS BY BUYING EVERYTHING THAT I CREATE!
POOF
......

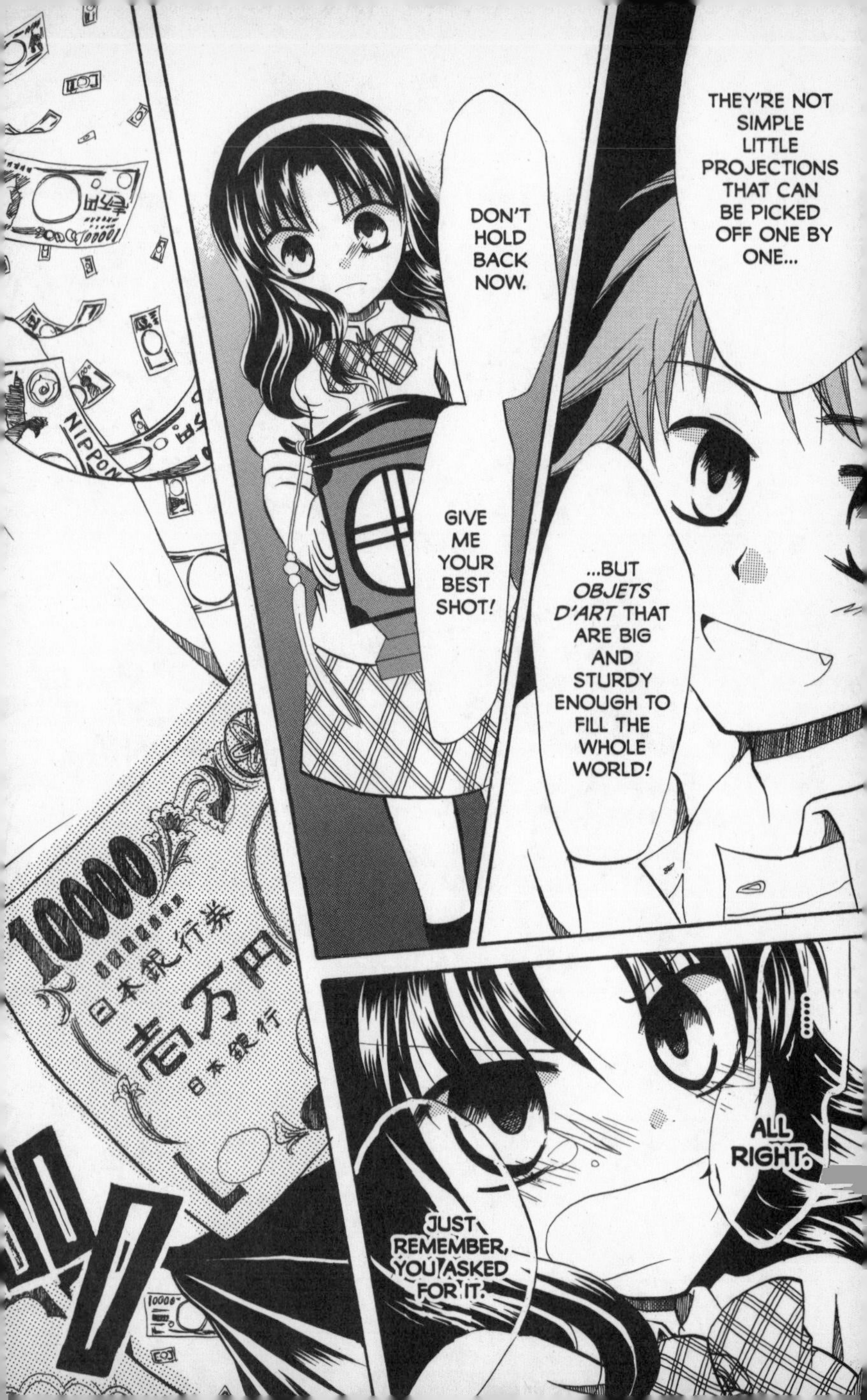
THEY'RE NOT SIMPLE LITTLE PROJECTIONS THAT CAN BE PICKED OFF ONE BY ONE...
...BUT *OBJETS D'ART* THAT ARE BIG AND STURDY ENOUGH TO FILL THE WHOLE WORLD!
DON'T HOLD BACK NOW.
GIVE ME YOUR BEST SHOT!
......
ALL RIGHT.
JUST REMEMBER, YOU ASKED FOR IT.
NIPPON
10000
日本銀行券
壱万円
日本銀行

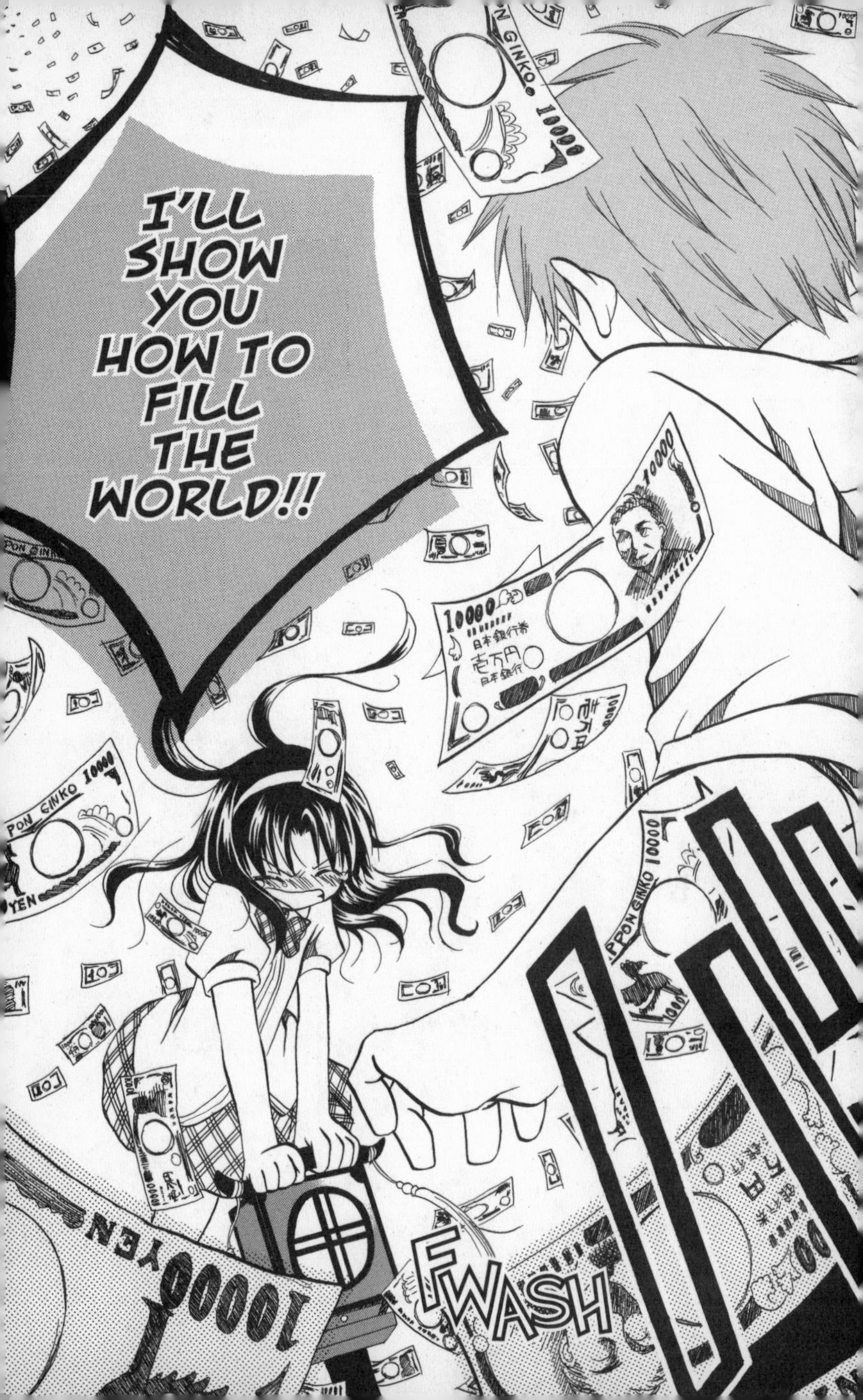
I'LL SHOW YOU HOW TO FILL THE WORLD!!
FWASH

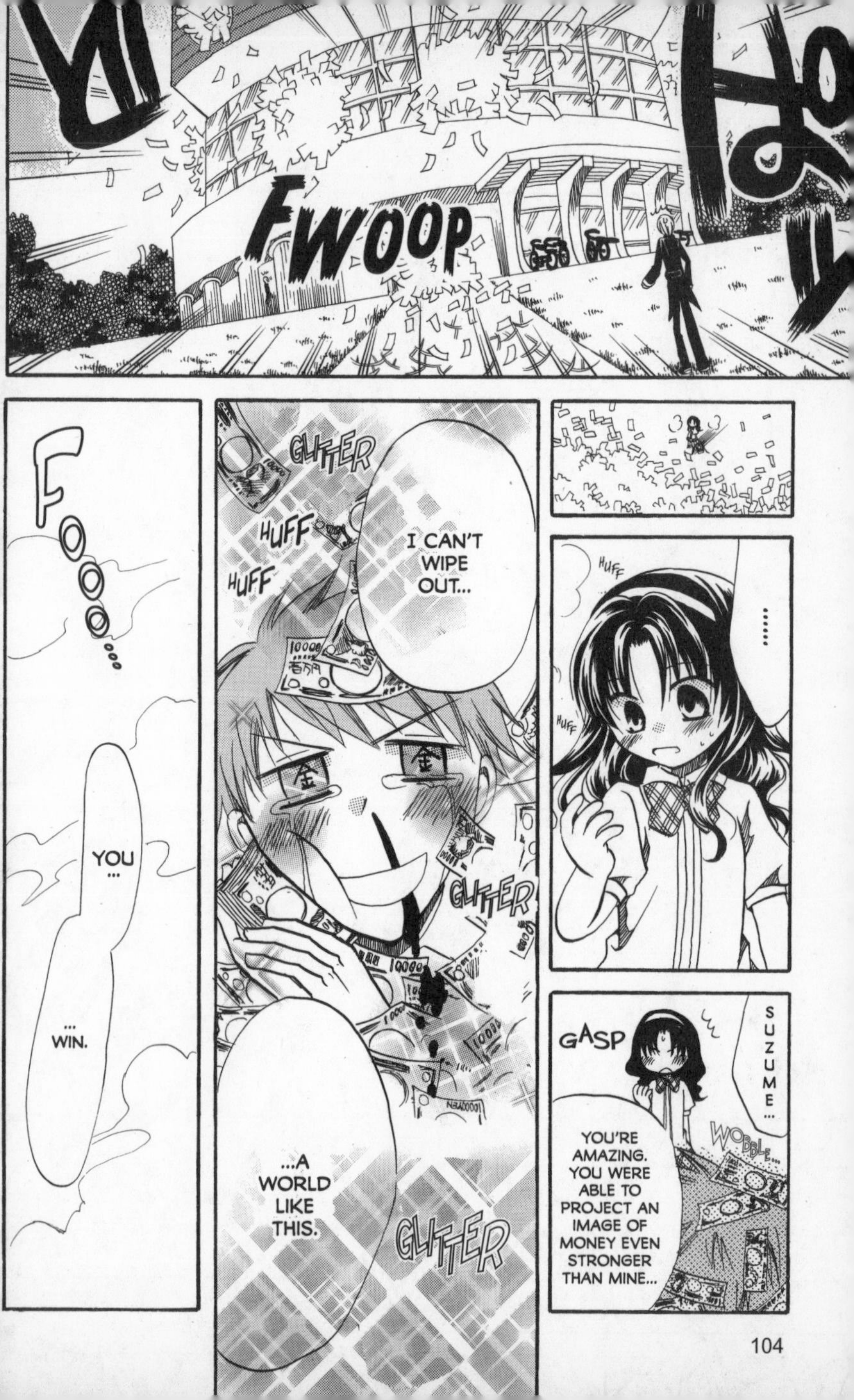
FWOOP
HUFF
HUFF
......
SUZUME...
GASP
WOBBLE...
YOU'RE AMAZING. YOU WERE ABLE TO PROJECT AN IMAGE OF MONEY EVEN STRONGER THAN MINE...
GLITTER
HUFF
HUFF
I CAN'T WIPE OUT...
GLITTER
...A WORLD LIKE THIS.
GLITTER
FOOOO...
YOU... ...WIN.

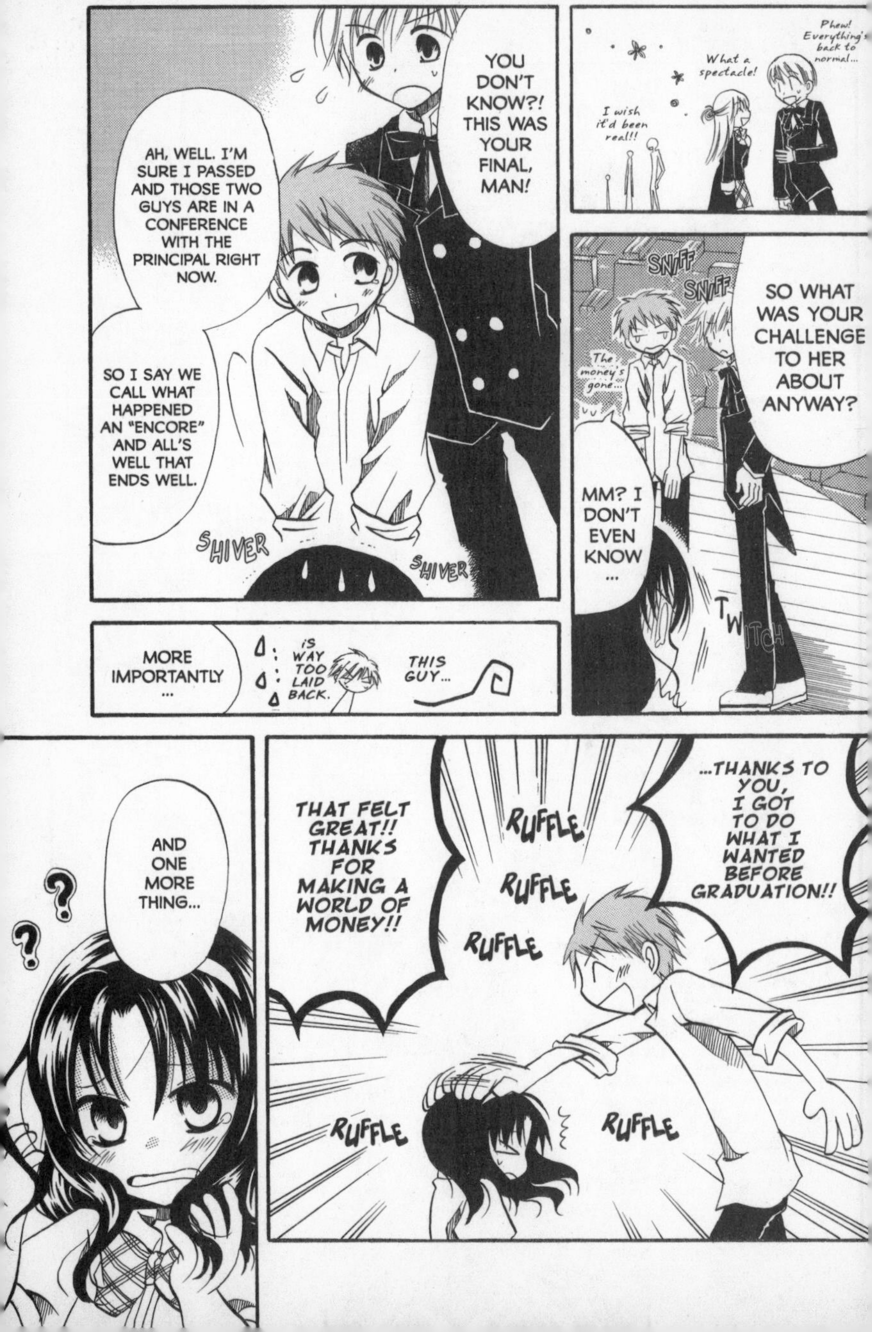
Phew! Everything's back to normal...
What a spectacle!
I wish it'd been real!!
SNIFF
SNIFF
SO WHAT WAS YOUR CHALLENGE TO HER ABOUT ANYWAY?
The money's gone...
MM? I DON'T EVEN KNOW ...
TWITCH
YOU DON'T KNOW?! THIS WAS YOUR FINAL, MAN!
AH, WELL. I'M SURE I PASSED AND THOSE TWO GUYS ARE IN A CONFERENCE WITH THE PRINCIPAL RIGHT NOW.
SO I SAY WE CALL WHAT HAPPENED AN "ENCORE" AND ALL'S WELL THAT ENDS WELL.
SHIVER
SHIVER
THIS GUY...
is WAY TOO LAID BACK.
MORE IMPORTANTLY ...
...THANKS TO YOU, I GOT TO DO WHAT I WANTED BEFORE GRADUATION!!
THAT FELT GREAT!! THANKS FOR MAKING A WORLD OF MONEY!!
RUFFLE
RUFFLE
RUFFLE
RUFFLE
RUFFLE
AND ONE MORE THING...
?
?

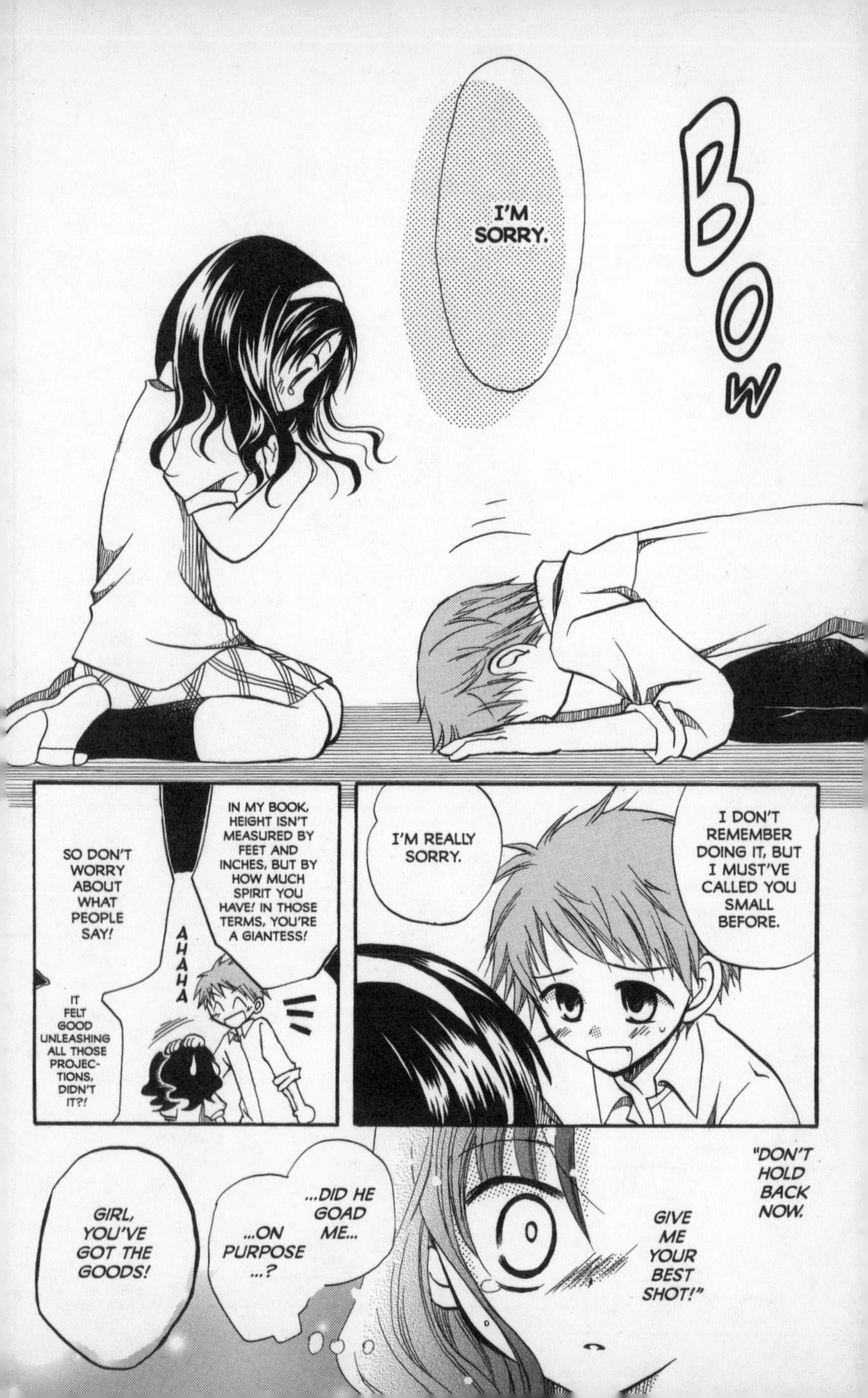
BOW
I'M SORRY.
I DON'T REMEMBER DOING IT, BUT I MUST'VE CALLED YOU SMALL BEFORE.
I'M REALLY SORRY.
IN MY BOOK, HEIGHT ISN'T MEASURED BY FEET AND INCHES, BUT BY HOW MUCH SPIRIT YOU HAVE! IN THOSE TERMS, YOU'RE A GIANTESS!
SO DON'T WORRY ABOUT WHAT PEOPLE SAY!
AHAHA
IT FELT GOOD UNLEASHING ALL THOSE PROJEC-TIONS, DIDN'T IT?!
"DON'T HOLD BACK NOW.
GIVE ME YOUR BEST SHOT!"
...DID HE GOAD ME...
...ON PURPOSE ...?
GIRL, YOU'VE GOT THE GOODS!

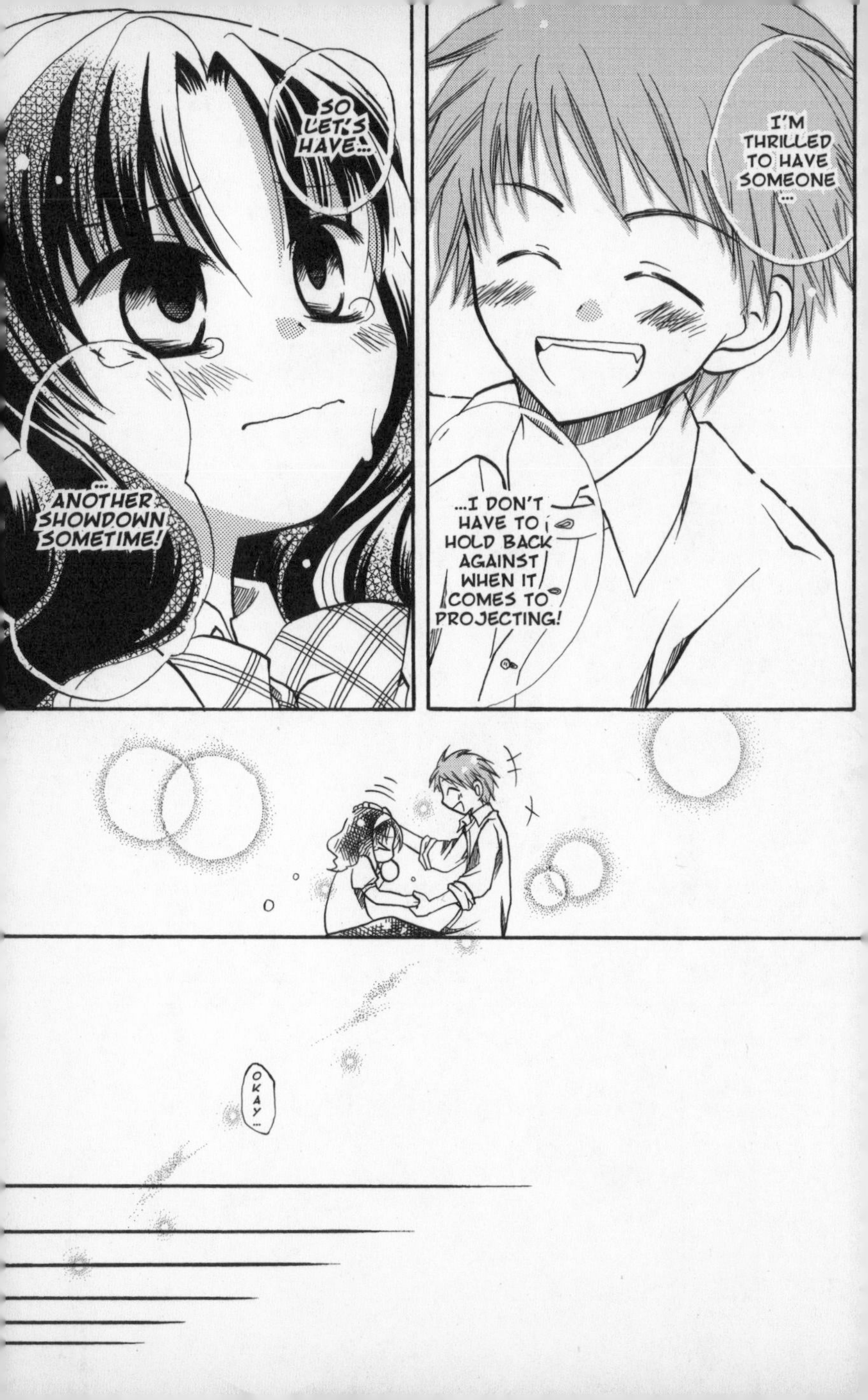
I'M THRILLED TO HAVE SOMEONE ...
...I DON'T HAVE TO HOLD BACK AGAINST WHEN IT COMES TO PROJECTING!
SO LET'S HAVE...
... ANOTHER SHOWDOWN SOMETIME!
OKAY...

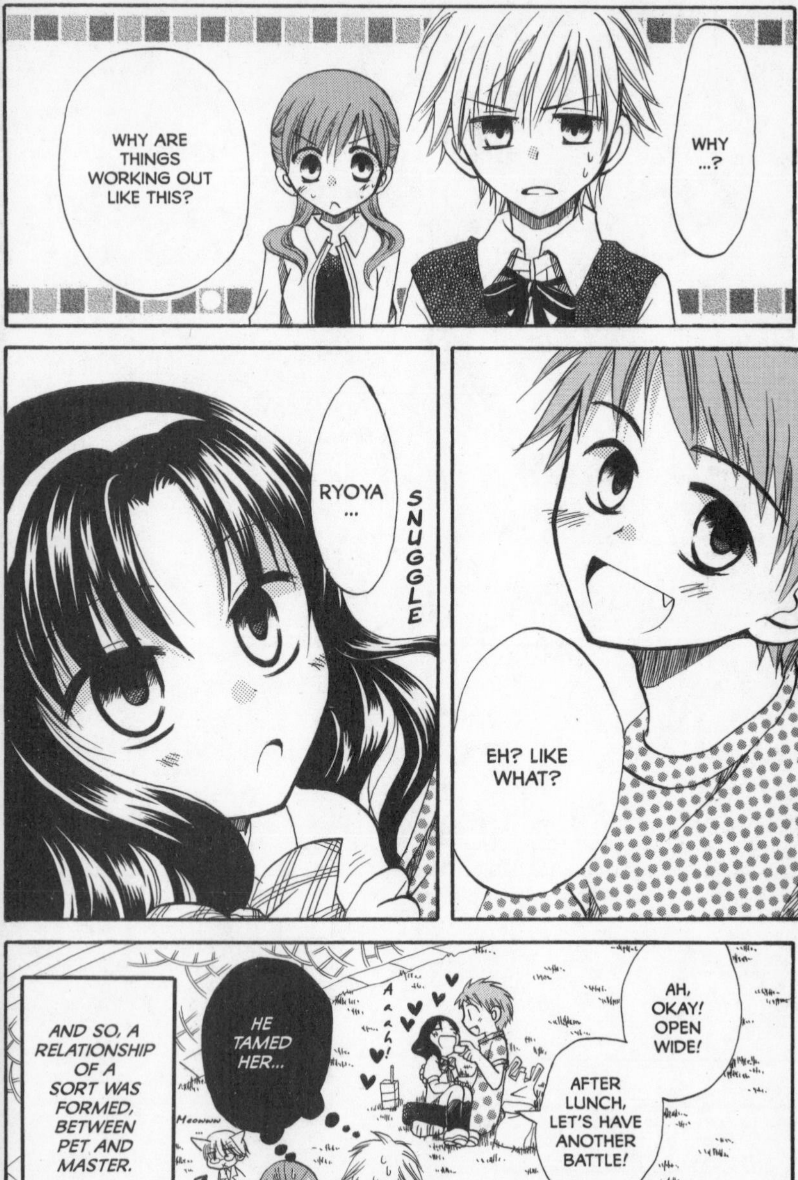
WHY ...?
WHY ARE THINGS WORKING OUT LIKE THIS?
EH? LIKE WHAT?
RYOYA ...
SNUGGLE
AH, OKAY! OPEN WIDE!
AFTER LUNCH, LET'S HAVE ANOTHER BATTLE!
Aaah!
HE TAMED HER...
Meowww ...
That reminds me of somebody...
AND SO, A RELATIONSHIP OF A SORT WAS FORMED, BETWEEN PET AND MASTER.

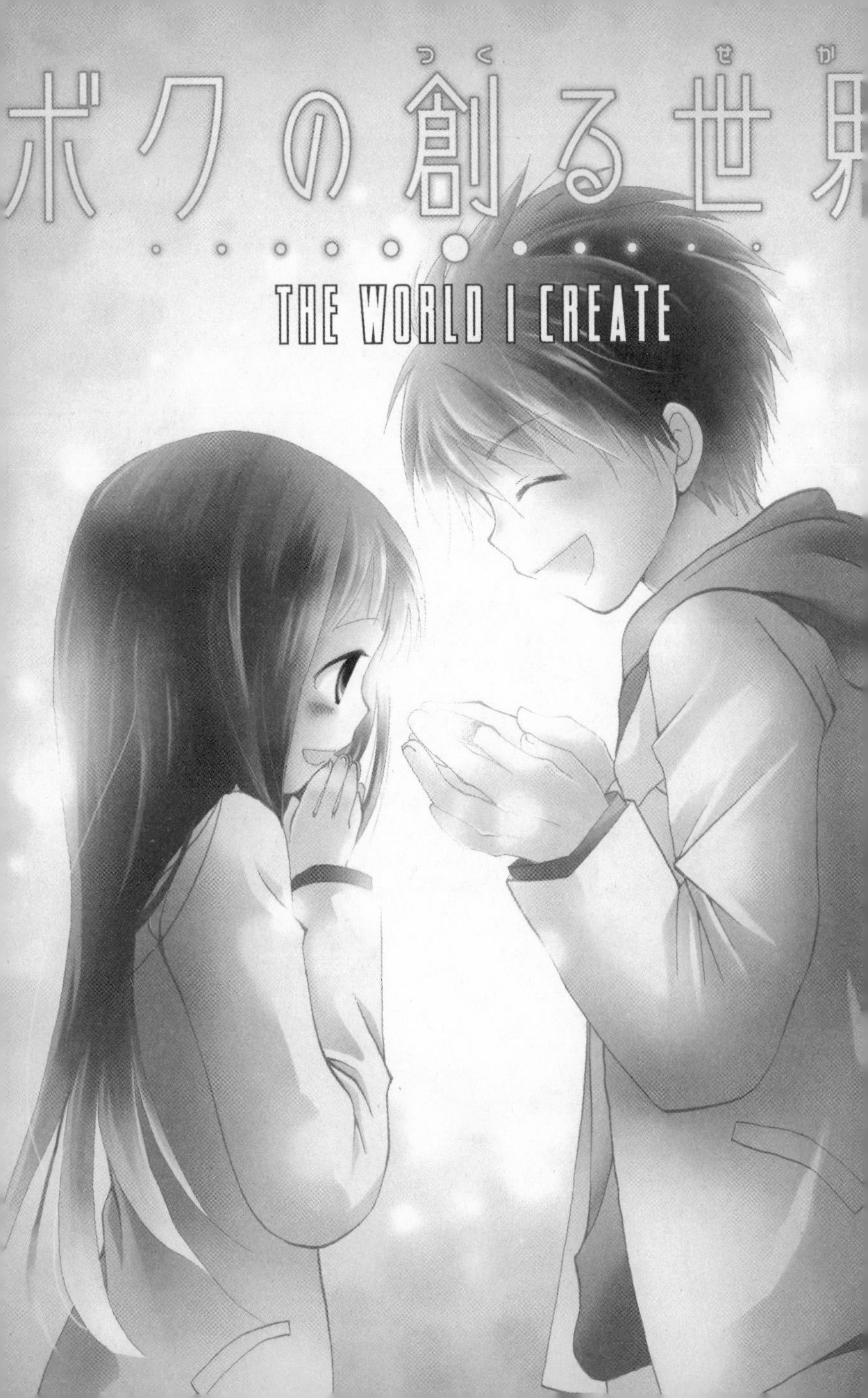
ボクの創る世界
THE WORLD I CREATE

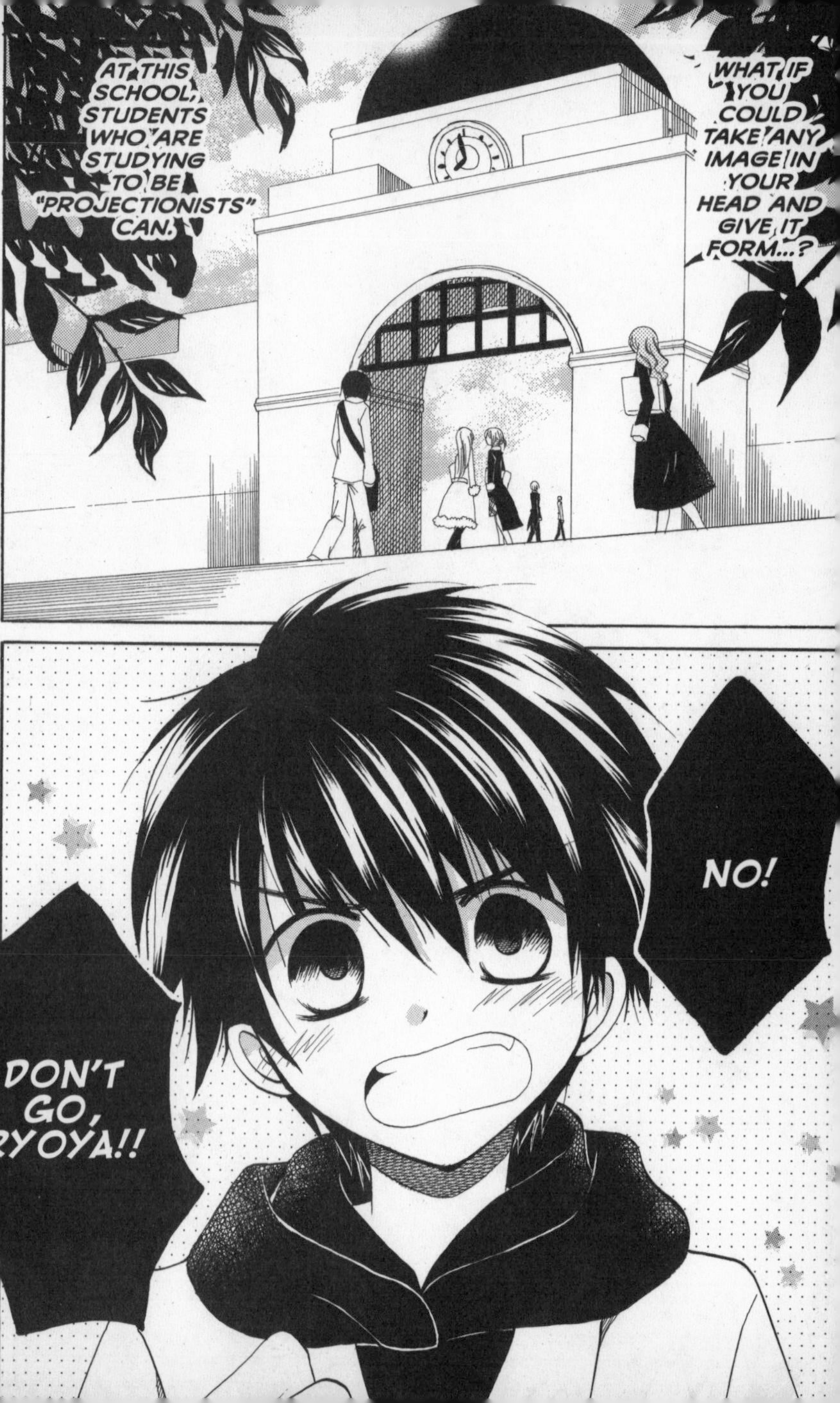
WHAT IF YOU COULD TAKE ANY IMAGE IN YOUR HEAD AND GIVE IT FORM...?
AT THIS SCHOOL, STUDENTS WHO ARE STUDYING TO BE "PROJECTIONISTS" CAN.
NO!
DON'T GO, RYOYA!!

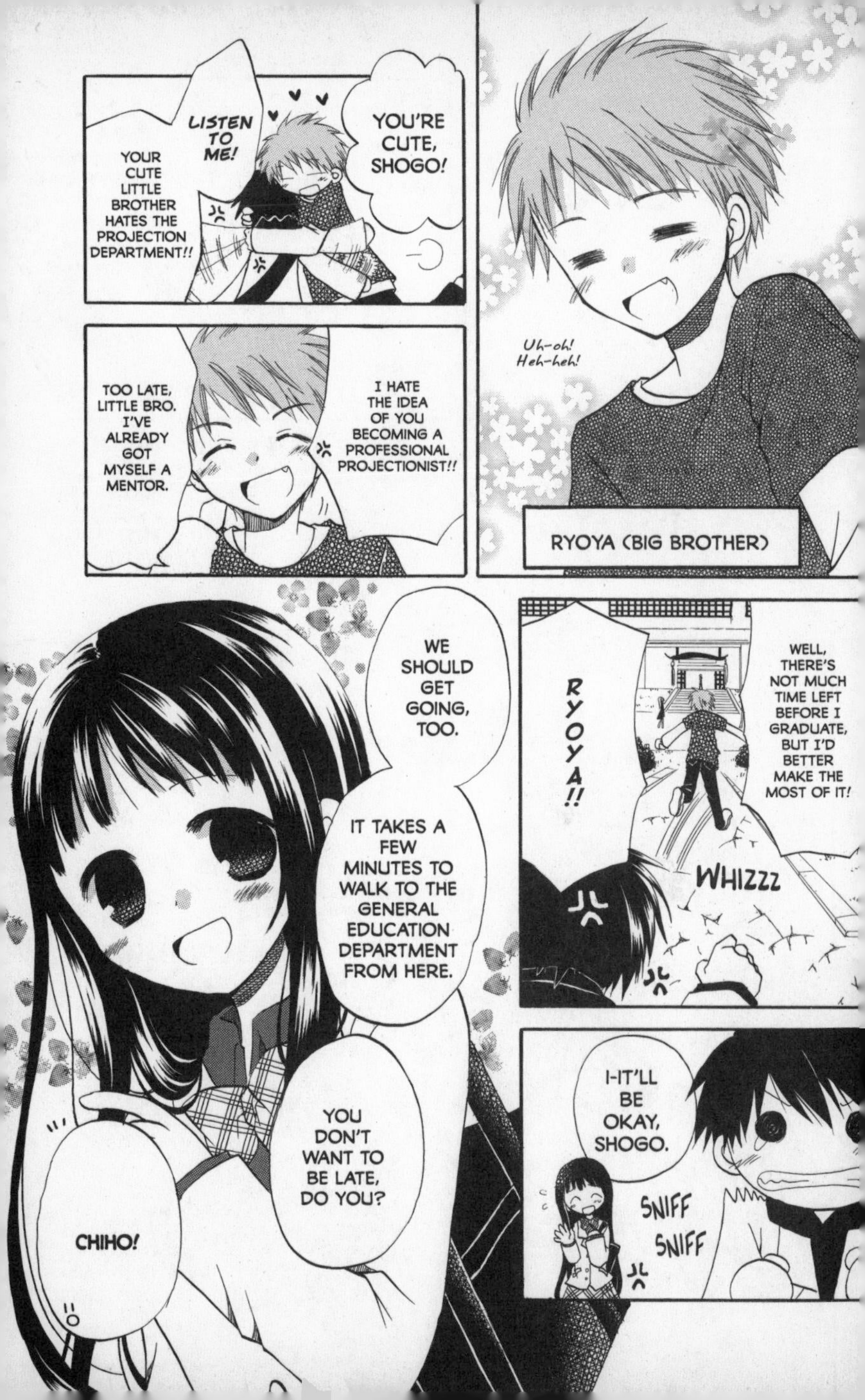
Uh-oh! Heh-heh!
RYOYA (BIG BROTHER)
YOU'RE CUTE, SHOGO!
LISTEN TO ME!
YOUR CUTE LITTLE BROTHER HATES THE PROJECTION DEPARTMENT!!
I HATE THE IDEA OF YOU BECOMING A PROFESSIONAL PROJECTIONIST!!
TOO LATE, LITTLE BRO. I'VE ALREADY GOT MYSELF A MENTOR.
WELL, THERE'S NOT MUCH TIME LEFT BEFORE I GRADUATE, BUT I'D BETTER MAKE THE MOST OF IT!
RYOYA!!
WHIZZZ
I-IT'LL BE OKAY, SHOGO.
SNIFF SNIFF
WE SHOULD GET GOING, TOO.
IT TAKES A FEW MINUTES TO WALK TO THE GENERAL EDUCATION DEPARTMENT FROM HERE.
YOU DON'T WANT TO BE LATE, DO YOU?
CHIHO!

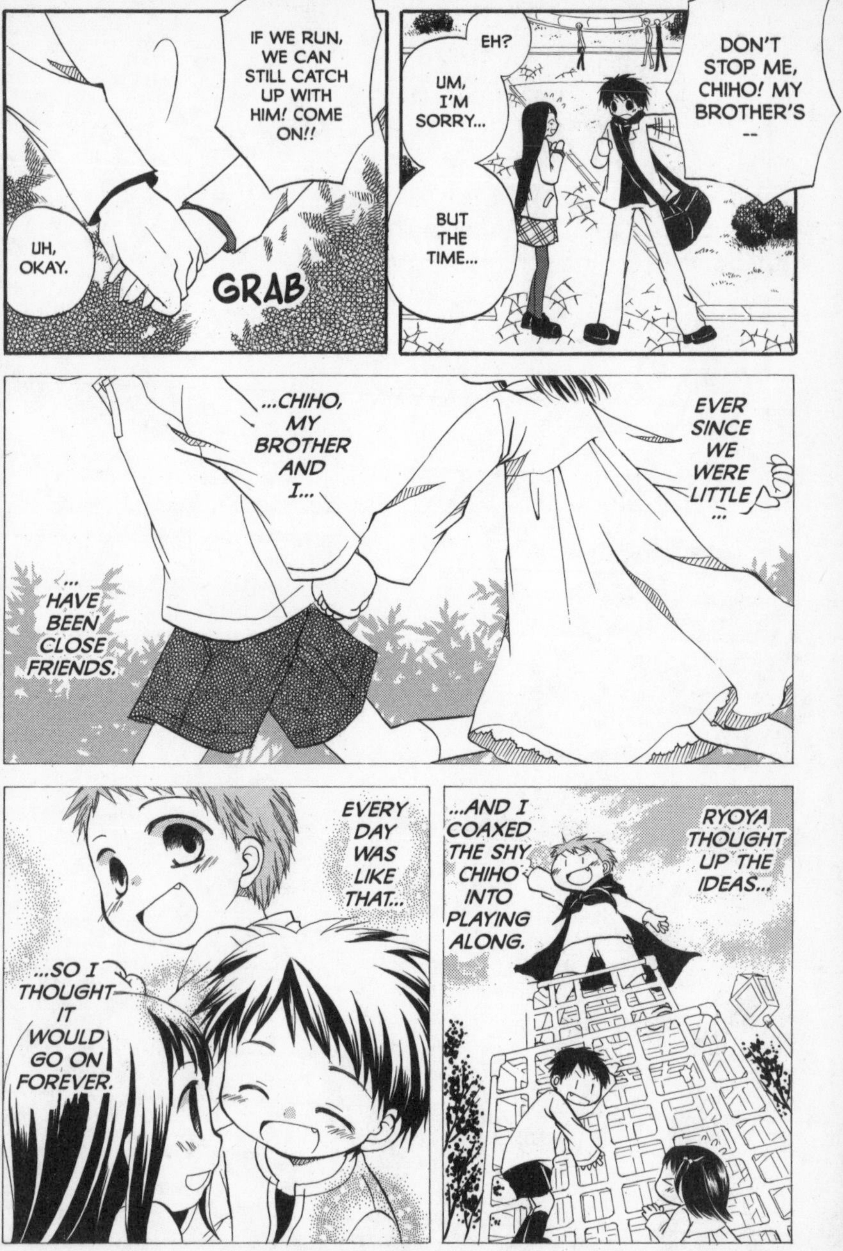
DON'T STOP ME, CHIHO! MY BROTHER'S --
EH?
UM, I'M SORRY...
BUT THE TIME...
IF WE RUN, WE CAN STILL CATCH UP WITH HIM! COME ON!!
UH, OKAY.
GRAB
EVER SINCE WE WERE LITTLE...
...CHIHO, MY BROTHER AND I...
...HAVE BEEN CLOSE FRIENDS.
RYOYA THOUGHT UP THE IDEAS...
...AND I COAXED THE SHY CHIHO INTO PLAYING ALONG.
EVERY DAY WAS LIKE THAT...
...SO I THOUGHT IT WOULD GO ON FOREVER.

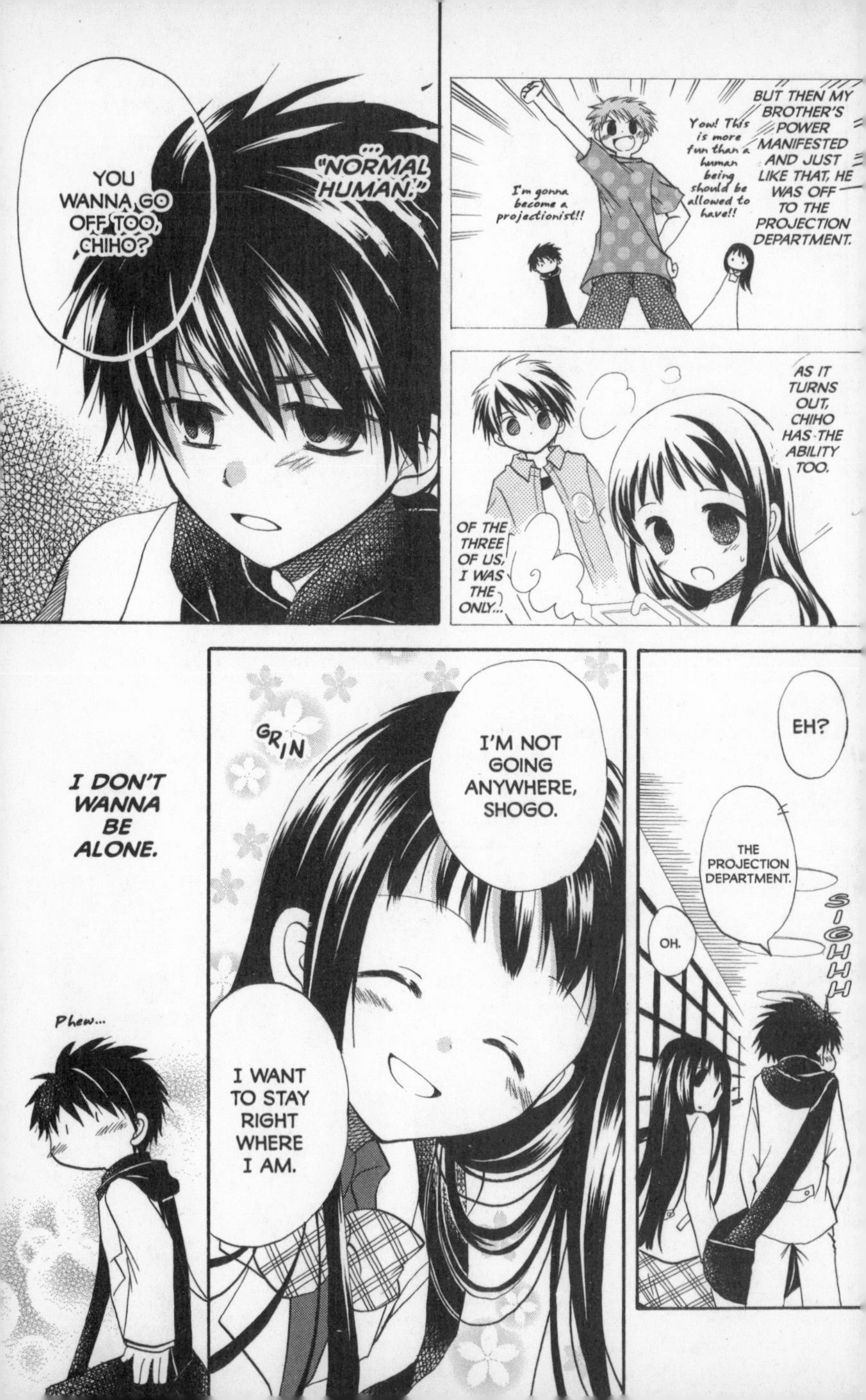
BUT THEN MY BROTHER'S POWER MANIFESTED AND JUST LIKE THAT, HE WAS OFF TO THE PROJECTION DEPARTMENT.
Yow! This is more fun than a human being should be allowed to have!!
I'm gonna become a projectionist!!
AS IT TURNS OUT, CHIHO HAS THE ABILITY TOO.
OF THE THREE OF US, I WAS THE ONLY...
..."NORMAL HUMAN."
YOU WANNA GO OFF TOO, CHIHO?
EH?
THE PROJECTION DEPARTMENT.
SIGHHH
OH.
GRIN
I'M NOT GOING ANYWHERE, SHOGO.
I WANT TO STAY RIGHT WHERE I AM.
I DON'T WANNA BE ALONE.
Phew...

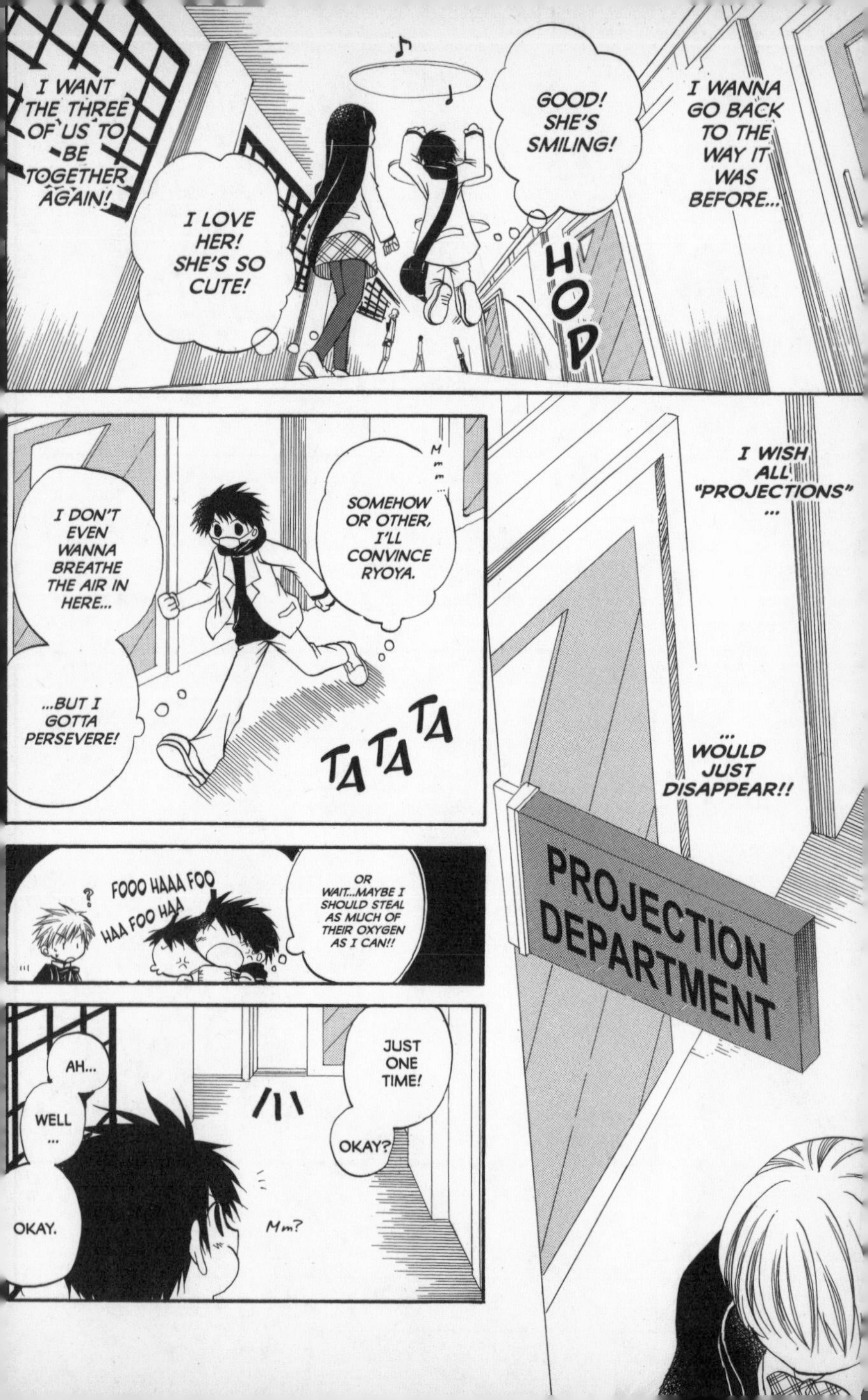
I WANNA GO BACK TO THE WAY IT WAS BEFORE...
GOOD! SHE'S SMILING!
HOP
I LOVE HER! SHE'S SO CUTE!
I WANT THE THREE OF US TO BE TOGETHER AGAIN!
I WISH ALL "PROJECTIONS" ...
... WOULD JUST DISAPPEAR!!
PROJECTION DEPARTMENT
Mmm...
SOMEHOW OR OTHER, I'LL CONVINCE RYOYA.
I DON'T EVEN WANNA BREATHE THE AIR IN HERE...
TA TA TA
...BUT I GOTTA PERSEVERE!
OR WAIT...MAYBE I SHOULD STEAL AS MUCH OF THEIR OXYGEN AS I CAN!!
FOOO HAAA FOO
HAA FOO HAA
?
JUST ONE TIME!
OKAY?
AH...
WELL ...
Mm?
OKAY.

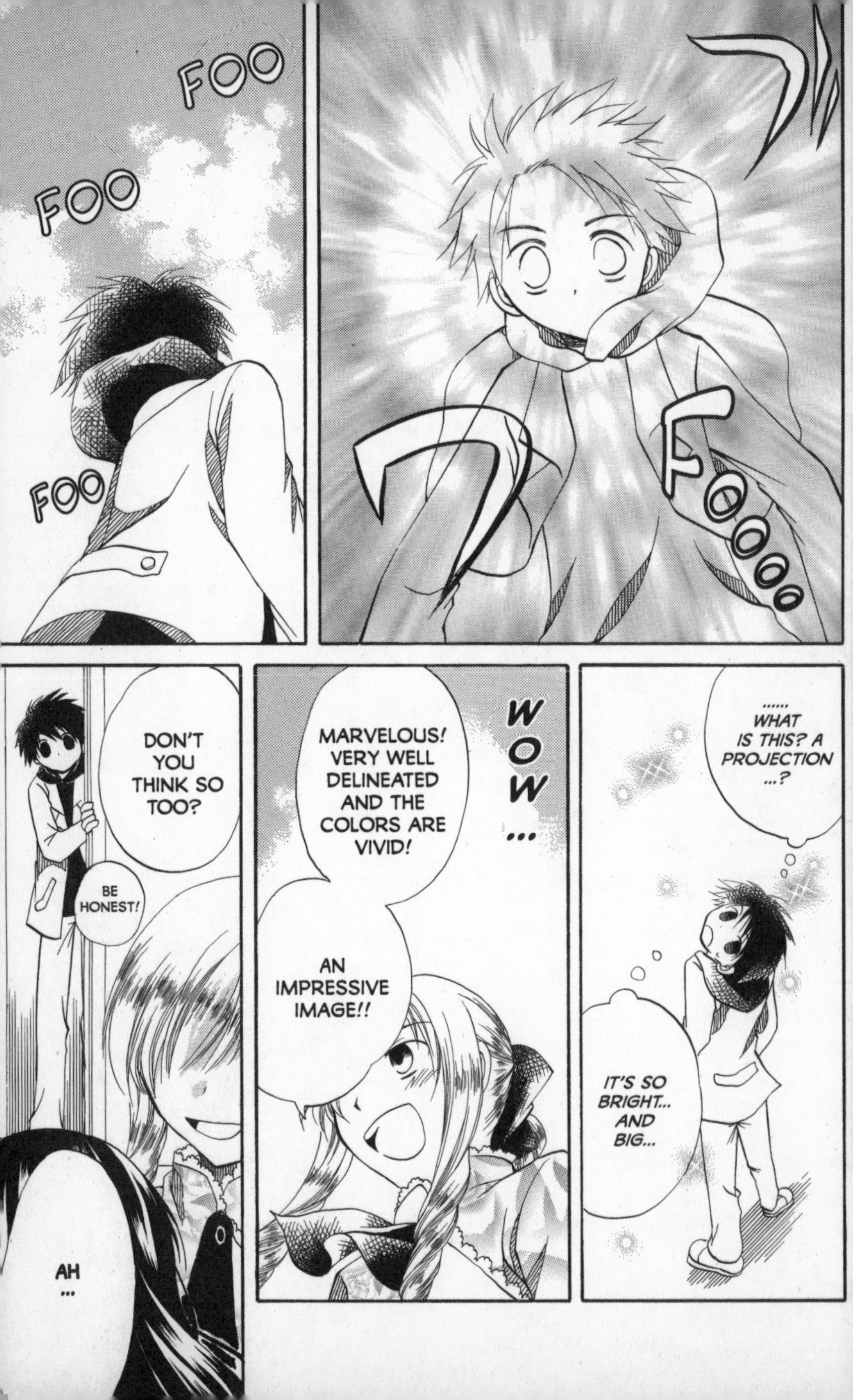
Foooo
FOO
FOO
FOO
......
WHAT IS THIS? A PROJECTION ...?
IT'S SO BRIGHT... AND BIG...
WOW ...
MARVELOUS! VERY WELL DELINEATED AND THE COLORS ARE VIVID!
AN IMPRESSIVE IMAGE!!
DON'T YOU THINK SO TOO?
BE HONEST!
AH ...

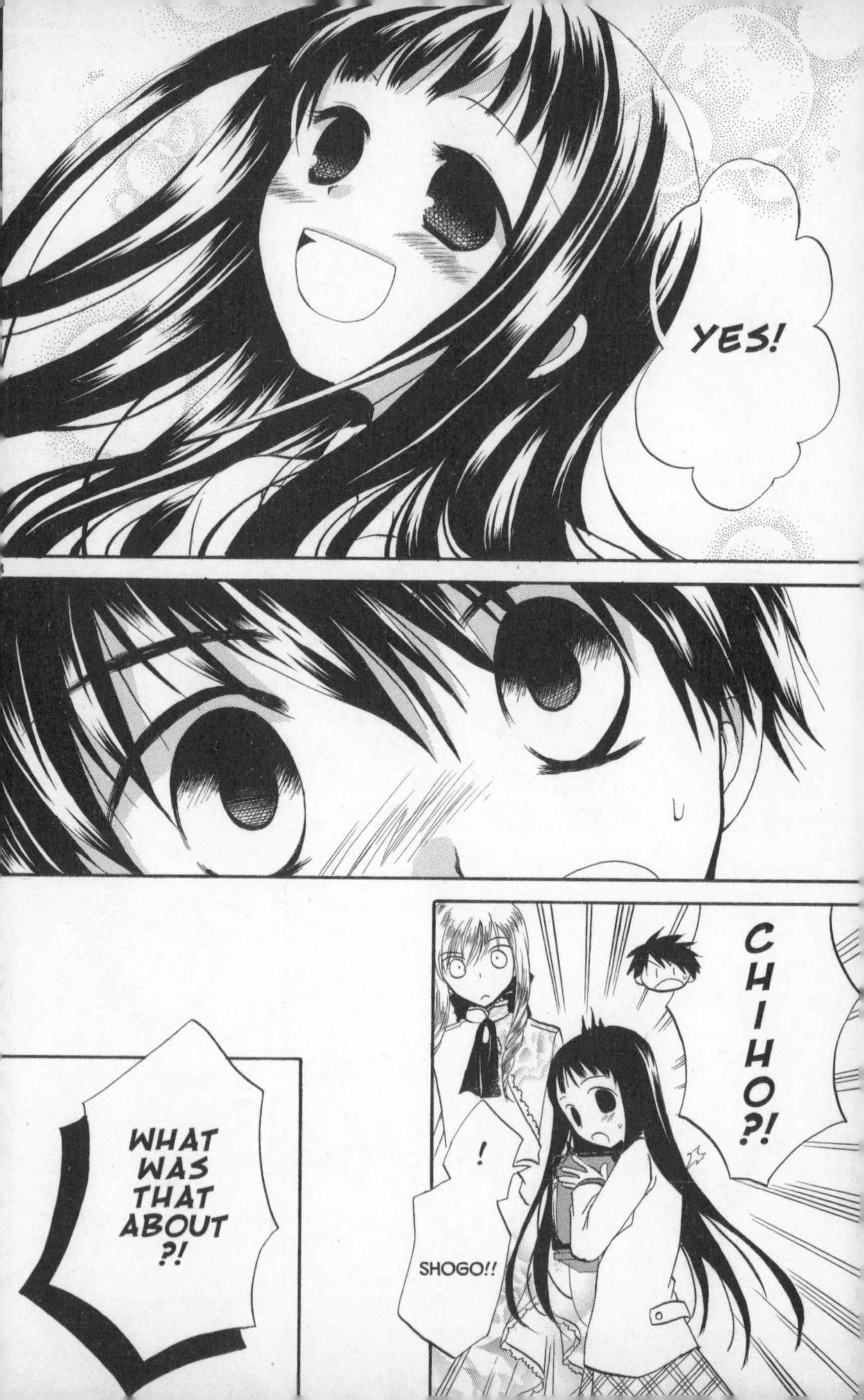
YES!
CHIHO?!
!
SHOGO!!
WHAT WAS THAT ABOUT?!

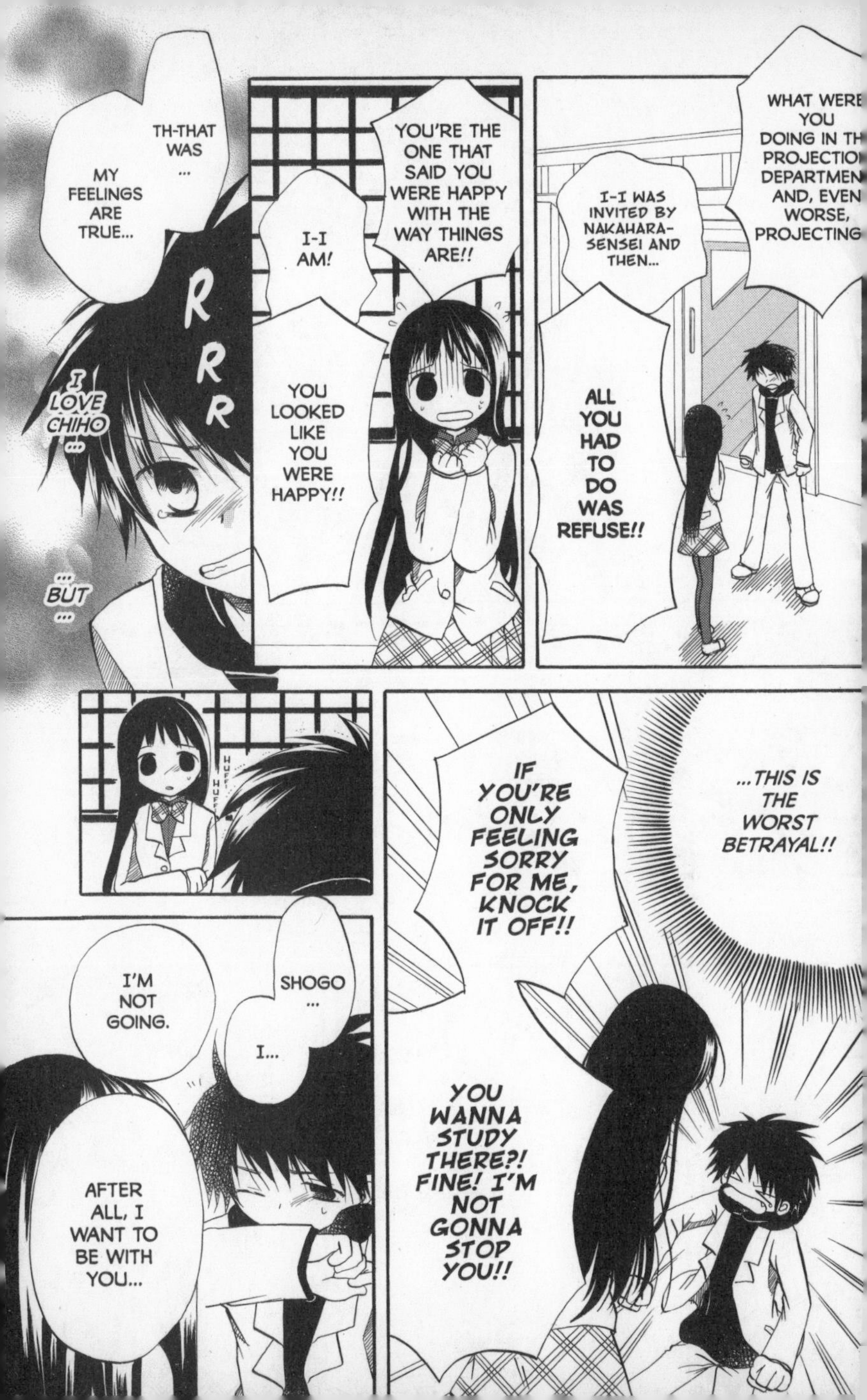
WHAT WERE YOU DOING IN TH PROJECTIO DEPARTMEN AND, EVEN WORSE, PROJECTING
I-I WAS INVITED BY NAKAHARA-SENSEI AND THEN...
ALL YOU HAD TO DO WAS REFUSE!!
YOU'RE THE ONE THAT SAID YOU WERE HAPPY WITH THE WAY THINGS ARE!!
I-I AM!
YOU LOOKED LIKE YOU WERE HAPPY!!
TH-THAT WAS ...
MY FEELINGS ARE TRUE...
RRR
I LOVE CHIHO ...
... BUT ...
...THIS IS THE WORST BETRAYAL!!
IF YOU'RE ONLY FEELING SORRY FOR ME, KNOCK IT OFF!!
YOU WANNA STUDY THERE?! FINE! I'M NOT GONNA STOP YOU!!
HUFF HUFF
SHOGO ...
I...
I'M NOT GOING.
AFTER ALL, I WANT TO BE WITH YOU...

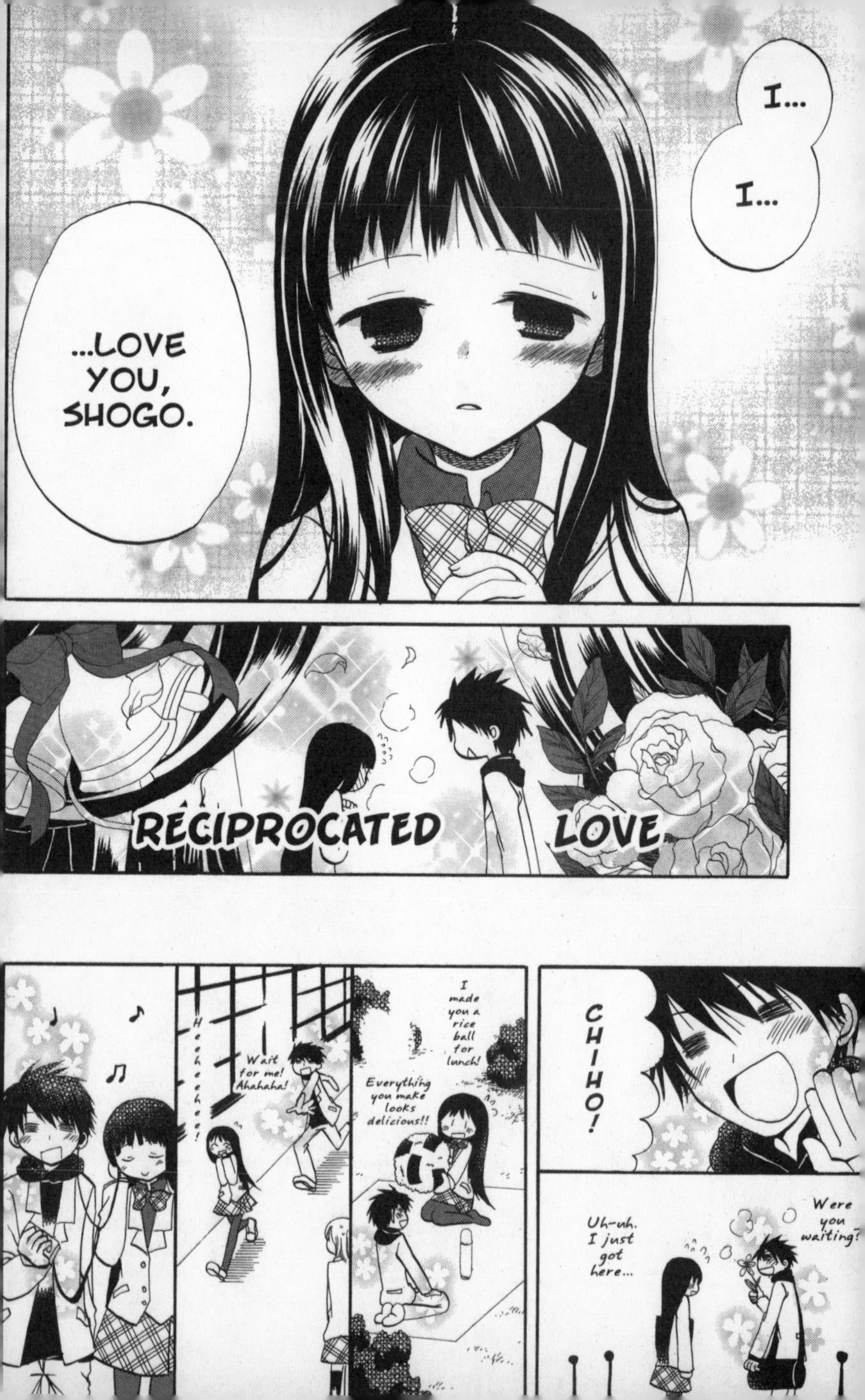
I...
I...
...LOVE YOU, SHOGO.
RECIPROCATED LOVE
CHIHO!
Were you waiting?
Uh-uh. I just got here...
I made you a rice ball for lunch!
Everything you make looks delicious!!
Wait for me! Ahahaha!
Heeheehee!

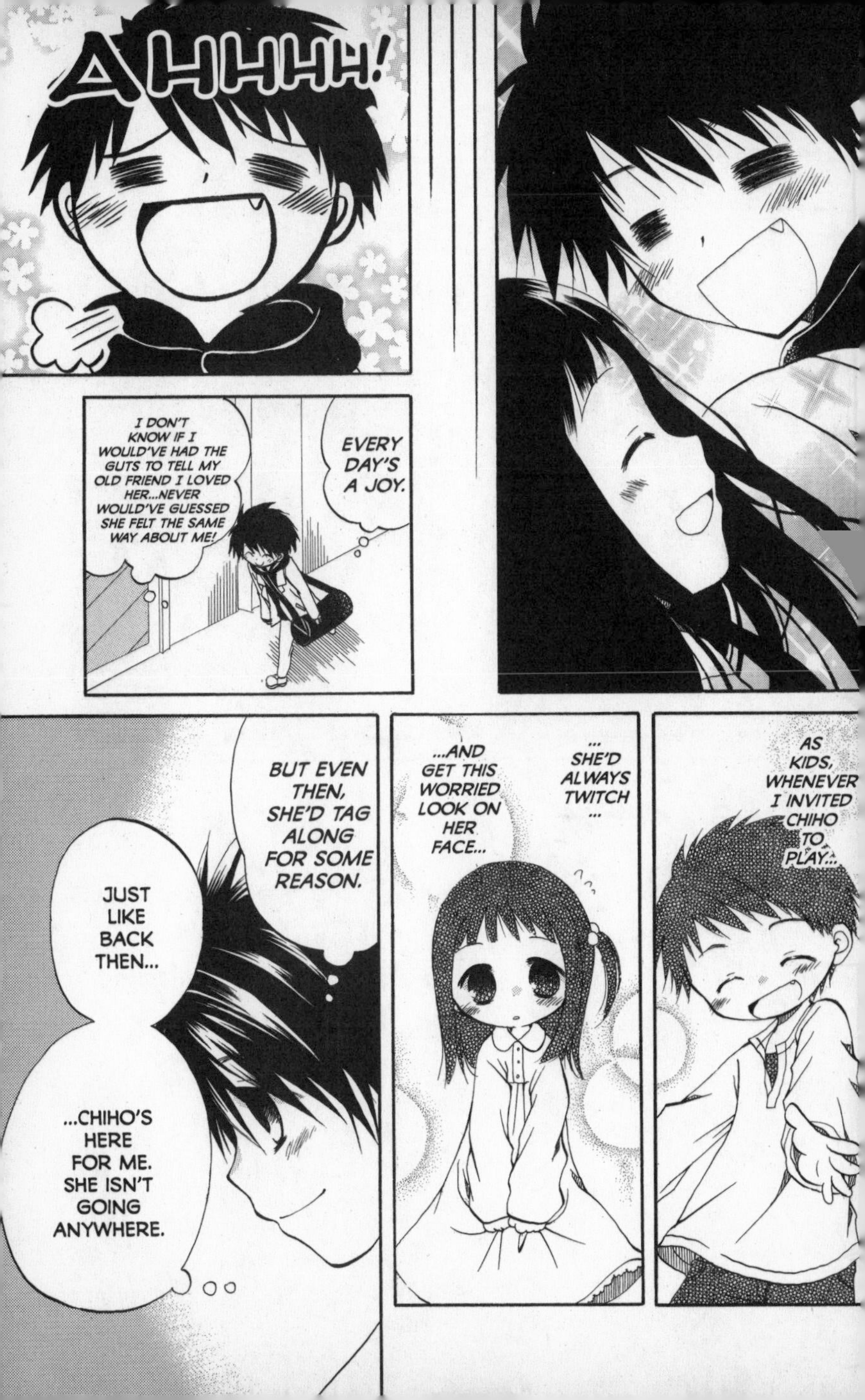
AHHHH!
EVERY DAY'S A JOY.
I DON'T KNOW IF I WOULD'VE HAD THE GUTS TO TELL MY OLD FRIEND I LOVED HER...NEVER WOULD'VE GUESSED SHE FELT THE SAME WAY ABOUT ME!
AS KIDS, WHENEVER I INVITED CHIHO TO PLAY...
...SHE'D ALWAYS TWITCH...
...AND GET THIS WORRIED LOOK ON HER FACE...
BUT EVEN THEN, SHE'D TAG ALONG FOR SOME REASON.
JUST LIKE BACK THEN...
...CHIHO'S HERE FOR ME. SHE ISN'T GOING ANYWHERE.

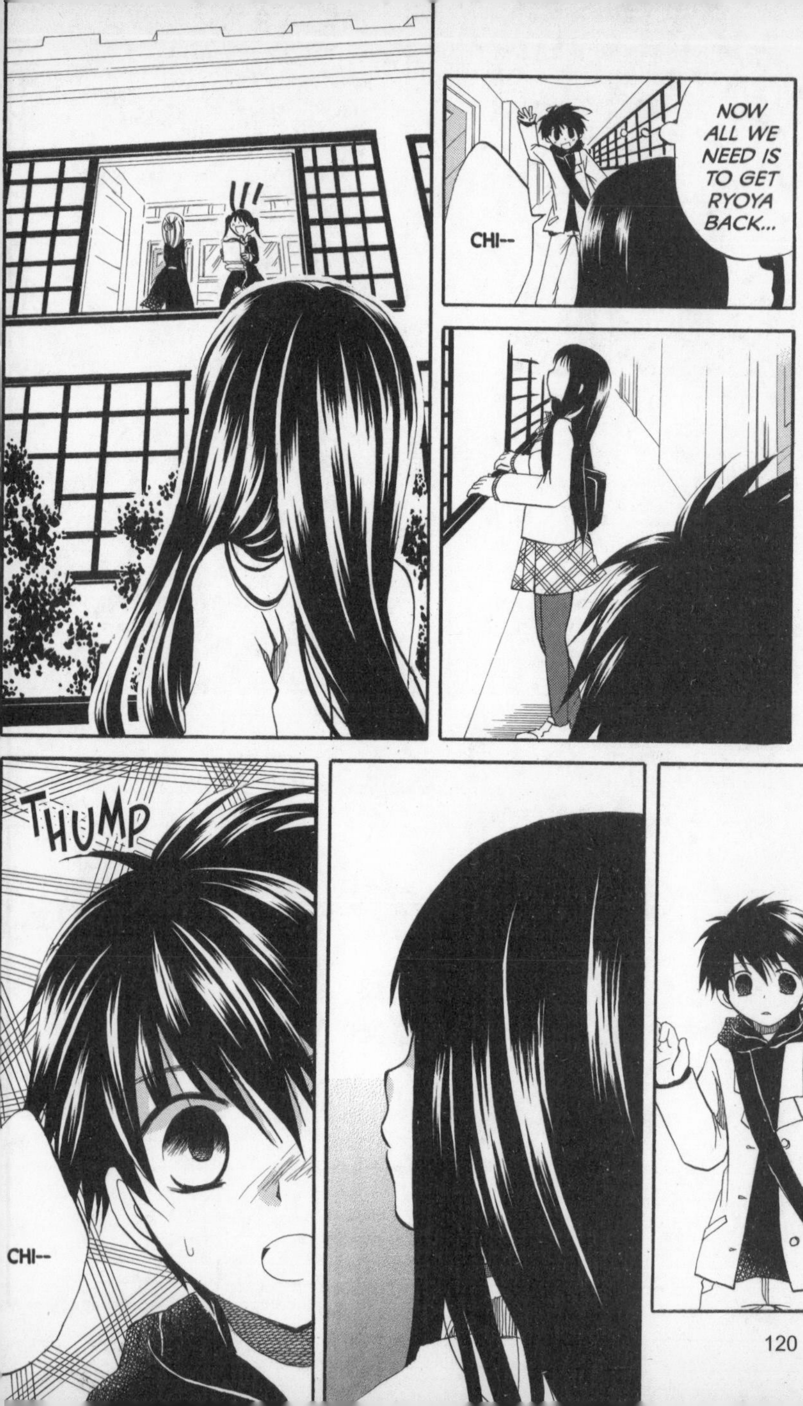
NOW ALL WE NEED IS TO GET RYOYA BACK...
CHI--
THUMP
CHI--

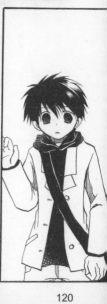

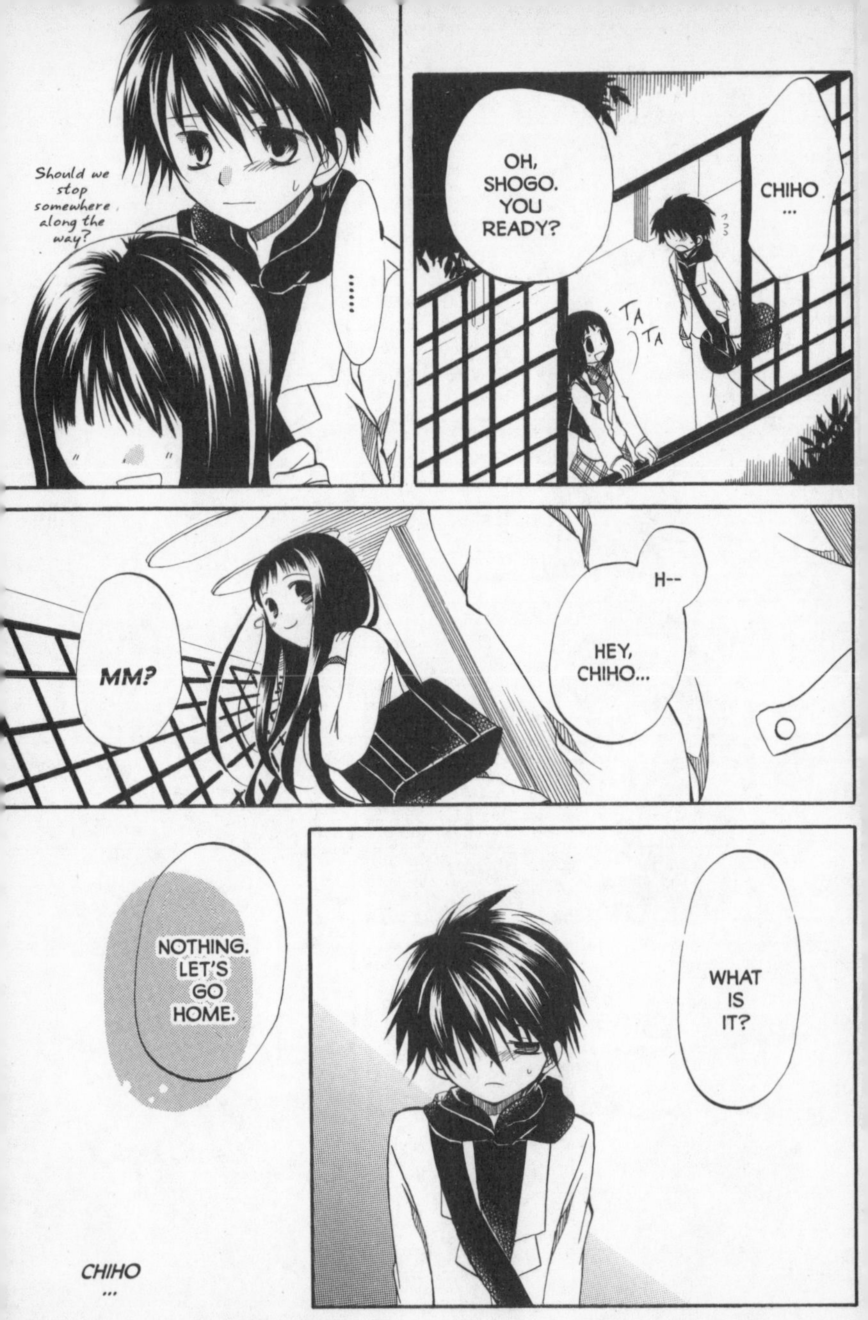
CHIHO ...
OH, SHOGO. YOU READY?
TA TA
......
Should we stop somewhere along the way?
H--
HEY, CHIHO...
MM?
WHAT IS IT?
NOTHING. LET'S GO HOME.
CHIHO ...

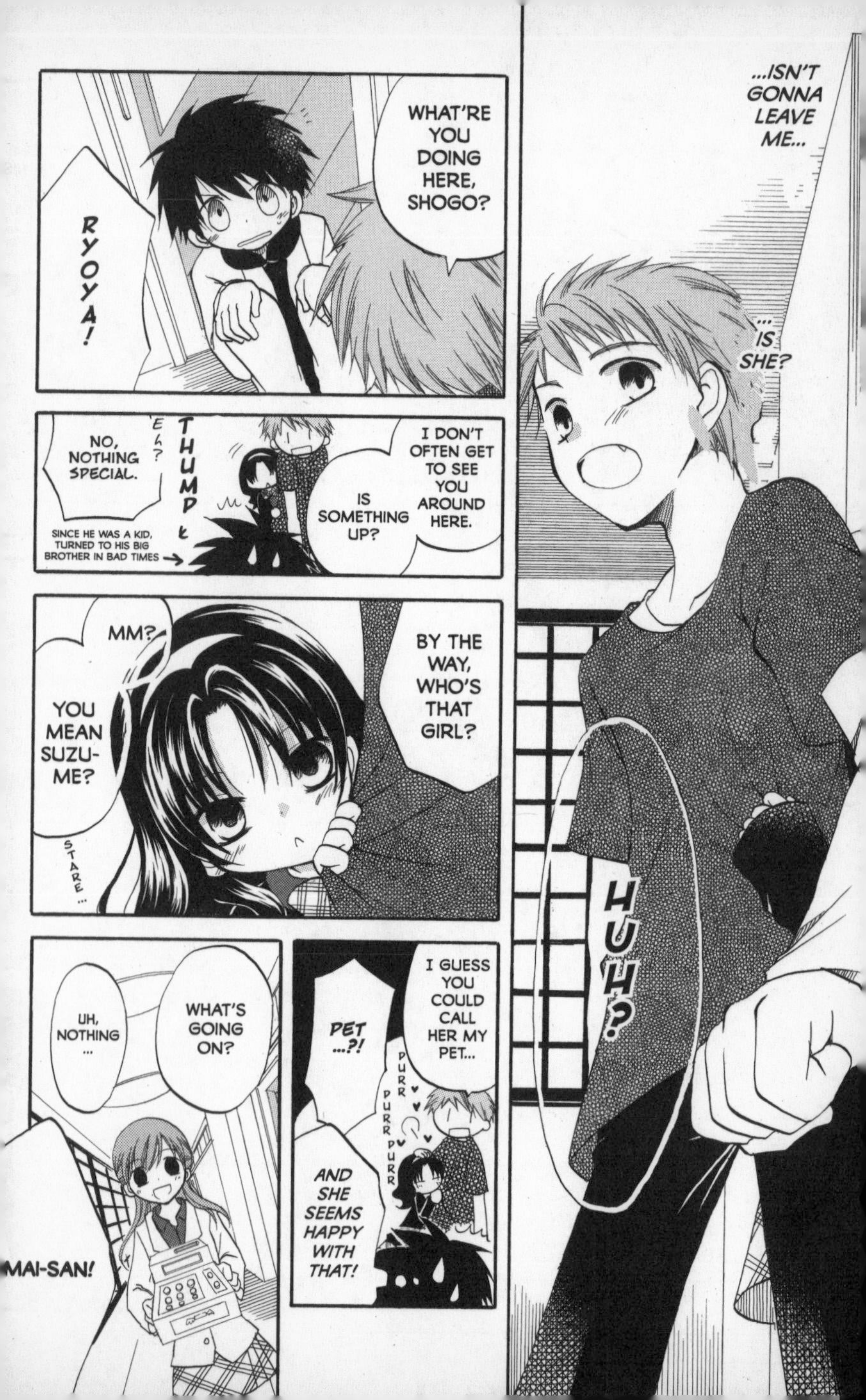
...ISN'T GONNA LEAVE ME...
...IS SHE?
HUH?
WHAT'RE YOU DOING HERE, SHOGO?
RYOYA!
I DON'T OFTEN GET TO SEE YOU AROUND HERE.
IS SOMETHING UP?
THUMP
NO, NOTHING SPECIAL.
SINCE HE WAS A KID, TURNED TO HIS BIG BROTHER IN BAD TIMES
BY THE WAY, WHO'S THAT GIRL?
MM?
YOU MEAN SUZUME?
STARE...
I GUESS YOU COULD CALL HER MY PET...
PET...?!
PURR PURR PURR
AND SHE SEEMS HAPPY WITH THAT!
WHAT'S GOING ON?
UH, NOTHING...
MAI-SAN!

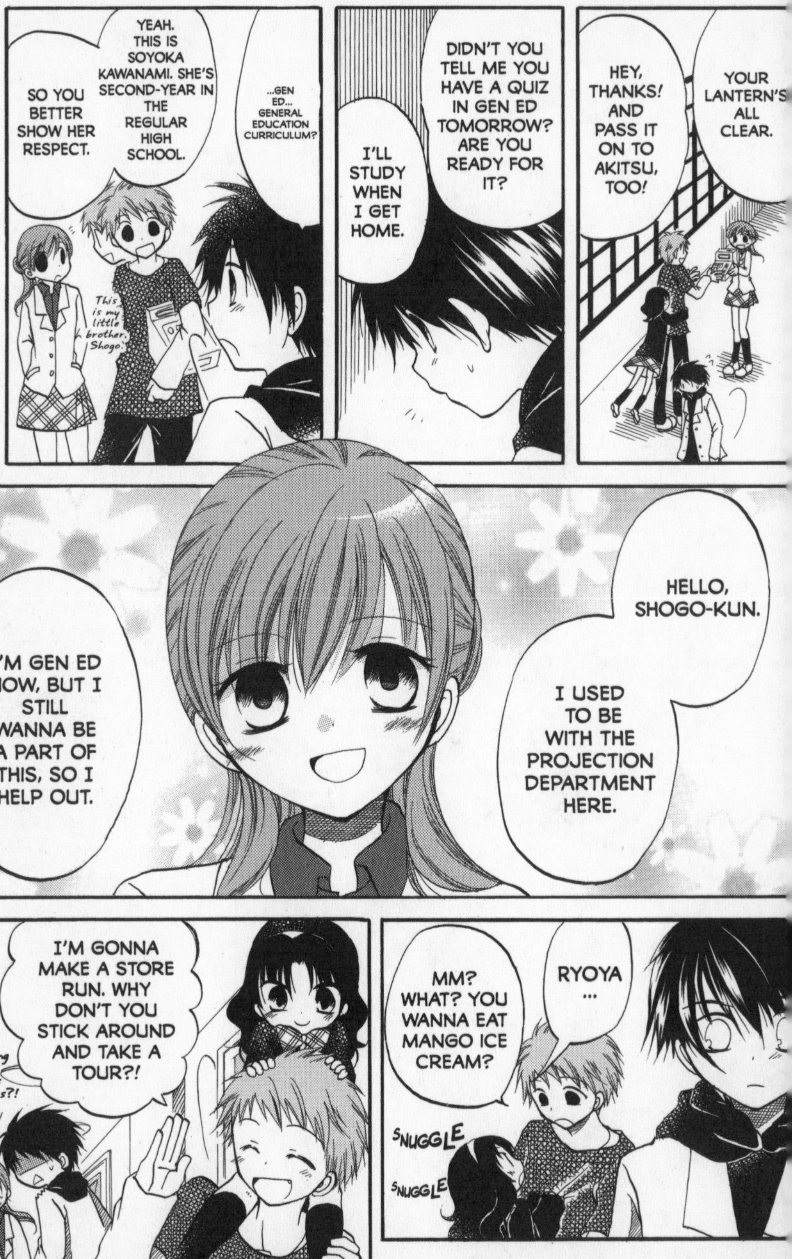
YOUR LANTERN'S ALL CLEAR.
HEY, THANKS! AND PASS IT ON TO AKITSU, TOO!
DIDN'T YOU TELL ME YOU HAVE A QUIZ IN GEN ED TOMORROW? ARE YOU READY FOR IT?
I'LL STUDY WHEN I GET HOME.
...GEN ED... GENERAL EDUCATION CURRICULUM?
YEAH. THIS IS SOYOKA KAWANAMI. SHE'S SECOND-YEAR IN THE REGULAR HIGH SCHOOL.
SO YOU BETTER SHOW HER RESPECT.
This is my little brother, Shogo.
HELLO, SHOGO-KUN.
I USED TO BE WITH THE PROJECTION DEPARTMENT HERE.
I'M GEN ED NOW, BUT I STILL WANNA BE A PART OF THIS, SO I HELP OUT.
RYOYA ...
MM? WHAT? YOU WANNA EAT MANGO ICE CREAM?
SNUGGLE
SNUGGLE
I'M GONNA MAKE A STORE RUN. WHY DON'T YOU STICK AROUND AND TAKE A TOUR?!
He's carrying her on his shoulders?!

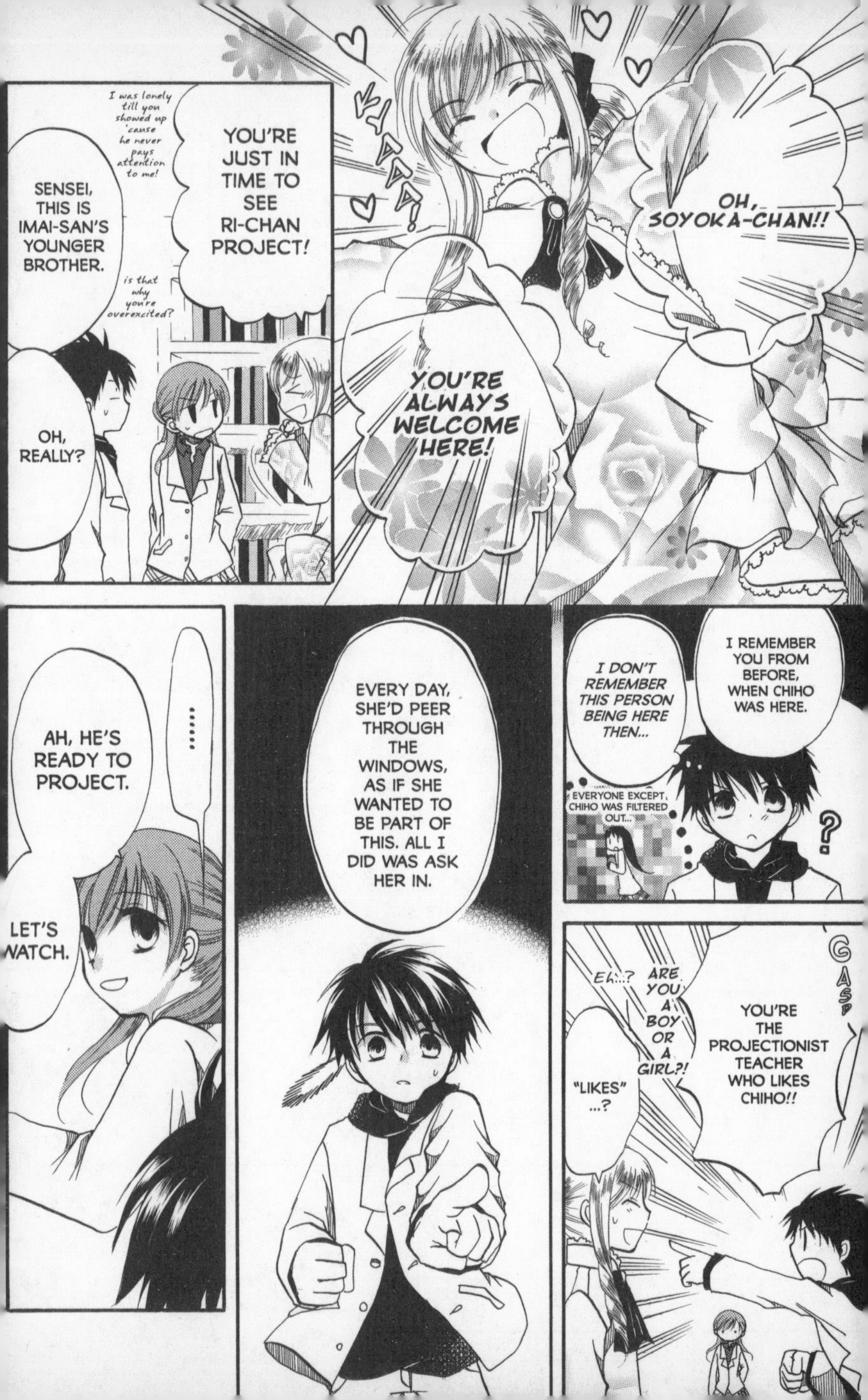
OH, SOYOKA-CHAN!!
KYAAA!
YOU'RE ALWAYS WELCOME HERE!
YOU'RE JUST IN TIME TO SEE RI-CHAN PROJECT!
I was lonely till you showed up 'cause he never pays attention to me!
SENSEI, THIS IS IMAI-SAN'S YOUNGER BROTHER.
is that why you're overexcited?
OH, REALLY?
I REMEMBER YOU FROM BEFORE, WHEN CHIHO WAS HERE.
I DON'T REMEMBER THIS PERSON BEING HERE THEN...
EVERYONE EXCEPT CHIHO WAS FILTERED OUT...
?
GASP
YOU'RE THE PROJECTIONIST TEACHER WHO LIKES CHIHO!!
ARE YOU A BOY OR A GIRL?!
Eh...?
"LIKES" ...?
EVERY DAY, SHE'D PEER THROUGH THE WINDOWS, AS IF SHE WANTED TO BE PART OF THIS. ALL I DID WAS ASK HER IN.
......
AH, HE'S READY TO PROJECT.
LET'S WATCH.

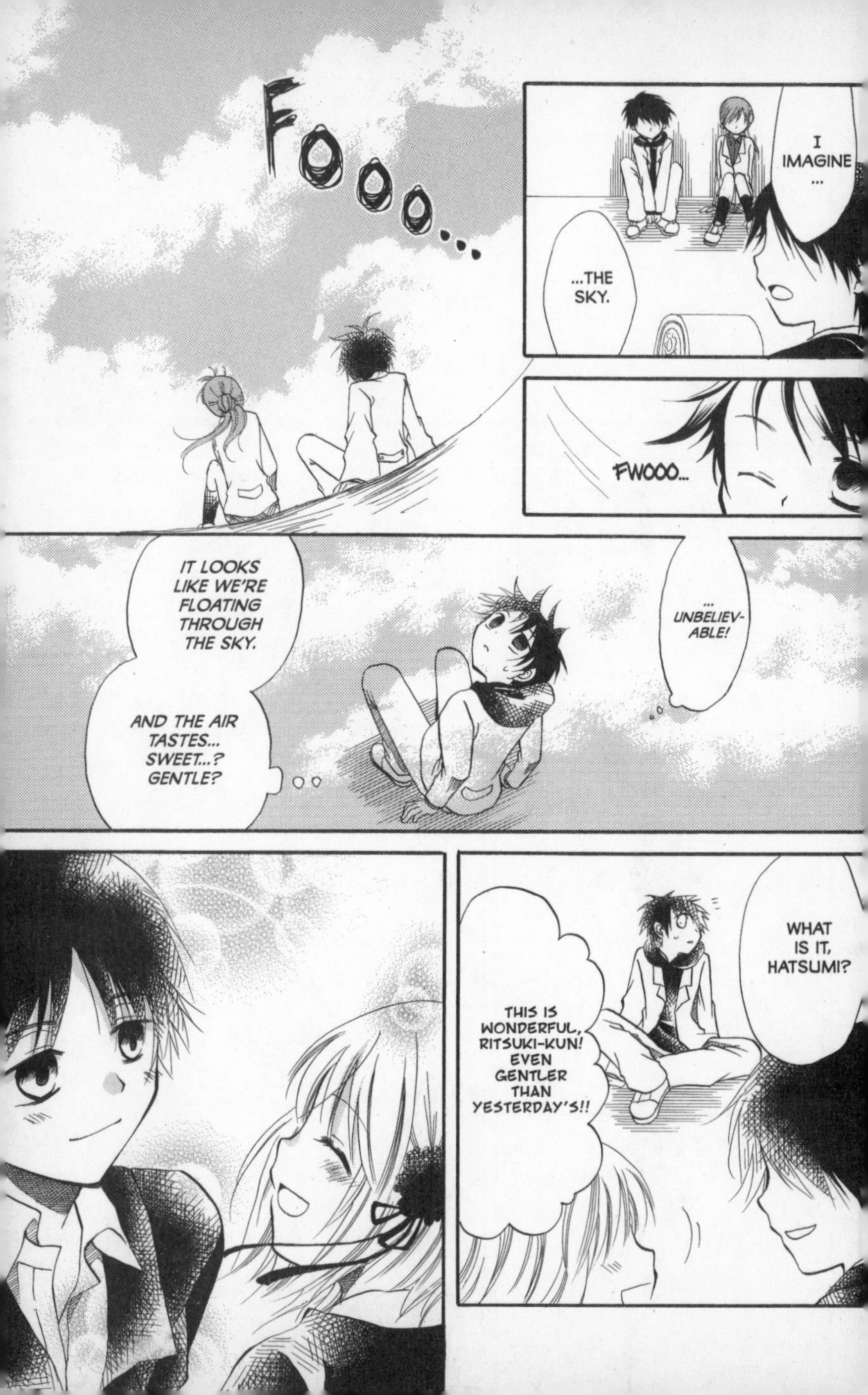
I IMAGINE ...
...THE SKY.
FWOOO...
FOOOO...
... UNBELIEVABLE!
IT LOOKS LIKE WE'RE FLOATING THROUGH THE SKY.
AND THE AIR TASTES... SWEET...? GENTLE?
WHAT IS IT, HATSUMI?
THIS IS WONDERFUL, RITSUKI-KUN! EVEN GENTLER THAN YESTERDAY'S!!

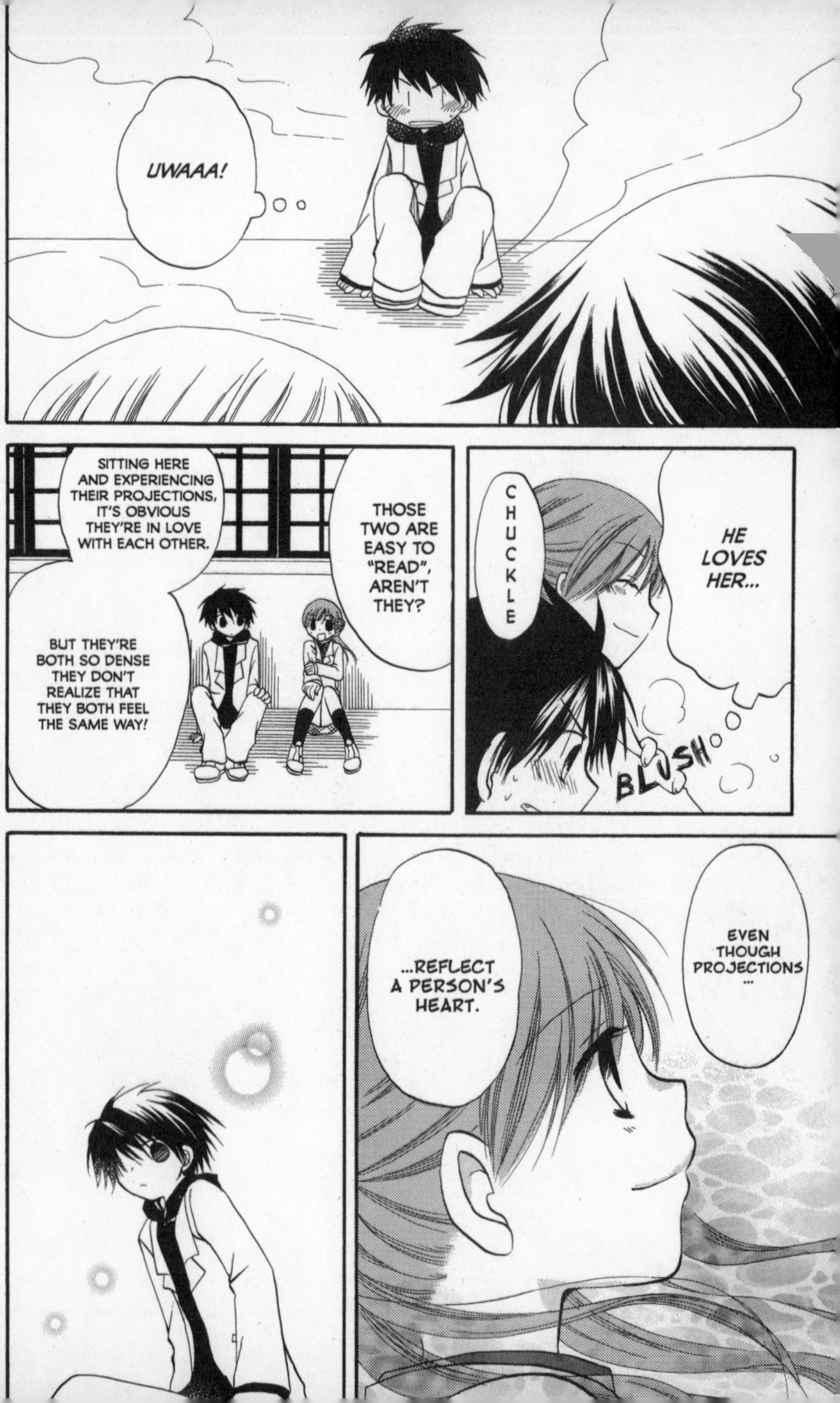
UWAAA!
HE LOVES HER...
CHUCKLE
BLUSH
THOSE TWO ARE EASY TO "READ", AREN'T THEY?
SITTING HERE AND EXPERIENCING THEIR PROJECTIONS, IT'S OBVIOUS THEY'RE IN LOVE WITH EACH OTHER.
BUT THEY'RE BOTH SO DENSE THEY DON'T REALIZE THAT THEY BOTH FEEL THE SAME WAY!
EVEN THOUGH PROJECTIONS ...
...REFLECT A PERSON'S HEART.

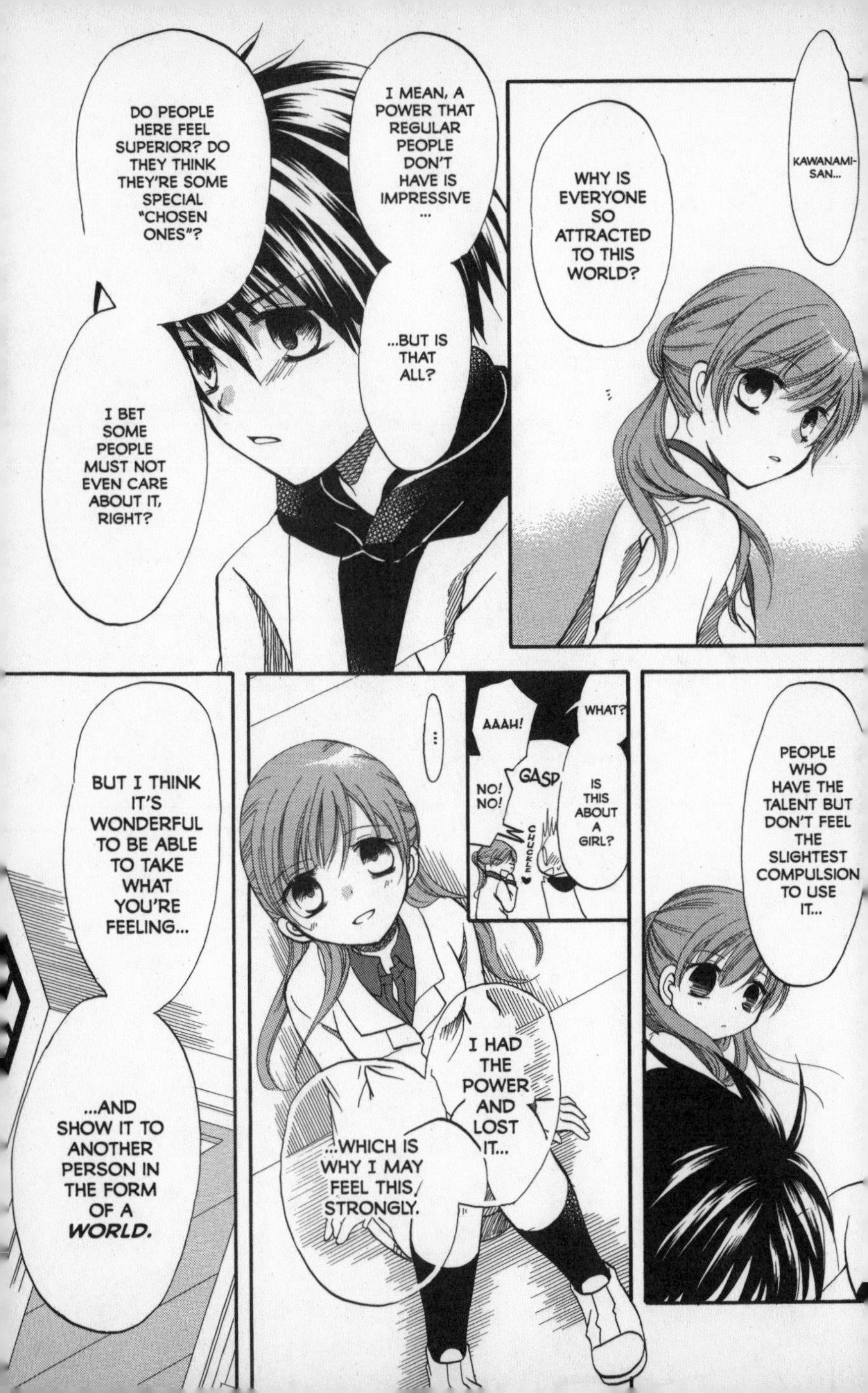
KAWANAMI-SAN...
WHY IS EVERYONE SO ATTRACTED TO THIS WORLD?
I MEAN, A POWER THAT REGULAR PEOPLE DON'T HAVE IS IMPRESSIVE...
DO PEOPLE HERE FEEL SUPERIOR? DO THEY THINK THEY'RE SOME SPECIAL "CHOSEN ONES"?
...BUT IS THAT ALL?
I BET SOME PEOPLE MUST NOT EVEN CARE ABOUT IT, RIGHT?
PEOPLE WHO HAVE THE TALENT BUT DON'T FEEL THE SLIGHTEST COMPULSION TO USE IT...
WHAT?
IS THIS ABOUT A GIRL?
AAAH!
GASP
NO! NO!
CHUCKLE
...
I HAD THE POWER AND LOST IT...
...WHICH IS WHY I MAY FEEL THIS STRONGLY.
BUT I THINK IT'S WONDERFUL TO BE ABLE TO TAKE WHAT YOU'RE FEELING...
...AND SHOW IT TO ANOTHER PERSON IN THE FORM OF A *WORLD.*

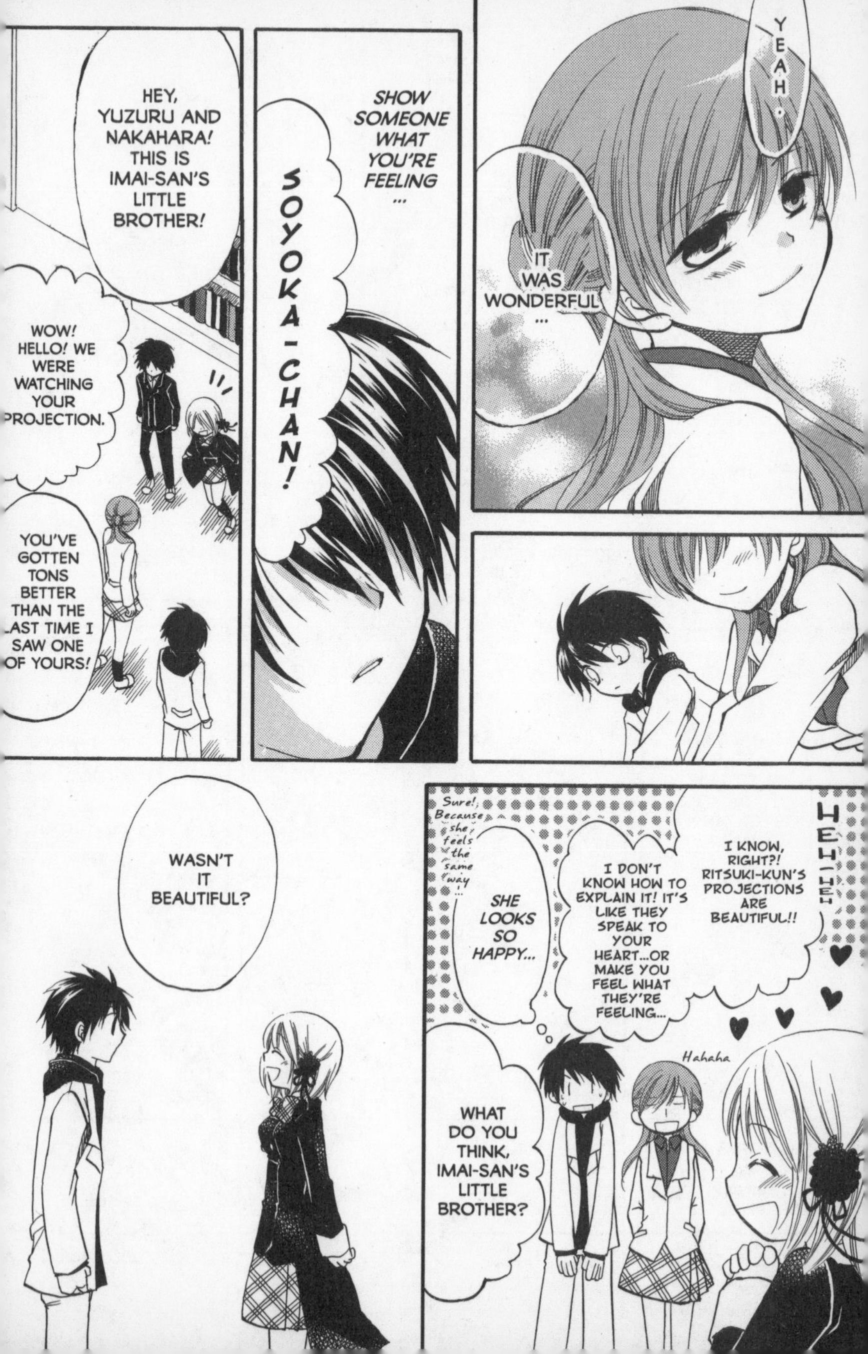
YEAH.
IT WAS WONDERFUL...
SHOW SOMEONE WHAT YOU'RE FEELING...
SOYOKA-CHAN!
HEY, YUZURU AND NAKAHARA! THIS IS IMAI-SAN'S LITTLE BROTHER!
WOW! HELLO! WE WERE WATCHING YOUR PROJECTION.
YOU'VE GOTTEN TONS BETTER THAN THE LAST TIME I SAW ONE OF YOURS!
HEH-HEH
I KNOW, RIGHT?! RITSUKI-KUN'S PROJECTIONS ARE BEAUTIFUL!!
I DON'T KNOW HOW TO EXPLAIN IT! IT'S LIKE THEY SPEAK TO YOUR HEART...OR MAKE YOU FEEL WHAT THEY'RE FEELING...
SHE LOOKS SO HAPPY...
Sure! Because she feels the same way...
Hahaha
WHAT DO YOU THINK, IMAI-SAN'S LITTLE BROTHER?
WASN'T IT BEAUTIFUL?

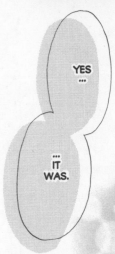

YES
...

...
IT
WAS.

I HATE
PROJECTIONISTS...
...BECAUSE THEY STEAL
EVERYTHING...

...IMPORTANT
FROM ME.
AND BECAUSE...

...I CAN'T BE PART
OF THEIR WORLD.

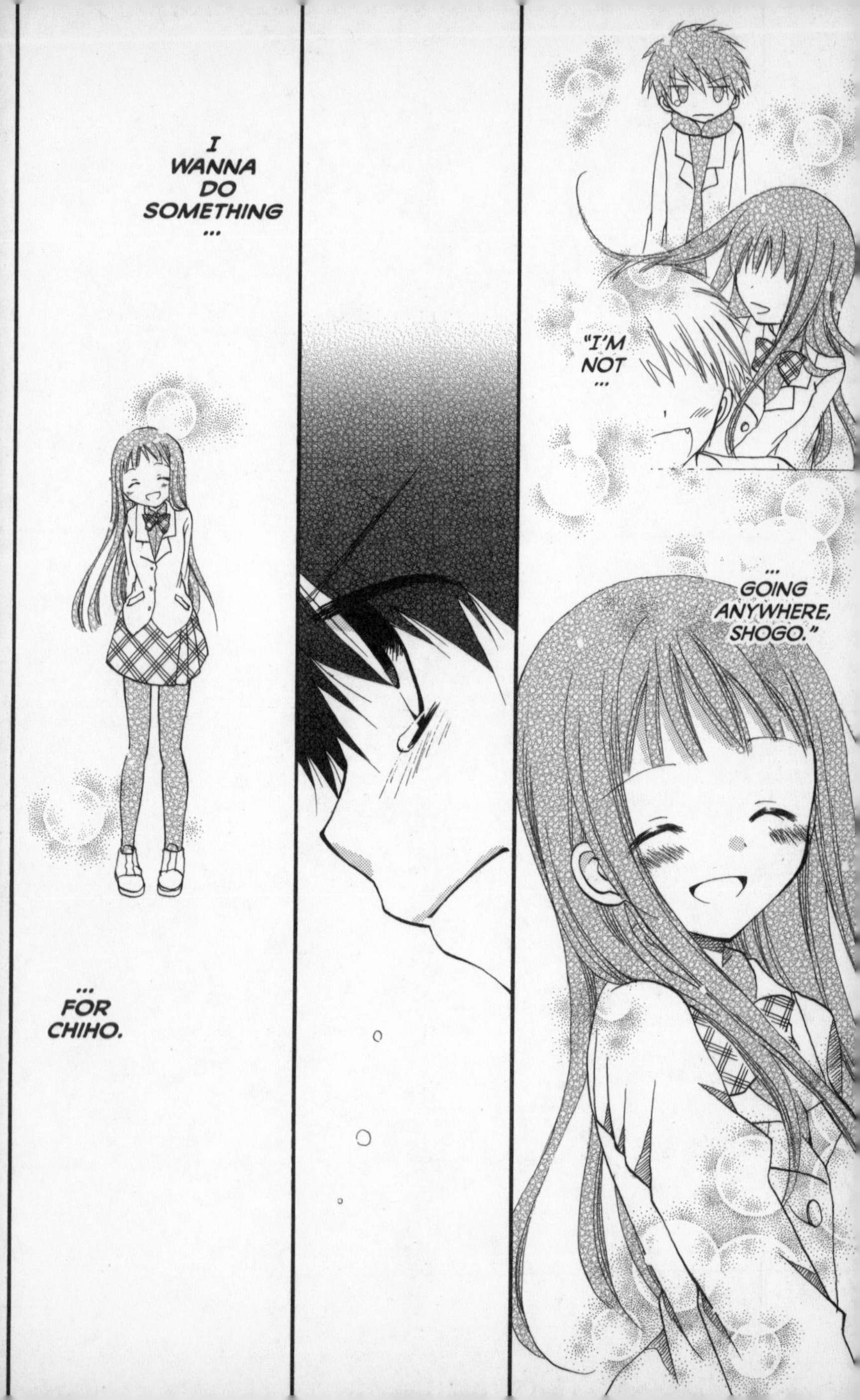
"I'M NOT ...
... GOING ANYWHERE, SHOGO."
I WANNA DO SOMETHING ...
... FOR CHIHO.

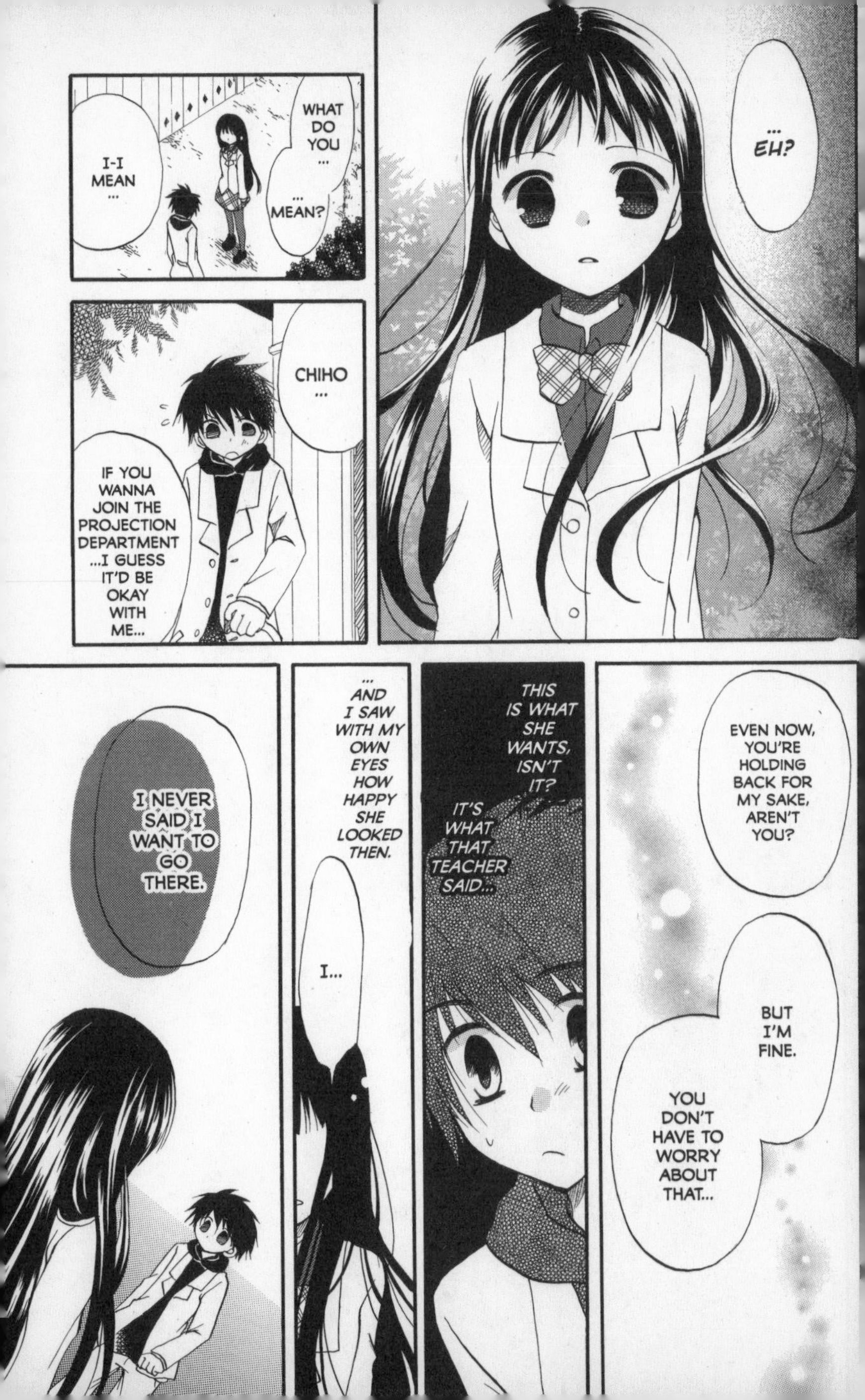
... EH?
WHAT DO YOU ... ... MEAN?
I-I MEAN ...
CHIHO ...
IF YOU WANNA JOIN THE PROJECTION DEPARTMENT ...I GUESS IT'D BE OKAY WITH ME...
EVEN NOW, YOU'RE HOLDING BACK FOR MY SAKE, AREN'T YOU?
BUT I'M FINE.
YOU DON'T HAVE TO WORRY ABOUT THAT...
THIS IS WHAT SHE WANTS, ISN'T IT?
IT'S WHAT THAT TEACHER SAID...
... AND I SAW WITH MY OWN EYES HOW HAPPY SHE LOOKED THEN.
I...
I NEVER SAID I WANT TO GO THERE.

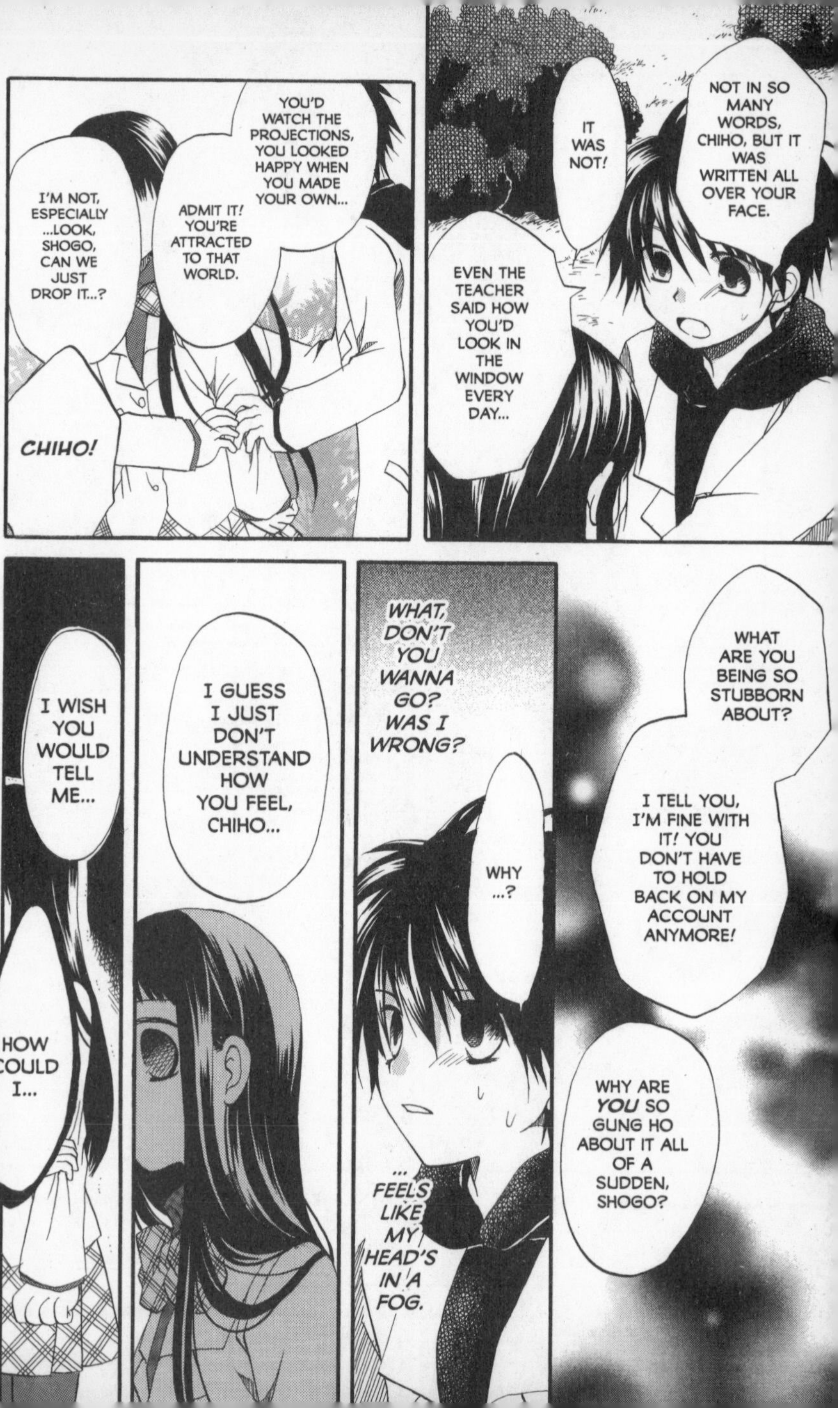
NOT IN SO MANY WORDS, CHIHO, BUT IT WAS WRITTEN ALL OVER YOUR FACE.
IT WAS NOT!
EVEN THE TEACHER SAID HOW YOU'D LOOK IN THE WINDOW EVERY DAY...
YOU'D WATCH THE PROJECTIONS, YOU LOOKED HAPPY WHEN YOU MADE YOUR OWN...
ADMIT IT! YOU'RE ATTRACTED TO THAT WORLD.
I'M NOT, ESPECIALLY ...LOOK, SHOGO, CAN WE JUST DROP IT...?
CHIHO!
WHAT ARE YOU BEING SO STUBBORN ABOUT?
I TELL YOU, I'M FINE WITH IT! YOU DON'T HAVE TO HOLD BACK ON MY ACCOUNT ANYMORE!
WHY ARE YOU SO GUNG HO ABOUT IT ALL OF A SUDDEN, SHOGO?
WHAT, DON'T YOU WANNA GO? WAS I WRONG?
WHY ...?
...FEELS LIKE MY HEAD'S IN A FOG.
I GUESS I JUST DON'T UNDERSTAND HOW YOU FEEL, CHIHO...
I WISH YOU WOULD TELL ME...
HOW COULD I...

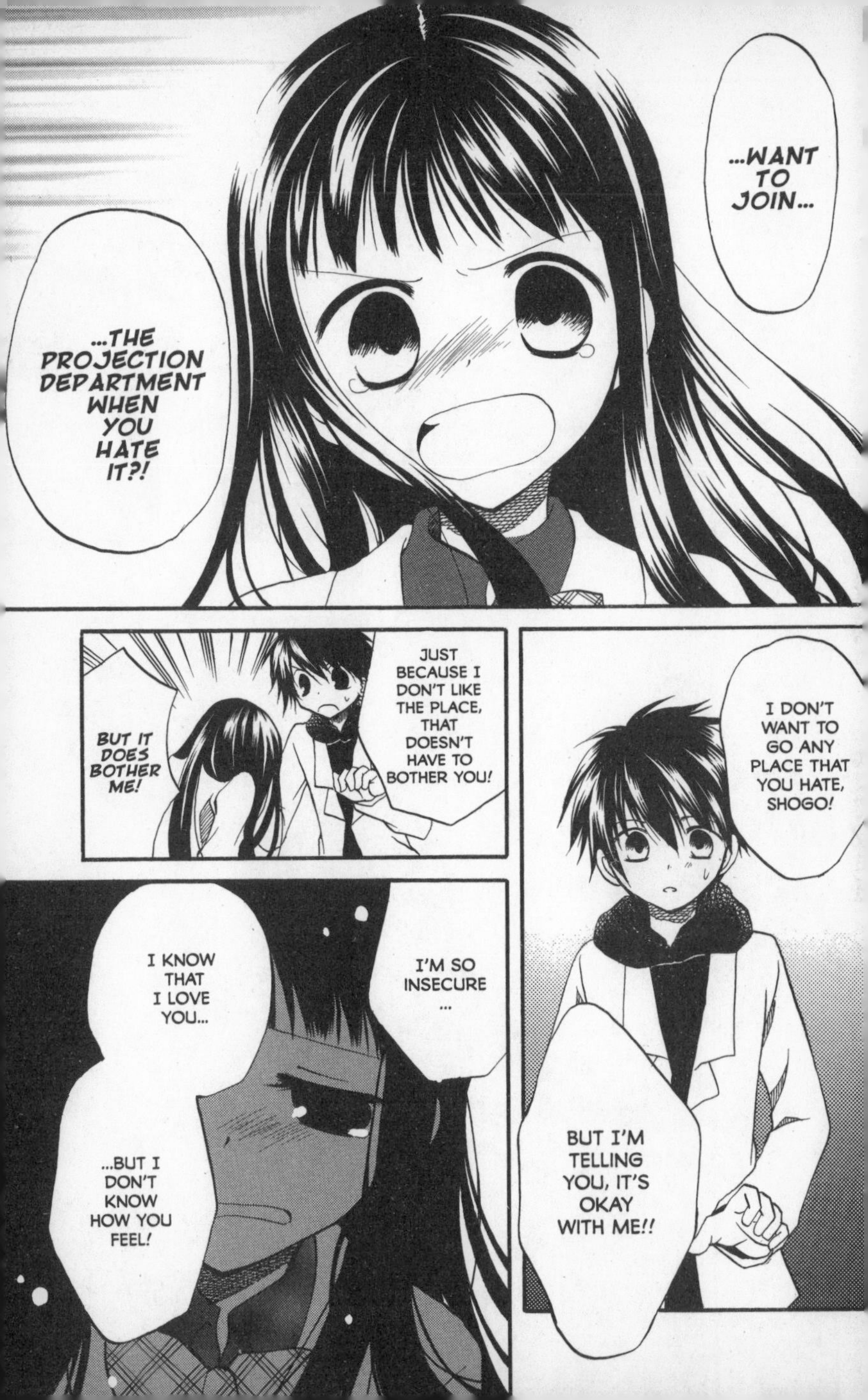
...WANT TO JOIN...
...THE PROJECTION DEPARTMENT WHEN YOU HATE IT?!
I DON'T WANT TO GO ANY PLACE THAT YOU HATE, SHOGO!
BUT I'M TELLING YOU, IT'S OKAY WITH ME!!
JUST BECAUSE I DON'T LIKE THE PLACE, THAT DOESN'T HAVE TO BOTHER YOU!
BUT IT DOES BOTHER ME!
I'M SO INSECURE ...
I KNOW THAT I LOVE YOU...
...BUT I DON'T KNOW HOW YOU FEEL!

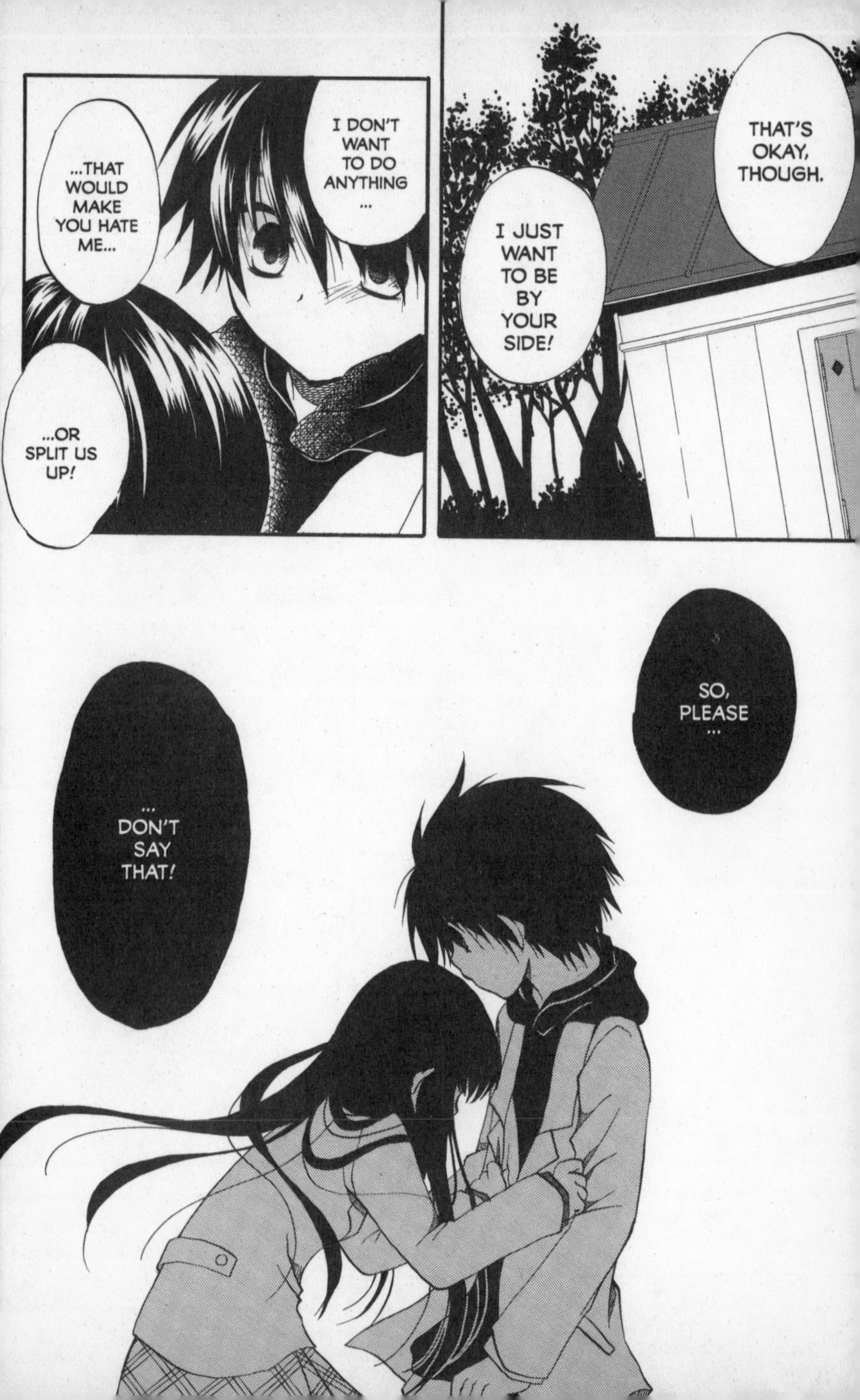
THAT'S OKAY, THOUGH.
I JUST WANT TO BE BY YOUR SIDE!
I DON'T WANT TO DO ANYTHING...
...THAT WOULD MAKE YOU HATE ME...
...OR SPLIT US UP!
SO, PLEASE...
...DON'T SAY THAT!

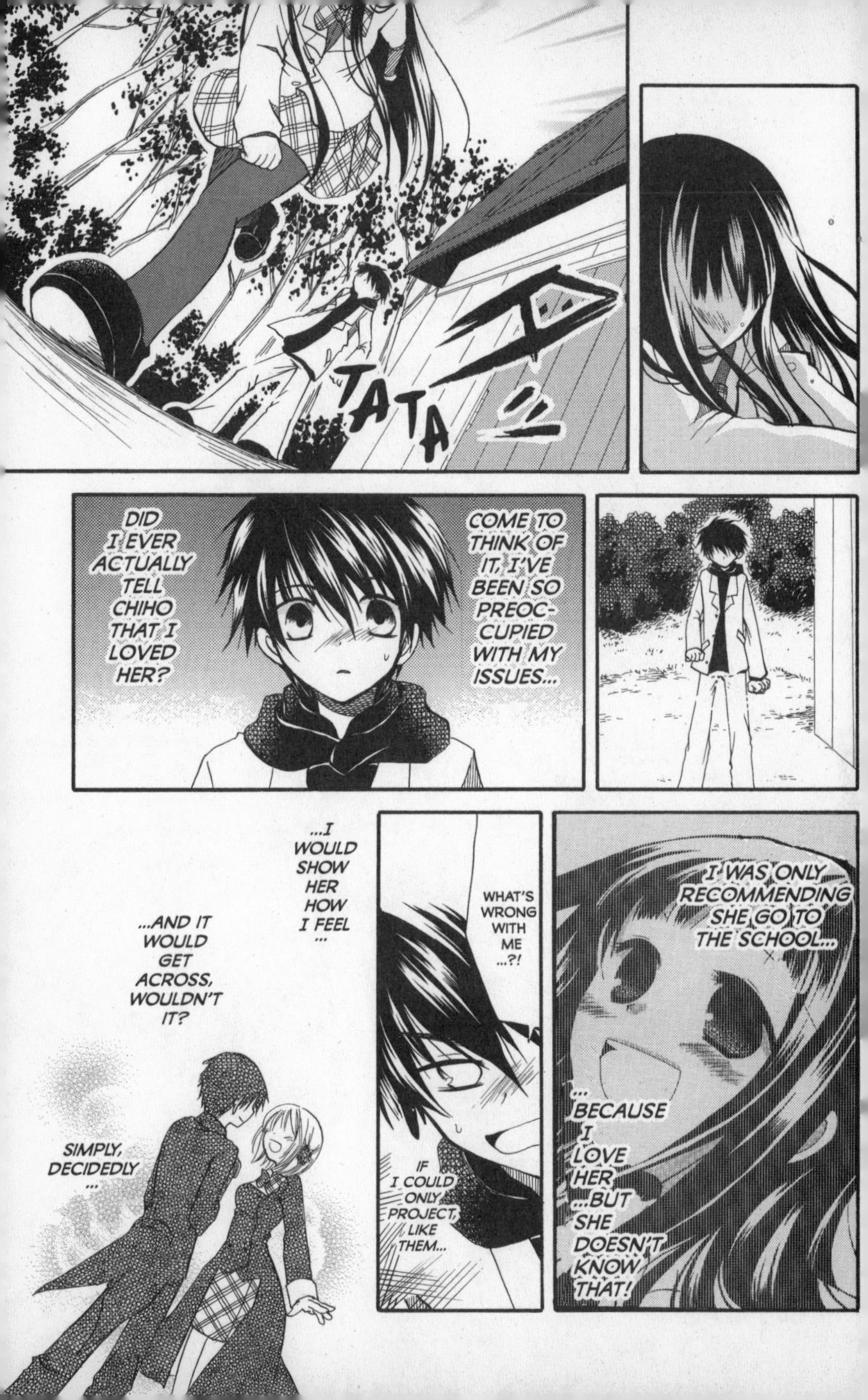
TATA
COME TO THINK OF IT, I'VE BEEN SO PREOCCUPIED WITH MY ISSUES...
DID I EVER ACTUALLY TELL CHIHO THAT I LOVED HER?
I WAS ONLY RECOMMENDING SHE GO TO THE SCHOOL...
...BECAUSE I LOVE HER ...BUT SHE DOESN'T KNOW THAT!
WHAT'S WRONG WITH ME ...?!
IF I COULD ONLY PROJECT, LIKE THEM...
...I WOULD SHOW HER HOW I FEEL...
...AND IT WOULD GET ACROSS, WOULDN'T IT?
SIMPLY, DECIDEDLY...

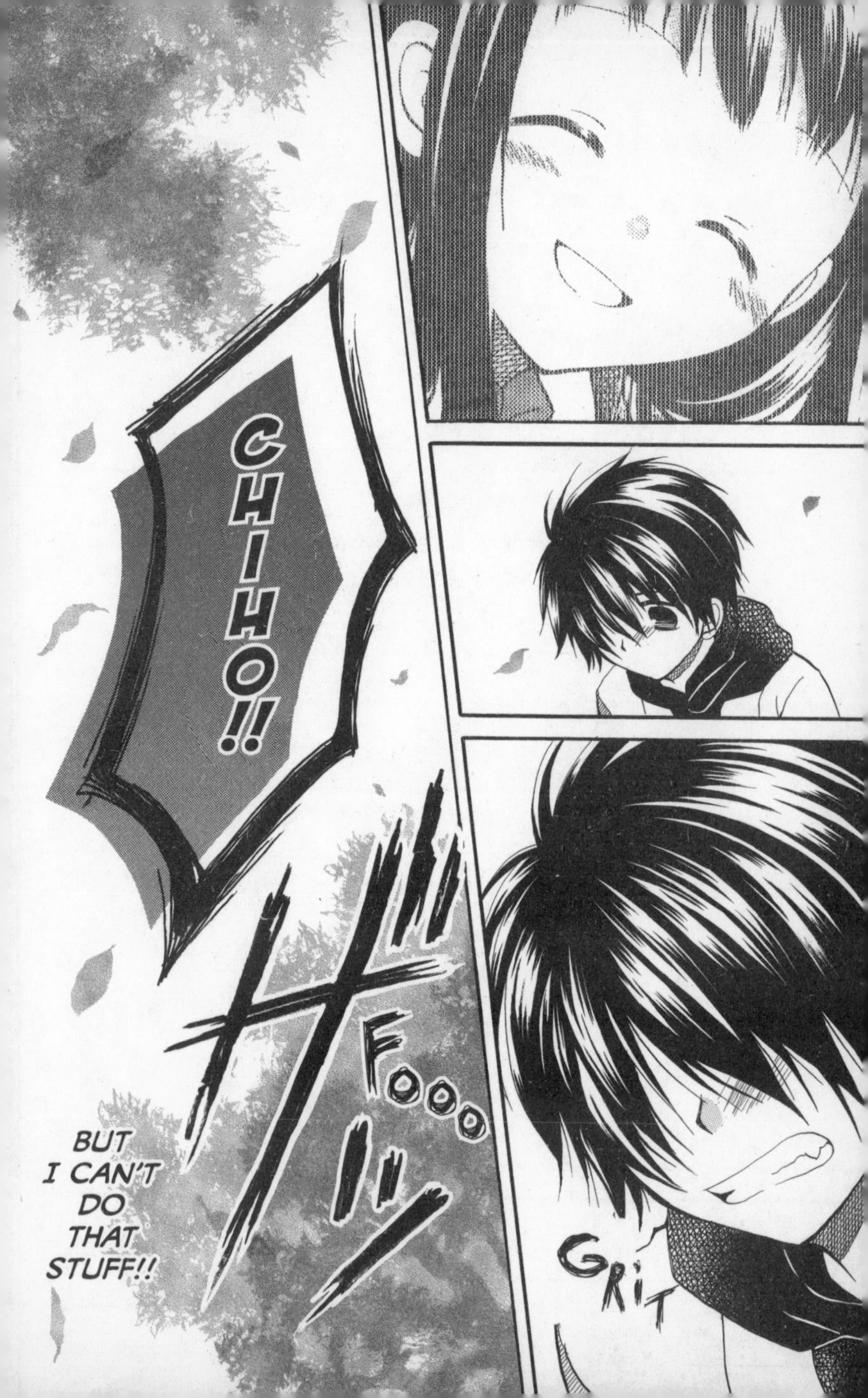
GRIT
CHIHO!!
FOOO
BUT I CAN'T DO THAT STUFF!!

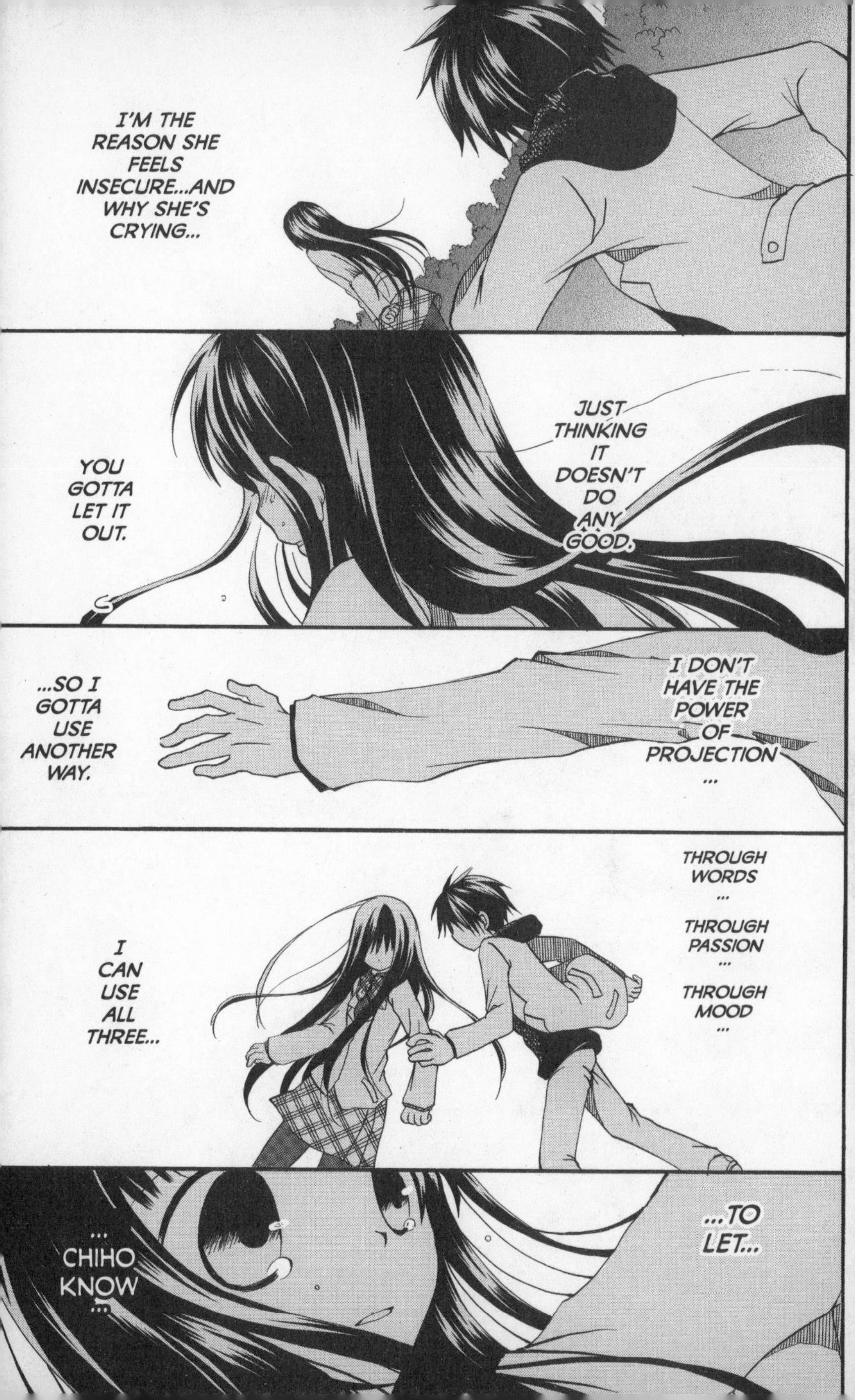

I'M THE REASON SHE FEELS INSECURE...AND WHY SHE'S CRYING...
JUST THINKING IT DOESN'T DO ANY GOOD.
YOU GOTTA LET IT OUT.
I DON'T HAVE THE POWER OF PROJECTION ...
...SO I GOTTA USE ANOTHER WAY.
THROUGH WORDS ...
THROUGH PASSION ...
THROUGH MOOD ...
I CAN USE ALL THREE...
...TO LET...
... CHIHO KNOW ...

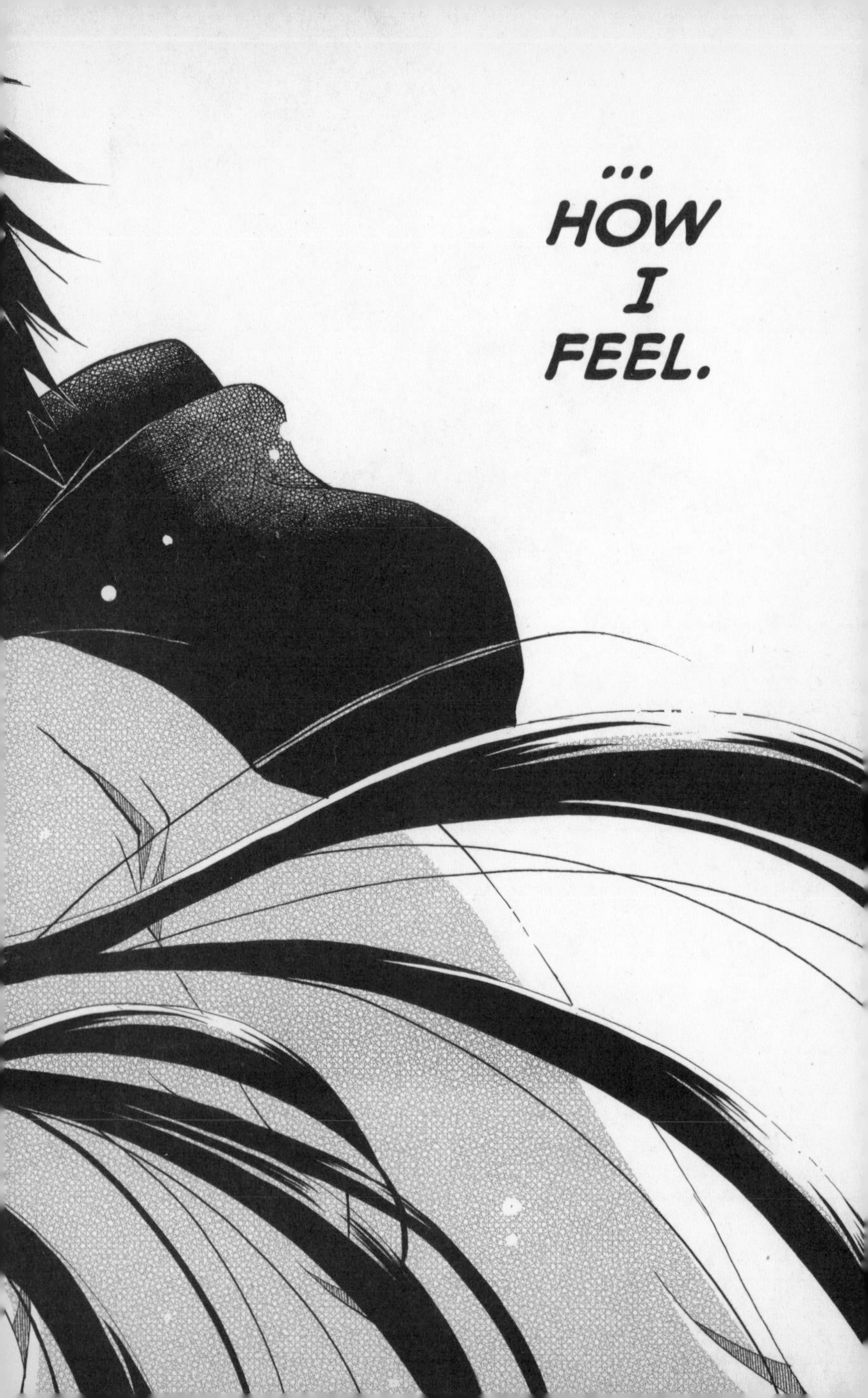
...HOW I FEEL.

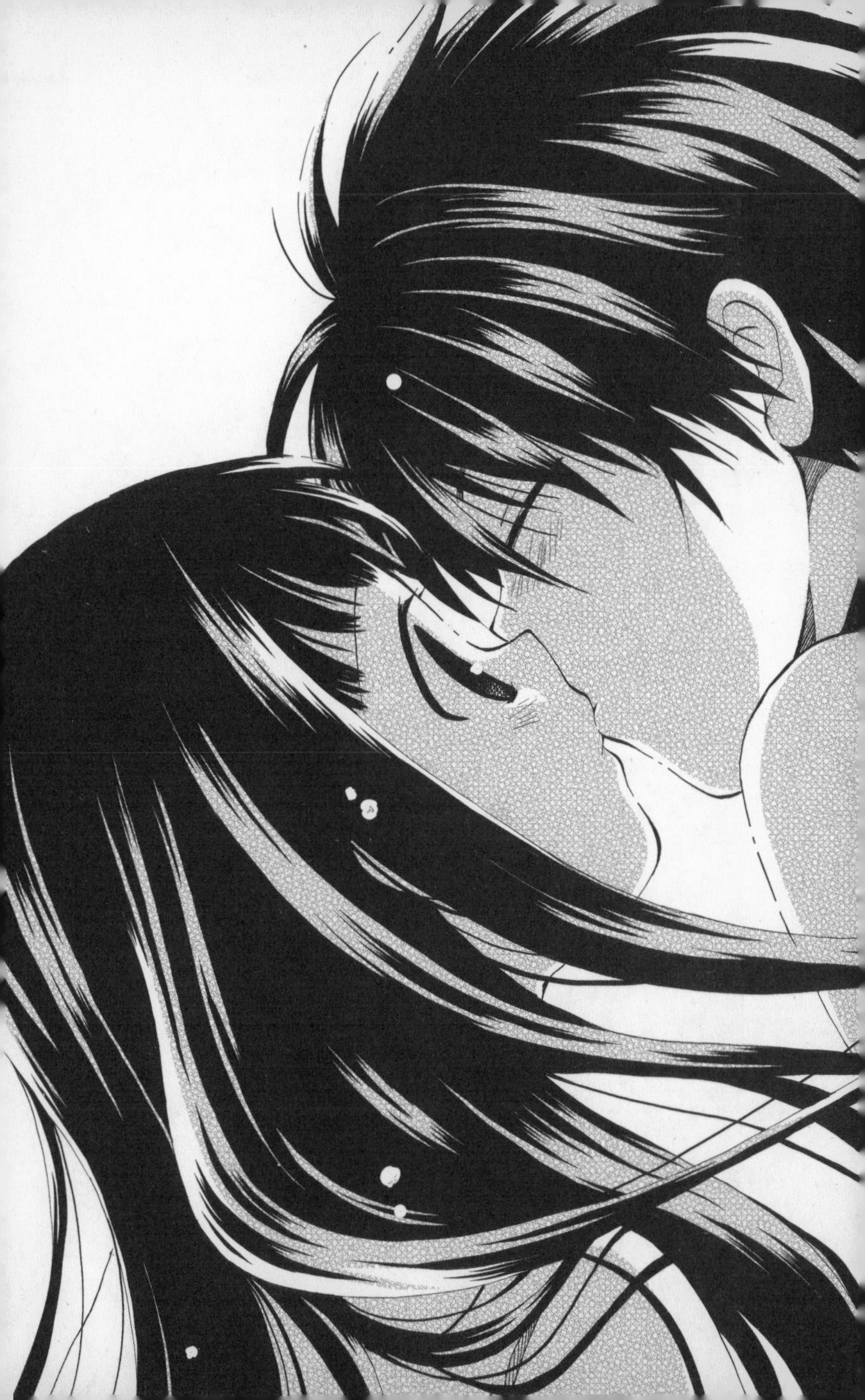

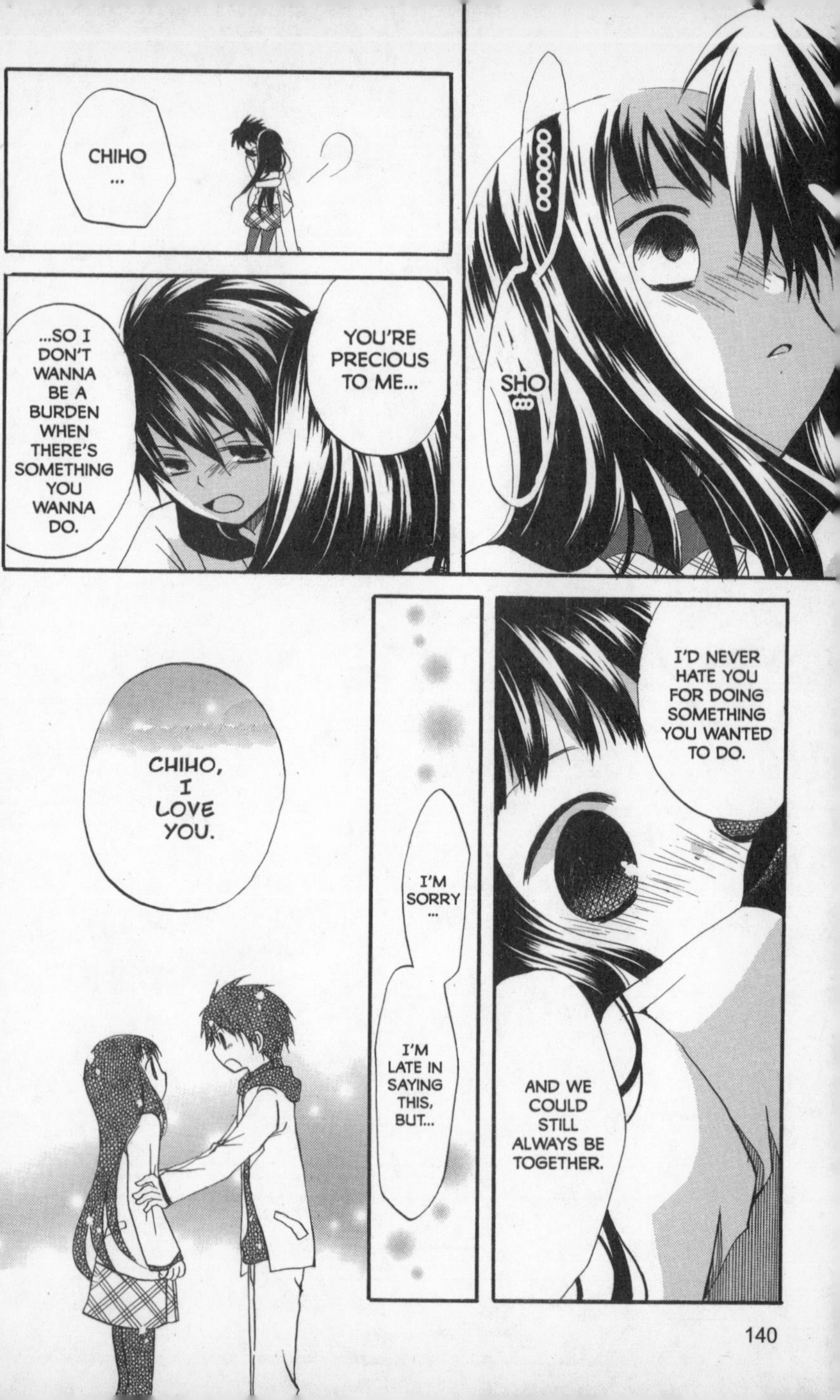
SHO...
CHIHO ...
YOU'RE PRECIOUS TO ME...
...SO I DON'T WANNA BE A BURDEN WHEN THERE'S SOMETHING YOU WANNA DO.
I'D NEVER HATE YOU FOR DOING SOMETHING YOU WANTED TO DO.
AND WE COULD STILL ALWAYS BE TOGETHER.
I'M SORRY ...
I'M LATE IN SAYING THIS, BUT...
CHIHO, I LOVE YOU.

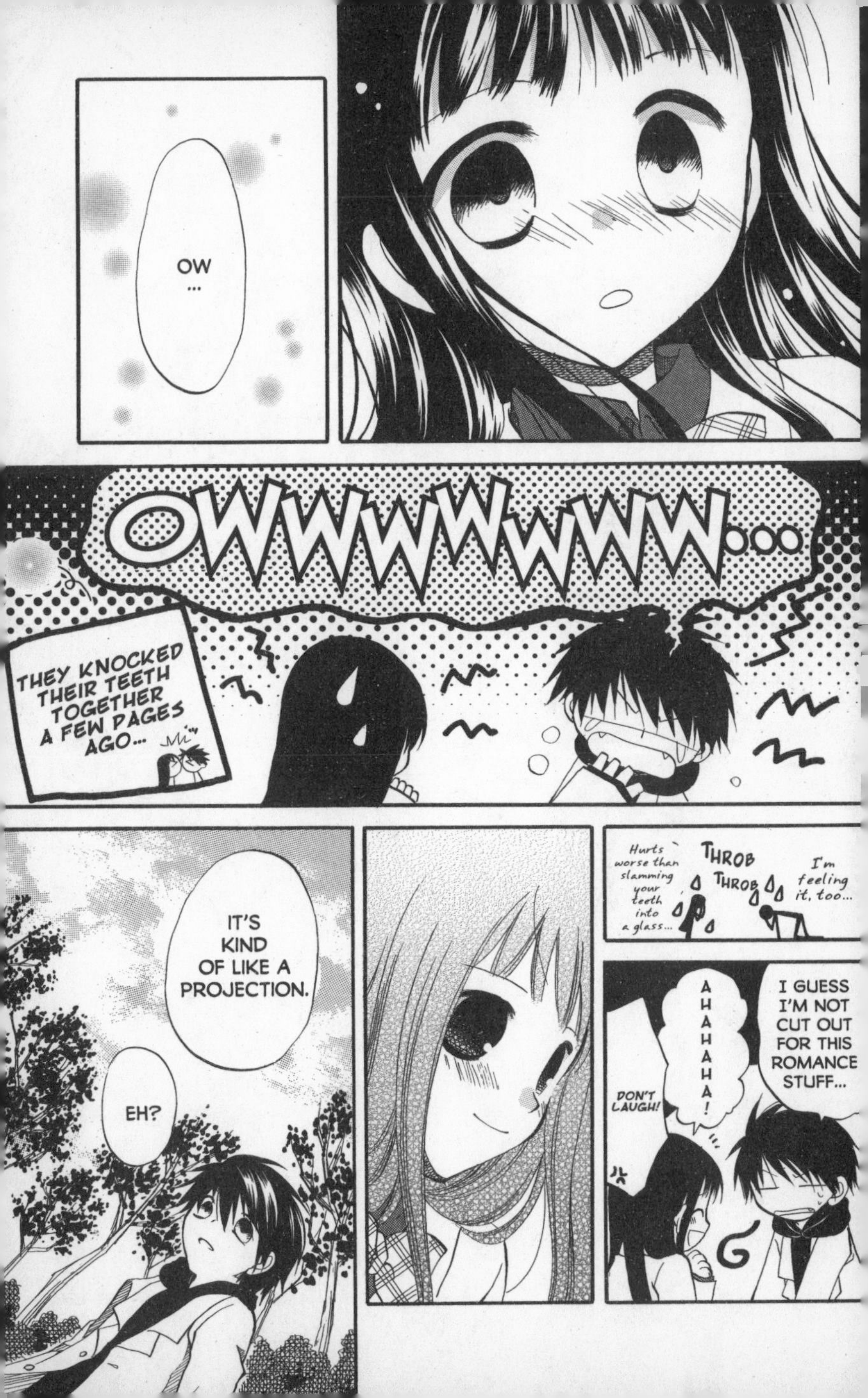
OW ...
OWWWWWWW...
THEY KNOCKED THEIR TEETH TOGETHER A FEW PAGES AGO...
I'm feeling it, too...
THROB THROB
Hurts worse than slamming your teeth into a glass...
I GUESS I'M NOT CUT OUT FOR THIS ROMANCE STUFF...
AHAHAHAHA!
DON'T LAUGH!
IT'S KIND OF LIKE A PROJECTION.
EH?

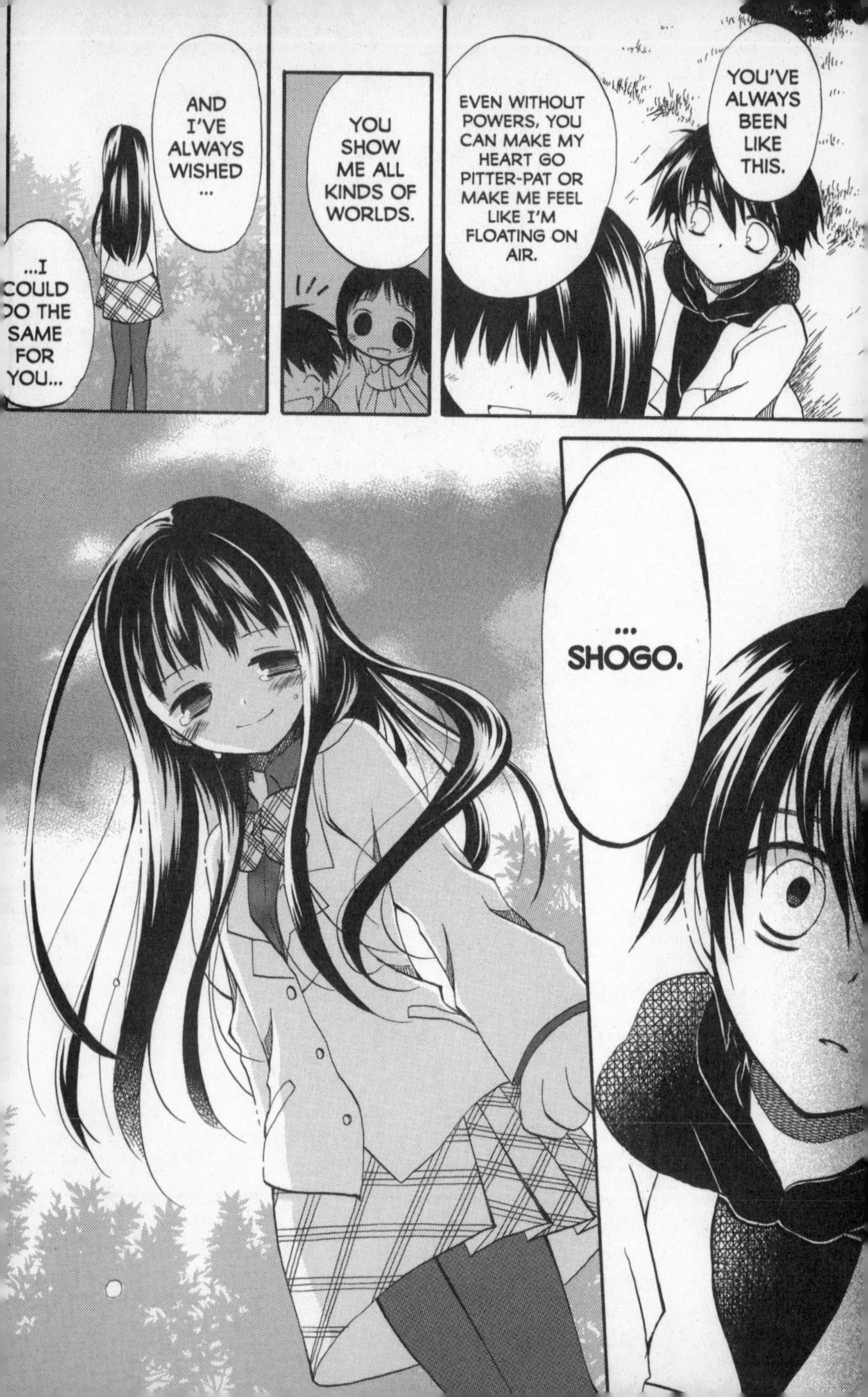
YOU'VE ALWAYS BEEN LIKE THIS.
EVEN WITHOUT POWERS, YOU CAN MAKE MY HEART GO PITTER-PAT OR MAKE ME FEEL LIKE I'M FLOATING ON AIR.
YOU SHOW ME ALL KINDS OF WORLDS.
AND I'VE ALWAYS WISHED ...
...I COULD DO THE SAME FOR YOU...
... SHOGO.

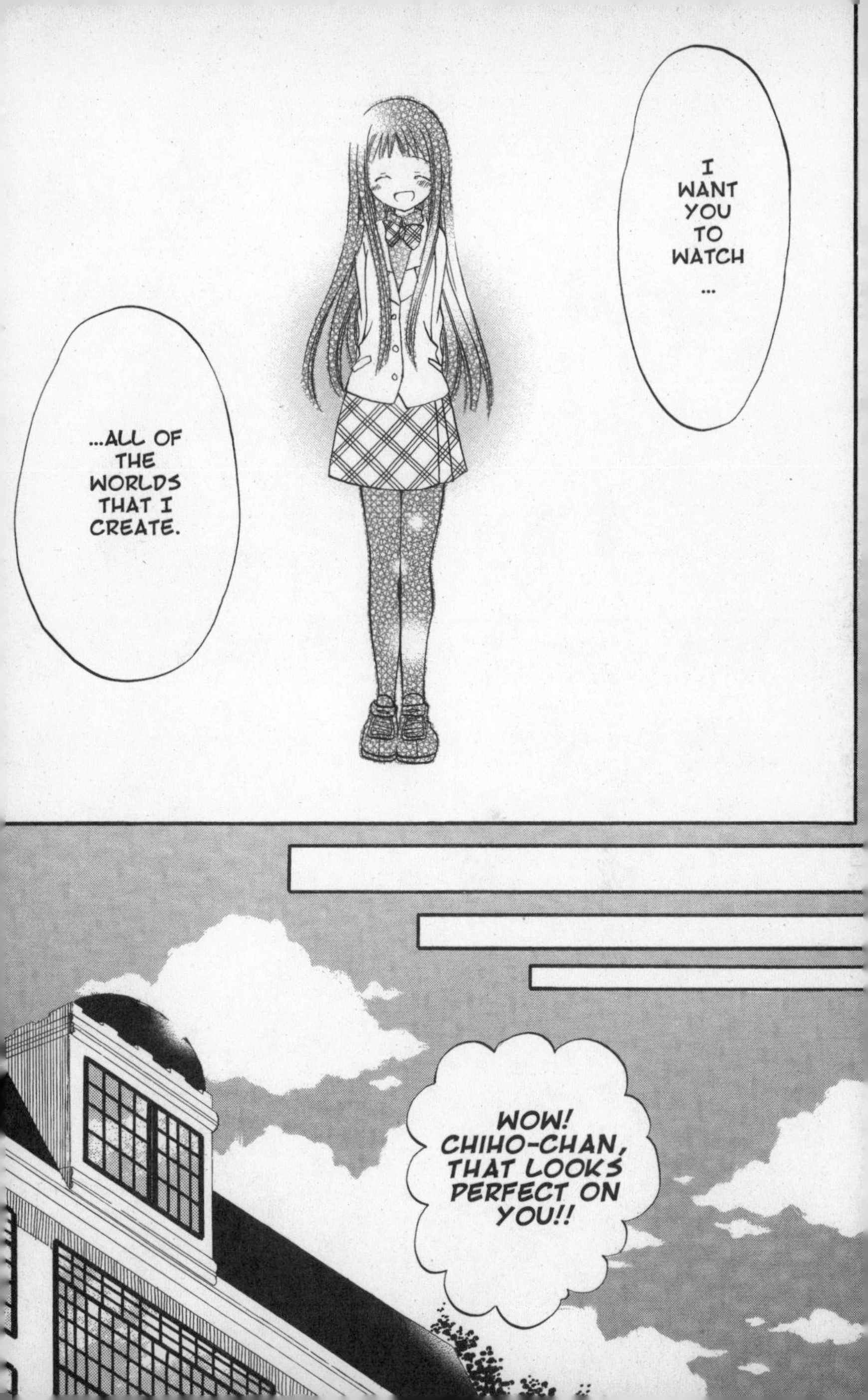
I WANT YOU TO WATCH...
...ALL OF THE WORLDS THAT I CREATE.
WOW! CHIHO-CHAN, THAT LOOKS PERFECT ON YOU!!

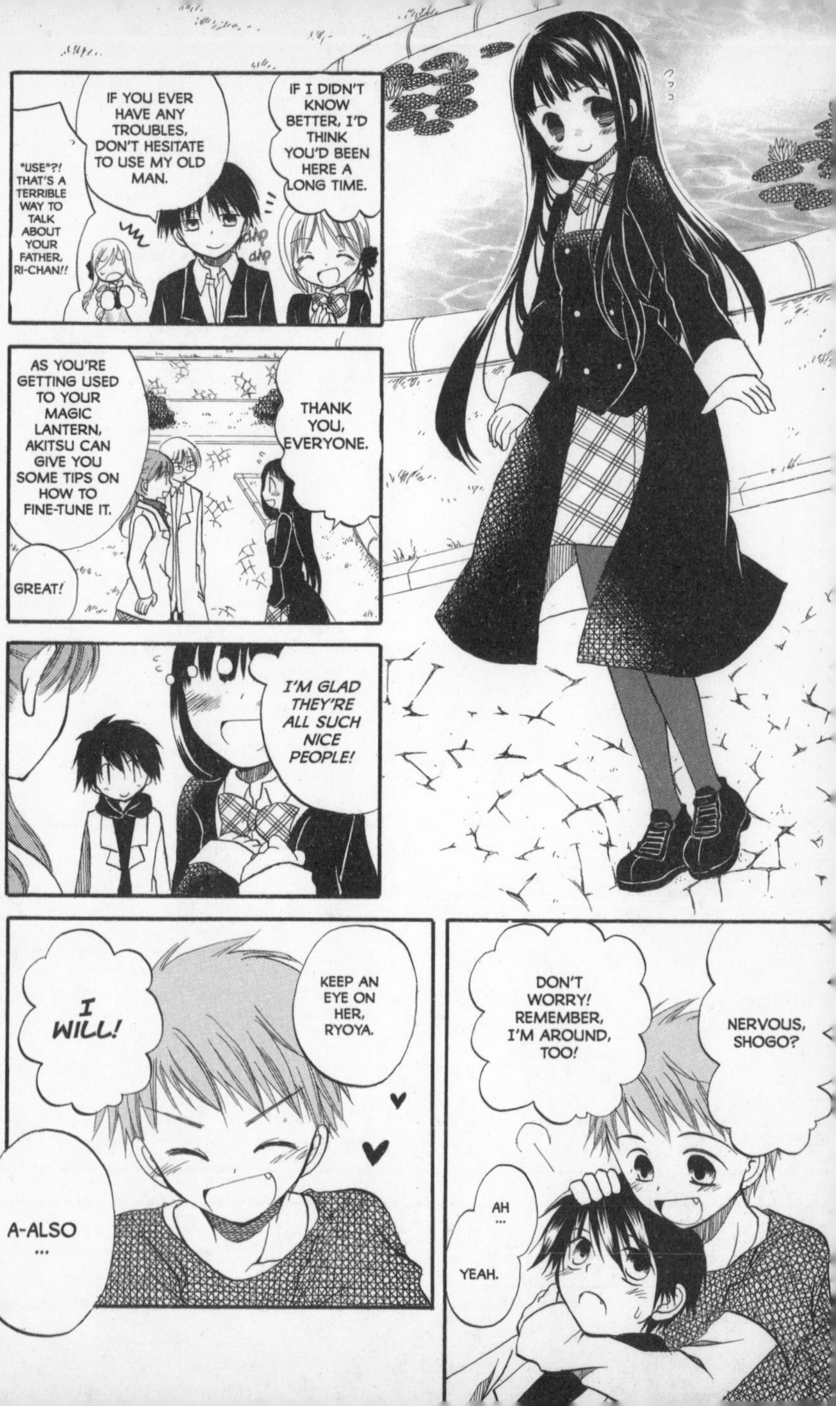
IF I DIDN'T KNOW BETTER, I'D THINK YOU'D BEEN HERE A LONG TIME.
IF YOU EVER HAVE ANY TROUBLES, DON'T HESITATE TO USE MY OLD MAN.
"USE"?! THAT'S A TERRIBLE WAY TO TALK ABOUT YOUR FATHER, RI-CHAN!!
THANK YOU, EVERYONE.
AS YOU'RE GETTING USED TO YOUR MAGIC LANTERN, AKITSU CAN GIVE YOU SOME TIPS ON HOW TO FINE-TUNE IT.
GREAT!
I'M GLAD THEY'RE ALL SUCH NICE PEOPLE!
NERVOUS, SHOGO?
DON'T WORRY! REMEMBER, I'M AROUND, TOO!
AH ...
YEAH.
KEEP AN EYE ON HER, RYOYA.
I WILL!
A-ALSO ...

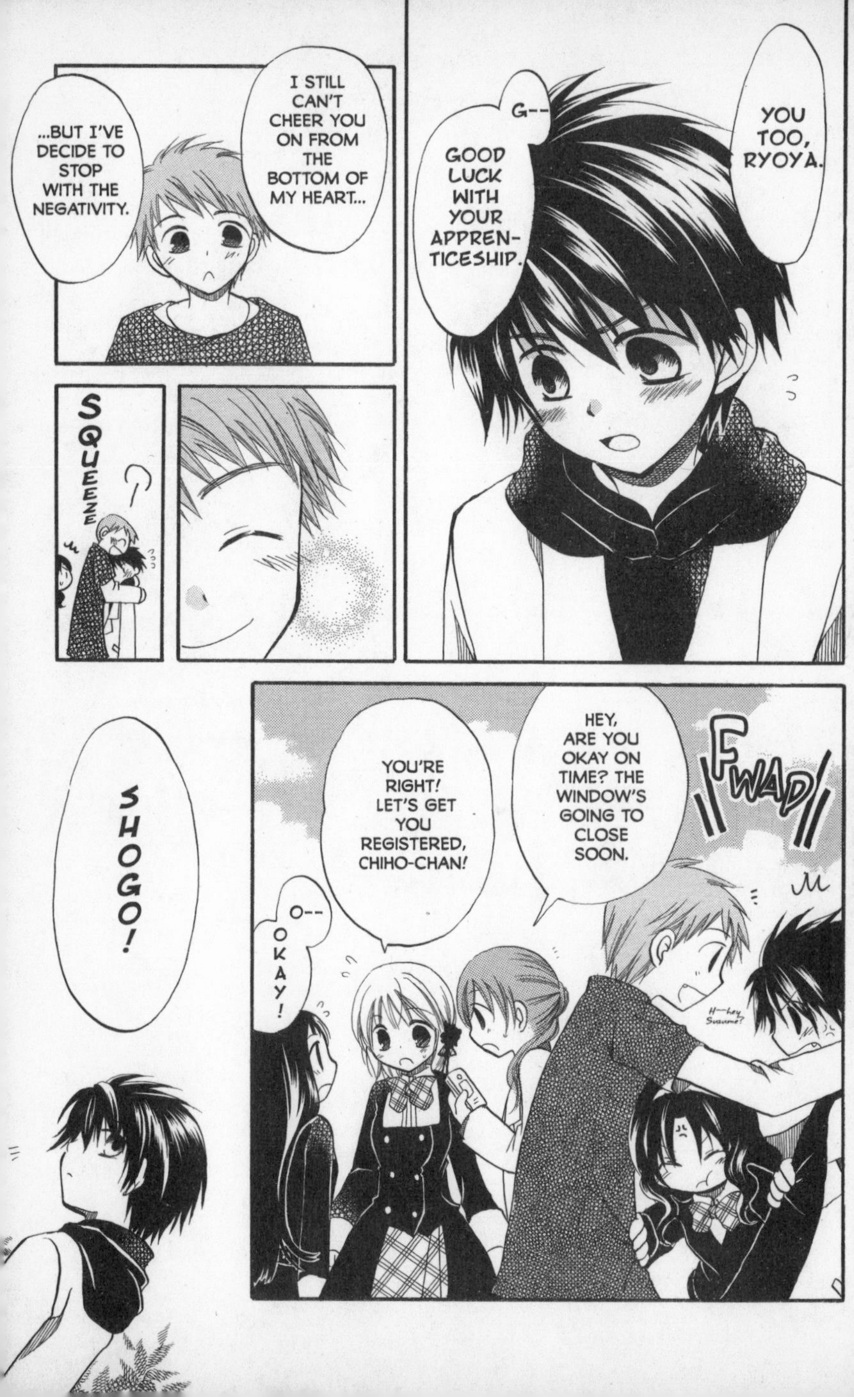
YOU TOO, RYOYA.
G--
GOOD LUCK WITH YOUR APPREN-TICESHIP.
I STILL CAN'T CHEER YOU ON FROM THE BOTTOM OF MY HEART...
...BUT I'VE DECIDE TO STOP WITH THE NEGATIVITY.
SQUEEZE
FWAD
HEY, ARE YOU OKAY ON TIME? THE WINDOW'S GOING TO CLOSE SOON.
H--hey Susume?
YOU'RE RIGHT! LET'S GET YOU REGISTERED, CHIHO-CHAN!
O-- OKAY!
SHOGO!

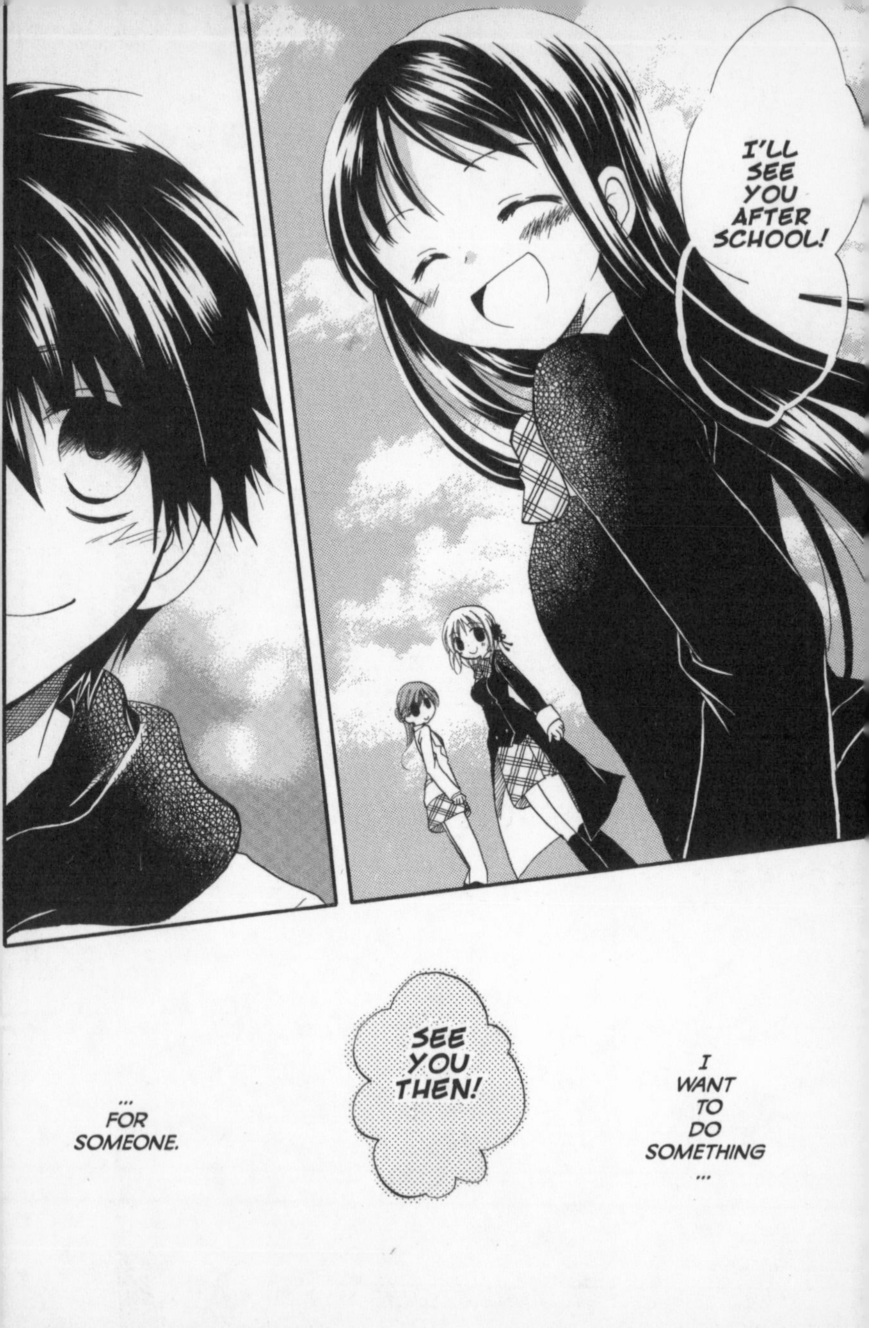
I'LL SEE YOU AFTER SCHOOL!
I WANT TO DO SOMETHING ...
SEE YOU THEN!
... FOR SOMEONE.

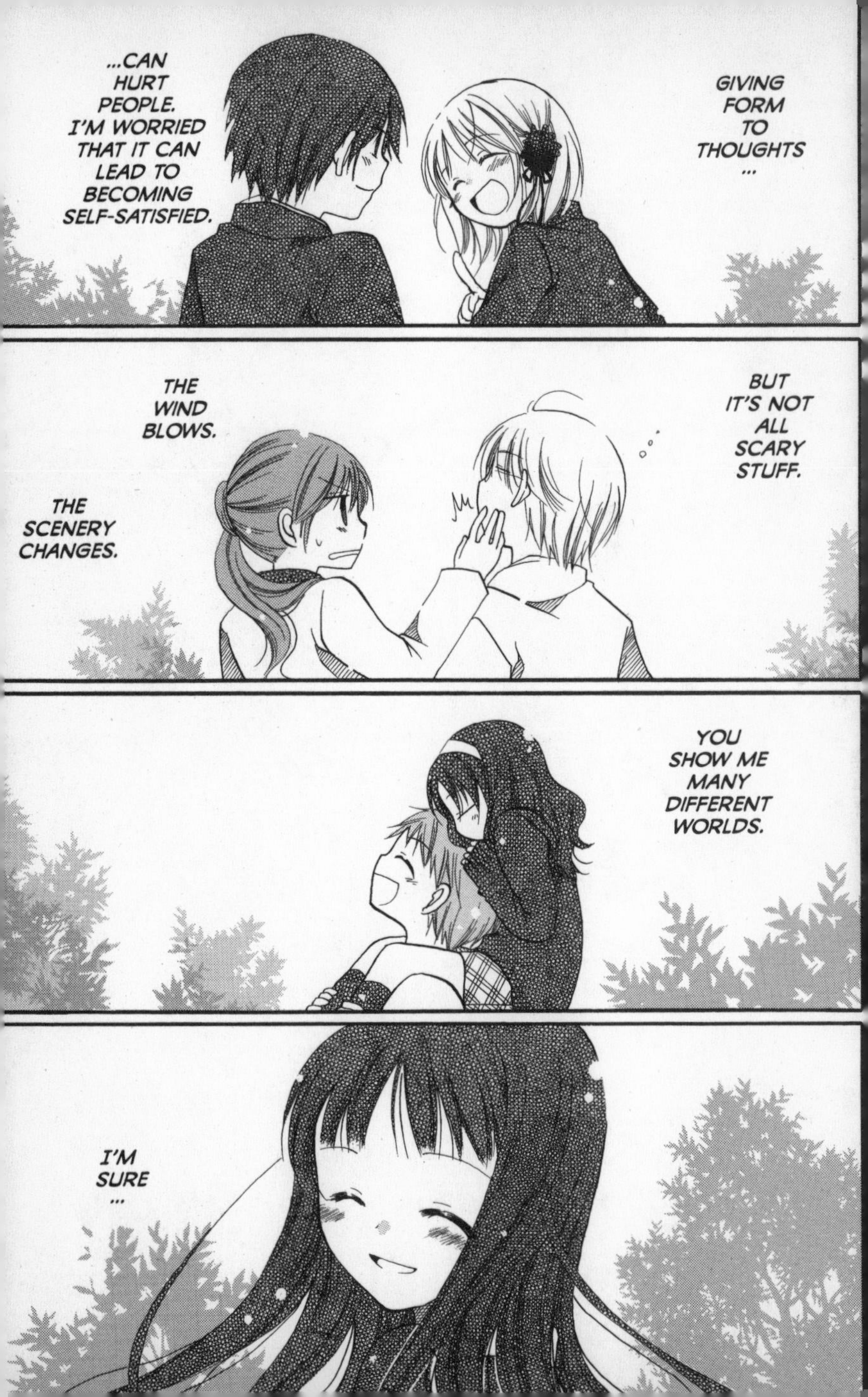
GIVING FORM TO THOUGHTS ...
...CAN HURT PEOPLE. I'M WORRIED THAT IT CAN LEAD TO BECOMING SELF-SATISFIED.
BUT IT'S NOT ALL SCARY STUFF.
THE WIND BLOWS.
THE SCENERY CHANGES.
YOU SHOW ME MANY DIFFERENT WORLDS.
I'M SURE ...

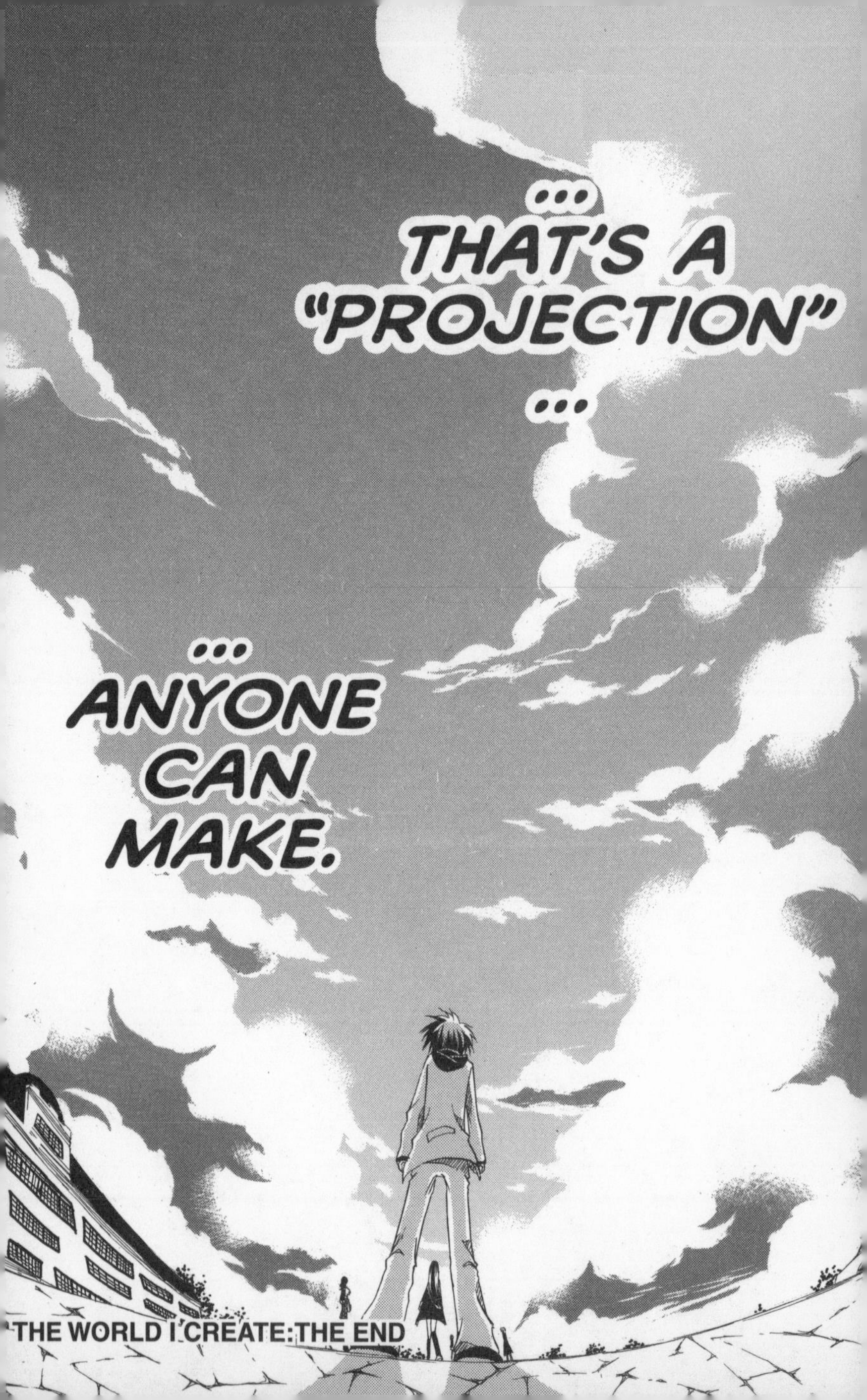
...THAT'S A "PROJECTION"...
...ANYONE CAN MAKE.
THE WORLD I CREATE: THE END

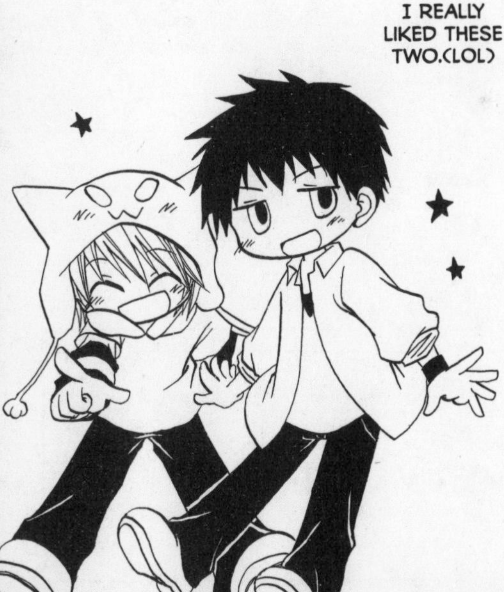
I REALLY LIKED THESE TWO.(LOL)

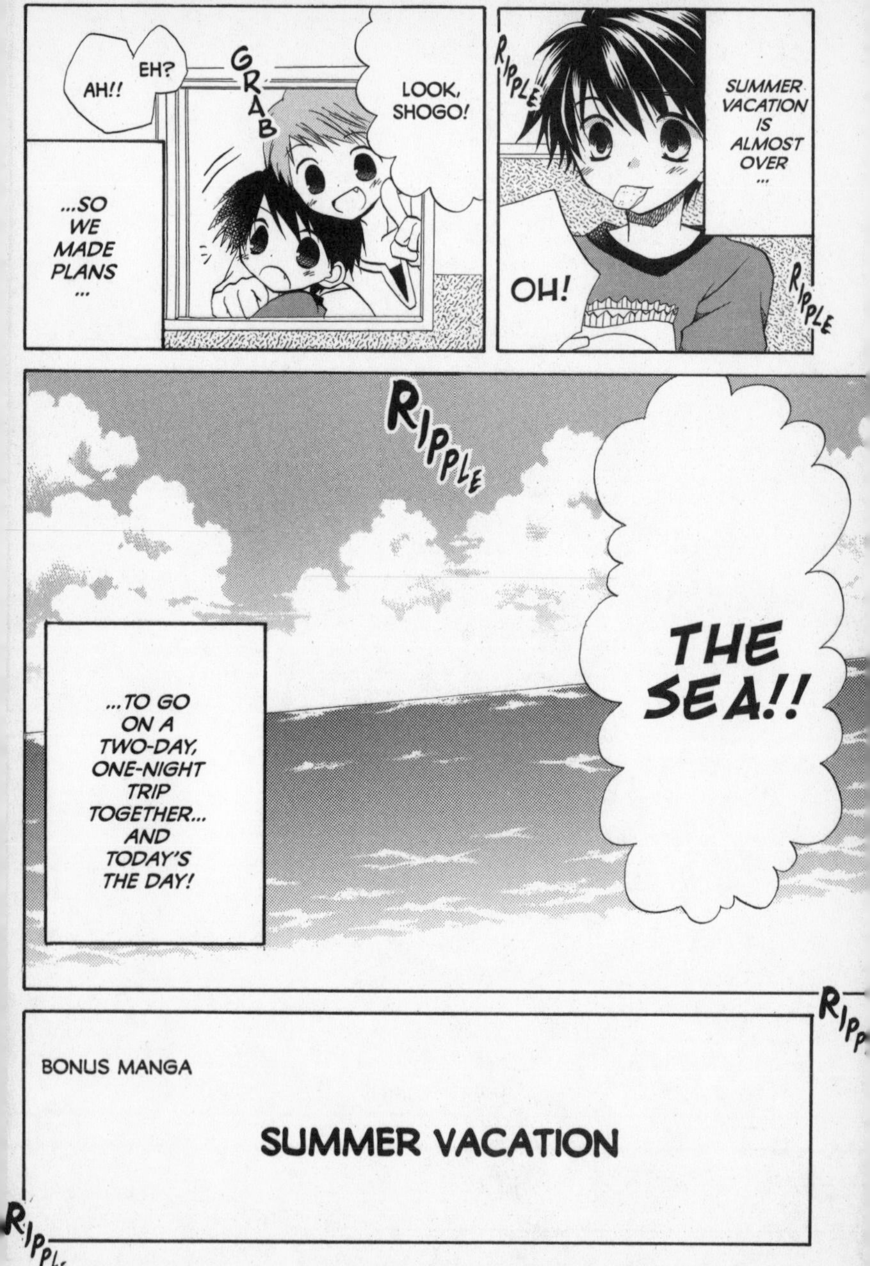
RIPPLE
SUMMER VACATION IS ALMOST OVER ...
OH!
RIPPLE
LOOK, SHOGO!
GRAB
EH?
AH!!
...SO WE MADE PLANS ...
RIPPLE
THE SEA!!
...TO GO ON A TWO-DAY, ONE-NIGHT TRIP TOGETHER... AND TODAY'S THE DAY!
BONUS MANGA
SUMMER VACATION
RIPPLE

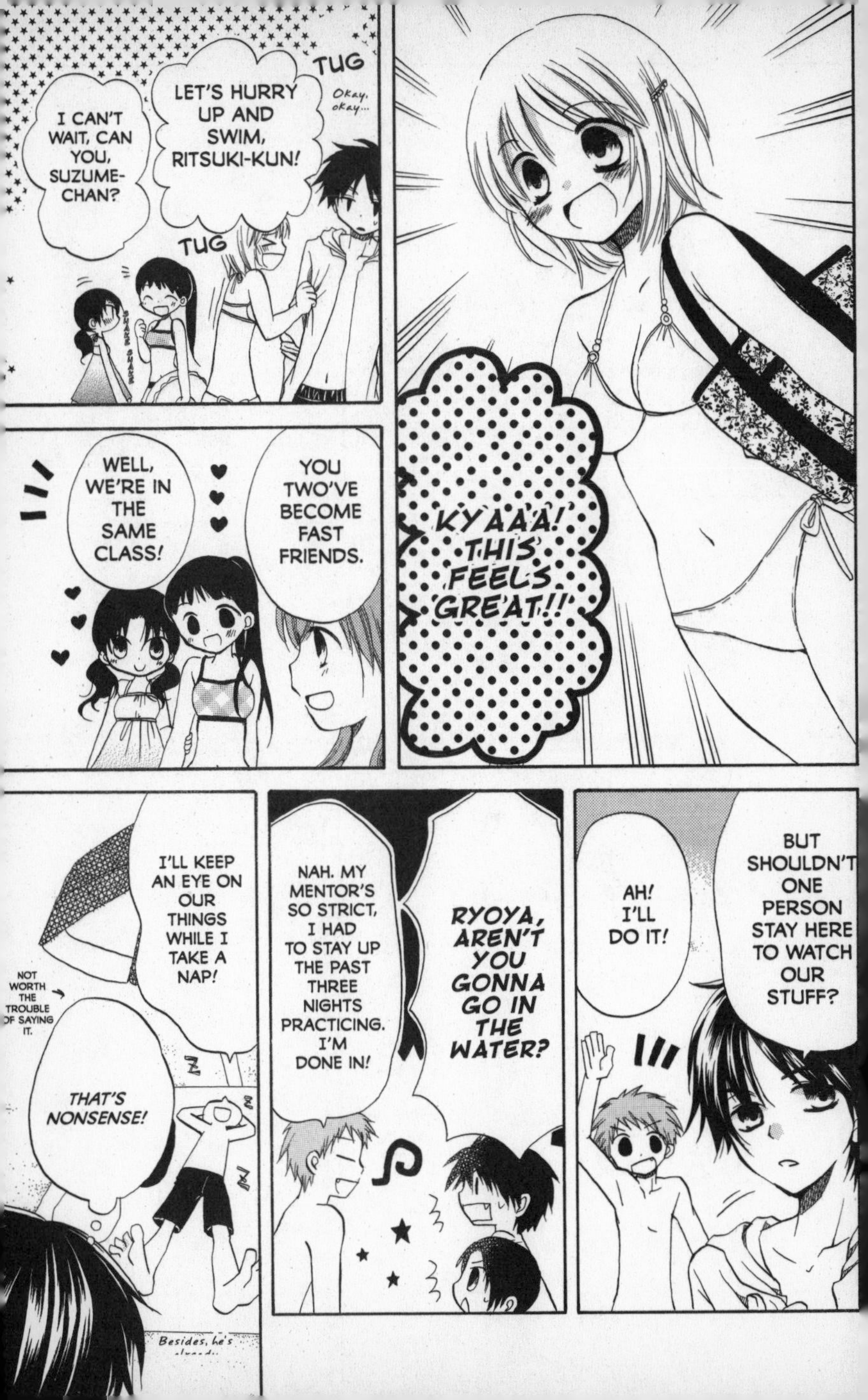
KYAAA! THIS FEELS GREAT!!
TUG
Okay, okay...
LET'S HURRY UP AND SWIM, RITSUKI-KUN!
I CAN'T WAIT, CAN YOU, SUZUME-CHAN?
TUG
YOU TWO'VE BECOME FAST FRIENDS.
WELL, WE'RE IN THE SAME CLASS!
BUT SHOULDN'T ONE PERSON STAY HERE TO WATCH OUR STUFF?
AH! I'LL DO IT!
RYOYA, AREN'T YOU GONNA GO IN THE WATER?
NAH. MY MENTOR'S SO STRICT, I HAD TO STAY UP THE PAST THREE NIGHTS PRACTICING. I'M DONE IN!
I'LL KEEP AN EYE ON OUR THINGS WHILE I TAKE A NAP!
NOT WORTH THE TROUBLE OF SAYING IT.
THAT'S NONSENSE!
Besides, he's

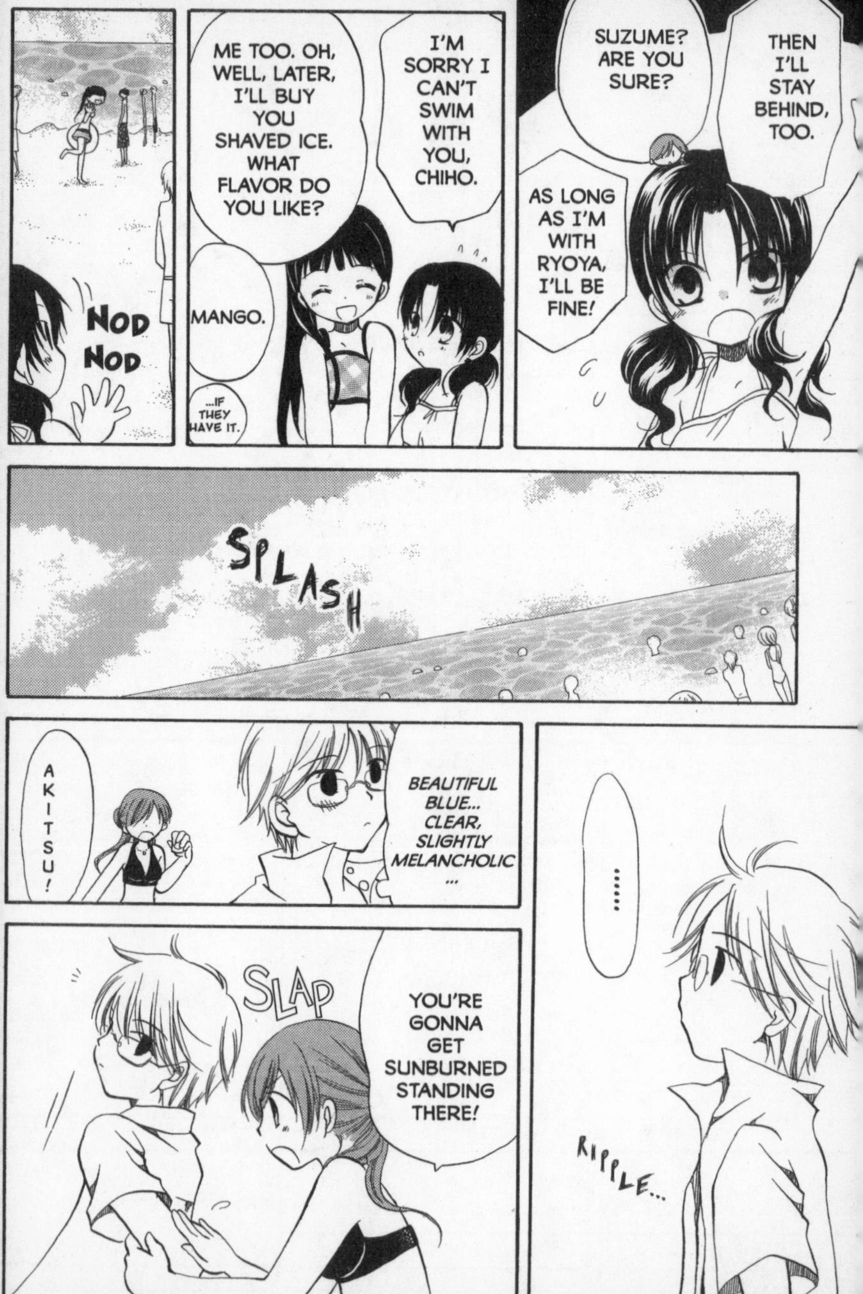
THEN I'LL STAY BEHIND, TOO.
SUZUME? ARE YOU SURE?
AS LONG AS I'M WITH RYOYA, I'LL BE FINE!
I'M SORRY I CAN'T SWIM WITH YOU, CHIHO.
ME TOO. OH, WELL, LATER, I'LL BUY YOU SHAVED ICE. WHAT FLAVOR DO YOU LIKE?
MANGO.
...IF THEY HAVE IT.
NOD NOD
SPLASH
......
RIPPLE...
BEAUTIFUL BLUE... CLEAR, SLIGHTLY MELANCHOLIC ...
AKITSU!
SLAP
YOU'RE GONNA GET SUNBURNED STANDING THERE!

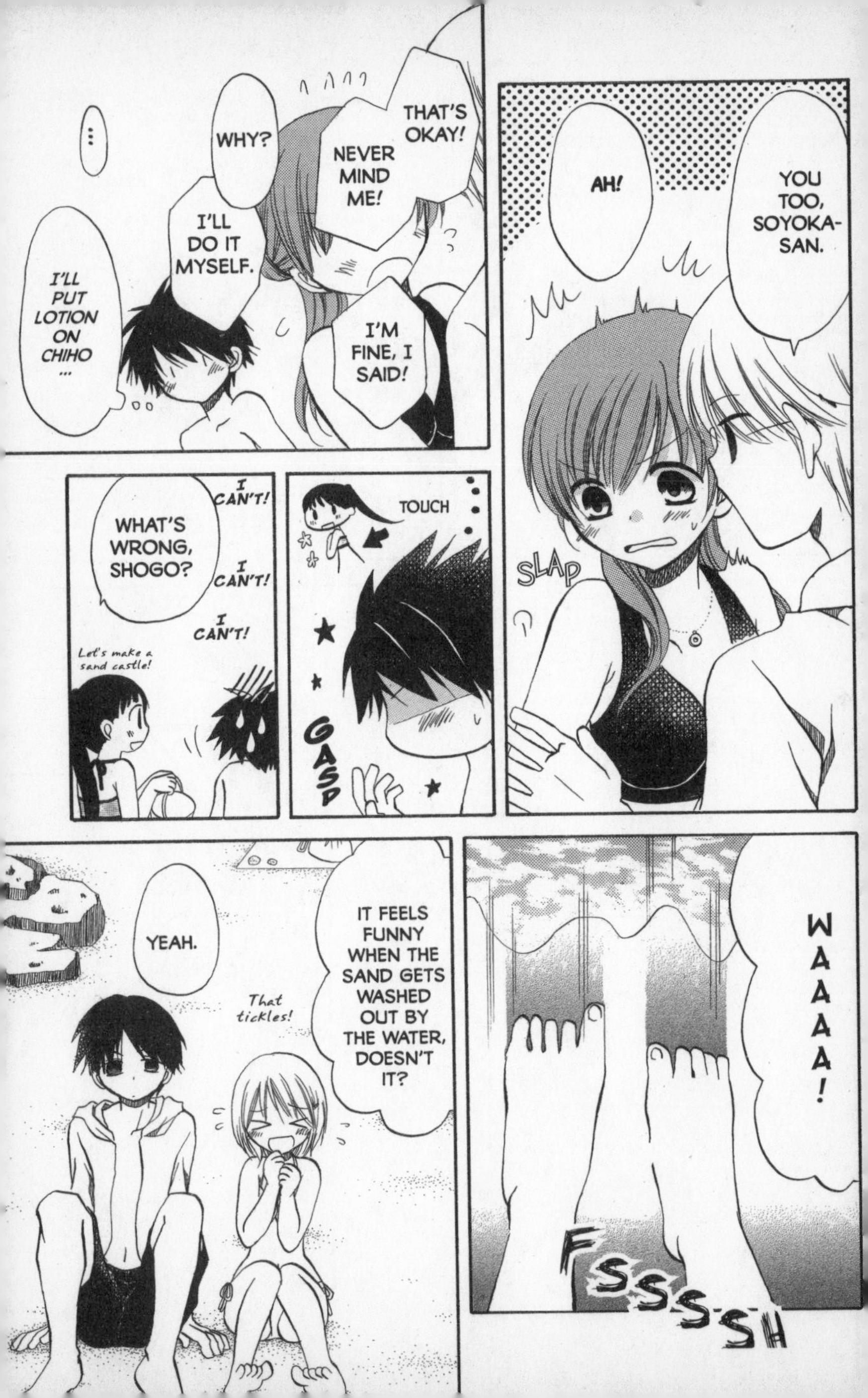
YOU TOO, SOYOKA-SAN.
AH!
SLAP
THAT'S OKAY!
NEVER MIND ME!
WHY?
...
I'LL DO IT MYSELF.
I'M FINE, I SAID!
I'LL PUT LOTION ON CHIHO...
TOUCH
GASP
I CAN'T!
I CAN'T!
I CAN'T!
WHAT'S WRONG, SHOGO?
Let's make a sand castle!
WAAAAA!
FSSSSSH
IT FEELS FUNNY WHEN THE SAND GETS WASHED OUT BY THE WATER, DOESN'T IT?
That tickles!
YEAH.

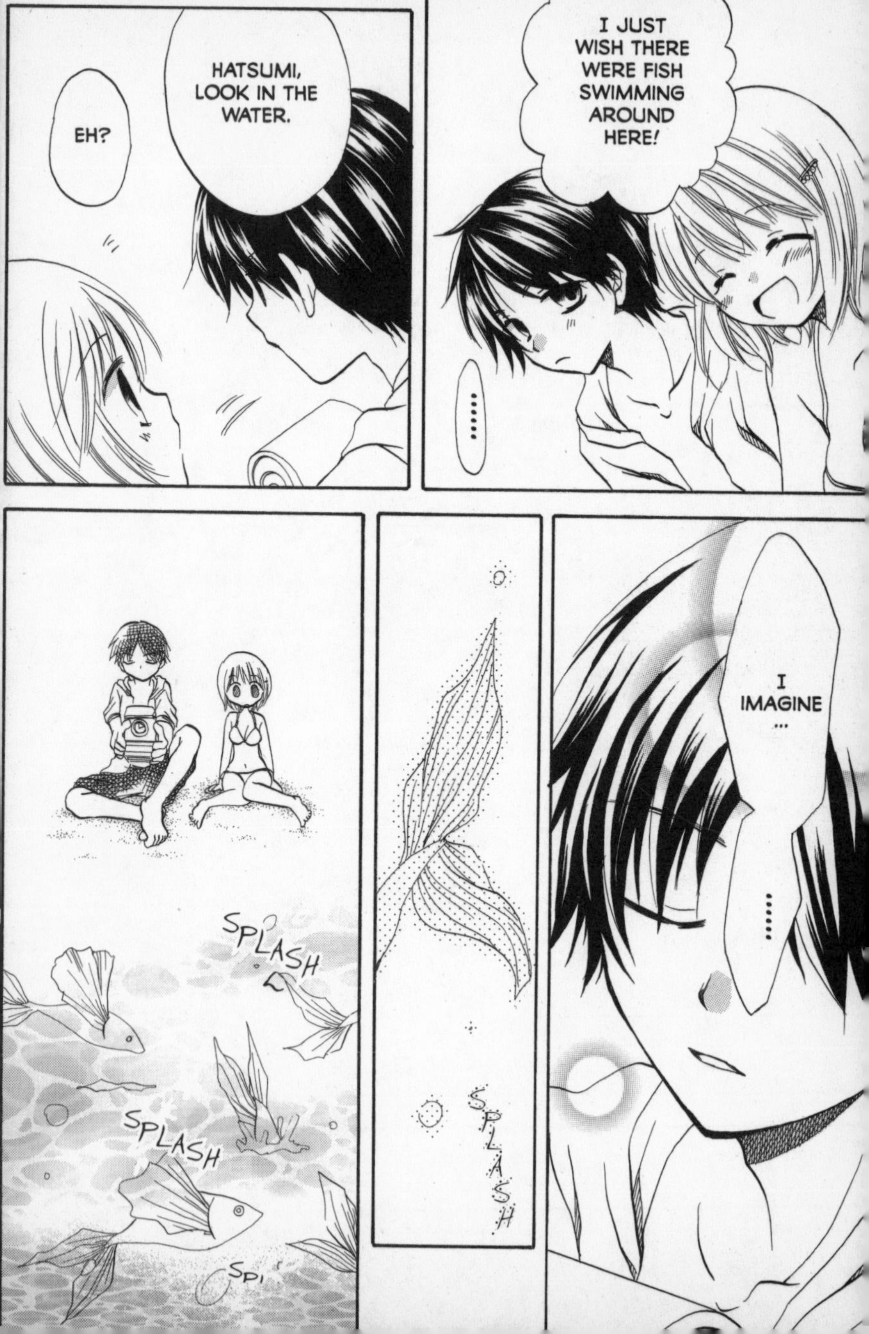
I JUST WISH THERE WERE FISH SWIMMING AROUND HERE!
......
HATSUMI, LOOK IN THE WATER.
EH?
I IMAGINE ...
......
SPLASH
SPLASH
SPLASH
SPL

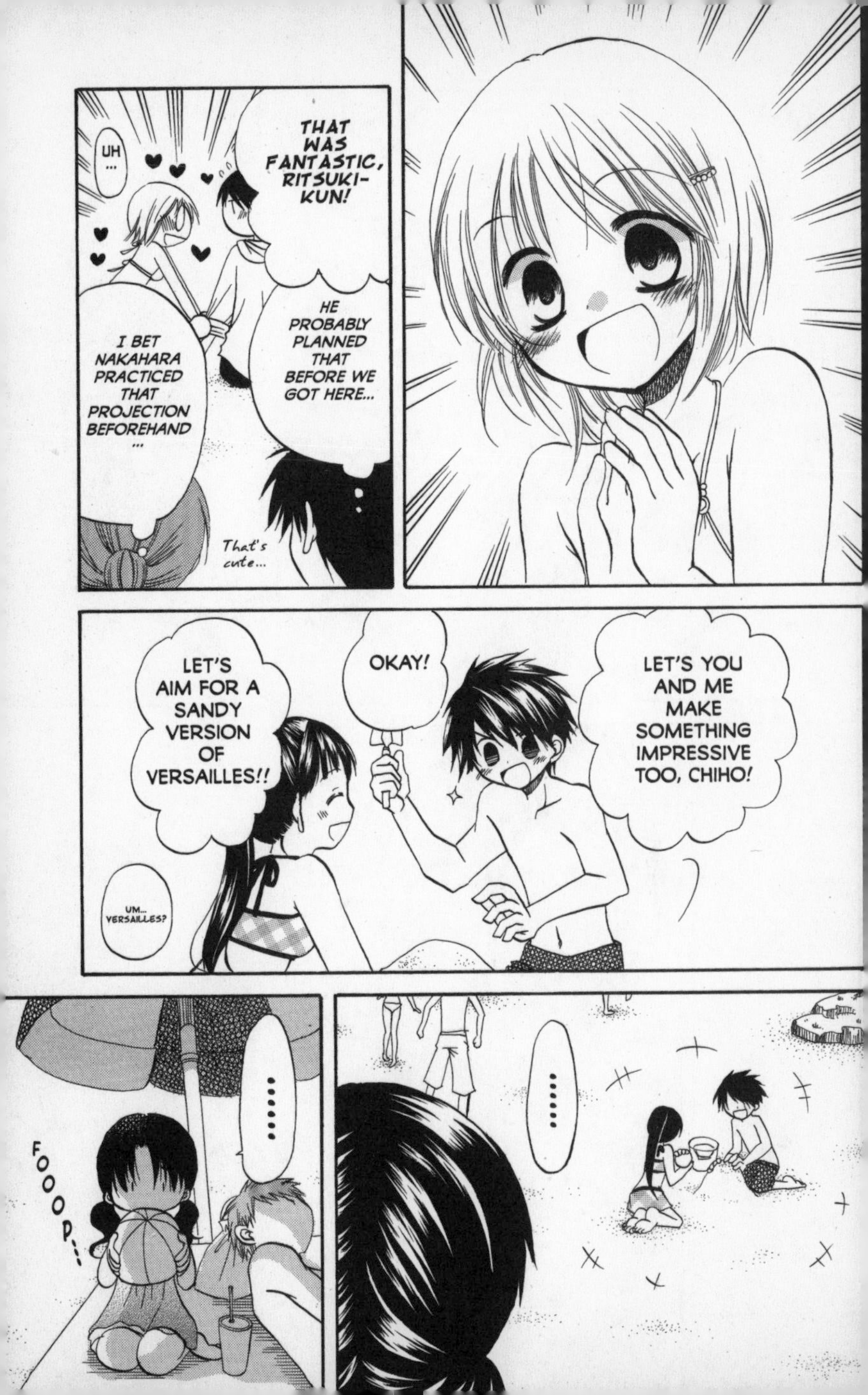
THAT WAS FANTASTIC, RITSUKI-KUN!
UH ...
HE PROBABLY PLANNED THAT BEFORE WE GOT HERE...
I BET NAKAHARA PRACTICED THAT PROJECTION BEFOREHAND ...
That's cute...
LET'S YOU AND ME MAKE SOMETHING IMPRESSIVE TOO, CHIHO!
OKAY!
LET'S AIM FOR A SANDY VERSION OF VERSAILLES!!
UM... VERSAILLES?
......
......
FOOOP!!

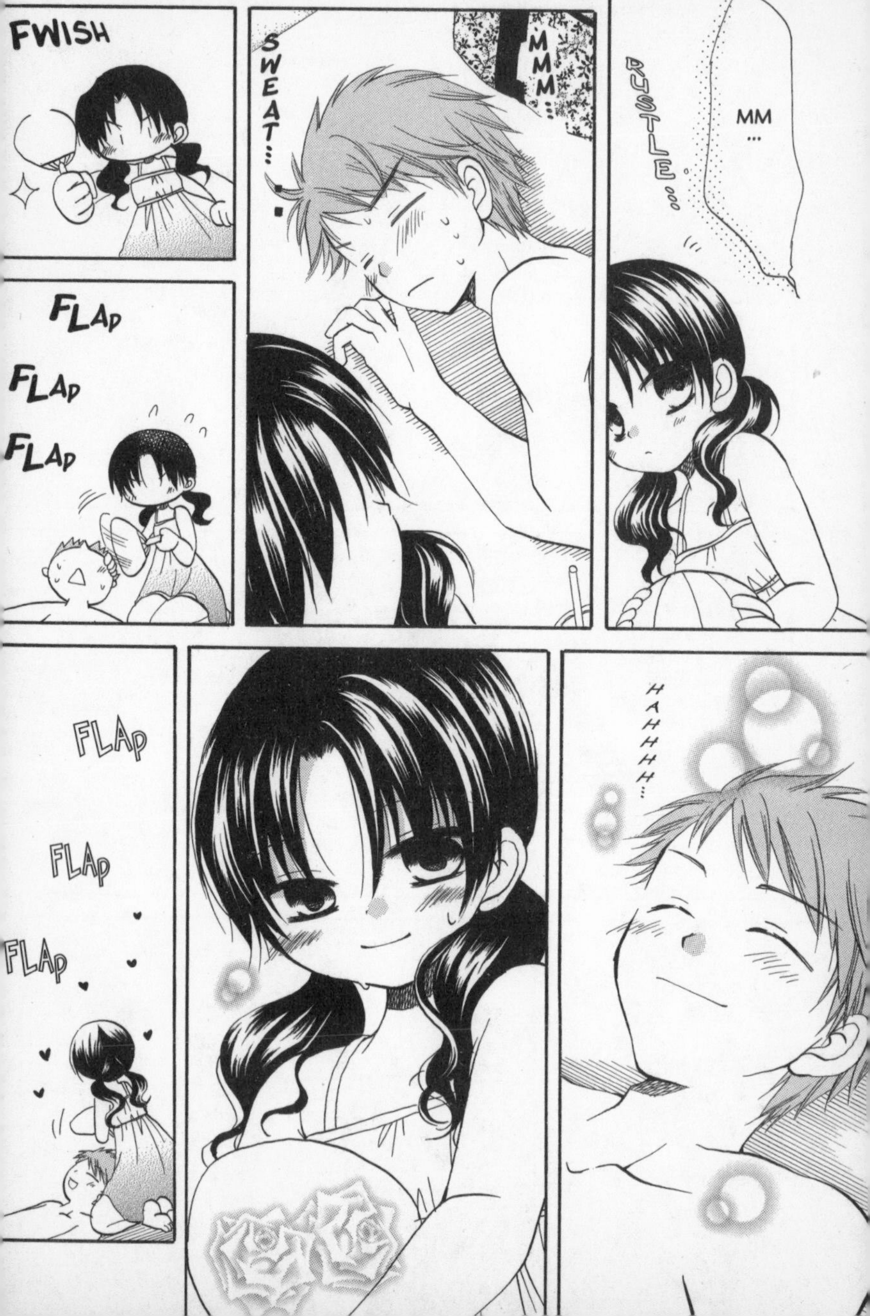

RUSTLE...
MM...
MMM...
SWEAT...
FWISH
FLAP
FLAP
FLAP
HAHHHH...
FLAP
FLAP
FLAP

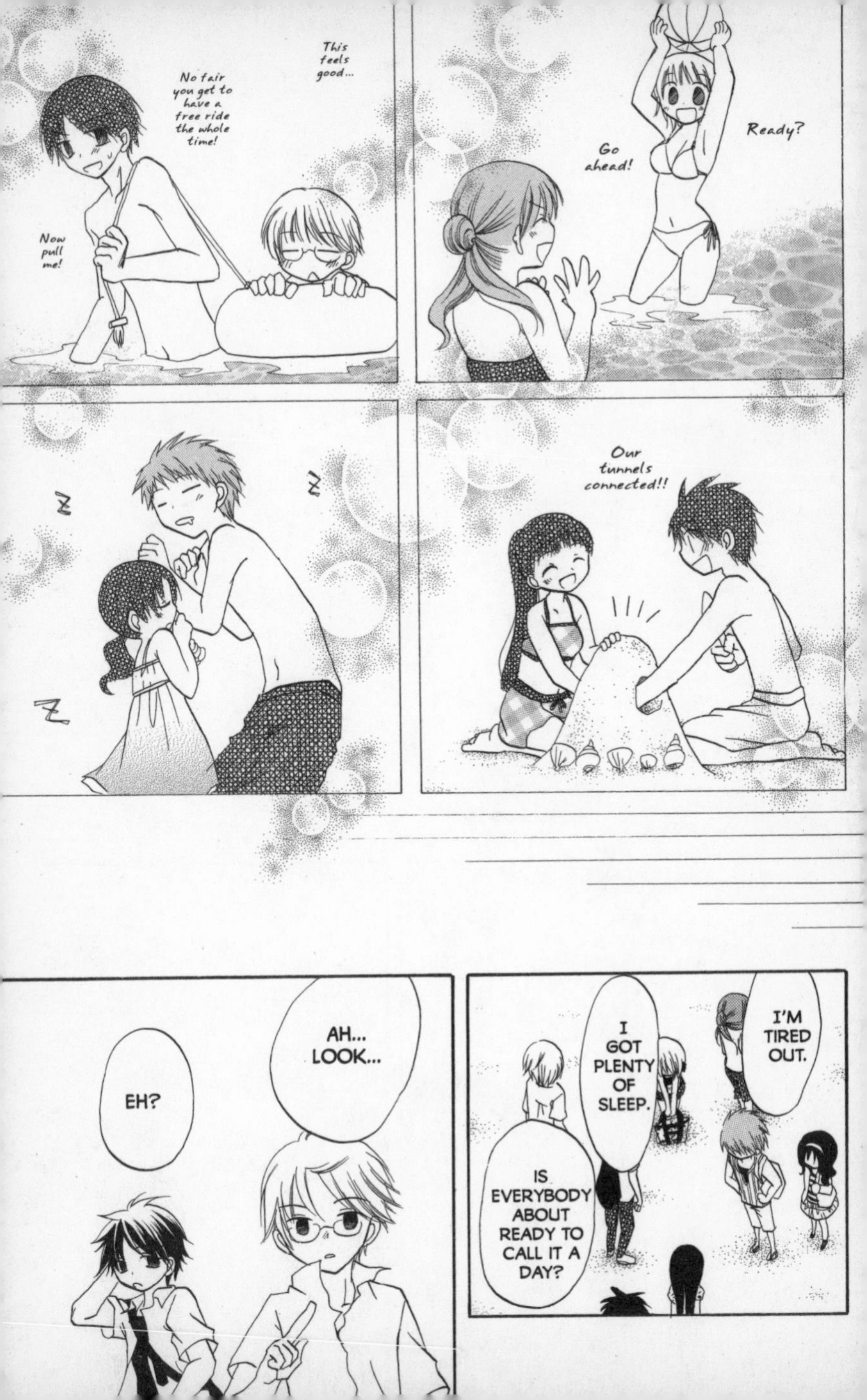
Ready?
Go ahead!
This feels good...
No fair you get to have a free ride the whole time!
Now pull me!
Our tunnels connected!!
Z
Z
Z
I'M TIRED OUT.
I GOT PLENTY OF SLEEP.
IS EVERYBODY ABOUT READY TO CALL IT A DAY?
AH... LOOK...
EH?

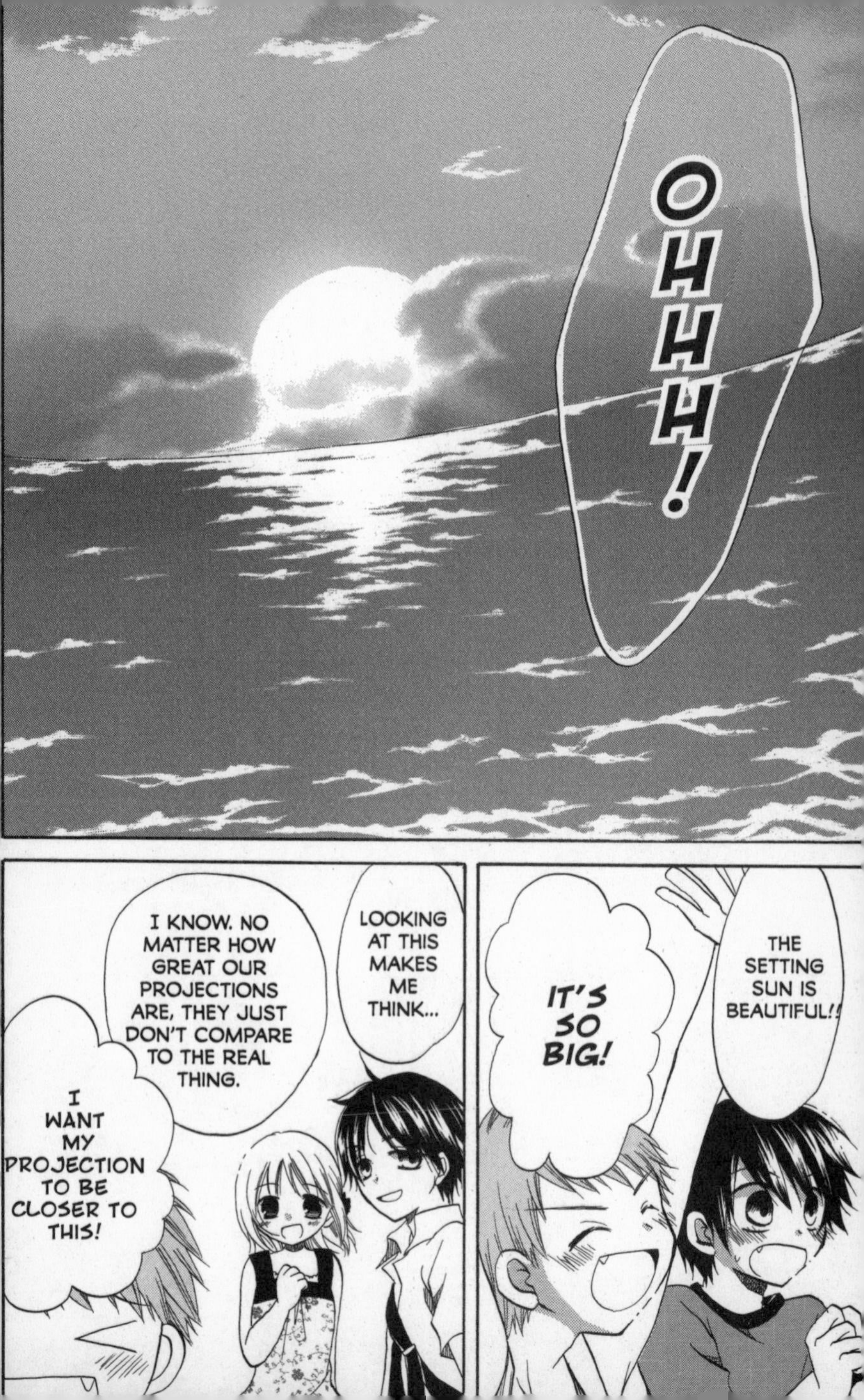
OHHHH!
THE SETTING SUN IS BEAUTIFUL!!
IT'S SO BIG!
LOOKING AT THIS MAKES ME THINK...
I KNOW. NO MATTER HOW GREAT OUR PROJECTIONS ARE, THEY JUST DON'T COMPARE TO THE REAL THING.
I WANT MY PROJECTION TO BE CLOSER TO THIS!

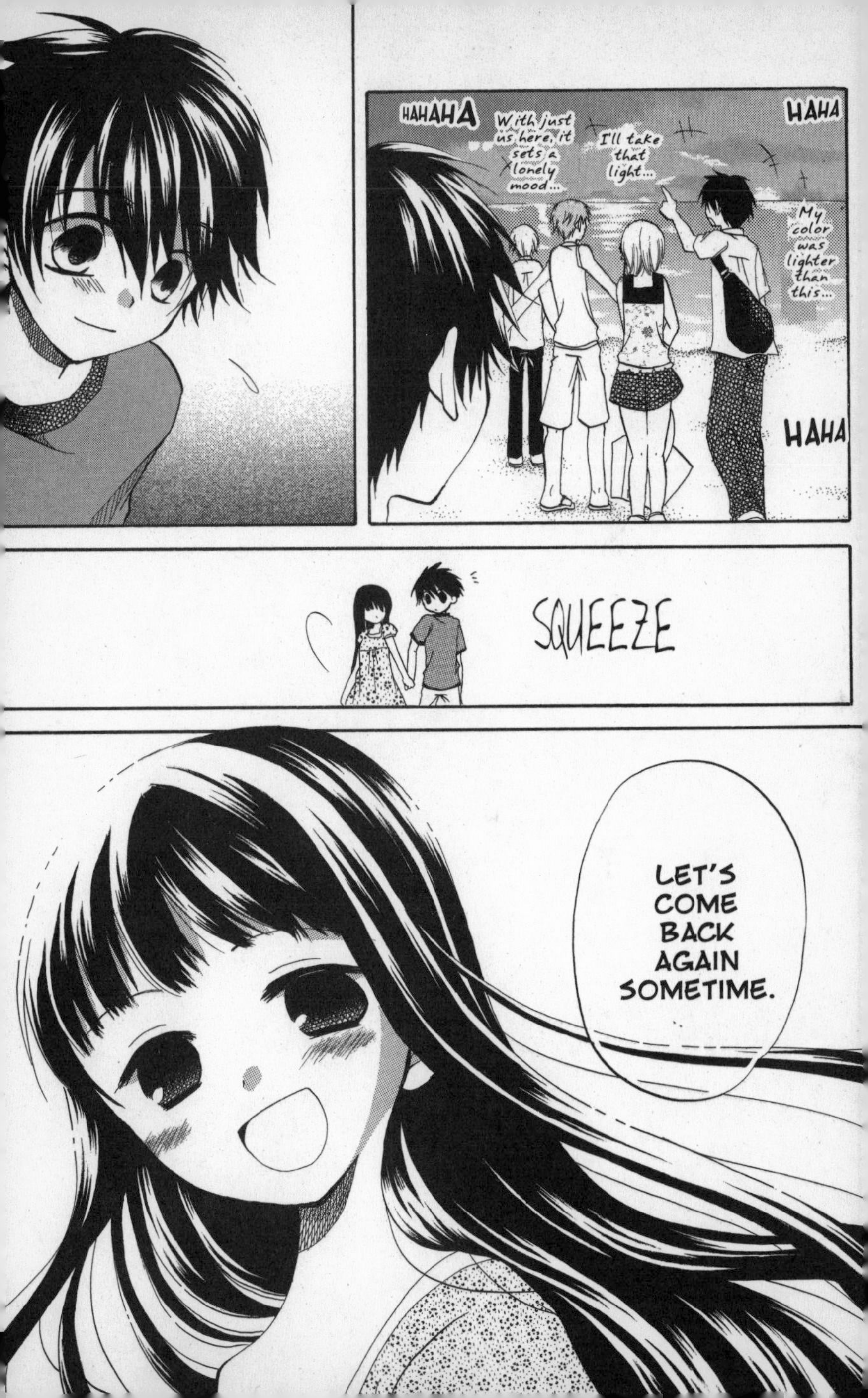
HAHA
My color was lighter than this...
I'll take that light...
With just us here, it sets a lonely mood...
HAHAHA
HAHA
SQUEEZE
LET'S COME BACK AGAIN SOMETIME.

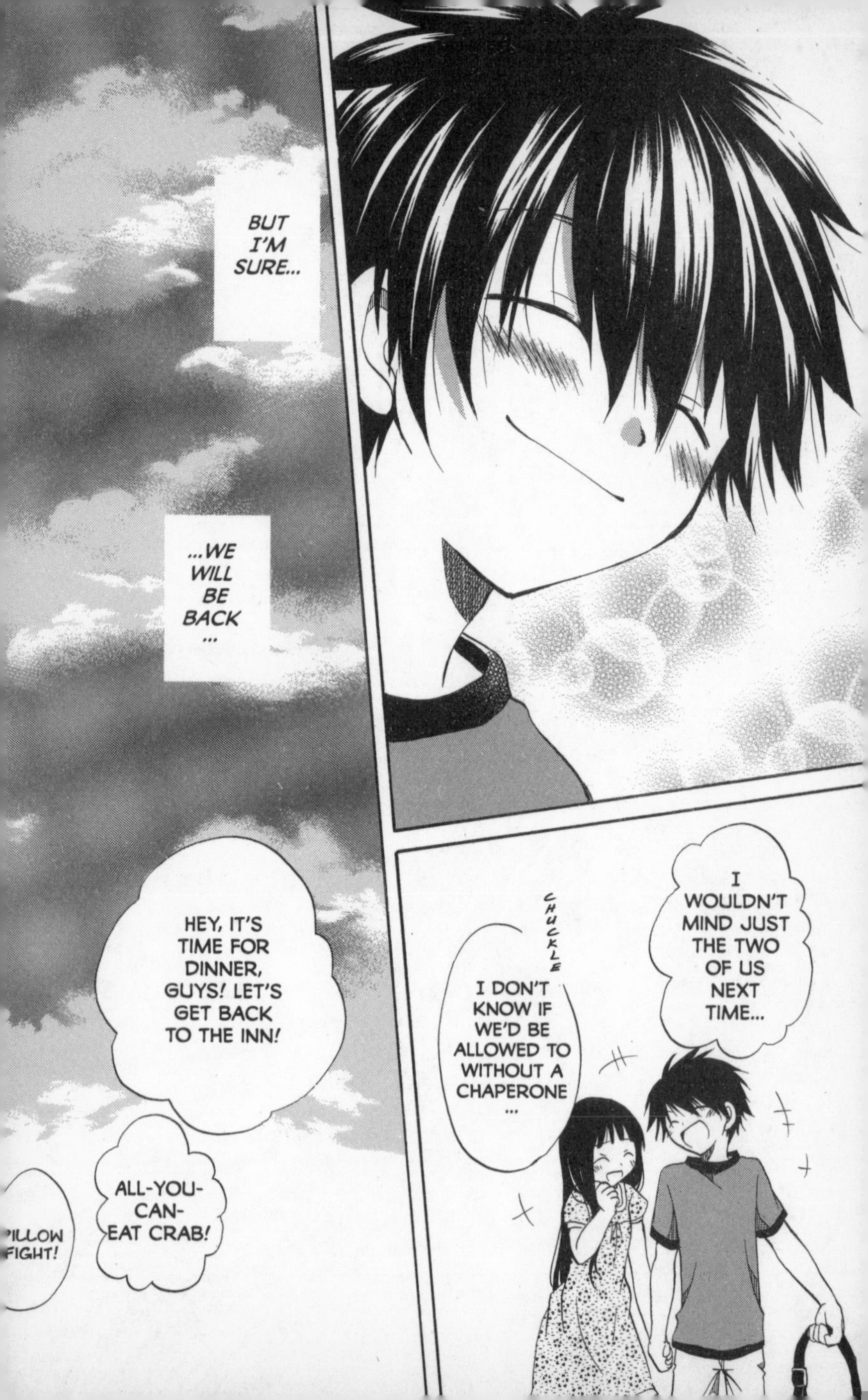
I WOULDN'T MIND JUST THE TWO OF US NEXT TIME...
CHUCKLE
I DON'T KNOW IF WE'D BE ALLOWED TO WITHOUT A CHAPERONE...
BUT I'M SURE...
...WE WILL BE BACK...
HEY, IT'S TIME FOR DINNER, GUYS! LET'S GET BACK TO THE INN!
ALL-YOU-CAN-EAT CRAB!
PILLOW FIGHT!

THANK YOU FOR GETTING "THE WORLD I CREATE." I'M AYAMI KAZAMA. I WAS SOOO, SOOO HAPPY TO HAVE MY STORIES COLLECTED INTO ONE VOLUME LIKE THIS. I WAS NERVOUS AT FIRST TO DO THIS SERIES, BECAUSE IT WAS THE FIRST TIME I HAD A CONTINUING STORY, BUT MY STRONGEST FEELNG WHILE DOING IT WAS, "THIS IS FUN!"(LOL) THE BONUS STORY FEATURED THE YOUNG PROJECTIONISTS IN THE SUMMER, A SEASON I DIDN'T COVER WITHIN THE ACTUAL SERIES. I HOPE YOU ENJOYED THAT, TOO.

AGAIN, THANK YOU VERY MUCH!!!

SEPTEMBER 2007

AYAMI KAZAMA

SPECIAL THANKS TO:

IKEJIMA-SAN, MY LITTLE SISTER, SAKI-CHAN, ASA-CHAN, ASAKI-SAN, ISHIKURA-SAN, KOZAWA-SAN, TAKKI-SAN, MY FAMILY, MY FRIENDS, MY ACQUAINTANCES, AND EVERYONE WHO HAD ANYTHING TO DO WITH THIS SERIES...♥

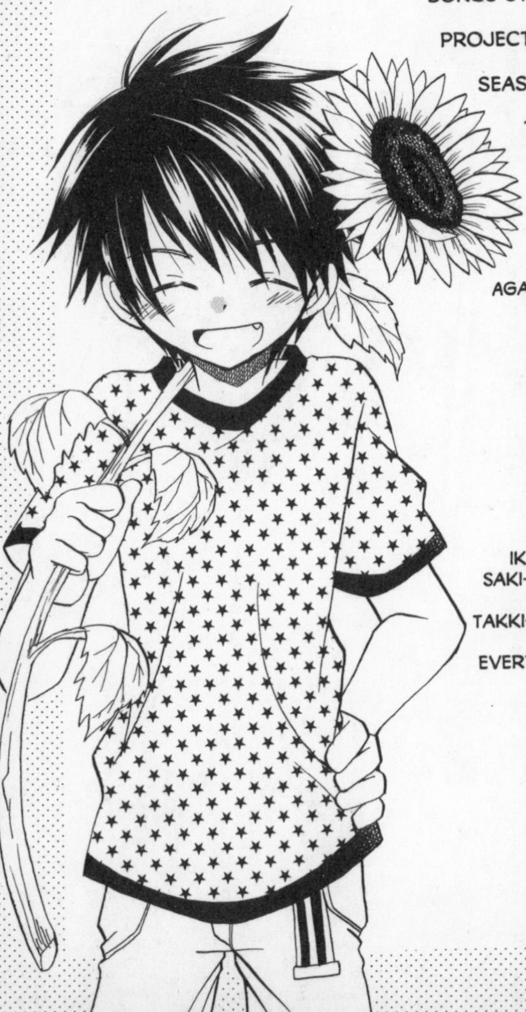

Sheldon Drzka
Translation and Adaptation
MPS Ad Studio
Lettering
Larry Berry
Art Director
Chynna Clugston Flores
Assistant Editor
Jim Chadwick
Editor

Jim Lee
Editorial Director
Hank Kanalz
VP—General Manager
Paul Levitz
President & Publisher
Richard Bruning
SVP—Creative Director
Patrick Caldon
EVP—Finance & Operations
Amy Genkins
SVP—Business & Legal Affairs
Gregory Noveck
SVP—Creative Affairs
Steve Rotterdam
SVP—Sales & Marketing
Cheryl Rubin
SVP—Brand Management

ISBN: 978-1-4012-2449-3